About this book

Global Prescriptions is a critical yet optimistic analysis of the role of trans-national women's groups in setting the agendas for women's health, and especially reproductive and sexual rights, in the international and the various national settings. A political theorist by training, Rosalind Petchesky's perspective is deeply embedded in feminist, postcolonial and ethical theory as well as current debates on globalization.

The book reviews a decade of women's participation in UN conferences, transnational networks, national advocacy efforts and sexual and reproductive health provision, assessing both their strengths and weaknesses. It contains trenchant critiques of the Cairo, Beijing and Copenhagen conference documents and of World Bank, WHO and health sector reform policies. It also offers case studies of national-level reform and advocacy efforts and appraises the controversy concerning TRIPs, trade, and essential AIDS drugs. That controversy, Petchesky argues, starkly illuminates the 'collision course' of transnational corporate and global trade agendas with the struggle for gender, racial and regional equity and the human right to health.

The author takes into account the formidable political and ideological forces with which global justice movements have had to contend: neoliberal economic policies; the trend toward privatization; population control, with its racist underpinnings; fundamentalisms of all stripes; and now resurgent militarism and neo-imperialism under the guise of the 'war against terrorism'. At the same time, she offers a sobering reassessment of transnational women's NGOs themselves and such problems as 'NGOization', fragmentation and donor dependency. Petchesky argues that the power of women's transnational coalitions for gender and global justice is only as great as their organic connection with local and national social movements and their commitment to addressing the need for not only major redistribution of the world's huge concentrations of wealth but also a mobilization of political will.

About the author

ROSALIND POLLACK PETCHESKY is Distinguished Professor of Political Science, Hunter College and the Graduate Center, City University of New York. Co-author of *Negotiating Reproductive Rights: Women's Perspectives across Countries and Cultures*, she is the founder and past international co-ordinator of the International Reproductive Rights Research Action Group (IRRRAG) and a MacArthur Fellow. Her recent response to 9.11, 'Phantom Towers', has had an extraordinary impact, being published in a large number of print and media sites in the US, Europe, Latin America and India. Professor Petchesky has long been active in women's, social justice and peace efforts and is a board member of the Women's Environment and Development Organization and the international journal, *Reproductive Health Matters*.

About UNRISD

The United Nations Research Institute for Social Development (UNRISD) is an autonomous agency engaging in multidisciplinary research on the social dimensions of contemporary problems affecting development. Its work is guided by the conviction that, for effective development policies to be formulated, an understanding of the social and political context is crucial. The Institute attempts to provide governments, development agencies, grassroots organizations and scholars with a better understanding of how development policies and processes of economic, social and environmental change affect different social groups. Working through an extensive network of national research centres, UNRISD aims to promote original research and strengthen research capacity in developing countries.

Current research programmes include: Gender Equity, Civil Society and Social Movements; Democracy, Governance and Human Rights; Identities, Conflict and Cohesion; Social Policy and Development; and Technology, Business and Society.

A list of UNRISD's free and priced publications can be obtained by contacting the Reference Centre, UNRISD, Palais des Nations, 1211 Geneva 10, Switzerland; Phone: (41 22) 917 3020; Fax: (41 22) 917 0650; E-mail: info@unrisd.org; Web: http://www.unrisd.org

UNRISD thanks the governments of Denmark, Finland, Mexico, the Netherlands, Norway, Sweden, Switzerland and the United Kingdom for its core funding.

Global Prescriptions
Gendering Health and Human Rights

Rosalind Pollack Petchesky

Zed Books
LONDON & NEW YORK

in association with

**United Nations Research Institute
for Social Development**

Global Prescriptions was first published in 2003 by
Zed Books Ltd, 7 Cynthia Street, London N1 9JF, UK and
Room 400, 175 Fifth Avenue, New York, NY 10010
www.zedbooks.demon.co.uk

In association with the United Nations Research Institute
for Social Development (UNRISD),
Palais des Nations, 1211 Geneva 10, Switzerland
www.unrisd.org

Cover designed by Andrew Corbett
Set in 9.6/12.6 pt Goudy
by Long House, Cumbria, UK
Printed and bound in Malaysia

Distributed in the USA exclusively by Palgrave, a division of
St Martin's Press, LLC,175 Fifth Avenue, New York, NY 10010

A catalogue record for this book
is available from the British Library

US Cataloging-in-Publication Data
is available from the Library of Congress

ISBN   Hb 1 84277 004 7
       Pb 1 84277 007 1

Contents

Boxes

Acronyms

ACT UP	AIDS Coalition to Unleash Power
AHI	Action Health Incorporated (Nigeria)
ANC	African National Congress (South Africa)
ART (ARV)	Antiretroviral therapy
ATTAC	Association for the Taxation of Financial Transactions for the Benefit of Citizens
CBO	Community-based organization
CDF	Comprehensive Development Framework (World Bank)
CEDAW	Convention on the Elimination of All Forms of Discrimination Against Women
CESCR	Committee on Economic, Social and Cultural Rights (United Nations)
CLADEM	Latin American and Caribbean Committee for the Defence of Women's Rights
CMH	Commission on Macroeconomics and Health
CNDP	National Commission on Population and Development (Brazil)
CPT	Consumer Project on Technology
CRLP	Center for Reproductive Law and Policy (Center for Reproductive Policy, 1993)
DALY	Disability Adjusted Life Years
DAWN	Development Alternatives for Women in a New Era
DNDi	Drugs for Neglected Diseases Initiative (MSF)
DOH	Department of Health
ECOSOC	Economic and Social Council (United Nations)
FDI	Foreign direct investment
FfD	Financing for Development Conference (United Nations)
FGM	Female genital mutilation
FINRRAGE	Feminist International Network for Reproductive Rights and Against Genetic Engineering
FWCW	Fourth World Conference on Women (Beijing)
GATS	General Agreement on Trade in Services
GAD	Gender and Development
GATT	General Agreement on Tariffs and Trade
GAVI	Global AIDS Vaccine Initiative
GBD	Global burden of disease
GEAR	Growth, Employment and Redistribution Policy (South Africa)
G-77	Group of 77 (United Nations)
HERA	Health, Empowerment, Rights and Accountability
HIPC	Heavily indebted poor country
HIV/AIDS	Human Immunodeficiency Virus/Acquired Immunodeficiency Syndrome
HNP	Health, Nutrition and Population (World Bank unit)
HSR	Health sector reform
ICC	International Criminal Court
ICESCR	International Covenant on Economic, Social and Cultural Rights
ICPD	International Conference on Population and Development (Cairo)
IFI	International financial institution
IGLHRC	International Gay and Lesbian Human Rights Commission
IGO	Intergovernmental organization
IPPF	International Planned Parenthood Federation
IPR	Intellectual property right
IRRRAG	International Reproductive Rights Research Action Group

IWHC	International Women's Health Coalition
IWHM	International Women and Health Meeting
JUSCANZ	Japan, United States, Canada, Australia & New Zealand (UN group)
LACWHN	Latin American and Caribbean Women's Health Network
MCH	Maternal and child health
MDGs	Millennium Development Goals
MoH	Ministry/Minister of Health
MSF	Médecins sans Frontières (Doctors without Borders)
MTCT	Mother-to-Child Transmission
NAF	National Abortion Federation (United States)
NAWO	National Alliance of Women's Organizations (India)
NGO	Nongovernmental organization
PAISM	Comprehensive Women's Health Programme (Brazil)
PMA	Pharmaceutical Manufacturers' Association (South Africa)
POA	Programme of Action
PrepCom	Preparatory Committee (United Nations)
PRSP	Population Reduction Strategy Paper (World Bank)
PWA	People with AIDS
RCH	Reproductive and Child Health Programme (India)
RDP	Reconstruction and Development Programme (South Africa)
RHM	Reproductive Health Matters
RTI	Reproductive tract infection
SAP	Structural Adjustment Programme
SHAPE	Schools HIV/AIDS & Population Education Programme (Swaziland)
STD, STI	Sexually transmitted disease, sexually transmitted infection
SUS	Universal Health System (Brazil)
SWAP	Sector-wide approach
TAC	Treatment Access Campaign (South Africa)
TFA	Target-Free Approach (India)
TNC	Transnational corporation
TRAC	Transnational Resource and Action Center (United States)
TRIPs	Trade-Related Aspects of Intellectual Property Rights (Agreement)
UDHR	Universal Declaration of Human Rights
UNAIDS	United Nations Joint AIDS Programme
UNCED	United Nations Conference on Environment and Development
UNDP	United Nations Development Programme
UNFPA	United Nations Population Fund
UNGASS	United Nations General Assembly Special Session
UNICEF	United Nations Children's Fund
UNIFEM	United Nations Development Programme for Women
UNRISD	United Nations Research Institute for Social Development
USTR	United States Trade Representative
WCAR	World Conference Against Racism
WDR	World Development Report (World Bank)
WEDO	Women's Environment and Development Organization
WGNRR	Women's Global Network for Reproductive Rights
WHA	World Health Assembly
WHO	World Health Organization
WHP	Women's Health Project (South Africa)
WID	Women in Development
WILDAF	Women in Law and Development – Africa
WSF	World Social Forum
WSSD	World Summit on Social Development; World Summit on Sustainable Development
WTO	World Trade Organization

Foreword

As part of the preparation by the United Nations Research Institute for Social Development (UNRISD) for the UN's five-year review of the World Summit for Social Development (WSSD) in 2000, we asked Rosalind Petchesky to prepare a paper for us on the interface between reproductive rights and social development. This paper was published in our Occasional Paper Series (OP8), and also contributed directly to the UNRISD Report for Geneva 2000, *Visible Hands: Taking Responsibility for Social Development*. Rosalind Petchesky, however, took the initiative to turn the work that she had done for us into the present book-length manuscript, which is a valuable contribution to current debates on the gendering of health and human rights.

The manuscript provides a poignant analysis of three decades of feminist struggles for gender equality, women's health, and reproductive rights and freedoms, which converged in different countries and then became increasingly globalized. These struggles are a powerful reminder of the indispensability of rights as the moral expression of political claims. What is also clear from Rosalind Petchesky's insightful analysis is the important ways in which struggles for rights can provide an entry point for contesting processes associated with neoliberal globalization. *Global Prescriptions* elaborates and underlines the interconnections between areas more commonly thought of as 'feminist enclaves' – reproductive and sexual rights and women's health movements – and the macroeconomic arena that neoliberals would like to keep insulated from public debate and scrutiny.

I would like to thank the United Nations Division for Social Policy and Development, and the governments of the Netherlands, Sweden and Switzerland for their financial contribution to UNRISD's activities for Geneva 2000. I also acknowledge the support of these governments and those of Denmark, Finland, Mexico, Norway and the United Kingdom, which provide UNRISD's core funding.

Thandika Mkandawire
Director, UNRISD
Geneva

Preface and Acknowledgements

This book has been three years in the making, but its origins really go back much further. They are embedded in a process of accretion and layering that happened during the 1970s, 1980s and 1990s, when movements for gender equality, women's health, and the rights and freedoms associated with 'owning our bodies' converged in different countries at different moments, then gradually 'went global' with increasing momentum. I entered this convergence of ideas and movements from my own location as a North American feminist of the left living in New York. I was born during the Second World War; came of age during the US civil rights movement that forever instilled in me the indispensability of rights as the moral expression of political claims; and was present as a young mother and academic at a moment when feminists in the US mobilized to defend the recently won right to safe, legal abortion from a mounting volley of conservative attacks. I remember vividly the angry and chaotic gathering of some 200 of us, almost all women, crowded into the basement of a West Village cabaret in New York City in 1977, determined to fight the passage through the US Congress that week of an amendment that would deny provision of federal medical insurance for abortion. It was a policy that effectively barred poor women (who are disproportionately African-American and Latina in the United States) from access to safe abortion even as it attempted to set in motion a political process that would abolish legal abortion for all women.[1] We understood that night, over a quarter-century ago, that a precious value was at stake, a value we soon named 'reproductive rights,' and that it was not only about gender but also inextricably about class and race.

My involvement in thinking about the meanings of reproductive and sexual rights and their interlinkages with issues of social justice, economic development and public policy thus has deep and tangled roots. From the start I was propelled into this thinking primarily as an activist who later sought to use my tools as a scholar to analyse more deeply, and situate in a broader context, ideas that really grew out of a collective process of concept formation and strategic action. I have been fortunate to be a participant in this process and to learn from many of the individuals and groups who have been its catalysts. Like all my previous work, *Global Prescriptions* is the product of the thought and activity of hundreds of people – colleagues, friends, organizations, historic gatherings – who should not be held responsible for its weaknesses and omissions but without whose labours, help and example the book would not exist.

In a more immediate way, the book grew out of a request from Shahra Razavi at the United Nations Research Institute for Social Development (UNRISD) that I contribute a commissioned paper to a series UNRISD was developing for the UN's five-year review of the World Summit for Social Development (WSSD) in 2000. Thanks to Shahra's encouragement and the painstaking work of editors at UNRISD, a long and bulky manuscript became the scaled-down original version of this work, published as an UNRISD occasional paper for WSSD+5 (Petchesky 2000a). I owe enormous gratitude to Shahra and UNRISD for their initial stimulus and support and for superb editorial suggestions during the early phase of this project. Meanwhile the bulky version – including the country case studies in Chapter 5 that had to be omitted from the UNRISD paper – still clamoured to see the light of day. Robert Molteno at Zed was kind enough to agree to publish it in a much revised and expanded form, with the addition of Chapter 3 and the Conclusion and a good deal of new material in Chapters 4 and 5. Robert and Zed have been the publisher of one's dreams – patient with my delays, efficient and always reassuring. UNRISD happily agreed to co-publish this final version. And Joseph Phelan, one of my amazing students at Hunter College, gave me tremendous help in assembling the bibliography.

During the process of revision, September 11 happened, and it was like a cataclysm – not only for the world but also, on a tiny scale, for the manuscript. What had been a hopeful story of feminist and social movement achievement suddenly seemed overwhelmed by a kind of death dance of global capitalism and global terrorism, which rapidly prompted a new era of militarism and neo-imperialist power. Agendas for health and human rights and the resources to realize them got swept aside in the wake of this new call for perpetual war, and I felt pulled by the urgent need to write, act and join with millions of others across the globe in a movement – so reminiscent of yet so different from the anti-Vietnam War era – to resist that call. A fortuitous invitation from Macalester College in Minnesota to participate in their International Roundtable on 'The Body: Meditations on Global Health' in October of 2001, gave me the opportunity to think my way through to the many ways in which war stands as an irreconcilable enemy of global health and human rights.[2] And an invitation by former Dean Robert Marino at Hunter College to deliver the first Distinguished Professor Lecture at my own institution enabled me to think about these deadly intersections more deeply. It became obvious then that finishing the book and resisting US unilateralism and warmongering were part of the same lifelong work. So I thank Hunter College and Macalester College for believing in that work and providing the occasions for me to better understand how its priorities fit together.

Throughout the process of researching and writing *Global Prescriptions*, many people generously shared with me materials, personal reflections and helpful suggestions not easily available in libraries or on the Internet. Many thanks to these angels scattered around the globe: Sonia Corrêa, Vera Paiva and Richard Parker in Brazil; Sandra Vallenas in Peru; Jane Cottingham in Geneva; Diane Elson in the UK; Kalpana and Vasanth Kannabiran of the Asmita Resource Centre for Women, Vanita Mukherjee, Radhika Ramasubban, T. K. Sundari Ravindran and all the gracious staff of RUWSEC, and Gita Sen in India; Jonathan Berger, Barbara Klugman and Fatima Pandy in South Africa; 'Nike O. Esiet and Bene Madunagu in Nigeria; Mercy Fabros and the staff of Womanhealth in the Philippines; Carol Barton, the Center for Reproductive Rights; Rhonda Copelon, Marilen Danguilan, Harold Edgar, Françoise Girard, the International Women's Health Coalition, Amy Kapczynski, Frances Kissling, Rita Raj, Bharati Sadasivam, Jael Silliman, and my graduate students at CUNY – Nirit Ben-Ari, Anne Marie Campbell, Jersey Garcia and Billy Kamaras – in the US. I am especially grateful to the wonderfully thoughtful collaborators who contributed original boxed essays and waited three years to see them appear in print: Frescia Carrasco and members of Movimiento Manuela Ramos in Peru and Colette Harris, formerly in Tajikistan and now at Virginia Tech University. In addition, I owe a special thanks to the journal with which I am associated, *Reproductive Health Matters*, its indefatigable editor, Marge Berer, and all the participants in RHM's February 2002 Bellagio meeting on health sector reforms for countless insights and up-to-date facts.

On another level, this book drew constant inspiration from dozens of women's groups with which I have had the privilege of working, both formally and informally, over the years, but especially the women of DAWN, IRRRAG, the Global Center at Rutgers University, HERA, IWHC, WEDO, and the women's caucuses of many UN conferences. Thanks to them, and most special thanks to my dear friends, Zillah Eisenstein and Sonia Corrêa, for being always there and unfailing in their personal support and their political and intellectual wisdom. Finally, thanks to my companion, Ronald June, and my son, Jonah, for making my life joyful however hard the work and however dangerous the world.

Rosalind P. Petchesky, November 2002

Notes

1 See Petchesky 1990 for a full analysis of the history, social and legal dimensions, and moral and political consequences of the Hyde Amendment and its aftermath in the US courts.
2 The proceedings of the 2001 Macalester International Roundtable, and my own contribution to it, can be found in *Macalester International*, Vol. 11 (Macalester College, Summer 2002).

1 / Transnationalizing Women's Health Movements

One of the highlights [of the World Social Forum in Porto Alegre, Brazil] was a surprise demonstration staged by 100 women against the conservative [new] Bush administration that [was] expected to overturn legislation on abortion and overseas programs on reproductive health. Shouting 'there is no justice without gender justice' and 'abortion legalization is possible!', the women paraded around the conference venue with placards flagging political calls for sexual difference, diversity, women's rights, autonomy, and reproductive choice. (DAWN 2001a: 1)

Notably, this event was happening at a meeting of some 10,000 critics of globalization, focused on ways to democratize macroeconomic decision-making and create global social justice. The participants were predominantly women from the global South, and the time was January 2001 – the beginning of the new millennium. It was a moment that encapsulated the historic convergence of women's health, human rights, and the critique of global capitalism.

In the last two decades of the twentieth century, women's health movements achieved a transnational presence and their ideas and strategies – initially focused on reproductive health and rights – took a broader shape as leadership came more strongly from the global South. Three major contextual influences informed this transnationalizing process: (1) the deleterious impacts of global capitalism and macroeconomic restructuring on poverty levels and health; (2) the rise of explicitly antifeminist, fundamentalist politico-religious forces; and (3) the HIV/AIDS pandemic, as it began to change indelibly the discourses of sexuality and the meanings of a human rights approach to health.

Women's health NGOs and transnational coalitions have been the central authors, advocates, custodians and implementers of a politics of reproductive

1

health and rights, and, to a somewhat lesser degree, of sexual health and rights.[1] Especially with regard to the 1994 International Conference on Population and Development (ICPD) in Cairo, whose Programme of Action (POA) was the first and most comprehensive international document to embody these concepts, the vigilance of women's organizations has been crucial not only to monitoring enforcement but to keeping the concepts 'alive' (DAWN 1999; Sadasivam 1999). While other groups, such as population and family planning organizations, have taken up these ideas in the pre- and post-Cairo era, their purposes and understandings are often much narrower and more instrumental than those of self-identified women's groups. Chapter 2 examines these differences in greater detail. An important task of this chapter is to discern what is distinct about women's movement perspectives, what ethical and social visions lie at their core.

Yet there is a prior question concerning just which women's movements we are talking about. How do movements become 'transnationalized'? Who claims to speak for them and with what degree of authenticity? In so far as the very notions of reproductive and sexual rights, and some of the key principles underlying them (for example, control of one's body), have been widely disparaged as emanations of Western individualism and its brand of middle-class feminism-for-export, these questions inevitably lurk around the margins of this inquiry. During and after the Cairo conference, not only religious fundamentalists but also some women's groups from the North as well as the South harshly criticized the 'Cairo consensus' as simply co-opting feminists and their ideas in order to legitimate old-style population control (see Akhter 1994; Hartmann 1994; Keysers 1999; Silliman 1999; Spivak 1999; Petchesky 1995a).

Regardless of their merits, such charges indicate that women's movements are far from homogeneous or conflict-free. Like all social movements, they are riddled with conflicts that reflect and cut across regional, class and ideological differences while raising serious issues of ownership and representation. Critical feminist theory and practice require attention to how concepts such as reproductive and sexual rights travel across various boundaries and whether those concepts can be said to have any universal validity.[2] At the very least, we can begin by looking at the different meanings and resonances they have taken on when women from the South, and from communities of colour in the North, have adapted them to their own circumstances.

From North to South: de-centring leadership, shifting vantage points

A language and politics of 'reproductive rights' had their historical origins in Northern-based women's health movements in Europe and the United States during the 1970s and early 1980s.[3] These movements were galvanized by conservative attacks on women's access to abortion as well as a feminist political framework privileging women's right to 'control over their bodies' in matters of reproduction and sexuality. But even within the United States in the early decades of 'second wave' feminism a significant diversity marked the construction of a reproductive rights politics. Women-of-colour groups, especially Puerto Rican and indigenous women, were strong leaders in the campaign to end sterilization abuse as well as to extend reproductive rights to include access to prenatal care (Shapiro 1985; Petchesky 1990). Black and Puerto Rican women in Westchester and New York City stressed motherhood rights, including entitlement to the necessary economic and social resources to care 'for all the children of their community' (Baxandall 2001: 239; Polatnick 1996; Benmayor, Torruellas and Juarbe 1992). For these women-of-colour activists, reproductive rights meant the right to have and raise children in decent, supportive conditions. Even with regard to the demands for legal abortion and contraception – commonly associated with white middle-class feminists in the US context – it is often forgotten that Black feminists and grassroots activists were among the pioneers in this movement and fought strenuously for the right of women in their communities to make their own decisions about pregnancy and childbearing (see Cade 1970; Rodrique 1990; Ross 1996; Fried 1990; Petchesky 1990). By the 1980s, women-of-colour groups such as the National Black Women's Health Project and the National Latina Health Organization exercised critical leadership in defining a broad platform linking reproductive rights to issues of poverty, racism and social welfare; and in 1994 they brought a distinct and powerful vision to the ICPD in Cairo (US Women of Color Delegation 1994; Fried 1990).

From a more global perspective as well, to dismiss the concepts of reproductive and sexual health/rights as being a 'Western' import makes little sense unless we are ready to repudiate 'democracy', 'freedom', 'national sovereignty' and 'development' for the same reason. Ideas are not the property of any one nation or culture; they 'travel', take on new meanings in diverse circumstances, and indeed may be used creatively to oppose the very (colonial or post-colonial) powers that once bred those ideas (Ram 1999; Grewal and Kaplan 1994; Bhasin and Khan 1986). Garcia-Moreno and Claro, who document the diverse trajectories and concerns of women's health movements around the world, make this argument persuasively: 'While Western ideas have played a role, women in Southern countries have generated their own analyses, organizations and movements, with and without exposure to the West, and there has been considerable cross-fertilization of ideas – across many countries and continents' (Garcia-Moreno and Claro 1994: 48; also Higer 1999; Silliman 1997; Chen 1996; Corrêa 1994; G. Sen 1994a, 1994b; M. Fried 1990; Petchesky 1990).

During the 1980s and 1990s, especially in the period of the UN conferences, this cross-fertilization contributed to the growing breadth and political sophistication of transnational women's health movements. Women's movements in the global South began to mobilize in their own ways and out of their own situations around reproductive health and rights. They formed national, regional and international networks whose purpose was entirely or in part to secure women's reproductive and sexual health and rights within a broad context of social development and gender equality.[4] Women from the South not only embraced the concept of reproductive rights but also enlarged that concept to include a broad perspective on women's reproductive health needs. It was participants from Latin America, Asia and Africa at the third International Women and Health Meeting in 1984 who urged that the newly formed Women's Global Network for Reproductive Rights (WGNRR) address a wide range of issues concerning maternal health, mortality and childbearing, and not only control over fertility (Corrêa 1994). At later forums Southern participants promoted an approach that would address women's health across the total life cycle rather than just during the 'reproductive years' (Diniz et al. 1998).

One interesting sign of how the movement's geography shifted over these years is the triennial International Women and Health Meetings (IWHM). Convened for the first time in Italy in 1975 to advocate for decriminalized abortion, the following three IWHMs were also held in Europe and the majority of their participants likewise were from Europe and North America. Beginning with the 1987 meeting, however, the IWHM was located and organized in the global South (Costa Rica, 1987; Philippines, 1990; Uganda, 1993; and Brazil, 1997), and its central themes increasingly related women's health to internationalism, economic and population policies, sexual abuse and violence, and national and global poverty. By the period preceding Cairo, a framework firmly linking reproductive and sexual health issues to both human rights and macroeconomic policies had clearly emerged, and women from the

South were a leading and majority presence (Corrêa 1994; Garcia-Moreno and Claro 1994 and http://www.iwhm-rifs.org/eng/program.htm#goals).[5]

In its earlier years, the transnational women's health movement tended to focus its energies on specific campaigns. These campaigns were primarily defences of women's right to make their own decisions about childbearing, contraception and sexuality, and were aimed at both (pronatalist) religious and fundamentalist forces and (antinatalist) population control and medical interests. Thus women activists have attempted to secure access to safe, legal and affordable abortion, contraception and maternal health services at the same time as they have opposed such abusive family planning practices as targets and 'incentives' for female sterilization and medical technologies considered harmful or inadequately tested in clinical trials. While such focused campaigns continue (for example, recent initiatives that secured a ban on the chemical sterilization method, quinacrine, in India and Chile), several major influences have stimulated the movement to develop a more comprehensive and affirmative agenda. First are the harsh economic conditions women have suffered as care givers and receivers, especially in developing countries, under structural adjustment policies and declining access to affordable health services (see Chapter 4). Second is the fury of right-wing religious and fundamentalist movements that aim to resurrect traditional patriarchal values and gender roles in societies undergoing rapid commercialization. Third is the devastating impact of HIV/AIDS, especially on women and youth in sub-Saharan Africa and the Caribbean, which has forced women's health groups as well as policy makers to address women's sexuality and sexual rights head-on. Finally, and on a more positive note, the series of UN conferences, particularly in Cairo and Beijing, provided a historic purpose and occasion for women's health activists working trans-nationally to develop a broader vision that could be implemented at the international, national and local levels.

Despite political differences and disparities in access to power and resources (both within and among countries and regions), I would argue that activists and thinkers from the South assumed intellectual and political leadership in shaping a more holistic and integrative direction for the trans-national women's health movement in the 1990s. As Jael Silliman (1999) writes:

Through the eighties and nineties women activists in the North became educated about issues of international debt, structural adjustment and US trade policies and the impact they were having on women's health worldwide. In fact, calls to reconsider debt repayments, international trade agreements and structural adjustment programs together with greater government investment in health and other basic needs were the strongest demands made by 'third world' women health activists. By the time of the series of international United Nations conferences, women's health activists saw health as an integral component of a broader development agenda.

One group that has been especially vocal in urging that 'women's reproductive health must be placed within a comprehensive human development framework' is Development Alternatives for Women in a New Era (DAWN), a network of women activists from all regions of the South (Corrêa 1994: 64). DAWN's 'holistic analysis' of reproductive health and rights links women's health needs – for 'access to contraceptive information and methods and legal abortion ... STD and cancer prevention, prenatal care and mental health services' – to a wide range of enabling conditions, including 'access to housing, education, employment, property rights and legal equality in all spheres' as well as 'freedom from physical abuse, harassment, genital mutilation and all forms of gender-based violence'. Moreover, that analysis revolves around a vision of universally available 'comprehensive health services' that would restore 'state responsibility for basic needs' and take priority over 'market forces' (Corrêa 1994: 58). As the Indian economist Gita Sen, one of DAWN's international coordinators, puts it: 'Reproductive health programs are ... likely to be more efficacious when general health and development are served. A poor female agricultural wage-laborer, ill-nourished and anemic, is likely to respond better to reproductive health care if her nutritional status and overall health improve at the same time' (G. Sen 1994a: 223).

Such basic conditions as clean water and decent, uncrowded habitations are surely integral to reproductive and sexual health and well-being – for example, using condoms or barrier methods safely, delivering and rearing healthy babies, or avoiding sexual abuse. Their absence puts women in untenable dilemmas, such as HIV+ pregnant women who must choose between breastfeeding their infants and exposing them to the risk of AIDS, or bottle-feeding them and exposing them to deadly bacterial infection from contaminated drinking water (Berer 1999).[6] The Women's Health Project in South Africa reports that 'according to the 1998 census, 20 per cent of African households [in South Africa] live in a single room and 46 per cent live in three or fewer rooms', while over half of such households are without adequate water and indoor toilets. They thus conclude: 'Currently water and sanitation services, quality of life, and the absence of disease may be sounder indicators of health than access to formal medical care' (Sadasivam 1999: 56). But why should women (or budget planners in resource-scarce societies) have to choose between safe water and sanitation on one hand and access to trained nurse-midwives, counselling and condoms on the other? Clearly, reproductive and sexual health requires both access to quality services and a reliable physical infrastructure.

Contrast this assessment with the statement of a US delegate participating in the Third Preparatory Committee Meeting (Prep Com) for Beijing in March 1995. She asserted that the US delegation must oppose a provision of the draft Platform's chapter on health urging governments to 'ensure access to safe drinking water and sanitation and put in place effective public distribution systems by the year 2000'. This, she argued, was an 'infra-structural problem', and such time-based targets were 'unrealistic' (Petchesky 1995a).[7] Yet, belying the pragmatic tone of the US position and underlying the public health concerns of the Women's Health Project is a profoundly *ethical* truth. For if infrastructural conditions and macroeconomic policies create the indispensable enabling environment for reproductive and sexual rights to become practical realities, then those conditions and policies must be incorporated into our ethical framework and seen not only as 'basic needs' but as fundamental human rights. Such social and economic rights are neither more nor less important than the personal rights more intimately related to reproduction, sexuality and health; together they form a single fabric of rights that are interdependent and indivisible.

Ethical frameworks of reproductive and sexual rights

Women's movements in different countries and regions often have very different priorities in regard to the aspects of reproductive and sexual health/ rights they seek to address. Latin American women's health organizations, for example, emerged as part of the broader movement towards democracy in a political climate emphasizing a robust concept of citizenship. Their emphasis has been on access to quality reproductive and sexual health services for women as part of their rights as citizens. South Asian women have been primarily concerned with problems of demographic targeting, coercion and promotion of sterilization and long-acting hormonal contraceptives; for them, reproductive rights resonate in the context of donor-driven policies in which the national government is often collusive. Health activists in Africa, facing dire poverty and the lack of basic services, have been preoccupied by issues of survival – high maternal and infant mortality rates, safe motherhood, and, more recently, stemming the tide of HIV/AIDS and reproductive tract infections that are killing so many young women and impairing their fertility (Alvarez 1990; Silliman 1997; Dixon-Mueller 1993). Nonetheless, the process of working together in networks and coalitions over the past decade and a half has produced common understandings that constitute a shared ethical core. Informing every aspect of this ethical core is a realization drawn from women's everyday experience: that, particularly for women, all human rights – rights to political and bodily self-determination, health, and development – have both personal and social dimensions, and these are integrally connected.

In an article written in preparation for the Cairo conference, Sonia Corrêa and I delineated four principles of a feminist ethical perspective on reproductive and sexual rights: (1) *bodily integrity*, or the right to dignity and respect for one's physical body and to be free from abuses and assaults, including unwanted pregnancy and unwanted sex; (2) *personhood*, which is closely associated with bodily integrity and implies the right to self-determination and respect in one's decisions about reproduction and sexuality; (3) *equality* in access to health services and all social resources, not only of women with men (gender equality) but of women with one another across lines of class, race, ethnicity, age, marital status, sexual orientation, physical ability, and other common social dividers; and (4) *diversity*, or the right to be respected in one's group affinities and cultural differences, in so far as these are freely chosen and women are empowered to speak on their own behalf, not subordinated to group claims in the name of tradition. All four aspects of this framework, we argued, depended on basic *enabling conditions* for women's empowerment and development. In other words, women's empowerment cannot be achieved without transforming the overall social, economic and cultural systems – including but not limited to family and reproductive systems – in which their subordination is entrenched (Corrêa and Petchesky 1994; see also Dixon-Mueller 1993). This means that not only the negative but also the *affirmative* dimensions of rights deserve priority; thus, sexual rights involve the right to free expression, pleasure and satisfaction as much as the right to freedom from abuse (Petchesky 2000; Klugman 2000). It also means that 'differences based on race, power, class and access to resources' (as well as ethnicity and age) must be factored into the calculations of gender differences, including in the gathering of data; and that women must never be 'treated as a unitary category ... in the international policy dialogue' (Silliman 1997).

The concepts of bodily integrity and personhood, while often seen as the hallmarks of Western liberal philosophy and the value it places on individualism and property ownership, are firmly ensconced in international human rights instruments.[8] The 'right to life, liberty and security of person' was first recognized in the 1948 Universal Declaration of Human Rights (UDHR), repeated in the International Covenant on Economic, Social and Cultural Rights (ICESCR, 1967) and various regional human rights conventions, and reaffirmed in the Cairo POA's Principle 2. It is the foundation for a wide range of reproductive and sexual rights, including fully informed consent and freedom from coercion with regard to family planning methods (that is, 'freedom from forced pregnancy, sterilization and abortion'); freedom from female genital mutilation (FGM), child marriage or other harmful traditional practices; freedom from sexual abuse, gender violence, and sexual trafficking; and the freedom of all persons 'to enjoy and control their sexual and reproductive life, having due regard to the rights of others' (IPPF 1995).[9] This genealogy refutes the claim sometimes made in UN conferences that reproductive and sexual rights are 'new inventions'.

Based on such established human rights principles, feminists affirm that women's health, pleasure and empowerment must be treated as ends in themselves and not merely as means towards other social goals – for example, reducing population numbers, producing more healthy babies, or helping to create expanded markets and cheap labour pools. Unfortunately, too many population specialists, economists and public health officials have latched onto the mantra of 'women's empowerment' for precisely these instrumentalist reasons. As Mahmoud Fathalla (1999) observes, 'The concept of MCH [maternal and child health] focuses special attention on women when and if they are reproducing, to ensure that society gets a healthy child, but often neglects their other reproduction-related health needs.' Likewise, Silliman points out that 'Investing in Women' has become the 'catch-phrase ... of all the major development organizations including the World Bank', as well as bilateral donor agencies and government ministries, who see women's education and reproductive health as efficient means towards their own aims rather than as fundamental human rights (Silliman 1997).

Such instrumentalism conflicts sharply with the ways in which women's movements in the South have embraced the concepts of women's self-determination and right to control over their bodies and adapted those concepts to local women's situations. For example, the campaign against FGM conducted by women's groups in the Middle East has taken the idea of bodily integrity as its ethical centrepiece and presents itself unequivocally in national and global arenas as a human rights campaign (see Toubia 1995; Magdy 1999; Seif El Dawla 1999). In a different context, Kalpana Ram charts the transnationality of the discourse of 'owning our bodies' through the recurrent uses of this slogan by Indian women's health activists from the 1930s until the 1990s. Her project is to document how 'key terms such as choice, autonomy and freedom are taken up and given different meanings' by women's groups and the state in different social and cultural settings; and how they are mediated by colonialism, postcolonialism, class and caste. As an example, she cites the Indian feminist campaign during the 1980s against prenatal sex selection through amniocentesis, used by middle-class Indian couples to abort female foetuses in the interests of son preference. That campaign, she suggests, did not reject notions of autonomy and women's right to control their bodies; rather, it recast those concepts in the framework of women's collective interests and rights to be valued as persons. Such diasporic travelling of feminist ideas, she argues, '[testifies] to a lasting vitality in certain concepts engendered by modernity' (Ram 1999: 626–8; Petchesky 1995b).

Like the feminist health movement in India, other Southern women's groups and, following their lead, the transnational women's health movement as a whole have understood bodily integrity and *individual* rights of the body and person as deeply connected to *social* rights. They have rejected false theoretical assumptions, whether from liberals or cultural nationalists, that dichotomize individuals and communities and either associate human rights with the fiction of an abstract 'individual' or, conversely, deny the reality of the body's individuality altogether. Without the ability and means to control their fertility and to be self-determined, experience pleasure, and be free from abuse in their sexual lives, women and girls cannot function as responsible, fully participating members of their families and communities; they cannot exercise citizenship (Corrêa and Petchesky 1994). Conversely, being self-determined in their sexuality and fertility depends on many other social and economic components of women's health, development and empowerment. Corrêa expresses this complexity on behalf of DAWN:

> DAWN affirms that the 'self' reaches far beyond the notion of bodily integrity and must be understood in the context of all significant family, cultural, social and economic relationships. But the decision-making self

must remain at the core of reproductive rights (with bodily integrity), and our challenge now is to expand the framework without demolishing this conceptual cornerstone. (Corrêa 1994: 77–8)

A pivotal concept informing feminist standpoints on reproductive and sexual rights is that of *women's empowerment*. Batliwala (1994) gives the most cogent definition of this concept, which she calls 'the process of challenging existing power relations, and of gaining greater control over the sources of power'. While the rhetoric of empowerment now abounds nearly everywhere among development specialists and was incorporated into the language of the Cairo POA (thanks to feminist initiatives), its meanings in mainstream contexts have usually been diluted to become indistinguishable from raising women's status through piecemeal reforms. The discourses of 'gender mainstreaming' and 'gender sensitivity' likewise imply this mechanistic approach and its assumption that the problems of gender inequality can be fixed by redirecting some resources toward women's and girls' education, skills, and access to health services and improving 'communication' between women and men. Such an approach ignores the deep-lying imbalances of power and the social structures and practices of subordination that characterize relations between women and men in most societies. Critical feminist analysis (drawing from Foucault, Marxism and poststructuralism) understands power as not only socially constructed but also dynamic, fluid and always engaged in contestation through a wide range of tactics deployed by the 'oppressed' – including subversion, subterfuge and sometimes outright resistance.[10] It conceptualizes empowerment as entailing not only material but also human resources and social, collective interaction.

Feminist concepts of power and empowerment are closely related to their challenges to mainstream views of sustainable development.[11] These challenges include a strong critique of the neo-Malthusian doctrine attributing not only poverty and social unrest but, more recently, environmental destruction to uncontrolled population growth. From the standpoint of the feminist ethical framework outlined above, this doctrine is pernicious and often racist because it blames the victims of economic injustices (impoverished and dark-skinned women) for problems whose causes lie far from their villages and shanties. By focusing narrowly on strategies to lower fertility, the concept of 'overpopulation' provides one of the most enduring rationales for population control policies that target women in poverty, who are frequently women of racial and ethnic minorities or lower castes. Such policies too often use coercive methods and disregard the human rights and basic health needs of such women and their children (Bandarage 1997; CWPE 1993; Hartmann 1995; G. Sen 1994b). As De Barbieri stresses,

> population policies were introduced to slow population growth without altering the fundamental dimensions of social inequality. ... The unequal distribution of wealth has appeared to be taken for granted in the introduction of population policy. (1994: 259)

In addition to the ethical and social justice arguments, critics of neo-Malthusian doctrine and its most recent environmentalist incarnation have countered that position on devastating empirical grounds, citing such facts as:

- the highest fertility rates are in countries with the sparsest populations (for example, in sub-Saharan Africa);

- some of the world's most 'overcrowded' countries and cities have the highest *per capita* income levels and rates of economic growth (the Netherlands, Hong Kong and New York City);

- robust economic growth, fertility decline and high levels of contraceptive use can coexist with enormous income gaps and persistent poverty (Brazil and the US), whereas no or slow economic growth can coincide with low fertility and very positive health indicators (Kerala, Costa Rica and, earlier, Sri Lanka);

- some of the most environmentally polluted countries are those with severe population declines (Russia, Poland and Ukraine); and finally,

- fertility rates have lowered in nearly all countries, while the continued growth of the world's population is due mainly to the simultaneous *decline in mortality*.[12]

According to feminist economist Juliet Schor, economic growth itself plays a key role in environmental degradation: 'More production of steel and autos creates more air pollution and global warming, more newspapers and houses lead to the felling of more trees, more food generally implies more pesticides and increased output in the rise in toxic substances' (quoted in Harcourt 1994b: 12). Both environmentalists and feminists have pointed out that the worst source of global pollution is overconsumption by Northern, developed countries – an analysis accepted by government delegates in Copenhagen in 1995 and repeated many times in the World Summit for

Social Development (WSSD) Declaration and Programme of Action. In other words, contrary to the old Malthusian logic that 'fewer and better' children were the formula for prosperity, it would appear that the dominant path to modernity has meant more and more *things* in place of children; plenitude, not people, is the worst polluter (Amalric 1994; Mazur 1994; Mies and Shiva 1993).

Growth-centred models of development, particularly in so far as they privilege macroeconomic indicators of output and official employment levels, also contain an inherent gender bias, for they leave out of account the (often unpaid) labour of women in households, communities and the informal sector (Harcourt 1994a; Kabeer 1994; Elson 1995). From a feminist standpoint, a key criterion of sustainability must be a policy's or an industry's social as well as its environmental impacts, particularly including its impact on gender relations. In 1994 Emberson-Bain thus argued that the development of mining in the Pacific island economies must be considered unsustainable, in so far as it destroyed women's traditional land rights and reinforced male power and authority over women. Likewise, the US Women of Color Delegation to the ICPD, calling attention to 'the Southern conditions' of poor women and most women of color in the North, argued:

> Poverty and environmental degradation throughout the world inform us that European style 'economic development' is unsustainable; and that approaches to sustainable development cannot simply target 'population growth' alone, while overlooking critical issues of racism, sexism, bad development policies, resource overexploitation for the few, inequitable distribution of wealth, unbridled consumption, and environmentally harmful technologies, as factors impeding sustainable development for all people. (US Women of Color Delegation 1994: 2)

Also in 1994, Gita Sen, reviewing three decades of population and development policies, predicted that 'policies targeted at improving macroeconomic management or increasing gross national product growth while ignoring or worsening the incomes and livelihoods of the majority' – for example, through disinvestments in the social sector – were likely to fail in their own terms. 'In the longer term,' she wrote, 'improving health and education, along with meeting other basic needs, raises the quality of a country's labour force, which is critical in determining the economy's growth potential and competitiveness', besides helping to lower birth rates (Sen 1994b: 66–8).[13] This argument about human or social capital is one that, at the dawn of the twenty-first century and in the wake of the failures of earlier structural adjustment programmes (SAPs) and economic crisis in Asia, Russia, and Latin America, even economists at the World Bank have come to accept. But meeting basic needs such as health has to do with social justice, not just increasing productivity.

From the standpoint of transnational women's health movements seeking to empower women as reproductive, sexual and political actors, recent economic crises and cuts in public health services have brought home that 'market-driven policies and other macroeconomic issues can no longer be left off the table when sustainable development, women's rights, the environment and health are discussed' (Sadasivam 1999: 11). Feminists have condemned the ways that multilateral donor institutions, donor countries and developing country governments have allowed debt service, military expenditures and free-market priorities to override the desperate need for public investments in health care and other enabling conditions. Along with other groups, they have called for demilitarization, debt cancellation and international regulation of unsustainable, unhealthy economic practices through such devices as taxes on speculative capital flows. Women's health activists from the global South and Eastern Europe have sounded the alarm about reproductive and other health threats involved not only in environmental toxins released by industries but in unfair trade practices (for example, the US embargo on Cuba that prevents women there from receiving mammograms, or unregulated drug prices that prevent people with AIDS in Africa and Asia from receiving life-prolonging but economically unaffordable medications).

Such links between health and economic development policies, between sustainability and human needs, are now acknowledged by the major international agencies responsible for health funding, especially the World Bank. But we seldom hear from international economists that such needs are also basic human rights that must take priority over profits and growth-centred economic policies. In other words, there is little recognition that dominant macroeconomic models and entities 'are bearers of social relations and are imbued with social values' as well as power relations, and that these models, values, and power relations 'are not immutable' (Elson and Cagatay 2000: 28). In order for reproductive and sexual rights, or health rights more generally, to become a material reality, we can no longer afford to think of macroeconomic regimes (finance, trade, fiscal policy) and human rights regimes as entirely separate discourses or entirely separate worlds.

1.1

Reproductive health and sexual rights are human rights

Rights cannot be divorced from needs. Reproductive and sexual health and other basic human needs – education, sanitation, clean water, nutrition – are equally important and interdependent; all are human rights. Especially for women, good pre-natal and obstetric care, safe contraception, and other aspects of health are inseparable from such basic amenities as reliable transportation, hygienic conditions and clean water. At the same time, their rights to liberty, security of the person and development are unattainable without comprehensive, accessible and affordable reproductive and sexual health services and the freedom to make decisions about their fertility and sexuality. These rights form a seamless web, and all are grounded in basic human needs. To rank them denies the realities of women's lives, especially for poor women.

(Excerpt from flier, circulated at the UNGASS for ICPD+5, March 1999, by Women's Coalition for ICPD, made up of 80 NGOs from around the world.)

Ethical frameworks: relinking the body and social development, human rights and basic needs

At the March 1999 Prep Com meeting for the UN General Assembly Special Session's five-year review of the Cairo conference (Cairo+5), the 'pro-life' Catholic newspaper *Vivant!* published a feature article, replete with statistical data and graphics, condemning the 'flawed human rights-based approach to health'. Central to the article's attack was an argument touting the discourse of basic needs as the ethically and socially superior framework to that of human rights. Associating such infrastructural conditions as safe water and nutrition with the 'needs' approach and reproductive and sexual health with the 'rights' approach, it alleged that 'indiscriminate funding for the ICPD's idealistically high standards of reproductive and sexual health *rights*' had caused 'underfunding and deterioration of more basic, practicable and affordable health *needs*'. And it further insinuated that such 'flawed' priorities represent the agendas of the West and its blatant disregard for the genuine needs and priorities of women in the South (Joseph 1999).[14]

One does not have to defend the deplorable record of Western governments and corporations with regard to Southern women's health needs to see that this rhetoric has an underlying strategic aim: to demonstrate the alignment of Vatican concerns in the context of UN politics with those of the global South against the North, and in the bargain to discredit the transnational women's movements. I shall analyse these strategic alignments and power blocs in the next chapter. Here I want to consider the fallacies in any position or ethical framework – whether coming from a right-wing religious group or from orthodox Marxists – that asserts a dichotomy between rights and needs and, as part of that dichotomy, a hierarchy subordinating some health and bodily needs (especially those related to reproductive choice and sexual pleasure) to others. On its face, such a dichotomy contains an implicit gender bias, as the Women's Coalition for ICPD made clear in its response to the *Vivant!* polemic (see Box 1.1).

It is worth tracing the origins of this dichotomous thinking along with its gender and ethical implications.[15] Ironically, given the Vatican's historical anti-communism and anti-Marxism as well as the venerable natural rights tradition in Catholicism, the concept of a 'needs-based approach' distinct from a 'rights-based' one actually derives from classical Marxism. However unaware, it echoes the distinction Marx and Engels made between 'the satisfaction of human needs' and 'bourgeois rights'. According to the orthodox interpretation of Marx's division of social relations into a material 'base' and an ideological 'superstructure', the former not only determines the latter but also is the repository of the most basic necessities for the production of human life (that is, 'needs'). 'Rights', on the other hand, refer to the catalogue of civil and political freedoms that groups demand from those in power to assert their equal claims to citizenship. They are the means toward emancipation but not the ends; the conditions of 'mental life' and 'idealism' (note the *Vivant!* article's description of reproductive and sexual rights as 'idealistically high standards') but not of real social and material life (in other words, the difference between voting and eating).[16]

Of course there is a certain kernel of truth here, which is what makes both the Marxist and the *Vivant!* positions seem compelling at first. As I illustrated earlier, Western, developed countries, particularly the United States, surely do champion reproductive and sexual health rights to the virtual exclusion of health infrastructure needs such as safe water and sanitation. On the other hand, Southern governments and local officials tend to associate 'development' with large, publicly 'visible' and structural projects, 'such as building roads or digging wells', to the detriment of the less visible, less 'material' health needs of women and children (Mukhopadhyay and Sivaramayya 1999: 349). But the subordination of development to individual rights (seen by Northern countries primarily in terms of political and civil rights), and of human rights to economic development and poverty alleviation (associated by Southern countries and the Vatican with 'basic human needs') are *really two sides of a coin*. Both imply that individual needs and social needs, needs and rights, somehow belong to different realms.

This dichotomization was of course a major outgrowth of the Cold War political climate and has had a direct counterpart in debates over human rights generally. Feminist critics of mainstream human rights organizations and discourses have argued that the very concept of different 'generations' of rights implies the priority of civil and political over economic and social rights. Such prioritizing has a distinctly miserly side, as Florence Butegwa observes:

> Civil and political rights are characterized as negative and cost-free rights in that governments are only required to abstain from activities which would violate them. This is contrasted with economic, social and cultural rights which require governments to do something, thereby committing considerable resources, to ensure individuals the enjoyment of those rights. (Butegwa 1995: 34)

Yet this distinction is fallacious, since some economic and social rights – for example, legislation to uphold non-discrimination in health services – are quite low-cost, while civil and political rights require legal infrastructure and enforcement mechanisms and thus public financing. In fact, all human rights enforcement depends to some extent on resources, but economic resources alone are useless without political will (UNDP 2000a).

Although the World Conference on Human Rights in Vienna in 1993 endorsed the principle of indivisibility among the different kinds of rights and their respective international covenants, as well as affirming the right to development as fundamental and inalienable, there is still very little effective international enforcement of economic, social and cultural rights. The 'right to the highest attainable standard of physical and mental health' has been enshrined in the World Health Organization (WHO) Constitution and the ICESCR since their advent in the 1960s. But the human rights treaty bodies only began reviewing health, and specifically reproductive and sexual health, violations in around 1994–5, following the Cairo and Beijing conferences (Center for Reproductive Rights 2002; Stanchieri, Merali and Cook 1999). The main international bodies responsible for health and development – the World Bank and the WHO – rarely if ever cast their policies in human rights terms, preferring the supposed greater measurability and 'objectivity' of cost-benefit approaches (see Chapter 4). Only the United Nations Development Programme (UNDP) has attempted to make a serious departure from this economistic framework, devoting its entire *Human Development Report* for 2000 to analysing the complementarities between 'the ideas of human development and those of human rights' (UNDP 2000a: 20). By and large, rights and needs remain split even within the UN's institutional machinery.

Underlying the rights–needs dichotomy is a basic fallacy. What it ignores is that rights are merely the codification of needs, reformulating them as ethical and/or legal norms and thus implying a duty on the part of those in power to provide all the means necessary to make sure those needs are met. This duty is affirmative as well as negative; that is, 'states [and other centres of power] have an obligation not only to respect (to not do harm) but also to take positive measures to ensure [the enjoyment of rights]' (Copelon and Petchesky 1995: 358). Rights are meaningless, in other words, without needs. But neither can needs stand on their own as ethical principles, because they lack any intrinsic methods for (a) determining whose and which needs should take precedence, (b) assigning obligations to specific parties for fulfilling those needs, and (c) empowering those whose needs are at stake to speak for themselves. Without some principle of personhood or moral agency, which is only available through a human rights framework, there is nothing to prevent the state, medical experts or religious authorities from deciding what is good for me on the basis of political expediency, aggregate data or fundamentalist interpretations of scripture. Rights bearers (who may be groups as well as individuals) are by definition those who are authorized – *or who may be self-authorized through a process of popular politicization and mobilization* – to make claims in defence of their own needs, now discursively if not officially formulated as rights.

This may seem to beg the question of whether some needs, and their corresponding rights, are more 'basic' or 'fundamental' than others. But my whole point is the logical interconnection between rights and needs and the indivisibility of different forms of rights, so that prioritizing makes no sense. This is especially apparent when we look at specific reproductive and sexual rights and the ways in which they cluster together with other rights in women's everyday lives. Even deciding whether to classify such rights as 'social', 'economic', 'cultural' or also 'civil and political' is very difficult. The Cairo POA (Paragraph 7.3) defines 'reproductive rights' as the right of women 'to decide freely and responsibly the number, spacing and timing of their children and to have the information and means to do so'. But how can a woman avail herself of this right if she lacks the financial resources to pay for reproductive health services or the transport to get to them; if she is illiterate or given no

Eleven conditions for 'deciding freely and responsibly the number, spacing and timing of one's children'

- Safe, reliable maternal and child health services linked to a viable primary health care system;
- Adequate nutrition and general health conditions to avoid a wide range of risks and complications, from anaemia to HIV infection;
- Access to safe contraception, good information, counselling and follow-up care;
- Literacy and education (to read package inserts or clinic wall posters, for example);
- Access to jobs, health insurance or other financial resources to pay for services, especially with the demise of social benefits and the increase in user fees;
- Convenient transportation to reach the services;
- Freedom from oppressive religious and traditional codes that constrain choice;
- The right to decide on and express one's sexuality, 'free of coercion, discrimination and violence' (Beijing Platform, Paragraph 96);
- Freedom from domestic violence or forced pregnancy through war rape and ethnic violence;
- Abrogation of restrictive trade and patent monopolies or political embargoes that impede access of poor countries to essential medicines, medical equipment and commodities;
- Participation of women in community groups and women's NGOs and in all levels of government policy making about reproductive and sexual health.

information in a language she understands; if her workplace is contaminated with pollutants that have an adverse effect on pregnancy; or if she is harassed by parents, a husband or in-laws who will abuse or beat her if they find out she uses birth control? (See **Box 1.2**.) The 'means to do so' contain a universe of freedoms and capabilities out of reach for many women and girls.

We might visualize these different aspects of reproductive health rights as a series of concentric circles, beginning with the most intimate relations and radiating out to the most societal and even global. Women with their own jobs and incomes may still be dependent on a husband (if they have one) to get access to health insurance that will cover maternity care, since so many women work in marginal, informal or uninsured sectors (Sadasivam 1999). Nor does having adequate information and clinic services for contraception protect women from domestic threats that put their well-being (or their marriage) in danger if they dare to utilize those services. As one rural worker in North-east Brazil reported to IRRRAG researchers:

He used to snoop in my things [until he found birth control pills hidden in a suitcase].... He asked me, 'What do you have these for? Don't you want to live with me anymore?... Then he took the pills, put them in water, dissolved them and buried them, saying, 'If I see these pills again you will pay me.' Now, 'pay me' means he will beat me. (Diniz *et al.* 1998: 59–60)

A substantial literature documents the intersections between violence against women, both domestic and clinic-based, and threats or impairments to their reproductive health (see Heise 1995; Heise, Moore and Toubia 1995; Weiss and Rao Gupta 1998; CRLP/CLADEM 1999). But the barriers to enjoyment of reproductive and sexual health rights may run deeper. Studies show that grassroots women like those active in local government councils, or *panchayats*, in India often comply with the hierarchy of priorities that puts road building before, say, preventing reproductive tract infections (RTIs). Many women tend to see their own health problems as less important 'when cost is an issue' or even as natural and inevitable, thus 'seeking medical care too late or not at all' (Mukhopadhyay and Sivaramayya 1999: 347; Sadasivam 1999: 11). But don't the very roots of such compliance and self-denial involve issues that directly affect women's right to development? How can the right to development be separated from the right to education, the right to political participation and participation in women's NGOs, and the cultural changes necessary to nourish women's empowerment and self-worth? What about the women in Iran who endure infertility, birth complications or stillbirths because of working since childhood in the carpet-weaving industry and suffering underdeveloped pelvises? (Sadasivam 1999) If they could bring their case before the UN human rights bodies, would they cite violations of their health rights, their reproductive rights, their right to education or their right not to be exploited by child labour practices or involuntary servitude? On the other hand, how can governments in debt-burdened poor countries address all these rights at once? Don't such countries have a right to a more equitable share of global resources? But, of course, all these rights apply here, are interconnected and indivisible, and are grounded in basic needs.

The critical importance of this indivisibility principle and the ways in which poverty creates insurmountable barriers to women's reproductive and sexual health become evident even in the famously 'healthy' state of Kerala in southern India. There, Vanita Nayak Mukherjee (DAWN's regional coordinator for South Asia) has been conducting qualitative research among women in poor fishing communities on the possible links between their high incidence of RTIs and menstrual and toilet practices. Her findings tell a grim story in which the combination of lack of sanitary or toilet facilities and culturally embedded gender discrimination seem to exacerbate reproductive, urinary and gastric morbidity among poor women. Poverty and the absence of toilets affect both sexes. But women alone are condemned by the norms of modesty and shame to suffer bladder retention and postponed defecation until they can sneak outdoors in the dark of night, whereas men apparently feel free at any time of day to defecate on the beach and urinate by the roadside. In addition, because of the lack of sanitary pads and private places to put them on during menstruation, women feel compelled to go about their lives with unhygienic layers of soiled garments underneath their skirts (Mukherjee 2002). What could be more graphic evidence that access to clean water and sanitation ('infrastructure') is a right essential, not only for health in general, but also for reproductive health and gender equality?

For *dalit* women in Andhra Pradesh, issues of health and reproductive and sexual rights form a seamless web with land issues, indebtedness and caste discrimination. One of the biggest concerns for activists is to organize and politicize dispossessed agricultural labourers, many of whom have lost the small plots allocated to them through land reform measures because of debt. But debt itself is inextricable from the unjust economics of the health care system. As a recent survey confirms, 'the second most common cause of rural indebtedness' in India is 'the increased cost of medical care' due to cost recovery and privatization trends in the health sector (Sadasivam 1999: 11). The more endemic violations of health and reproductive rights that *dalits* face as a result of poverty and discrimination include no water or sanitation in rural villages; persistently high infant and maternal mortality; and a growing incidence of not only RTIs but now HIV, as more and more *dalit* women have become migrant workers and been recruited into the international sex trade.[17]

Yet these very examples from India suggest that the meanings of human rights and their potential violations, far from being universal and inalienable, are malleable and specific to multiple intersections of class, gender, caste, ethnicity, geography, age, marital status, and so on. If they are to have any relevance to real life, rights must be seen as dense, dynamic, concrete, and above all in perpetual motion within spirals of contextualized political discourse and action.

A note on the irrepressibility of rights – deeper into the thicket

[T]he irreducible contamination of the subject of human rights indicates that we can no longer theorize the normativity of rights claims in terms of the rational universality of a pure, atemporal and context-independent human dignity that is ultimately separated from economics or politics.... Yet, *[rights] are the only way for the disenfranchised to mobilize*. (Cheah 1997: 261, my italics)

Until now I have spoken as though a 'human rights approach' were a taken-for-granted, unproblematic terrain. But I am by no means oblivious to the enormous contestation surrounding human rights discourse and to the very real limitations, both theoretical and political, with which the legacy of human rights is encumbered. This is neither the time nor the place for a review of the voluminous literature both defending and critiquing 'rights talk'.[18] My purpose here is briefly to explain my own understanding of what makes human rights so troublesome and at the same time so irrepressible – and ultimately indispensable to movements for social change. The paradox we confront is that, while numerous cultural, Marxist and postcolonial critics, especially in India and the United States, excoriate the Western, individualist, state-centred and legalistic biases of mainstream human rights traditions, the very social movements that many of those critics support – including feminist, anti-globalization, anti-racist, *dalit*, indigenous, and others – continue to invoke the language of human rights. What are we to make of this, and what theoretical assumptions are embedded in all I have said thus far that make me believe there is a politically defensible and philosophically coherent way of framing human rights as an oppositional discourse?

The first task is that we must stop thinking of human rights as either a fixed body of principles agreed by assembled rational reflectors, in a Rawlsian 'original condition' detached from all worldly identities and interests; or a bag of normative tools and weapons that the legions of innocent oppressed and disenfranchised wield against their subjugators. Rather, we should think of human rights as a discursive field of power relations that operate within the domain of racialized, gendered global capital in its present form – relations that are constantly in a process of realignment and change. In rethinking the meanings and philosophical ground of human rights, I am indebted not only, obviously, to Foucault's concept of power but to Pheng Cheah's very thoughtful reflection on 'Posit(ion)ing Human Rights in the Current Global Conjuncture' (1997). In that essay, Cheah not only challenges the false dichotomy between a cultural relativist (presumably Asian) and a universalist (presumably Western) view of human rights, which many feminists have also done; he also goes further to insist on 'the irreducible imbrication of *all* claims to human rights' – including those of transnational NGOs – 'within the force-field of global capitalism'. By invoking human rights claims (to reproductive and sexual health care, gender equality, sexual freedom, non-discrimination, etcetera), we do not position ourselves *outside* the power relations of global capitalism, markets, and their institutional bulwarks. Rather, we ourselves, and the very human rights claims we assert, are inevitably conditioned and 'contaminated' by these same forces; we exist within them even as we work to transform them (Cheah 1997: 255, 265).

Cheah outlines what he calls the 'three voices' of current human rights discourse: (1) that of 'the economically hegemonic North or West', which espouses a Kantian universalism grounded in the common endowment of *individuals* with human dignity and reason; (2) that of Asian governments (presented in the Bangkok Declaration during the 1993 preparatory process for the World Conference on Human Rights in Vienna), whose position resembles Hegel's *corporate state* and is grounded in national sovereignty, cultural particularity, and political will; and (3) that of transnational human rights NGOs, whose own variant of universalism 'is mindful of systemic economic inequality, genuine cultural diversity and gender' and is grounded in a vision of a *'global civil society'* or 'public sphere' that transcends 'particularistic interests' (245–7, 253). Though speaking on behalf of different sets of political actors and from different political locations, 'all three voices share the same normative framework', Cheah argues, since all '[claim] to be the pure voice of reason representing genuine universality' and believe in the use of reason to transform 'existing institutional structures' and achieve universal human dignity.

Although he insists on the inevitable complicity and interiority of all three voices in 'the globalization of capital', Cheah's project is not to repudiate human rights. Rather, he seeks to affirm the irresistibility of human rights as a discourse for negotiating globalization, at the same time re-examining the normative basis of that discourse. What is interesting about his argument is that, while sharing the values of feminist and human rights NGOs, he wants to go 'beyond a critical analysis of positionality' or location that would simply unmask the hypocrisies of the Western individualist or nationalist-communitarian human rights claims. It is not difficult to expose the ways in which the US uses a carrot-and-stick approach to alleged human rights violations by China or other countries to bargain for favourable trade conditions or patent rights for its transnational corporations and to shore up its own political and moral as well as economic hegemony. Nor do we lack countless examples of the ways in which Asian, African and Latin American governments not only accommodate patriarchal values and religious institutions but also, in their eagerness to court foreign investment and aid, abet multinationals' exploitation of cheap (female) labour and the sacrifice of small local producers to the export economy. It is much trickier, however, for transnational women's and human rights NGOs to admit that our own positioning *vis-à-vis* national and international institutions and our own conceptual frameworks are imbricated in global capitalist power relations, that there is no pure and innocent place to be.

Cheah's critical reassessment of the positioning of human rights discourse has three important implications for transnational women's (and other) NGOs – implications that offer both a more realistic and a more open-ended scenario for political activism. First, with regard to the institutional framework where debates over human rights norms and claims are most intensively fought out, Cheah calls into question whether a 'global civil society' or an 'international public sphere' really exists.[19] We might imagine such a sphere – a site where 'consensual rational procedures of political decision making and law enactment' occur (1997: 253) – in the series of UN conferences of the past decade, or in claims brought before UN human rights bodies, in both of which transnational NGOs have played an increasingly effective part. But Cheah's warning to us that 'no international public sphere or global civil society *in the full sense* has come into existence' (1997: 258, my italics) calls forth the stark reality of such proceedings, undeniable to anyone who has witnessed them. For they are still mired in statist posturing; appeals to religion, tradition and national sovereignty; and the dominance of neoliberal macroeconomic ideology (see Chapter 2). At the same time, Cheah's realism contains a hopeful note. It leaves open the possibility that the very imperfect UN procedures in which many women's and human rights NGOs are currently engaged may be an inchoate form of the more democratic and participatory global governance we would like to envision.[20]

The second implication of Cheah's realist-cosmopolitan analysis of human rights has to do with defining who are its actors or agents and the inevitable particularity of their voices. A global civil society does not yet exist for the simple reason that there is no reliable mechanism for representing the 'voices of the oppressed', and the oppositional movements and organizations that now claim to act in their name are themselves divided by multiple identities, interests and ideological positions. Cheah again brings us down to earth by recalling the 'impossibility of locating a pure voice of the subject of oppression or a genuinely popular voice, and therefore, of any vision of human rights claiming an all-encompassing universal validity' (1997: 256). This reminder has been a constant theme sounded for over two decades by women of colour, Third World and postcolonial feminists, whose theories of difference, location and intersectionality (of race, class, ethnicity, age, geography, etcetera) have irrevocably fractured the hegemonic image of 'woman' or 'global feminism'.[21] Even taking the infinitesimal fragment of the world's women represented at, much less able to participate in, UN conferences, it is obvious that innumerable divisions of region, class, race/ethnicity, culture, positioning within global capitalism, and access to power and resources divide them. Yet the absence of any universality among the claimants to human rights precludes neither 'the very real normative power that human rights exert on various types of actors' (1997: 260) nor the very real political power that transnational coalitions, organized across such differences, can mobilize. Such coalitions can use human rights norms both to give those norms themselves greater clarity and efficacy and to transform the global balance of forces.

The question of subjects and the ineluctable fact that human rights subjects must be created within particular historical conjunctures brings us to a third implication of Cheah's analysis, a kind of paradox. This is that the collective subjects of human rights do not exist *a priori* but are themselves constituted by the very (performative) process of articulating and demanding enforcement of human rights claims. In Cheah's terms, 'They are constituted as an institutionally recognizable collective, which they were previously not, so that they can have leverage as the subjects/ objects of institutional decision making' (1997: 257). This dependence on the very procedures and institutional forces that one is challenging to act (in the case of national judiciaries, international organizations and human rights treaty bodies), or to concede responsibility (in the case of states, transnational corporations and international financial institutions), brings us back to the 'contamination' referred to earlier. To become legitimized and, indeed, realized as actors within the UN system, transnational women's NGOs have had to learn and in many ways internalize the rules and procedures of that system. To participate in international and regional gatherings, they have had to rely on and compete among themselves for resources and recognition from various international donors, including not only government agencies and private foundations but also the World Bank. Even counter-hegemonic groups and social movements asserting human rights demands in the streets – against the World Trade Organization (WTO) or the G-8, in favour of a moratorium on debt or access to essential medicines (see Chapters 3 and 5) – do so in response to institutional frameworks and agendas set by those in power.

But here, too, acknowledging that we act – and even achieve our identities as actors – within existing power regimes has a liberating potential. To misname this process 'cooptation' is simply to reduce all power to a zero-sum game and therefore to misconstrue the nature of power. For, to the extent that the historical conjuncture within which we operate (in this case globalized, racialized, gendered capitalism) is always in flux, 'no single actor' – neither the US government, nor Pfizer, nor Nike, nor the World Bank, nor the WTO – totally controls it. If our ideas and 'points of resistance' (reproductive and sexual rights, sustainable development, gender equality) are continually being 'reinscribed into the text of global capitalism' (1997: 265), those same ideas and resistance points, framed as human rights, also have the power to change existing historical conditions and power relations. As Cheah puts it, drawing on the work of Jacques Derrida:

> The 'historicity' or 'finitude' of reason … refers to reason's constitutive inscription within a shifting field of historical forces that it cannot control or transcend. But at the same time, this moving base also holds the ineradicable promise of ethical transformation because it exceeds and cannot be captured by the hegemonic forces of any given historical present. (1997: 263)[22]

The understanding of power as fluid, dynamic and open-ended has relevance to the form and effectiveness of human rights claims. Human rights, rather than being a transcendent body of norms that we (rational actors) create and 'can choose to either embrace or repudiate' (1997: 264), are simply the rhetorical structure 'given to us' in the present historical conditions for asserting counter-hegemonic statements of justice. In this sense, they are a necessary and irrepressible element of contemporary movements for social change. This awareness puts the usual objections to human rights in a very different light. For one thing, we no longer have to waste time arguing over 'the sterile opposition between universalism and cultural relativism' (1997: 235), since the 'historicity' of human rights claims means they always must be *both at once*. This is similar to the argument I made earlier about the necessary interdependence between rights and needs, and between individual and social rights. Attempts to concretize universalist principles by adapting them to particular circumstances of particular (gendered, contextualized) bodies can only strengthen the possibilities for their material enforcement. Attempts to transform the individualist, state-centred conceptions of human rights derived from Western traditions into models that reflect local diversities and community-based decision making become vibrant expansions rather than denials of human rights discourse, developing its constitutive potential to empower disenfranchised groups (see Kothari and Sethi 1991).

Other criticisms frequently levelled at human rights have to do with the absence of effective instruments and mechanisms of enforcement and thus with their status as merely moral imperatives rather than justiciable, legally binding rules.[23] But rethinking human rights as a discursive field in which the terms of power and authority are continually shifting, depending 'on the constellation of forces at a given conjuncture' (Cheah 1997: 266), means reinserting action and volition, as well as a certain amount of unpredictability, into our conceptual framework. More concretely, it means that the process of defining with greater and greater specificity who is responsible for rights violations and where and how restitution should be made is part of an ongoing political struggle.

We can see the tenuous yet potentially transformative effects of this struggle in efforts by transnational development NGOs to devise strategies for holding corporations accountable for their human rights violations, or by transnational women's NGOs to bring not only state agents but 'private' perpetrators of violence against women under the jurisdiction of the International Criminal Court. Closer to the concerns of this book are efforts to define and secure international recognition of reproductive and sexual rights through the Cairo and Beijing processes and their national implementation (Chapters 2 and 5) and the more recent campaign to recognize access to life-prolonging medicines as a part of the human right to 'the highest attainable standard of health' (Chapter 3). In each of these instances, transnational activists have found their work limited, their words appropriated, their world circumscribed by a global constellation of forces they could not control. And at the same time, their work and their words have changed that world in surprising ways, opening up new strategic possibilities.

Notes

1 'NGOs' encompass a broad-ranging spectrum, from (1) grassroots or community-based organizations, to (2) service or advocacy organizations dependent largely on

private donors, to (3) giant non-profit organizations that are funded mainly through public resources and sometimes have budgets larger than those of some poor countries (for example, the International Red Cross or CARE International) (Weiss and Gordenker 1996). Transnational women's NGOs primarily belong to the second category, although they often grow out of women's movements whose real strength is in the first, and sometimes they form working alliances with mega-organizations that fit the third.

2 The International Reproductive Rights Research Action Group, or IRRRAG, which I coordinated for seven years, had to address these kinds of questions continually. Made up of researchers, health providers and women's health activists from Brazil, Egypt, Malaysia, Mexico, Nigeria, the Philippines and the US, the IRRRAG project encountered many differences among ourselves and our respondents over rights, reproduction and sexuality. See *Negotiating Reproductive Rights* (Petchesky and Judd 1998), and *Catalysts and Messengers* (IRRRAG 1999). On questions of how ideas travel and the ambiguities of transnational feminisms, see also Grewal and Kaplan 1994 and Narayan 1997. On the Beijing conference as a focal point for these issues, see Eisenstein 1998.

3 In the US, the Committee for Abortion Rights and Against Sterilization Abuse (CARASA) was formed in 1977 in response to the Hyde Amendment restricting federal health insurance (Medicaid) payments for abortions. CARASA was followed by the US-based Reproductive Rights National Network (R2N2) and the European International Campaign on Abortion, Sterilization and Contraception (ICASC), both formed in 1978.

4 These included DAWN (Development Alternatives for Women in a New Era), Isis International, the Latin American and Caribbean Women's Health Network (LACWHN), the Caribbean Association for Feminist Research and Action (CAFRA), the East and South-east Asia–Pacific Regional Women and Health Network, the Feminist International Network for Reproductive Rights and Against Genetic Engineering (FINRRAGE, based in Dhaka), Women in Law and Development–Africa (WILDAF), and Women Living Under Muslim Laws Network.

5 Another indicator of the impact of Southern women's perspectives on the movement is the changing content of the newsletters published by such major networks as the WGNRR and the LACWHN. Beginning in the mid-1990s, articles in these publications increasingly covered such issues as women's working conditions, the environment, prostitution and sexual trafficking, health needs of women migrants and refugees, the health impact of SAPs and globalization, HIV/AIDS and racism, along with the usual topics of abortion, contraception, maternal mortality, etcetera.

6 With antiretroviral medications, treatment is now possible to prevent HIV transmission in pregnancy; but the medications are still too costly and inaccessible to many women in poor countries. See Chapter 3 below.

7 In the final Platform for Action, in a concession to the US objection, the target date was omitted and replaced by the vague phrase 'as soon as possible'; see Beijing POA, Paragraph 106(x).

8 See Petchesky 1995b and Ram 1999 for further discussion.

9 The ICPD POA comes closest to articulating the principle of bodily integrity when it links 'equal relationships between men and women in matters of sexual relations

and reproduction' to 'full respect for the physical integrity of the human body' (Paragraph 7.34).

10 Corrêa (1997) makes this point with great clarity in her analysis of 'women's power' and 'male transformation'. See also Scott 1990.

11 According to Harcourt (1994: 1, 22, n. 2), Gro Harlem Brundtland, now head of the World Health Organization, originated the concept of 'sustainable development'. This was in 1987 when she was still Norwegian Prime Minister and before the UNCED in Rio de Janeiro, when it was brought into official UN parlance. The term itself is 'highly contested' but in mainstream usage refers 'to a concern with balancing conservation of economic resources with economic growth based on industrialization and the need to safeguard earth's resources for future generations'.

12 For fuller discussion, see Bandarage 1997; A. Sen 1994; Committee on Women, Population and the Environment 1993; CNPD 1999; and Mazur 1994.

13 Sen's arguments here, of course, were prophetic, written five years before the economic crises of the late 1990s and the beginning of soul-searching by the World Bank and IMF about whether their austerity regimes and SAPs of the previous years had gone too far.

14 The article prominently displays a photograph of a dark-skinned woman smiling happily as she gathers wheat in a field, with the caption: 'Women in developing countries have a far greater need for nutrition, safe water, and other health services than for the 'reproductive' products and services treated as a priority by Western nations.'

15 One of the earliest and most forceful voices opposing such a dichotomization between rights and needs was that of the Indian economist and Nobel laureate Amartya Sen (see Sen 1994 and 1999). Sen's argument, however, identifies 'rights' only with political rights and civil liberties, which he argues are integral to achieving economic needs and development. In this way, rather than rejecting both terms of the North–South debate, he mediates them.

16 This is a very oversimplified summary of ideas contained variously in the 1859 Preface to A Contribution to the Critique of Political Economy; The German Ideology, Part I; and The Communist Manifesto (see Marx 1994). I do not mean to suggest that Vivant! (whose editorial policy is clearly aligned with the Vatican) is deliberately or knowingly drawing from Marxism. Its polemic against 'rights' and in favour of 'needs' no doubt has a more circuitous genealogy. In the 1960s and 1970s, the concept of 'basic human needs' was taken up by left-wing developmentalists and Third World countries as a shorthand for giving priority to poverty alleviation over corporate profits (G. Sen 1994b). In the Vatican's zeal to identify itself with the South, its spokesmen may not be thinking of the socialist and Marxist derivations of concepts of development that prevail in many Southern countries.

17 Personal interview with D. L. Jaya of VEDIKA, Amal Charles of the Society to Train and Educate People's Participation in Development, and R. Girija of SHARADA Women's Organization (March 2000). I am grateful to Asmita Resource Centre for Women in Andhra Pradesh, especially to Kalpana and Vasant Kannabiran, for their hospitality and making it possible for me to meet these extraordinary dalit women leaders.

18 For a sampling of various positions in this long-standing debate – including liberal, critical race theory, feminist and postcolonial – see Dworkin 1978; Tushnet 1984;

Olsen 1984; Williams 1991; Kothari and Sethi 1991; Peters and Wolper 1995; Cook 1994 (especially articles by Charlesworth and Coomaraswamy); Cheah 1997; A. Sen 1999; Dutt 1998 and Grewal 1998.

19 Compare the discussion of 'global civil society' in Stienstra 1999: 261–2, which makes similar points.

20 I am adopting Weiss and Gordenker's definition of 'global governance' as 'efforts to bring more orderly and reliable responses to social and political issues that go beyond capacities of states to address individually' (1996: 18).

21 Again, only a small sampling of this enormous and rich literature is possible here – for example, Lorde 1984; hooks 1989 and 1997; Anzaldúa 1990; Mohanty 1997; Eisenstein 1996; Alexander and Mohanty 1997; Crenshaw 1997; Grewal and Kaplan 1994; Shohat 1998.

22 Cheah is drawing especially here from Derrida's 1990 essay, 'Force of Law – the "Mystical Foundation of Authority"', *Cardozo Law Review*, 2: 919–1045. 'Reason' in this passage can be read as the voices of transnational activists making human rights claims.

23 Amartya Sen calls this the 'legitimacy' and 'coherence critiques' – see Sen 1999: 227–31.

2

The UN Conferences as Sites of Discursive Struggle

Gains and Fault Lines

Efforts by transnational women's NGOs to concretize reproductive and sexual rights into practical policies and programmes that will improve women's lives have taken place at international and national/local levels. This chapter reviews the international work the women's coalitions have carried out, and the forms of opposition they met, during the UN conferences of the 1990s and their five-year follow-up meetings in 1999–2000. My aim will be to assess both the strengths and the weaknesses of that activity and the larger structural, strategic and political obstacles that still prevent women's movements from realizing their visions.

The new visibility of NGOs as international actors is a subject of growing interest among international relations scholars. Weiss and Gordenker define NGOs as 'a special set of organizations that are private in their form but public in their purpose', thus distinguishing them from either intergovernmental organizations (IGOs) or transnational corporations (TNCs). NGOs, they assert, 'have become crucial to the UN's future' and 'a salient phenomenon in international policy making and execution'. The 'expertise, commitment and grassroots perceptions' they bring to the international arena have made them a bridge between the UN, governments and other NGOs. In addition, the organizational form through which transnational NGOs most often work – networks or coalitions that allow their constituents both autonomy and inter-dependence – has proved a flexible and effective model for global governance (1996: 18–24).

In the past decade, no NGO coalition fits this description better or has had a greater impact on UN norms and procedures than that of women organized transnationally (West 1999). In fact, it was nineteenth- and early twentieth-century feminists who pioneered the collaborative organizational structure that Weiss and Gordenker hail (Rupp 1997 and Meyer 1999). But, while the history of women's organizations 'lobbying the international community' predates the recent UN conferences by at least a century, their effectiveness and influence grew dramatically during the 1990s. Chen finds the roots of this influence in the previous UN Decade for Women conferences that culminated in Nairobi in 1985, with 'over 14,000 women from some 150 countries' attending the NGO Forum. That historic moment – the first international women's conference held in Africa – marks the foundation of a truly 'global women's movement' whose 'leadership shifted perceptibly – although not entirely – from North to South' (Chen 1996: 142).[1] Silliman takes a more critical view of this process, aware of the hierarchies and imbalances that still prevail alongside coalition building and diversity. She makes an important distinction between NGOs and social movements, suggesting that the former tend to be service- and project-oriented within existing systems while the latter pursue alternative visions to transform those systems (1999: 156; also Stienstra 1999). I would put it somewhat differently, arguing that the relationship between NGOs and social movements is precisely what is at issue. In so far as NGOs maintain close ties and accountability to the social movements that more often than not gave them birth, they can contribute significantly to transformative and oppositional projects.

Transnational women's NGOs working in the field of reproductive and sexual rights were already having a significant impact on international policy-making prior to the Cairo conference in 1994. For two decades women's health movements had disseminated strong critiques of family planning abuses, coercive practices, and the health risks of some methods, and argued the need for comprehensive and user-sensitive services. These critiques directly or indirectly influenced a number of powerful institutions that set the agenda for international population programmes (for example, the Ford and MacArthur Foundations, the International Planned Parenthood Foundation [IPPF] and the Population Council). These institutions began to apply a gender perspective to their international funding, to incorporate feminist critiques into their research agendas, and to hire staff and consultants who are knowledgeable within this perspective.[2] Moreover, UN and donor agencies – including the WHO, UNFPA, the World Bank and USAID – appointed 'gender advisory groups' from selected women's health researchers and NGOs to help them reorient their policies. Although such advisory groups have often been more symbolic than real and are in no way representative of women's movements, they do signal a new credibility of

Methodology of women's coalitions at the United Nations in the 1990s

1 Preliminary organizing and strategic planning 'to build consensus and coalitions' among women's groups across all regions through transnational communications and meetings (for example, the World Women's Conference for a Healthy Planet that preceded UNCED, and the Women's Voices '94 conference that preceded Cairo).

2 Mounting global campaigns, petition drives and lobbying efforts at the national, regional and international levels to publicize women's views on the issues.

3 Utilizing transnational women's networks to ensure that sympathetic women, and especially women's NGOs, from all the regions are represented on official government delegations and in liaison with the UN secretariat for the conference.

4 Participating not only in the separate NGO Forum but also in all the preparatory committee meetings (prep coms) and the official conference itself.

5 Drafting policy documents and recommendations and using these through a structure of task forces 'to monitor all amendments and rewrites of [official] draft documents' and make sure they reflect women's perspectives and concerns.

6 Supplementing the drafting and monitoring tasks with rigorous lobbying of delegations, daily meetings between the Women's Caucus and delegates, and acting as 'a bridge between the official deliberations and the parallel NGO deliberations'.

7 Monitoring the documents' implementation by national governments, by mobilizing and surveying both the governments themselves and local women's groups.

Source: Chen 1996: 142–51.

those movements that has goaded international population, health and development organizations to demonstrate 'gender sensitivity' in their public self-presentations.

Precedents for the gains and shortcomings of the women's coalition in Cairo were also set in the work of women's groups at the UNCED conference in Rio de Janeiro (1992) and the World Conference on Human Rights in Vienna (1993). Women's groups participating in those meetings created a strategic process and methodology that would be applied in all the subsequent conferences (see **Box 2.1**). Utilizing this strategy and their own Women's

Action Agenda 21, transnational women's groups in Rio were able for the first time to 'effectively put women's issues and concerns on the official global agenda'. Through their influence, the official Agenda 21 took some steps towards reframing the concept of sustainable development to encompass not only environmental protection but also the right to health, gender equality, reduction of military expenditures, alleviation of poverty, and the concerns of women in all these areas (Chen 1996).

The idea that 'women's rights are human rights' and that violence against women contradicts universal norms that supersede either 'tradition' or national sovereignty was firmly established as a result of transnational women's organizing prior to and during the Vienna Human Rights conference (see Bunch and Reilly 1994; Center for Women's Global Leadership 1995; Chen 1996). The Vienna Declaration and Programme of Action and the Declaration on the Elimination of Violence against Women (adopted by the General Assembly the same year) express the consensus of governments that 'gender-based violence and all forms of sexual harassment and exploitation' constitute violations of human rights. Their focus on women as subjects of human rights and women's bodies as the objects of human rights violations was a vital step toward legitimating the discourses of reproductive and sexual rights developed in Cairo and Beijing. The Vienna Declaration is the first UN document in history to make explicit reference to sexuality (as opposed to biological sexes) and implicitly to draw on the principle of bodily integrity in relation to sexual matters. Thus the sexual and gender violence claims were precursors in opening up the space for any talk about sexual rights, including affirmative rights of enjoyment and satisfaction, in international arenas (Petchesky 2000). Vienna also provided the foundation for the international codification of crimes against women. Building on women's insistence that the International Criminal Tribunals for the Former Yugoslavia and Rwanda prosecute sexual violence, the Women's Caucus for Gender Justice won recognition of rape, sexual slavery, forced pregnancy, forced sterilization, trafficking and other forms of sexual and reproductive violence as crimes against humanity – and in some cases as war crimes or genocide – in the Rome Treaty for an International Criminal Court (see Rome Statute 1998: Articles 6, 7 & 8; Copelon 2001; Women's Caucus for Gender Justice 2000; Sajor 1995).

The Women's Caucus model worked successfully to influence the outcomes of all the 1990s UN conferences for two main reasons. First, it was well organized and had focused, knowledgeable leadership that provided strategic guidance and lobbying skills to women less familiar with the UN process.[3] Second, women's NGOs have something the official delegations need and often lack: extensive knowledge and experience of the issues under debate. Nowhere is this truer than in the field of human rights, despite the political sensitivity of human rights issues. As Gaer demonstrates, 'human rights NGOs [have been] the engine for virtually every advance made by the UN in the field of human rights since its founding' (1996: 51). Women's human rights groups have been instrumental in supplying the human rights treaty bodies with cases, background information and clarification of norms and concepts, especially in regard to issues of violence against women and reproductive health and rights. More generally, they have explained such concepts as 'reproductive health' and 'gender equality' to population and development organizations, government delegates, and UN organizations; contested the distinction between 'public' and 'private' spheres; and '[pressured] intergovernmental bodies within the UN to live up to their rhetoric on women's rights' (Miller 1999: 165). The prominence of women's human rights and gender perspectives throughout the Cairo, World Summit for Social Development (WSSD) and Beijing documents – and more recently, the General Assembly's Declaration of Commitment on HIV/AIDS (2001) – is a direct legacy of the work done by women's caucuses in Rio de Janeiro and Vienna.

.Reassessing Cairo and Beijing: substantive achievements and shortfalls

Shortly after the ICPD in Cairo, both its achievements and its limitations from a gender and human rights perspective were evident. On the positive side, the transnational women's coalition had succeeded in winning a real paradigm shift embodied in three aspects of the POA. First, the Cairo document moves firmly from an approach based on demographic targets and narrow family planning methods to a comprehensive reproductive health approach. Second, it integrates the principles of gender equality, equity and women's empowerment into population and development strategies. Third, it explicitly recognizes reproductive rights, very broadly defined and linked to primary health care, as fundamental human rights (Germain and Kyte 1995; Petchesky 1995a). At the same time, however, the fault lines in the Cairo Programme continue to block any real progress in transforming the reproductive and sexual health/rights agenda from noble rhetoric into actual policies and services. In addition to the weakness of sexual rights in the document and the continued absence of recognition for women's right to safe, legal abortion, these fault lines consist of the ICPD's failure to address macroeconomic inequities and the inability of prevailing neoliberal, market-oriented approaches to deliver reproductive and sexual health for the vast majority. To understand how these contradictions occurred in Cairo and persisted in Beijing and the ICPD+5 and Beijing+5 review processes, it is necessary to analyse the opposing political forces that transnational women's groups confronted in all these arenas.

Fundamentalist agendas/feminist responses. Foremost in the field of players contesting reproductive and sexual rights is the cluster of ideological positions and their advocates I will call, for want of a better term, 'fundamentalist'. Following a number of commentators, I take contemporary fundamentalisms to be political movements that cut across all major religions and geographical regions, although they typically use religious language and symbols as rhetorical tools. While their methods are technologically and politically sophisticated, their objectives are conservative, in the sense of trying to restore a real or imagined past against the encroachments of a perceived external enemy (imperialism, 'Western decadence', 'feminazis', 'satanism'). Central to this project is the restoration of a patriarchal form of family and authority, including the subordination of women to men and their confinement to traditional social roles, dress codes and norms of sexual behaviour. As floor speeches by numerous delegations in Cairo and Beijing illustrate, appeals to 'national sovereignty' and to 'tradition' – signifying men's control over the state and over women – are integrally linked in the fundamentalist worldview. This adherence to doctrinaire patriarchalism, through an 'absolutist approach to law' and religious texts, is the cord that ties together very diverse fundamentalist adherents – whether Christian, Islamic, Jewish, Hindu or other (see Freedman 1996; Marty and Appleby 1993).

During the Cairo Prep Coms and conference in 1994 (and again in Beijing and during Cairo+5 and Beijing+5), a number of delegations representing Christian or Islamist varieties of fundamentalism joined together to oppose elements of the draft POA they claimed were offensive to their own traditions or laws. Often led by the Vatican (identified as the Holy See for UN purposes), these delegations were supported by numerous right-wing NGOs with 'women' in the title (such as Coalition for Women and the Family) who lobbied delegates and distributed fliers.[4] Fundamentalists took particular objection to any language under debate they interpreted as tending to (1) legitimate or facilitate abortion; (2) give women or adolescents the possibility of making reproductive and sexual decisions independently of men or parents; (3) condone 'diverse forms of the family' (other than the patriarchal, hetero-sexual kind); and (4) extend the concepts of reproductive and sexual health, reproductive rights or sexual rights to unmarried adolescents or gays and lesbians. As Freedman observes, the central problem sparking the opposition by fundamentalists to the Cairo POA 'was not fertility regulation itself' but rather 'the challenge to "traditional" patriarchal social structures posed by the commitment to women's empowerment' (1996: 66). It was also, one must add, the challenge of unorthodox sexualities.

Freedman's point, although it neglects the homophobic dimension of fundamentalist views, is very important in clarifying that we are not in fact looking at 'the historical pro-natalist versus anti-natalist controversy' here (DAWN 1999: 8). To be sure, many fundamentalist groups oppose modern methods of contraception, especially for unmarried or childless married women. But some – for example, the Iranian government – actively promote such methods. The deeper object of their common hostility is what they would call a 'Western feminist' or 'individualist' philosophy of sexual and family relations, and most especially women's authority over sexual and reproductive decisions. Vatican spokespeople frame this position in the language of 'parental rights and responsibilities' and adherence to 'family values', and they deployed this language vigorously throughout the Cairo, Beijing and 'plus five' processes.

Nonetheless, although women's groups failed to win explicit reference in the documents to freedom of sexual orientation or sexual expression – or even the words 'sexual rights' – their gains on behalf of a sexual rights discourse woven through the Cairo and Beijing texts are little short of revolutionary. Thus 'reproductive health' includes the ability 'to have a satisfying and safe sex life', and 'sexual health' involves 'the enhancement of life and personal relations, and not merely [disease prevention]' (ICPD, Paragraph 7.2; Beijing, Paragraph 95). Nowhere does Cairo restrict these principles to heterosexual married adults. Rather, it seeks 'to enable [adolescents] to deal in a positive and responsible way with their sexuality' and urges governments to provide adolescents with appropriate services and counselling with regard to reproductive health, 'responsible sexual behaviour', contraception and prevention of HIV/AIDS and other STDs (Paragraphs 7.3 and 7.47). Paragraph 7.33 states: 'Promotion and the reliable supply and distribution of high-quality condoms should become integral components of *all* reproductive health-care services.' But the Beijing Platform goes furthest towards defining a concept of sexual rights:

> The human rights of women include their right to have control over and decide freely and responsibly on matters related to their sexuality, including sexual and reproductive health, free of coercion, discrimination and violence. Equal relationships between women and men in matters of sexual relations and reproduction, including full respect for the integrity of the person, require mutual respect, consent and shared responsibility for sexual behaviour and its consequences. (Paragraph 96)

Even this much concession to the 'right to experience a *pleasurable* sexuality' as 'essential in and of itself' (HERA 1998) probably owes more to the devastating effects of the HIV epidemic during the 1990s (especially in sub-Saharan African countries) and the tireless work of transnational AIDS activists than it does to women's movements. Nonetheless, it is indicative of a surprising realignment of forces within UN debates – a shift in government attitudes, a setback for fundamentalists, and a strengthening in the position of the women's health and human rights coalition. As Barbara Klugman, a member of the South African delegations in both Cairo and Beijing, has written:

> Ultimately, sexual rights took prominence in Beijing as a topic of serious negotiation because so many non-Western groups supported the language. The African position in support of sexual rights, the willingness of many delegates from other southern countries at the Conference (particularly from the Caribbean) to speak explicitly for this position, and the presence of an organized lobby for sexual rights made up of NGOs from both North and South ... undermined the fundamentalist argument that sexual rights was a Western construct irrelevant to developing countries. (Klugman 2000: 152)

Nonetheless, Klugman makes clear that, had the African delegations understood the meaning of 'sexual rights' to include freedom of sexual orientation, 'they would have retracted their support as a result of their own prejudices' (2000: 153). Five years later, much further into the HIV/AIDS disaster in Africa, a strenuous campaign by the women's coalition to insert the words 'sexual rights' and 'sexual orientation' in the 'Further Actions and Initiatives' document for Beijing+5 failed (see IWHC 2000). Still, by the end of the Cairo+5 meeting, sexual rights had become an indelible part of the international human rights discourse and substance, regardless of the absence of the actual words from any document.[5] This achievement, the result of persistent efforts by women's health and human rights NGOs, is more than a symbolic victory. A compilation of the work relevant to reproductive and sexual health of the five UN human rights treaty bodies indicates dozens of instances since the Cairo and Beijing conferences in which the human rights committees have cited countries for their failure to prevent sexual and other forms of violence against women; or to provide sex education, sexual and HIV/AIDS counselling for men and women or more funds for sexual health services.[6] And the political struggle to enlarge the meaning of 'sexual rights' within accepted human rights discourse to encompass sexual diversity and pleasure continues.

On the highly contentious issue of abortion, the transnational women's movements also gained some advances if we read the Cairo Programme and the Beijing Platform together. The greatly compromised Paragraph 8.25 from ICPD acknowledges that 'unsafe abortion [is] a major public health concern', on one hand, yet refuses to see abortion 'as a method of family planning' on the other.[7] Yet, even within its limitations, Paragraph 8.25 urges governments to make all abortions safe where they are 'not against the law' and to provide 'access to quality services for the management of complications arising from [unsafe] abortion' in any circumstances. Moreover, the Beijing Platform goes beyond Cairo in providing that governments should 'consider reviewing laws containing punitive measures against women who have undergone illegal abortions' (Paragraph 106k). Such provisions opened a wedge in the late 1990s enabling women's health activists in countries with restrictive abortion laws to win an expansion of safe, legal services (for example, in Brazil and Bolivia). The Cairo+5 'Key Actions' document (1999) takes this progress one step further. Delegates at that meeting adopted a new provision, advanced by the Women's Coalition, that 'in circumstances where abortion is not against the law, health systems should train and equip health service providers' to ensure that abortion 'is safe and accessible' (Paragraph 63, iii). Given the frequent absence of such training and access, even in countries like the United States where abortion is a legal right, this provision has great practical importance.

Slowly and incrementally, women's determination in all eras, countries and cultures to seek abortions, even at great risk to their lives and health, in order to gain some control over their fertility and bodies was starting to make an impact on international human rights standards.[8] Or so it was until the US Congress in 1999 passed the infamous law known as the 'global gag rule', suspended for a time during the Clinton administration but signed and sealed by newly elected President Bush as his first official presidential act. Under that law, no government or NGO project overseas can receive US funds if it provides or makes referrals for abortions, 'actively promotes' abortion, or even advocates for reform of its country's abortion laws – even if it does so with non-US funds (Cohen 2000; Mann 2000; CRLP 2001; Toner 2001). Thus have a handful of conservative US politicians beholden to religious right-wing fundamentalists sought to muzzle women's health movements around the world.

During the Cairo+5 (1999) and Beijing+5 (2000) proceedings, the fundamentalist contingent put forward even more vigorously than in 1994–5 their position asserting a singular patriarchal-nuclear family form, parental rights and non-recognition of (unmarried) adolescent sexuality. Indeed, throughout Beijing+5, Vatican supporters among the NGO participants sported big red buttons saying 'MOTHER' to assert 'that women's primary role in society is motherhood and caring for the home and family'. Yet, as in Cairo, language recognizing 'various forms of the family' and women's 'multiple roles', as well as men's shared responsibility with women for the care of children, carried the day (IWHC 2000: 4). During Cairo+5 the funda-mentalist position on parental rights and adolescent sexuality also failed, thanks to the vocal presence of a large and diverse Youth Coalition in alliance with the Women's Coalition. [9] As a result, the Cairo+5 document takes a strong, proactive stand to address the growing catastrophe of HIV/ AIDS and other STDs. It sets out concrete targets and indicators for policies and services that governments should have applied by 2005 and 2010, especially for women and young people, including male and female condoms and anti-retroviral drugs for pregnant HIV+ women (Girard 1999).[10] Grim reality, if not feminist politics, seemed to be deflecting the fundamentalist agenda.

Populationist agendas/feminist responses. While less vocal than the fundamentalist contingents (whom they regard as enemies), US-based population control organizations – whose principal aim is to disseminate contraceptives and reduce numbers among the world's poor – were very much present in Cairo. These groups seemed content to let the Women's Coalition do the work of directly confronting the fundamentalist opposition and crafting a 'consensus' document that would resonate with new language, new ideas and (they hoped) renewed funding in the face of years of conservative opposition in the US Congress. But it would be a mistake to regard mainstream population and family planning groups as in some way passive or outside the debates in Cairo. Their lingering (though, I would argue, waning) influence and ideology are clearly evident in the contradictions within the Cairo document between the rhetoric of reproductive and sexual health/ rights and an approach to resources still focused on prioritizing family planning within publicly supported services and relying on the market for everything else.

In principle the Cairo Programme avoids the old neo-Malthusian numerical projections and panic about 'population explosions'. The document's text is refreshingly free of direct causal links between population growth and either poverty, migration or environmental deterioration, presenting instead a more complex picture in which population growth is one variable among many interconnected social and economic problems. In regard to the enabling conditions for reproductive and sexual rights, the POA makes a significant advance beyond previous population conferences by directing governments to provide reproductive health services 'through the primary health-care system' and to make these accessible 'to all individuals of appropriate ages ... no later than the year 2015' (Paragraph 7.6). It adopts a holistic approach, urging that reproductive health services be 'integrated' so that maternal health and prenatal care, gynaecological health, child health, family planning, programmes to improve women's and children's nutritional status, and programmes to prevent HIV infection and other STDs are fully coordinated (Paragraphs 8.8 and 8.17). Above all, the POA text, especially in Chapters 7 and 8, abandons any notion of family planning, much less population control, as an end in itself. Instead it makes fertility simply one element within a broad framework governed by the principles of 'informed free choice' and 'equitable access to basic health care for all', repudiating demographic targets, incentives and disincentives (Paragraphs 7.12, 7.22, 8.3 and 8.8).[11] And, in the context of equalizing life expectancy across countries and reducing infant, child and maternal mortality, Chapter 8 urges governments to ensure improvements in structural conditions that have an impact on health – 'particularly that of vulnerable groups' – such as housing, water, sanitation, and workplace and neighbourhood environments (Paragraph 8.10).

The Beijing Platform's chapter on 'Women and Health' improves upon the Cairo Programme in a number of respects. First, it embeds reproductive and sexual health/rights in the general principles of equality and non-discrimination and specifically in women's human right to 'enjoyment of the highest standard of health ... throughout the whole life cycle in equality with men' (Paragraph 92). Second, it fully adopts the reproductive health and rights provisions of the Cairo document but incorporates them into an overall health and environmental protection agenda instead of separating these into distinct chapters. Third, it introduces a number of concrete actions absent from the Cairo POA, such as programmes and services for prevention and early detection of breast, cervical and other gynaecological cancers and programmes to ensure household and national food security (Paragraphs 106–7). The attention both documents give to the larger physical and environmental context of health should be linked to their emphasis (Chapter 4 in the Cairo POA and throughout the Beijing Platform) on creating gender equality and empowering women in all realms of social life – including education, work, politics, community development, household labour and decisions, and sexuality.

As feminist human rights advocates remind us, human rights are 'evolving, not static'; they build on one another cumulatively and need to be seen as a whole (Copelon and Petchesky 1995: 357). This means reading all the UN conference documents – including Beijing's improvements in regard to abortion access and sexual rights – as an interwoven fabric. When we do so, it would appear that international policies have moved very far indeed from a normative framework that privileges populationist aims toward one in which gender justice and a holistic, integrative view of health and sustainable development take priority.

But, while this is true with regard to the normative principles and goals of the Cairo POA, when we examine the sections devoted to *resources* and *implementation* a different picture emerges. As **Box 2.2** indicates, in spite of all the language relegating family planning to a broader reproductive and primary health agenda, when it comes to actual allocations of resources the 'family planning component' (contraception and sterilization) still receives the lion's share. Indeed, family planning is projected as costing nearly twice as much in 2015 as all of reproductive health, maternal and child health, gynaecological health, prevention and treatment of HIV/AIDS and other STDs, and adolescent reproductive and sexual health and education combined (Paragraphs 13.14–15).[12] Admittedly, the ICPD POA is the only conference document of the 1990s that sets a precise money target, a positive step in principle. But the fact that family planning is the only area in which the financial calculations of 'experts' are accepted seems more a victory for the population establishment than for women's health movements. As for primary health care, emergency services, education, sanitation, water, housing, and all the other aspects of the 'development' side of ICPD – much less any programmes for gender equality and women's empowerment – these are dismissed with the gratuitous comment that 'additional resources will be needed' (Paragraphs 13.17–18). Feminist critics attending the NGO Forum had good reason to demonstrate outside the official meeting with signs that angrily queried, 'Where is the "D" in ICPD?'

Even more troubling is the ICPD's overall approach to implementation and enforcement. While the chapter on health recognizes the devastating impact that SAPs, 'public-sector retrenchment' and 'the transition to market economies' have had on health indicators, especially among the poor, the implementation chapters revert to the market-oriented policies that have actually widened income gaps and mortality and morbidity gaps globally and within countries. In order to improve 'cost-effectiveness', 'cost-recovery' and quality of services, governments are urged to reintroduce user fees and social marketing schemes; 'promote the role of the private sector in service delivery and in the production and distribution ... of high-quality reproductive health and family-planning commodities'; and 'review legal, regulatory and import policies ... that unnecessarily prevent or restrict the greater involvement of the private sector' (Paragraphs 13.22, 15.15 and 15.18). There is a cautionary word about providing adequate 'safety nets' but no indication of their scope or duration. Nor does the Cairo POA anywhere address the need for multi-sectoral approaches at the level of national health systems, so that health, population and development ministries do not continue to function as separate, competing entities. In sum, 'development' in the ICPD framework remains stuck within free-market capitalist priorities.

The market-oriented perspective within the POA signifies, not so much any conscious plan, but the hegemony of global capitalism in the post-Cold War world. That perspective is unquestioned dogma among the major donor governments – particularly the US and the European Union (EU) – and the international financial institutions (IFIs). Their presence in the ICPD-related meetings may have intimidated any very outspoken opposition among the 'Group of 77' (G-77) countries, who are desperately seeking foreign investments and debt relief.[13] The fundamentalist contingents, despite all their rhetoric about 'basic needs' (see Chapter 1), were too preoccupied with opposing the reproductive and sexual rights language to have taken an outspoken position on the macroeconomic issues. As for the Women's Coalition its position on these questions was also contradictory in practice. On one hand, the Coalition proposed language strongly criticizing SAPs and their adverse impact on women, recommending demilitarization and social

A feminist report card on the Cairo Programme of Action

New achievements	Remaining gaps and challenges
• Shift from population control to 'reproductive rights and reproductive health' paradigm; comprehensive definition of reproductive health, including sexual health, integrated with primary health services for all (Ch. 7; Paras 7.2, 8.8).	• Access to safe, legal abortion not recognized as part of reproductive health and rights; deference to national laws; where illegal, requirement of treatment for complications only (Para. 8.25).
• Definition of 'reproductive rights' as part of 'already recognized inter-national human rights'; includes 'the right to attain the highest standard of reproductive and sexual health', 'the *means* to do so', 'informed choice' and freedom from 'discrimination, coercion and violence'; end to targets and incentives (Paras 7.3, 7.12, 7.22).	• Reliance on private market mechanisms (cost-recovery schemes, user fees, health reform to assure 'cost-effectiveness'), increased involvement of private sector and deregulation, rather than measures for global macroeconomic restructuring to generate resources and assure accountability (Paras 8.8, 13.22, 15.15, 15.18).
• Recognition of adolescent rights to all reproductive and sexual health services, including 'sexual education' and full protection against unwanted pregnancy, HIV/AIDS and other STDs (Paras 7.2, 7.37, 7.45, 7.47).	• Ambiguous language about 'the rights, duties and responsibilities of parents' could compromise right to confidentiality; inadequate resource allocations; absence of multisectoral integration (in the health and education sectors, for example).
• 'Gender equality, equity and empowerment of women' as a separate chapter; recognition of 'the empowerment and autonomy of women and the improvement of their political, social, economic and health status' as 'a highly important end in itself' (Para. 4.1).	• No resource allocations or specified amounts for any aspect of sustainable development, primary health care, women's empowerment and improved status, poverty alleviation or environment (Ch. 13).
• Recognition of all forms of violence against women, including FGM, and measures to end them as integral to reproductive health (Paras 4.4, 4.9, 4.22, 4.23, 7.3, 7.6, 7.17).	• Treatment of 'women' as a unitary category; failure to recognize racial, ethnic and class divisions in access to resources and services and health risks (except HIV/AIDS).

Box 2.2 cont.

New achievements	Remaining gaps and challenges
• Shared male responsibility for child care, housework and reproductive and sexual health as essential to gender equality (Ch. 4c).	• No concrete strategies for implementation, no resource allocations.
• Encouragement of governments to expand and strengthen 'grassroots, community-based and activist groups for women' (Para. 4.12).	• No resource allocations or specified targets.
• Recognition of the 'diversity of family forms', including female-headed households, and the need for government policies to benefit all, especially the most vulnerable (Paras 5.1, 5.2).	• Failure to expressly recognize affirmative sexual rights along with reproductive rights, including right to diversity of sexual expression and orientation.
• Definition of reproductive health services as integrating not only family planning but also antenatal and obstetric care, infertility treatment, prevention and treatment of HIV/AIDS, STDs and gynaecological cancers (Paras 7.6, 8.8).	• Specification of precise money target ($17 billion) but *imbalance* in resource allocations: twice as much specified for 'family planning component' as for all of 'reproductive health component' put together (Paras 13.14, 13.15).
• Target date of 2015 for reproductive health services, increasing life expectancy, reducing infant and child mortality and reducing maternal mortality (Paras 7.6, 7.16, 8.5, 8.16, 8.21).	• Inadequate allocation of resources to reproductive health component; no resources directed to necessary infrastructure, poverty alleviation and enabling conditions.

sector investments instead. On the other hand, its members were reluctant to push the US and the EU too hard on the resource questions because of needing those delegations as allies on reproductive and sexual health and rights. Among the civil society participants in Cairo, only the population and family planning groups had an unequivocal interest in accommodating the neoliberal agenda and placating the Northern donors.

To understand the quiet but critical role of population and family planning groups in abetting this agenda, we need to go back to De Barbieri's reminder that achieving social equality and the redistribution of wealth has never been their concern. Throughout its history, the international population establishment has pursued the aim it took on from its origins during the Cold War: to 'reduce Third World population growth through the diffusion of contraceptive technology' (Freedman 1996: 65; Greenhalgh 1996). Many of these organizations, including the UNFPA, have become much more sophisticated in their methods for achieving this aim, having been persuaded by massive research evidence that coercion and mistreatment too often drive women away from clinics while education and jobs motivate them to have fewer children. Hence they embrace feminist concepts such as 'the right to choose', gender equality, and women's empowerment. But while this 'feminization' of the populationist rhetoric is sincere, it is also opportunistic. On a purely strategic level, population and family planning organizations needed the expertise, commitment and ideas of the women's coalition throughout the Cairo process to act as a buttress against the fundamentalists; thus they pursued a marriage of convenience. But the primary interest of these groups is to rationalize their own existence and increase their budgets; for if family planning is just one part of reproductive health care, which is part of primary health care, one might ask, what is the rationale for separate 'population' programmes at all?

Given the right-wing congressional blocks to US funding for international family planning, it would seem that US-based population organizations are reluctant to give up the one card they still believe can sell their activities to government funders: popular fears of 'overpopulation' and the view that population growth in developing countries is a 'security threat' to US interests (see Hartmann 1999). Even as its own population growth projections declined year after year, the UNFPA in the late 1990s continued to preface its publications and media statements with figures projecting how many billions will inhabit Earth and correlating these with environmental and social disaster. A graphic exhibit during the Cairo+5 review, as well as a well-funded media campaign conducted by mainstream population organizations, warned that the world's population would reach 'six billion' by 12 October 1999 (Filmmakers Collaborative 1999; CRLP 1999). The UNFPA's commitment to the reproductive and sexual health and rights-based approach of Cairo is clear, but this is still seen as a *means* 'to slow population growth', 'to accelerate economic growth' and 'to reduce potential environmental damage', rather than a matter of basic human rights (UNFPA 1997a; UNFPA 1999).[14] The sacred cows it never wants to question are those of economic growth and free markets.

Much more tenacious and doctrinaire in their population control aims are US-based population and environmental groups such as Population Action International (PAI) and the National Audubon Society. In a flier produced for the Cairo+5 meetings, the Audubon Society falsely defines the 'consensus' reached in Cairo in crude neo-Malthusian terms: 'the need and the means to slow population growth and eventually stabilize human numbers' ('the means' being understood here as contraception, full stop). Warning that 'population will double before 2050', it reels off the imagined causal chain of dire consequences – economic crises, hunger and malnutrition, migration pressures, water scarcity, depletion of other natural resources, civil conflict, war and disease.[15] PAI, in a 1997 booklet directly addressed to the World Bank and its post-Cairo funding policies, berates the Bank for having given 'limited attention ... to the problem of rapid population growth in the last few years', sweeping population issues 'narrowly under the health sector', and redirecting its loans and research efforts towards health and education rather than family planning (Conly and Epp 1997).[16]

If population groups are accusing the World Bank of abandoning a population control agenda in favour of women's health and education, then the women's and development NGOs must have been doing something right in Cairo, Copenhagen and Beijing. Yet the fault lines in the Cairo POA, its unbalanced resource allocations, and its assumption that equitable population policies based on people's health and social needs are compatible with market-driven economic policies remain extremely problematic. They recall the criticisms by certain feminist groups who attended the NGO Forum in Cairo but remained distrustful of not only the official conference but also the Women's Coalition. These groups charged that the whole ICPD process was an exercise in cooptation; that it used the language of reproductive health and rights to legitimate old-style population control with a feminist face; and that, given the abusive history of population programmes, no population policy can ever be compatible with feminist values and goals.[17]

While mainstream organizations like PAI and the National Audubon Society give fuel to these charges, two countervailing trends indicate that feminist influences on the population and family planning field have been far from superficial. First, there is no logical necessity why population policies must be élitist, reductionist or aimed only at lowering numbers (especially among the poor, migrants and people of colour). Demography, after all, is a social science dealing not only with fertility and numbers but also with how people (populations) are distributed across age cohorts, genders, ethnic groups and geographic areas; their marriage, employment and cohabitation patterns; their deaths and diseases; as well as their access to goods, land and services. Numerous academic demographers reject coercive population control and instead apply their tools to identifying and eliminating inequities in these patterns of distribution, whether in treatment for HIV/AIDS or in access to affordable housing.[18] Mainstream journals in the field increasingly publish studies examining such topics as user perspectives on family planning services, racial inequities in education and health care, abortion laws across countries, male involvement in sexual and reproductive decisions, and STD prevention programmes.[19] These shifts in focus might never have happened without the impact of transnational feminist organizing and research.

Second, women's movements have influenced not only the research methods and concerns of mainstream population organizations but also their allocation of resources and service delivery programmes in countries around the world. An important example is the work of IPPF in its Western Hemisphere (Latin America and the Caribbean) and South Asian regions, where gender perspectives, quality of care, and most recently women's empowerment and development have become the major indices of successful programming. For instance, in reproductive health projects run by IPPF's affiliate, the Family Planning Association of India (FPAI) in Maharashtra state, project personnel say they never speak of 'family planning' but rather try to 'empower the women in the *mahila mandals* [local women's organizations] to think, express themselves, take decisions and act'. They have introduced training courses for young women to become beauticians and hospital aides, computer training and adult literacy classes, as well as encouraging young women's public involvement through the *mahila mandal* and the *panchayat*. The *mahila mandal* president, in her late twenties, reports that working with her group to get local officials to build them an office and to demand a health centre and toilets 'made me realize who I really am' (IPPF South Asia 1999: 14).

Such involvements have resulted in a dramatic rise in women's age at marriage and their literacy rates as well as their contraceptive use. Similar projects in Madhya Pradesh report that now '94 per cent of project clients are opting for temporary contraceptive methods (mainly the condom) in an area where the traditional emphasis has been on sterilization'. As IPPF's regional office puts it, 'the key to achieving these statistical triumphs was development, both attitudinal and material' (thus fulfilling the old notion that 'development is the best contraceptive'?) (IPPF South Asia 1999: 13). It hardly seems to matter whether in the minds of population planners these programmes are seen as means toward higher rates of contraceptive use when women are provided with the resources and encouragement to make, and realize, their own demands in their own voices.

What makes IPPF, by any criteria a Northern-based, 'mainstream' and powerful international family planning organization, different from PAI? To understand how IPPF priorities in some regions began to change in the 1990s, we need to look at the internal dynamics that link significant parts of that organization to women's movements.[20] In a valuable case study, Adriana Ortiz-Ortega and Judith Helzner attribute a decade of change in IPPF policies to the following factors: (1) 'the momentum of the feminist movement' in the mid to late 1980s; (2) the appointment of 'in-house feminists' in key staff and board positions; and (3) the building of close alliances with women's health networks and movements outside the organization (Ortiz-Ortega and Helzner 2003).[21] The experience of IPPF suggests two important conclusions. First, 'feminists working within mainstream institutions' can help to change policies and programmes in ways that directly benefit the lives of the most marginalized women – *if* their work is constantly informed by connections to grassroots and regional women's movements. Both progressive work within institutions and independent movements outside those institutions are crucial to social change, and they reinforce one another. Second, mainstream population and family planning organizations are no more monolithic than are women's NGOs. Some cling to their neo-Malthusian convictions while others are responding to feminist ideas and practices and attempting to incorporate them into their local projects.

By 1999 the Women's Coalition for ICPD had developed a much more sophisticated set of concepts and lobbying strategies and was able to strengthen the integrative reproductive health approach of Cairo, notwithstanding the single-mindedness of population groups. In fact, the media campaign by hard-core populationists failed to have an impact on the Cairo+5 'Key Actions' document. On the contrary, that document fortifies the broad reproductive and sexual health and rights provisions of the ICPD with time-bound targets and concrete indicators for measuring compliance. For example, Paragraph 53 states:

> Governments should strive to ensure that by 2015 all primary health-care and family planning facilities are able to provide, directly or through referral, the widest achievable range of safe and effective family planning

and contraceptive methods; essential obstetric care; prevention and management of reproductive tract infections, including sexually transmitted diseases, and barrier methods (such as male and female condoms and microbicides if available) to prevent infection. By 2005, 60 per cent of such facilities should be able to offer this range of services, and by 2010, 80 per cent of them should be able to offer such services. (Paragraph 53)

Responding to data showing that some 600,000 maternal deaths and 18 million incidents of maternal morbidity still occur annually worldwide, delegates at Cairo+5 also adopted 'births assisted by skilled attendants' as the benchmark for reducing maternal mortality, specifying that this benchmark be reached in five-year intervals and percentages, with a target of 90 per cent of all births by 2015 (Paragraph 64). Women's health and well-being *have* superseded population control in the framework of international health and development politics. But the global macroeconomic agenda remains as un-woman-friendly as ever.

Learning from the fault lines: political dynamics at the Social Summit and the 'Plus Fives'

As my analysis in the previous section tried to show, transnational women's movements working within the UN conferences were contending with hostile forces on all sides, in addition to coping with an alien system of rigid rules and procedures. In such a situation, tactical compromises and unholy alliances (for example, with mainstream population organizations or neoliberal governments) are hard to avoid (cf. Silliman 1999). More disturbing is the likelihood that the Women's Caucuses in Cairo and Beijing diverted disproportionate energy towards combating the fundamentalist and traditionalist attacks on reproductive, sexual and other women's human rights and less towards assuring the structural and macroeconomic conditions for those rights. This shortsightedness reflects not so much a wilful political choice or the dominance of Northern women's NGOs as deeper structural and cultural weaknesses of women's movements across the globe. First is the way in which those movements tend to be fragmented into single-issue ghettos, with some groups focused on reproductive and sexual health, others on violence against women, and still others on women's labour and economic conditions; 'women's health' becomes a specialized enclave that rarely interacts with 'Women in Development' (WID) or 'Alt-WID', and vice-versa. Second is the way in which international political institutions, and to some extent feminist activists, have internalized dominant gender norms so that macroeconomic issues (trade, finance and resource allocations), like military and security issues, are perceived as intrinsically masculine and insular terrain.

It is important not to minimize, however, the intense backlash that the very success of women's NGOs in inserting feminist ideas into the Cairo POA aroused. Organized in the name of national sovereignty and traditional morality, this backlash was mainly the work of the Vatican and some of its government allies but also expressed the misgivings of some member states about the growing influence of civil society groups on the UN deliberation process. As early as the Beijing preparatory meetings in 1995, women participants began facing restrictions on NGO access and accreditation to the official conferences, mostly closed-door negotiations and an overwhelming resort to brackets or filibustering tactics to avoid consensus over particularly contentious texts and to stall or even sabotage any final document. Even the word 'gender' became a bone of contention that had to be bracketed throughout the draft Platform (Petchesky 2000). And, of course, the most visible evidence of a determination to marginalize the effects of a massive radical feminist presence on the official proceedings (and on Chinese women) was the decision of the Chinese government to isolate the NGO Forum in the distant town of Huairou (Chen 1996: 152; West 1999; Runyan 1999).

With regard to reproductive and sexual rights specifically, such a backlash had already occurred in Copenhagen in March 1995. The Copenhagen Declaration and Programme of Action (POA) from the World Summit for Social Development (WSSD) in some ways reflects Cairo in reverse. Its comprehensive framework, integrating sustainable development, poverty eradication, health, education, human rights, and gender and racial equality, infuses the entire document instead of being concentrated within certain chapters. The 'Principles and Goals' section declares the empowerment of people, 'particularly women', to be 'a main objective of development and its principal resource'. It affirms the urgency of women's full participation in all spheres and levels of social, political and economic life and their 'access to all resources needed for the full exercise of their fundamental rights'. Chapter 4 on 'Social Integration' elaborates on these principles, linking them to a concept of pluralism and diversity in societies and inclusion of all vulnerable and marginalized groups.

And yet the Social Summit document virtually ignores not only sexuality but also the definition of reproductive and sexual health and choice as fundamental human rights. It incorporates 'full access to preventive and curative health care', especially for women and children, into its programmes for poverty eradication and social integration. But, deferring to the Vatican view, it qualifies every mention of such access with deference to 'parental rights and responsibilities' (Paragraphs 35c, 36h, 74g).[22] The items listed as necessary 'to meet the basic needs of all' are broad and comprehensive (everything from food security and employment to targets for reducing maternal mortality and raising life expectancy). But sexuality is nowhere among them, and the document's repeated commitment to a human rights approach is strangely silent throughout the section on 'basic human needs'.

In part these omissions reflect a practical reality: the stronger presence of Vatican forces in Copenhagen relative to that of women's health groups, who (with fewer human and financial resources) could not manage travelling to three UN conferences in a year. At the same time, behind this reality lurks a set of priorities in which the major funding agencies that support global feminist advocacy (and are located mostly in the North) do not put social development high on their agenda, and many feminist-identified organizations themselves still do not think of social development, macroeconomic, or global governance issues and 'women's issues' in the same breath. While a central argument of this chapter is that such bifurcated thinking among transnational women's health groups is gradually changing, it is not changing rapidly enough – in part because the fundamentalist challenge takes centre stage.

A fundamentalist, anti-feminist backlash was also highly visible during the ICPD+5 negotiations at United Nations headquarters in New York in 1999. Under the leadership of HERA (Health, Empowerment, Rights and Accountability), the Women's Coalition for ICPD mobilized over 100 organizations from both the South and the North in a strategic process very similar to that applied at the earlier UN meetings.[23] The familiar but intensified scenario presented the coalition with two new problems relative to the 1994–5 conferences. First, the G-77 countries decided to function throughout these meetings as a bloc with a single spokesperson – a tactic guaranteed to delay the proceedings endlessly since the G-77 could never agree on anything.[24] Second, many government delegates were New York-based mission bureaucrats rather than seasoned experts from the home countries who might be expected to know something about the ICPD and have experience in its implementation. Women's Coalition members soon began to realize they were lobbying among people who had not even been in Cairo, had never read the POA, and did not know the difference between reviewing practical actions to implement a document and redrafting that document all over again (Sen and Corrêa 2000). But of course these dynamics were really indications of the low level of governments' commitment to the review process and their growing resentment of NGO activity at the UN. Arguably, the work of the Women's NGO Coalition at these meetings was pivotal to producing any final report at all.

And yet a consensus document did finally emerge, one that not only holds the line on the major reproductive and sexual health/rights provisions of the Cairo POA but also goes well beyond these in specifying concrete targets and indicators (see above). This mainly positive outcome had two political catalysts. First, a realignment within the G-77, led by a strong group of Latin American and Caribbean countries, succeeded in isolating the fundamentalist partners of the Holy See and bolstering the voices of delegations whose national policies favour the Cairo agenda and were in uncomfortable tension with the backlash mentality.[25] Second, members of the Women's Coalition, far from being silenced in the 1999 meetings, worked in many resourceful ways to make their presence and ideas felt. These included numerous press conferences and interviews, an effective alliance with the Youth Coalition, forceful speeches before the conference plenaries and an 'Open Letter to the Vatican' signed by dozens of Latin American NGOs and others from the Women's Coalition.[26] Most dramatic of all, perhaps, was a silent demonstration during the Prep Com in March in which Women's and Youth Coalition members lined up outside the delegates' meeting room to protest against the stalling tactics being carried out by certain delegations and to insist that the review process move forward. That security guards were immediately deployed to remove the hundred or so demonstrators signifies that concerted silence in UN corridors may sometimes speak louder than words.

With regard to substance, the Beijing+5 process (with a broader set of concerns and issues at stake) yielded far less and was more disappointing than that of Cairo+5. Its 'Further Actions' document contained practically no time-bound targets, benchmarks, or resources for implementation and in many areas simply repeated the already agreed language of the Beijing Platform.[27] Yet, from a strategic point of view, women's groups involved in Beijing+5 made some significant gains that could have positive impacts in the future. Their effective work with sympathetic government delegations contributed to the further dissolution of the G-77 bloc and the formation of a new grouping of countries, led by Brazil and Peru, that called itself SLAC, later joined by all 14 CARICOM countries (thus becoming SLACC, Some Latin American and Caribbean Countries). This group, along with several African countries and India, took positions supporting not only gender equality and economic justice but also the phrase 'sexual rights' – which the EU and the JUSCANZ countries (Japan, US, Canada, Australia and New Zealand) also supported (IWHC 2000; Sen and Corrêa 2000). It is no accident that the countries involved in this new grouping, however ephemeral it may be, are those in which women's health movements have played a strong and enduring role.

In fact, I would argue that by 1999 transnational women's health NGOs had become far more sophisticated than they were in 1994 about the need for effective strategies to address the *structures of power* underlying existing patterns of global governance. One example of such a strategy is the international petition campaign launched by Catholics for a Free Choice (CFFC) during ICPD+5 to challenge the Vatican's status at the UN. Cleverly titled 'See Change' and using the Internet to gather adherents, the campaign had been endorsed by more than 550 organizations by Summer 2000. It raises hard questions about whether the Vatican (or Holy See) should have the status of a 'nonmember state permanent observer', since it is not a state under international law, any more than is Disney World or Exxon, and should not be uniquely privileged among all the world's religious groups (Rahman 1999; CFFC 2000).[28]

The increasing attention paid by women's health activists to the larger structures of global power also extends to the macroeconomic conditions of reproductive and sexual rights, or the fault lines of Cairo. In the years between Cairo and ICPD+5, transnational women's health NGOs became more committed to repairing those fault lines and to confronting directly the problems of privatization, unregulated transnational capital flows, debt service, inequitable trade patterns, and the resulting shrinkage of social resources to meet health needs. This was a response to several influences in the late 1990s, including growing evidence of the harsh impacts of globalization; large transnational coalitions demonstrating against the WTO in Seattle and elsewhere; and the leadership of Southern women's groups, whose work for reproductive and sexual rights has consistently been linked to a strong economic justice platform (see *Dawn Informs* 2000–2002). As a result, the Women's Coalition amendments to the Cairo+5 final outcomes document addressed the problem of additional resources for implementation by recommending:

(1) 'effective global and national regulation of capital flows so that their volatility does not continue to undermine local economies and national social policies, including sexual and reproductive health';

(2) efforts 'to create a more level playing field in international trade';

(3) 'immediate action regarding bilateral and multilateral debt relief of heavily indebted poor countries';

(4) 'socially responsible investments from [to replace 'increased involvement of '] the private sector'; and

(5) 'additional mechanisms to raise resources such as taxes on financial transactions at the global and national level whose proceeds would be earmarked for human development programmes including sexual and reproductive health'.

Four years earlier, at the Social Summit in Copenhagen, NGO participants had foreshadowed these proposals and in fact gone much further than in any UN conference before or since to seriously challenge global capitalism, resource inequities, and the structural gaps in global governance. Most far-reaching and visionary among their recommendations were these amendments to the draft WSSD Declaration and POA submitted by the Women's Caucus:

• Replace the document's emphasis on '[*promoting*] dynamic, open, free markets' with an emphasis on '[*regulating*] markets in the public interest with a view to reducing inequality, preventing instability, expanding employment, increasing the security of employment and establishing a socially acceptable minimum wage'.

• Establish the basis for international trade equity through 'effective regulations for the trade and investment activities of [TNCs]'.

• 'Initiate the foundation of a global fund for human security that would serve as a compensation mechanism for the social insecurity that results from the instability of the international market ... financed by a [tax on global finance capital].'

• 'Develop a globally agreed upon Code of Conduct for TNCs which includes labour rights and standards as well as community and environ-mental protection clauses, and invest the UN with appropriate powers of monitoring and enforcing.'

- Establish a cap of 1 per cent of GDP on military spending and annual reductions in military spending of 5 per cent of GDP to release funds for social needs.

- Integrate the goal of gender equality into 'all relevant policy areas and budgetary decisions' and create additional resources for women's empowerment in all spheres.

- Generate new financial resources through 'new forms of taxation that will promote sustainable social and economic development such as placing taxes on resource use, commodification of common resources, taxes to discourage the production of toxic products, taxes on international financial speculative transactions' [Tobin tax].[29]

Above all, the Women's Caucus amendments for the Copenhagen POA contain the design for an elaborate machinery that would make the IMF, the World Bank and the WTO, as well as governments and TNCs, accountable to both ECOSOC and the human rights treaty bodies for upholding international standards of economic and social rights, poverty elimination, gender equality, and trade equity. In addition, this machinery would include (1) a newly established juridical assembly able to hear cases and apply sanctions for non-compliance; (2) regular mechanisms for monitoring and correcting the impact of SAPs on women and poverty levels; and (3) an 'elected international assembly of representatives of social groups to meet in conjunction with governments under the existing General Assembly as a component of a new system of global governance' – thereby institutionalizing and democratizing NGO participation in the UN system. However utopian their vision may seem, by 1995 some transnational women's groups were quite aware that the international political and economic system would have to be entirely transformed in order to achieve a healthy world.

Both in 1995 and again in 1999, the official documents finally accepted by governments (including the G-77) reflected the existing realities of global power, ignoring nearly all of the Women's Caucus recommendations. When it comes to resources, implementation, and follow-up, the Copenhagen Declaration and POA echoes the Cairo POA in its concessions to the prevailing neoliberal, market-oriented doctrine. As Runyan puts it, 'the task is framed as a problem of managing the seemingly autonomous forces of globalization that are represented as a fait accompli', while underneath 'remains a commitment to the promotion of free markets and free trade'

(1999: 218). Although it is urged that SAPs 'include social development goals' and 'give priority to human resource development', they should also 'establish a more favourable climate for trade and investment' (Commitment 7). Nowhere are any economic principles framed in concepts such as social solidarity or social rights, nor is there a trace of the redistributive language or the imaginative resource generation strategies (beyond voluntary bilateral and multilateral aid and debt relief) of the Women's Caucus amendments.[30]

Likewise, the ICPD+5 final outcomes document (1999) relies on familiar appeals to donor countries and organizations to increase their contributions to ODA; to enact measures to relieve the debt burden of poor countries; and to build in 'adequate social safety net measures to promote access to services' by those who might be excluded (Paragraphs 95, 100, 105).[31] That document does call on the private sector (now assumed to be the main provider of health services everywhere) to 'ensure that its services and commodities … meet internationally accepted standards' and to conduct its activities in a manner that is 'socially responsible, culturally sensitive … cost-effective … [and consistent with] basic rights recognized by the international community' (Paragraph 86). But no formal international mechanisms yet exist to ensure that the private sector and the IFIs are held accountable for the ways their macroeconomic policies and practices affect human life and health. Nor, under the twentieth-century, state-centred UN model, are entities even more powerful than states responsible for upholding UN conference documents or human rights conventions. The twenty-first-century vision of an elected international assembly of civil society representatives as part of 'a new system of global governance' still seems a faraway dream.

Back to the future: Copenhagen+5 in 2000

Of all the Plus Five review processes, the one for the 1995 Social Summit probably embodies most starkly the contradictions of global governance in a new era. The WSSD+5 agenda addressed issues of the greatest importance: poverty eradication strategies, allocation of resources within and among countries, and the social and economic 'enabling environment' – including gender equality – for development to proceed. Yet these meetings, even in comparison with Beijing+5, were clearly downgraded in the eyes of governments, donors and the media. No heads of state or ministers from G-7 countries even attended, and the proceedings got very little attention in the mainstream media.

On the eve of the UN General Assembly Special Session (UNGASS), in an apparent attempt to pre-empt the proceedings, Secretary-General Annan himself joined with the OECD, the World Bank and the IMF to issue a report entitled '2000 – A Better World for All'. This was a glossy compilation of statistics and targets (based on already published sources) documenting the worsening in the previous five years of poverty, social and gender inequalities, infant and maternal mortality, environmental devastation, and HIV/AIDS and other epidemics. The message was clear: We, the senior managers of globalization and neoliberal macroeconomic policies, recognize that these unfortunate trends have accompanied globalization (though *not* that they bespeak its failures). And we recognize that they need to be brought under control (that is, managed). But goals and targets to reduce poverty '*cannot be imposed – they must be embraced*'; that is, through voluntary measures, not regulations and timetables. So women's and anti-poverty NGOs intending to use this General Assembly process as a forum to demand strong measures to regulate global capital flows, cancel debt, redistribute wealth, and promote gender and economic justice should be forewarned: your efforts will be of little consequence in the eyes of the world's opinion leaders.[32]

In this way, WSSD+5 in June 2000 (foreshadowed by Beijing+5) signified the ultimate backlash against the 1990s conference process and the increasingly vocal participation of civil society groups. In direct proportion to efforts by such groups (both within UN meetings and outside them) to challenge macroeconomic policies and to democratize global decision-making structures, we saw various moves to bifurcate the UN and multilateral decision-making systems as a whole. Under a dual regime, the 'hard' issues of globalization – including matters of resource allocation, finance, trade, and security – become the exclusive province of closed-door proceedings among the G-7 countries and their institutional strongholds, the WTO, World Bank, IMF, and Security Council, as well as occasional *ad hoc* ministerial-level meetings like the 2000 Millennium Forum. Meanwhile, broad principles concerning 'soft' issues such as poverty, health, social and gender equality, labour, racism and xenophobia – but not the funds and enforcement machinery to implement them – are debated endlessly within the more inclusive processes of the General Assembly, where developing country governments, civil society organizations, and sympathetic agencies like UNDP, the United Nations Development Programme for Women (UNIFEM) and the International Labour Organization (ILO) have a more prominent voice. But such open, relatively participatory debates become more constricted, and NGO input more confined to separate forums. Rarely do they address, much less adopt, the structural and transformative actions that would be necessary to make really progressive change.[33]

The reason for this paralysis is quite simply the normative hegemony of economic globalization and its pull on virtually all UN member states (with the possible exception of Cuba). It seems clear that international markets and globalizing institutions represent a fast train that developing countries and China are scrambling to board, not one they wish to slow down or redirect. In a similar way, many are scrambling for seats on the Security Council rather than trying to strengthen the more open, democratic processes within the UN system where civil society groups have some real access. As a result, neither the official debates nor the final outcome documents of Beijing+5 or WSSD+5 even hinted that the negative consequences of globalization might be systemic, endemic, and structural. Rather, reminiscent of decades of national welfare policies that focus on reforming poor people, the few paragraphs in the documents that address structural reforms emphasize the reduction of 'obstacles' *within* countries that prevent their further 'integration' into globalization's beneficent ambience.[34]

With regard to generating resources for social development, efforts by the Women's and Development Caucuses to replace the term 'debt relief' with 'debt *cancellation*' and to support a modest Canadian proposal for 'further study of the implications of a currency transaction tax', adding 'its use to generate revenue for a social development fund directed to the poorest', were thoroughly defeated.[35] Moreover, a strong proposal sponsored by the G-77 and introduced by the Women's Caucus that would have seriously challenged the IFIs by calling for their democratization and accountability within the UN system was dead in the water.[36] Not only did this proposal confront the adamant opposition of the EU and JUSCANZ; it also evoked little if any fighting spirit on the part of even the most critical among G-77 governments. (When the head of the US delegation in Geneva said she 'had trouble with this word democratization' in a paragraph on the Bretton Woods institutions, it provoked laughter at the political irony but not outrage.) Thus the absence of political will that women's and other NGOs observed during the con-ferences is very basic. It has to do not just with failure to implement the Cairo, Beijing and Copenhagen POAs but also with a non-critical stance toward the market-driven, corporate world we now live in, or else fear of voicing criticisms too openly and being denied a place on the train.

The WSSD+5 proceedings differed markedly from those of Beijing+5 in the assemblage of major actors participating, among NGOs as well as delegates, and therefore in both the alignment of forces and the substance of contentious debates. The first thing one noticed was the surprisingly low profile of the Holy See and its small bloc of fundamentalist and conservative NGO allies, who had played such a disruptive role in both the Cairo+5 and the Beijing+5 proceedings. The Vatican committed very little human and material resources to this conference, was represented by a noticeably small and inexperienced delegation, and had none of the battalions of front groups with big red 'Mother' buttons seen during Beijing+5. This lack of interest underlines how, contrary to its claims of commitment to the needs of the South and people in poverty, the Vatican's political passions are focused primarily on opposing abortion, adolescent sexuality and homosexuality, while championing 'parental authority' and traditional gender divisions. Yet, in a disturbing mirror image, feminist groups, too, particularly those dedicated to women's health and human rights, had a much smaller presence in the WSSD+5 review than they did in Beijing+5. This reflects not only the unfortunate back-to-back timing of the two conferences but also the failure of many Northern donor and women's groups to recognize the inseparability of 'gender justice' and 'economic justice' (Sen and Corrêa 2000).

The lack of a strong feminist presence in the WSSD+5 UNGASS resulted in some serious steps backward in the final document. These included a failure, in any of the ten paragraphs dealing with HIV/AIDS, to specify the particular vulnerability of women and girls to infection; the excision of proposed language referring to male and female condom distribution; the document's complete silence on unsafe abortion; and the refusal of some G-77 countries to acknowledge female-headed households as a group with particular needs in poverty eradication efforts, or women's unpaid household labour as part of the informal sector. Moreover, after many failed attempts by members of the Women's Caucus, the document ended up with no explicit reference anywhere to the need to assess the gender and social impacts of globalization and to ensure women's participation in macroeconomic decision making.[37]

Nonetheless, the absence of a feminist–fundamentalist centre-ring battle yielded three unexpected and mainly positive results. First, the revised configuration of players ironically contributed to a more unified and gender-egalitarian G-77 than existed in the overcharged context of Beijing+5. Building on the experience of the earlier SLACC grouping, but now including important leadership from South Africa, the Philippines, and other countries, some of whose delegations included experienced NGO members, the G-77 in the WSSD+5 process became on some issues one of the strongest allies of the Women's Caucus, pushing through some of its most critical proposals. This new alignment of countries and leadership is important because it dissolves the older, fallacious division between 'gender justice' (with globalization), supported by the North, and 'economic justice' (with traditional forms of patriarchy), supported by the South (Sen and Corrêa 2000). 'South-oriented economic positions and support for women's rights' can be understood as integrally linked (Sen 2000). But this change becomes possible only within the context of a highly mobilized and feminist anti-globalization movement supportive of Southern interests such as debt cancellation and – as I shall document below – access of poor countries to essential medicines. The shifting character of the G-77 thus illustrates that not only political alliances but also political positions and ideologies may be quite fluid within UN conference settings, reflecting shifting historical conjunctures.

Second, despite the small size of the Women's Caucus during WSSD+5, it managed to transform a draft in which gender was practically absent from much of the text into a document in which gender implications are scattered throughout. With support of not only the US and the EU but also the now friendlier G-77, the Caucus's proposed additions regarding gender equality in the workplace and household, feminization of poverty, gender-sensitive data and indicators, violence against women, maternal mortality reduction, and reproductive and sexual health were adopted (though none with specific, time-bound targets).[38]

The third and most ground-breaking development of the WSSD+5 process – one resulting directly from the newly forged alliance among the Women's Caucus, Development Caucus and G-77 – was the achievement of historically unprecedented language linking trade-related intellectual property rights (TRIPs),[39] access to essential medicines, and the fundamental human right to health. At the April Prep Com in New York, the Women's Caucus proposed the following language to be included in Paragraph 80, on TRIPs:

> Recognize that intellectual property rights under the TRIPs Agreement must not take precedence over the fundamental human right to the highest attainable standard of health care, as provided in many inter-national human rights and other multilateral instruments, nor the ethical responsibility to provide life-saving medications at affordable cost to developing countries and people living in poverty.

The Caucus saw this as a wedge issue that might raise the awareness of governments and development NGOs of the connections between health, human rights, and global trade. The issue also has important gender implica-tions because of the plight of HIV-infected pregnant women in poor countries and the greater susceptibility of women and girls to HIV infection generally. But there was little optimism that the proposal would be accepted, especially given the commitment of the US and EU governments to TRIPs and WTO authority. Thus Caucus members were both surprised and elated when the South African delegation took over their language verbatim and succeeded in winning its adoption by the entire G-77 and China during the intersessionals.

At the Geneva UNGASS, the paragraph quoted above became one of the most contentious issues dividing North from South, with the EU and JUSCANZ firmly stressing 'the importance of intellectual property rights (IPRs) to promote incentives for further research' and that exceptions in the TRIPs Agreement for 'national emergencies' were adequate to cover the HIV/AIDS crisis. NGO participants, however, pointed out that such except-ions depend for their interpretation and enforcement on the WTO, whose processes are closed and unaccountable. In contrast, subsuming TRIPs to international human rights standards – in particular the right to the highest attainable standard of physical and mental health embodied in the UDHR, the ICESCR and the WHO Constitution – means subjecting it to the potential jurisdiction of international customary law and the UN human rights treaty bodies.

With clear leadership from South Africa and strong lobbying support from the Women's Caucus and some development NGOs (particularly the Committee of Concern, Third World Network and Social Watch), the G-77 persisted in its fight for the principle that 'intellectual property' is not more valuable than human life and that access to affordable medicines is a matter, not only of exceptions to patent laws, but of fundamental human rights. The result, after long negotiations, was a compromise combining the G-77 and EU proposals but in a manner that *puts the human rights clause first* and includes the right of member states to exercise their options to bypass TRIPs (through cheaper imports or local manufacture) 'in an unrestricted manner'.[40] Although this compromise fell short of subjecting IPRs and global trade directly to human rights provisions regarding health, it nonetheless opened up a new arena of discourse and interpretation promoting this link and contributed to later victories on drugs and trade in South Africa, Brazil and globally (see Chapter 3 below). The achievement of this important provision in the WSSD+5 final document also marked an advance for transnational women's activism:

- For the first time in any international multilateral agreement, global trade, human rights and health have been connected – with important implications for women's health.

- For one of the few times within UN debates (the right to development being a notable exception), the G-77 and China adopted a human rights framework as the basis of their position.

- Through its key role in marshalling this dispute to a surprisingly successful conclusion, South Africa – one of the most progressive and 'feminist-friendly' governments in the world – strengthened its leadership position among the G-77.

- By taking the initiative in introducing this language, the Women's Caucus demonstrated its concern with linking gender and health issues to macroeconomic policies and global trade.

Transnational women's efforts around trade, health and human rights at the WSSD+5 meetings illustrate the critical necessity of 'strategic alliances formed across social movements' as well as between those movements and sympathetic IGO and government allies (Stienstra 1999: 269). But participants in the WSSD+5 meeting hardly foresaw that access to life-prolonging medicines, especially in regard to the HIV/AIDS pandemic, would become the most highly contested battlefield in the contest between (intellectual) property rights and human rights (to health). This is because it is an issue that directly engages international conflicts over trade inequities, pricing of goods essential for life and health, and the alleged prerogatives and benefits of corporate claims to exclusive ownership of patents and markets. The controversy over drug pricing and availability for HIV/AIDS patients, especially in sub-Saharan Africa, also has compelling gender implications because of the greater vulnerability of women and girls to infection and because of the proven effectiveness of antiretroviral drugs in preventing prenatal and perinatal transmission. In that sense, such access must be seen as an integral component of reproductive and sexual rights for women as well as of 'the human right to the highest attainable standard of physical and mental health', when 'attainability' is a matter chiefly of affordability and supply. This crucial issue thus illuminates the intersection of gender and reproductive/sexual rights with issues of poverty and class, racial and regional exclusions. And it lies at the heart of challenges to globalization's systemic and systematic reinforcement of multiple inequalities.

Towards polycentric strategies and multiform visions

Feminist critics of participation in lobbying UN conferences argue that, despite many gains achieved, 'by choosing the United Nations conferences as a site for NGO organizing, women's NGOs had to operate within the framework set by the United Nations and government representatives' and thus found themselves 'straitjacketed'. These critics also question 'using limited resources to respond to an agenda set by governments and UN agencies rather than using their resources to work for change outside of these international structures' (Silliman 1999: 151–2; Keysers 1999: 17). Yet the past few years of transnational feminist advocacy show that women's health and human rights groups have learned important lessons about (a) how to work most effectively within the UN system and (b) the importance of challenging global power arrangements. My argument is that we must find new ways of linking (a) to (b).

Certainly legitimate questions can be raised about the costs as well as benefits (human and material) of women's NGOs becoming involved in 'UN level diplomacy', just as they can with regard to lobbying and electoral politics within states. But women's work for social change has to occur both within and outside established institutions, and in global, national and grassroots contexts simultaneously. Far from competing, these different levels and forms of work are mutually reinforcing; they are complementary avenues for reaching the same goals. Indeed, they are often performed by the same people who gear themselves to different strategies to suit different political arenas, just as trade unionists know that negotiating contracts and marching on picket lines require different tactics and skills but are both indispensable and inter-dependent. This goes back to the previous chapter's analysis of the imbrication of all positionings – even the most critical and counter-hegemonic – within the power dynamics of global capitalism; there is no 'outside'. Claiming some privileged site from which radical social change inevitably and exclusively springs is at best an illusion, at worst a colossal arrogance.

To say this is not to give in to cynicism or despair but rather to learn some lessons from the twentieth century's failed revolutions and to rethink the processes of long-term social change, particularly at the global level. These processes are polycentric; they spring from many strategies and sites at once. Without denying that a global civil society is still embryonic, we can acknowledge that women's participation in UN conferences exemplifies an evolving bringing-into-being of global citizenship. Rather than 'mainstreaming the women's movements and strait-jacketing women's activism', the experience of participating in the conferences sharpened the strategic abilities and broadened the political awareness of many women's groups from North and South (compare Naples and Desai 2002, West 1999, and Keck and Sikkink 1998).

From this perspective, we can address more fruitfully the real divisions in power, resources and political priorities within and among transnational women's movements that surfaced during the 1990s UN conference activities. Many have commented on the fact that strategic leadership roles and behind-the-scenes planning tended to be dominated by Northern-based NGOs such as the Women's Environment and Development Organization (WEDO), the International Women's Health Coalition (IWHC) and the Center for Women's Global Leadership, groups that have greater access to funds, information and Internet technology than do most women's groups from the South (Silliman 1999; Higer 1999; Spivak 1999; Lang 1997). Moreover, as Higer points out, participation in the entire process of a UN conference, including the prep coms, is critical to keeping track of that process and making a significant impact. Such participation requires not only 'sufficient resources, foreign sponsors' and close knowledge of the UN system, but also time and freedom from other work and family responsibilities – a luxury only élite women usually have (Higer 1999: 139). As a result, the women's caucus at each of the major 1990s conferences tended to be divided between masses of NGO participants, who felt bewildered by the official proceedings and more comfortable attending informal panels and workshops; and seasoned NGO 'experts' immersed in the technical work of drafting and lobbying (see **Box 2.1**).

So how should we evaluate these realities? To ask the question is to confront once again the complexities of power and the inescapable operation of power divisions and conflicts within all social formations and movements, regardless of their location or scale. Existing global inequities determine that, like the countries and regions they inhabit, Southern-based women's health and human rights NGOs 'struggle against the dominant voices of Northern-based women's NGOs, which have greater resources, ease of movement, communication capabilities, and access to key information within IGOs' (Miller 1999: 165). Feminist NGOs in the North have a continual obligation to insist, in their relations with private donors and IGOs and among their own members, that resources and information be distributed more equitably and that the leadership roles of women's NGOs in the South be given direct and material recognition – that is, not through Northern NGOs as conduits and gatekeepers. Moreover, the women's caucus methodology, notwithstanding its important achievements, still requires the creative and committed efforts of both its Northern and its Southern adepts to become more inclusive and participatory (Higer 1999), through the Internet as well as open procedures. Finally, women's NGOs have to confront the global, systemic injustices that structure these intra-movement power imbalances in the first place, and to develop a more complex view of power relations as they infect all social movements and their various fragments.

An example of the kind of false political Manicheanism that divides 'insiders' pulling the strings from those righteously marching outside the gates is Amy Higer's split of the international women's health movement, particularly its activities before and during the Cairo conference, into 'pragmatists' and 'radicals'.[41] This oversimplified analysis ignores multiple grids and nuances that greatly complicate the picture:

- Many of the activists most deeply focused on drafting and lobbying to secure 'reproductive and sexual rights' language in the Cairo and Beijing documents were Southern women who have taken broad, outspoken stands against the impact of SAPs and trade inequities within their own countries and regions.

- Some of the most notoriously powerful leaders of women's NGOs based in the North have used their power to open up political spaces for many women around the globe.

- Some of the most vociferous critics of Northern-based women's NGOs for dominating the 'inside' process were themselves Northern-based women's NGOs who condemned that process as inherently cooptive and refused involvement in it.

- Others were prestigious academic feminists based in élite Northern institutions with ample resources to fly around the globe speaking on behalf of subjugated women from the South.

Who is uncontaminated or without contradiction here? Clearly there were leaders of some organizations at the Cairo and Beijing conferences who 'opted to focus their energies on gaining a foothold in the policy world' and 'credibility at the policy table' (Higer 1999: 133, 139). The important thing to understand, however, is that such individuals were unable to control the process, much less to '[tailor] the women's health agenda', even if they had wanted to. This was because both the process and the movement were much bigger and more complex than a few individuals and involved many diverse forces. As a result, the outcomes – the documents themselves and the uses of them as organizing tools by grassroots women's groups – were both more radical than many mainstream and fundamentalist interests wished and less transformative than feminist visions of social justice require.

Taking a much broader view of the relations among women's NGOs, social movements, and global governance, Stienstra argues, following Gramsci, that civil society entities are always 'in a dynamic relationship with states and intergovernmental organizations'. States and the dominant institutions of global capital (the World Bank, IMF and WTO) depend on transnational NGOs for their own legitimacy and for the construction of 'consensual hegemony' around norms and values. They 'need the NGOs and the movements they represent in the development of norms and standards' and, as we have seen, even in interpreting those standards. Hegemony is thus *relational*, not totalistic, and this means that transnational NGOs have a certain (limited) power in defining norms and the mechanisms for their enforcement (Stienstra 1999: 262, 268). We can apply this relational concept of power not only to the institutions of national and global governance but also to transnational women's NGOs and the complicated divisions and tensions within and among them. Thus the Northern-based women's health and human rights NGOs that played convening roles in Cairo and Beijing and the Plus Five conferences could only do so by forming networks of allied organizations from Africa, Asia-Pacific, Latin America and the Caribbean as well as Eastern–Central Europe. This was necessary in order to sustain their legitimacy and viability in a globalizing world, an instance perhaps of 'the North embracing the South' (Spivak, cited in Runyan 1999: 210). But the interesting thing is the ways in which the partner networks develop a life of their own, with their own outlooks and agendas and an independent, vocal leadership from the global South.[42]

According to Stienstra's analysis, women's transnational NGOs interact with and influence processes of global governance on three main levels: through 'the personal connections of some women in élite positions' to women's movements; through 'activism in relation to international conferences and organizations'; and through social movement activities that 'challenge the broader forces at work in global governance' (1999: 261). But none of these levels is self-sufficient. Relying on the first two without the third assures entrapment in a liberal mode of incremental reforms at best, whereas relying on the third without the first and second most often means that demands for radical, structural transformation remain disembodied from concrete institutional forms and practices. The tendency of 'élite NGOs that have much access to the United Nations ... [to] measure success by how many words or phrases of their own they were able to have inserted into international agreements', and to rate that more highly than 'monitoring and ensuring compliance', still falls very much within the liberal frame of political action (1999: 265). It does not yet address the problem that transnational women's groups, like all social movements, constantly face: how to create transformative politics embodying 'new meanings or alternative political and economic practices that challenge the [hegemonic] norms' (1999: 270).

Two key obstacles stand in the way of a feminist project of anti-racist and pro-global justice transformation in the current historical moment. The first is simply the ubiquitous reach of neoliberalism and the 'globalization of economies', which, at the end of the Cold War, joined military security as the double 'comprehensive norm' of international politics (Stienstra 1999: 269). The hegemony of this norm has become all too clear within the UN and the WTO, as most national governments, including those of the G-77 countries, have scrambled for inclusion in the global economy and Secretary-General Kofi Annan has courted transnational corporate 'partners' under the so-called Global Compact (see Chapter 6). A second obstacle is the fact that women's and human rights NGOs must contend with other actors and global forces – the TNCs, the IFIs and the G-8 countries, primarily the US – who not only dominate global capitalism but also conduct their international relations in closed-door processes that lack any accountability and to which NGOs have no access. Stienstra wisely cautions women's and other transnational NGOs not to 'overestimate their influence' or entertain the illusion that they have carved out a secure political space or 'place at the table' in the existing force field of UN politics. For '[they operate] in a broader context that [involves] the push and pull of other social forces, including transnational corporations and global finance' (1999: 268–70) – and, we should add, transnational fundamentalist forces aligned against women's reproductive and sexual rights.

The truth of this caveat became painfully clear in 2001, when the broad and integrative agenda achieved in Cairo, Beijing and their five-year follow-up meetings was watered down to a few narrow, disconnected but easily measurable 'targets' in the Millennium Development Goals (MDGs). The MDGs were formulated through a process that involved closed-door meetings with representatives of six UN agencies plus the IMF, OECD and World Bank. This effort was itself a follow-up to a closed ministerial-level UN meeting in 2000 that produced a (non-binding) document called the 'Millennium

Declaration'. The final document, the Secretary-General's 'Road Map of Millennium Development Goals', was published on 19 September 2001, just a week after the World Trade Center attacks and in a global climate that precluded virtually any protest or even public attention (UN General Assembly 2001c, 2001d). In other words, unlike the conference documents of the 1990s, the MDGs were produced in the total absence of civil society participation; women's and human rights groups were not invited to the table (Girard 1999, 2001; Berer 2001). Moreover, rather than an integrative human rights framework, the 'Road Map's' outcome goals and targets return to the narrow, vertically defined and presumably quantifiable parameters friendly to macroeconomists. Several of its targets for 2015 relate to health (reducing by two-thirds the under-five mortality rate and by three-quarters the maternal mortality rate; halting and beginning to reverse the spread of HIV/AIDS, malaria and other 'major diseases'; halving 'the proportion of people without sustainable access to safe drinking water'). Included among the eight goals are 'to promote gender equality and empower women', mainly through improving access to education for girls and women. However, gone entirely is the broader ICPD goal of access by 2015 for all who need it to reproductive health 'through the primary health care system', to say nothing of the wide range of specific targets for sexual and reproductive health services agreed in ICPD+5. Clearly this omission is not just an oversight but part of the backlash against the Cairo and Beijing frameworks and their human rights approach, spearheaded by the Holy See and its conservative allies and above all by the US government under the Bush administration (Girard 2001; Berer 2001).[43]

At the same time, recalling the fluidity and dynamism of the larger political and macroeconomic context stressed in the previous chapter, it is possible to identify certain strategic moves on the part of transnational women's and other NGO coalitions that are structural in nature and have a serious transformative potential. These include such recent trends as people's and women's budgets, calls for transparency and accountability on the part of TNCs and IFIs, proposals for regulation of transnational capital flows, and demands around access to essential medicines as part of the human right to health (see Chapters 3 and 6). Such moves have developed in the context of transnational anti-globalization struggles and, in the late 1990s and early twenty-first century, have been an increasingly important part of women's health movement strategies to mobilize resources and implementation mechanisms for reproductive and sexual rights.

The outcomes of the UN conferences I have just analysed give depressing confirmation that the UN system is not an arena that fundamentally challenges global structures of power. The market values and privatization that dominate the thinking of the IFIs, TNCs and major donor countries have also captured that of most Southern governments and seriously compromise the normative principles that the women's caucuses won. Moreover, one consequence of globalization is the hegemony of an economistic discourse that threatens to obscure principles of social justice and human rights, particularly in the domain of health.

At the same time, I would argue that participation in the UN conferences has been a critical vehicle for strengthening and broadening transnational women's coalitions. More importantly, it has raised their awareness about the macroeconomic priorities of global institutions and just how much remains to be done in order to change those priorities. Chapter 3 will chart the ways in which access to drugs for HIV/AIDS has become a powerful vehicle for beginning to demand corporate and international responsibility under international human rights principles. Chapter 5 will examine the impact of the UN conference documents at the national level and how the work of monitoring their implementation (albeit left largely to women) has affected NGOs. Without the principles and the documents, however, and the transformative values they contain despite their weaknesses and because of women's efforts, there would be little for which to hold corporations and governments accountable.

Notes

1 It was at the Nairobi conference, for example, that the DAWN network and UNIFEM (an independent UN development fund for women) were formed. See also the analysis by West in Meyer and Prügl 1999.
2 Two good examples are the widely used 'quality of care' framework designed by Judith Bruce and Anrudh Jain at the Population Council (see Bruce 1990) and the Ford Foundation's Reproductive Health and Population Programme, founded in 1989 by Dr José Barzelatto. Both would be unimaginable without two decades of women's health movement advocacy.
3 In Rio, the Women's Environment and Development Organization (WEDO) and its president, the late Bella Abzug, provided crucial organizational leadership. In Vienna, the Center for Women's Global Leadership (Rutgers University, US) played a central role. In Cairo and Beijing, while WEDO continued to convene the large, public Women's Caucus, the International Women's Health Coalition (IWHC) mobilized a strategic network of lobbyists, NGO delegates and text drafters who worked both behind the scenes and in the Women's Caucus.
4 See Kissling and O'Brien 2001 and CFFC 2000 for a critical analysis.

5 Even the Holy See, in its final interpretive statement at the UNGASS in July 1999, unwittingly reinforced this discourse when it announced its reservations to any provision making access to abortion part of 'sexual health, sexual rights, reproductive health or reproductive rights.'

6 The major human rights treaty bodies at the UN are the Committee on Economic, Social and Cultural Rights; the Committee on the Elimination of All Forms of Racial Discrimination; the Committee on the Elimination of All Forms of Discrimination Against Women (CEDAW); the Committee on the Rights of the Child; and the Human Rights Committee. See the useful compilation of their work on sexual and reproductive health rights in Center for Reproductive Rights (2002).

7 See Berer 1993, who points out the absurdity of this position, since preventing an unwanted birth (induced abortion) and preventing an unwanted pregnancy (contraception) obviously have the same end in view.

8 See Petchesky 1990, Chapter 1, for a historical and anthropological overview; and Petchesky and Judd 1998 for contemporary cross-cultural examples.

9 A dynamic, skilled and very vocal Youth Coalition, representing 132 NGOs in 111 countries, participated in all the ICPD+5 meetings. It argued that adolescents have the same sexual and reproductive rights, and the same right to participate in decisions that affect their lives, as adults. This was an important change from previous UN meetings.

10 Relevant paragraphs include: anti-discrimination policies towards people living with AIDS, 'including women and young people' (Paragraph 67); provision of anti-retroviral drugs and counselling on breastfeeding to pregnant women with HIV/AIDS (Paragraph 69); 'research and development of … female-controlled methods that both protect against sexually transmitted diseases … and prevent unwanted pregnancy' (Paragraph 59); and full access for young people aged 15–24 (90 per cent by 2005, 95 per cent by 2010) to all the necessary information and services to prevent HIV infection, including 'female and male condoms, voluntary testing, counselling and follow-up'. By 2005 'in the most affected countries' and by 2010 globally, the HIV infection rate among young people should have been reduced by 25 per cent (Paragraph 70).

11 The principle of 'basic health care for all' comes from the Alma Ata Declaration adopted by the International Conference on Primary Health Care in 1978.

12 That 'delivery-system costs' for reproductive health have been included under 'family planning' suggests that it remains the central budgetary programme and that vertical rather than integrated systems still prevail.

13 The G-77 'is an intergovernmental group established in 1964 to represent the interests of developing countries in the United Nations' (UNIFEM 1995). Today it consists of nearly 150 member states that differ vastly in culture, economic conditions, internal politics, and power position both within the UN and in the global arena.

14 Similarly, a WGNRR Position Paper (1999) on behalf of 30 women's groups and individuals around the world argues: 'Whilst the rhetoric has shifted through the Cairo process from a demographic, target-driven orientation in family planning programmes to one concerned with reproductive health, the drive to reduce the fertility of women in poor countries continues often to be the focus of health and population policies. Reproductive health and reproductive rights have become a "means to an end" instead of being an "end in themselves", i.e., instead of

acknowledging women's rights to health care as a basic human right.'

A striking exception in UNFPA documentation is the 1997 report titled 'The Right to Choose: Reproductive Rights and Reproductive Health', written by staff researcher Stan Bernstein and grounded in a strong human rights and gender equality framework (see UNFPA 1997b).

15 Perhaps the most outrageous and untenable claim here is the flier's attribution of 'the recent upsurge of infectious disease' – read, HIV/AIDS – to 'population growth'.

16 The report's authors even criticize the renaming in 1996 of the Bank's Population, Health and Nutrition (PHN) Department to 'Health, Nutrition and Population' (HNP) as an indicator of where the Bank's priorities now lie.

17 They included the WGNRR, UBINIG (Bangladesh), ANTIGENA (Switzerland), the Committee on Women, Population and the Environment (USA), and the Third World Network. See the joint booklet (published in 1993 by Isis International, Manila) critiquing the 'Women's Voices '94 Declaration on Population Policies' and Hartmann 1994; Keysers 1994; Spivak 1999; Silliman 1999; Higer 1999.

18 Marge Berer first addressed this argument to feminist colleagues over a decade ago (see Berer 1990; 1993).

19 Such journals in the US include *Studies in Family Planning, Population and Development Review, Demography* and *International Family Planning Perspectives*, the first three published by the Population Council and the latter by the Alan Guttmacher Institute, the research arm of the Planned Parenthood Federation of America. All appear to have been influenced to some extent by the more explicitly feminist *Reproductive Health Matters*, launched in 1993.

20 My argument here is not meant to suggest a revolution at the international policy level of IPPF but rather to emphasize the process by which progressive change begins to happen within institutions. Not only did IPPF's international office dissolve its Gender Advisory Panel, relegating gender to a lowly task force. It also has yet to commit general funds to the kinds of empowerment projects I describe here, which still depend largely on outside grants. In other words, a feminist transformation in IPPF's mission is far from having become institutionalized. (Many thanks to Judith Helzner for these insights.)

21 In the Western Hemisphere Region, the principal liaison group was the LACWHN. IPPF in South Asia maintains similar relations with local and national women's groups, who are very strong and well organized in that region.

22 The Women's Caucus proposed amendments to the draft Declaration and POA had inserted strong and consistent language reaffirming Cairo and calling for promotion of women's sexual and reproductive rights, but these proposals were virtually ignored in the final version of the WSSD document.

23 The ICPD+5 review process consisted of three stages over a five-month period in 1999. The Hague Forum (preceded by simultaneous Youth and NGO Forums) in early February was sponsored by UNFPA and was mainly convened to finalize background documents reviewing progress and obstacles in implementing the POA within countries. This was followed in March by a Prep Com in New York for the later UN General Assembly Special Session (UNGASS), held in late June–early July to review the Secretary-General's Final Report on Key Actions for Further Implementation of the Cairo POA. The March Prep Com, however, unable to

resolve many contentious issues, had to be carried over into several extended sessions in May and June. All three stages (including the NGO and Youth meetings) produced official documents that may be accessed through the UNFPA's website. My analysis is drawn from several sources: personal communications from Sonia Corrêa and Adrienne Germain; Corrêa's article in *DAWN Informs* No. 1/99; a report by SAGE (Strategic Analysis for Gender Equity), a consultant group whose members participated in all the 1990s UN conferences; and my own observations as a participant in all stages.

24 In Cairo and Beijing, the G-77 had agreed to speak in unison on economic issues but as individual countries on the 'controversial' issues related to gender equality and reproductive/sexual health (Sen and Corrêa 2000: 6).

25 In fact, only a handful of G-77 countries have allied consistently with the Holy See. These include Argentina, Egypt, Honduras, Libya, Malta and Sudan (see Corrêa 1999).

26 The Open Letter (1 July 1999) asked: 'Given that the Vatican is not a nation-state, is not involved in the implementation of the Cairo Programme of Action and, by its very nature, does not have women or children or sexual and reproductive problems, why is the Vatican delegation interested in blocking advances in contraception, sexual education, and HIV prevention that are beneficial to millions of women, especially … poor women?'

27 A statement issued by the Women's NGO Caucus titled 'La Lutta Continua!!!' (9 June 2000) registered 'our disappointment with the Outcomes Document' and expressed 'regret that there was not enough political will on the part of some governments and the UN system to agree on a stronger document with more concrete benchmarks, numerical goals, time-bound targets, indicators, and resources aimed at implementing the Beijing Platform.'

28 Rahman (1999) reviews the historical bases on which the Holy See's UN non-member state observer status has been grounded (international diplomatic, postal and telecommunications activity) and persuasively shows the fallacies in its claim to be a 'territory' (0.44 km) with a permanent 'citizenry' in any way comparable to that of legitimate states with permanent UN missions.

29 Many of these recommendations are similar to ones contained in 'The Copenhagen Alternative Declaration' (8 March 1995), a document emanating from the work of the NGO Development Caucus.

30 A provision in Chapter 5 to '[reduce], as appropriate, excessive military expenditures and investments for arms production and acquisition' not only has none of the budgetary percentages and time-goals specified by the Women's Caucus but also has the undermining phrase, 'consistent with national security requirements.'

31 The ICPD+5 final outcomes document did, however, incorporate one Women's Coalition recommendation on resources, urging that countries' increased contributions to ODA be earmarked 'in particular' for 'improvement in the status and empowerment of women, basic health care and education, emerging and continued health challenges', and poverty eradication (Paragraph 95).

32 A protest statement signed by 77 NGOs attending the UNGASS for WSSD+5 charged that 'A Better World for All' was attempting to 'derail' the UNGASS negotiations, 'reinforced the perspectives from the North and disempowered the South', and 'undermined the very concept of political inclusiveness that defines the UN'.

33 No exception to this trend was the conference known as 'Financing for Development', which culminated in Mexico in 2002. Financing for Development aims to mobilize domestic and international financial resources to implement the economic and social development goals of the 1990s UN conferences. But significant NGO lobbying, by transnational women's groups among others, has not succeeded in transforming the neoliberal priorities that have dominated previous UN conferences. See Chapter 6 below.

34 See Paragraphs 29, 30 and 30bis in the Beijing+5 'Final Outcome' document; and Paragraph 4 in the Political Declaration and Paragraph 8 in the 'Further Initiatives' document for WSSD+5.

35 Notwithstanding the encouraging pronouncements about a more equitable distribution of wealth within and among nations in the Political Declaration, this goal is almost entirely abandoned in the 'Further Actions and Initiatives' section of the document. Instead, the emphasis is almost entirely on restructuring national taxation systems, eliminating corruption and inefficiency on the part of national governments, and reaffirming Copenhagen's target of 0.7 per cent GNP for developed country foreign assistance – a target that is almost nowhere met to date.

36 The proposed paragraph stated: 'Reform the international financial structure, including a reexamination of current voting rights of the IMF and *creation of mechanisms to assure accountability of the international financial institutions, including the World Trade Organization, to the United Nations system, through the human rights treaty bodies as well as ECOSOC, and the compliance of their policies and programmes with social development concerns and internationally agreed human rights principles.'* This became the bland and almost meaningless Paragraph 123: 'Continue work on a wide range of reforms to create a strengthened and more stable international financial system, enabling it to deal more effectively and in a timely manner with the new challenges of development.'

37 This was especially egregious given the consensus reached to adopt already agreed Beijing+5 language. Compare Paragraphs 135a and 135h in the Beijing+5 Final Outcomes document, which urge 'effective measures to address the challenges of globalization, including … equal participation of women, in particular those from developing countries, in the process of macroeconomic decision making'; and 'social development funds, where appropriate, to alleviate the negative effects on women associated with structural adjustment programmes and trade liberalization'.

38 See Paragraphs 27bis, 39ter, 54bis, 72bis, 73bis, and 76, WWSD+5 'Further Initiatives' document (July 2000).

39 The TRIPs (Trade-Related Intellectual Property Rights) Agreement was enacted as part of the Uruguay Round of GATT (General Agreement on Tariffs and Trade, the precursor to the WTO) in 1994 and is binding on all WTO members. See Chapter 3 below and C. M. Correa 2000.

40 The full text of the agreed Paragraph 80 reads: '*Recognize the right of everyone to the enjoyment of the highest attainable standards of physical and mental health as contained in relevant international human rights instruments as well as in the WHO Constitution. Further recognize the critical importance of access to essential medicines at affordable prices.* Acknowledge the contribution of intellectual property rights to promote further research, development and distribution of drugs, and that these intellectual property rights should contribute to the mutual advantage of producers and users of technological knowledge and in a manner conducive to social and economic

welfare. Agree that Member States may freely exercise, consistent with national laws and international agreements acceded to, in an unrestricted manner, the options available to them under international agreements to protect and advance access to life-saving, essential medicines.' Paragraph 99a, pertaining to financial resources for 'ensuring the provision and affordability of drugs', also includes the Women's Caucus proposed amendment: *'encouragement of local manufacturing and import practices* consistent with national laws and international agreements acceded to ....' These paragraphs foreshadow the Doha Declaration on TRIPs (see below).

41 Higer implies that the 'Women's Voices '94' Declaration – which did generate much debate and opposition – was the product of one planning meeting of 19 people in 1992, failing to mention the circulation of that draft for a year and a half to gather comments, or the meeting of some 250 representatives of women's health NGOs from around the world in January 1993 in Rio de Janeiro to undertake the Herculean task of finalizing the document with direct democratic participation from as many groups as possible. Higer's use of the acronym 'IWHM' to stand for 'international women's health movement' is also misleading because (a) it implies a degree of coherence and organizational structure that the movement has never had, and (b) it appropriates the acronym used for the triennial International Women and Health Meetings.

42 A striking example is HERA (Health, Empowerment, Rights and Accountability), a transnational network of women's health activists from mainly Southern regions who served as core lobbyists and NGO members of official delegations in Cairo and Beijing, as well as leading the Women's Coalitions during ICPD+5 and Beijing+5. IWHC in New York served as HERA's secretariat without determining its politics or strategies.

43 In late 2002, the Secretary-General designated Professor Jeffrey Sachs of Colombia University, formerly director of the Commission on Macroeconomics and Health, to set up a series of advisory task forces to develop implementation guidelines for the various MDGs. Several prominent feminists involved in sexual and reproductive health and human rights work and based in the US have been appointed to these task forces. At this writing, it remains to be seen whether they will be able to restore some of the broader, more integrative health and human rights perspective to the MDG mandate, or whether the General Assembly and national governments will have the will to follow such an expanded 'road map'.

3/ HIV/AIDS and the Human Right to Health: on a Collision Course with Global Capitalism

[T]he debate on AIDS is increasingly becoming a debate on what kind of world we want to have: a world that nurtures our common humanity or a system that protects and promotes global minority rule. (Booker and Minter 2001: 12)

Many recent commentators have remarked that, with all its profoundly tragic and socially disruptive dimensions, the HIV/AIDS crisis has revolutionized how we think and what we know about sexuality and gender relations.[1] AIDS also has a 'silver lining', according to Mark Malloch Brown, the UNDP Administrator, in so far as 'it is forcing the West to engage with Africa' (Crossette 2001b). Analysing the global politics of HIV/AIDS is far beyond the scope of this book, yet rethinking women's health movement strategies to implement reproductive and sexual rights is impossible without putting HIV/AIDS squarely into the picture.

As we saw earlier, the pandemic has probably had a much greater impact in opening up a space within UN politics for talking about sexuality, sexual health and sexual rights than anything feminist health activists might have accomplished on their own. In this chapter I argue that the impact of the crisis has even wider ramifications, exploding the boundaries separating such previously distinct categories as health, gender, sexuality, trade, property rights and human rights, and affecting the future shape of global governance regimes. I attempt to document how that explosion began to reverberate during 2000–1, both within UN meetings on development and HIV/AIDS and beyond, in the global politics of trade. And I examine the 'silver lining' in the epidemic, in so far as it has brought the principle of health as a human right into debates about corporate global power.

'People's health before patents and profits':⁸ the global campaign for access to medicines

By the close of the 1990s conferences and their five-year reviews, the idea of health as a human right had started down a collision course with global capitalism. As the previous chapter showed, important elements of this contradiction were already in evidence at the WSSD+5 meetings in New York and Geneva. During 2000–1, the issue of access to essential medicines that had been such a bone of contention in those meetings became a central unifying cause not only for anti-globalization coalitions but also for WTO member states from the South seeking to challenge Northern dominance over trade regimes. In a drama that pitted such groupings against the hitherto presumed invincible might of transnational pharmaceutical companies and their Northern government patrons, the forces of global civil society and social justice won a number of surprising victories. Before examining the chronology and political dynamics of these victories in more detail, I should first explain why seemingly technical debates over intellectual property rights and trade rules are symptomatic of much deeper fissures within global capitalism. Out of these fissures, I argue, come openings for change.

The TRIPs Agreement originated in 1994 at the instigation of a group of US-based multinational corporations lobbying the Uruguay Round of GATT, which also created the WTO.³ Its ostensible purpose was to harmonize the variations in patent laws and their enforcement across countries. But, according to Argentine economist Carlos Correa, the main objective of these corporations was to combat the growth of Asian competitors (whom they accused of imitation and 'piracy') and 'to freeze the comparative advantages that had so far ensured US technological supremacy'. Their 'policy of "technological protectionism" aimed at consolidating an international division of labour whereunder Northern countries generate innovations and Southern countries constitute the market for the resulting products and services' (Correa 2000: 4–5). TRIPs would lock in this division by establishing a minimum global standard of patent, copyright and other protections like those already in existence in major industrialized countries, especially the US. The infotech and biotech industries – the most dynamic levers of US economic growth in the 1980s and 1990s and those for whom 'knowledge as property' was most vital to profits – and their US government patrons had a particular stake in this globalized patent regime.⁴

In both its origins and its potential consequences, the TRIPs agreement thus favours the economic and technological hegemony of the North. Its regime of patent protections also shuns cultural perspectives at odds with the spread of capitalist markets everywhere – such as the view of animal life, 'seeds, plants, and other living resources necessary for food and health' as part of the 'commons' belonging to all peoples, rather than bounty for private expropriation and commodification (Barker and Mander 1999: 32; Shiva 2001). As Vandana Shiva and others have warned for years, patents protecting corporate monopolies over such life forms (for agribusiness, genetic engineering and modern medicines) are covers for 'bioimperialism' or 'biopiracy'. Slightly altering or merely converting to commercial purposes a seed or rice variety or a healing herb known to indigenous people for centuries can constitute an 'invention', legally entitling TNCs to appropriate local and indigenous knowledges – those belonging to women farmers and healers in much of the Third World (Shiva 2001: 49; Barker and Mander 1999: 32). In other words, such knowledges, like whole inhabited lands in the past, are regarded as *terrae nulliae*, their communal owners and inventors rendered invisible since only private (corporate) forms of property count. Cheah calls this 'a legalized form of late-capitalist theft' (1997: 251); Shiva calls it 're-colonization' and likens it to Columbus's 'discovery' of America (2001: 12–13).

The defence of TRIPS and IPRs generally by Northern governments and corporations has from the beginning been riddled by contradictions, if not outright hypocrisy. In mobilizing that defence, US corporations – especially 'Big PhRMA' – continually make two conflicting arguments.[5] On one hand, they insist that IPRs are indispensable to sustain their own motivation to engage in research and technology development (R & D), implying that, without this incentive, no research for new medicines would take place. On the other hand, they claim that a globalized patent system will ultimately benefit developing countries, since it will bring them new technology, investment flows, and patent protections of their own. Yet, while the long-term consequences for developing countries have still to be understood, certainly in the short term this promise remains unfulfilled. Nearly all (97 per cent) of current patents are held by companies in industrialized countries; between 1977 and 1996, 95 per cent of all patents granted in the United States were conferred on applicants from only ten industrialized countries. What this means is that something like $20 billion a year in fees for technology use flow from the South to the North (UNDP 2000a; Correa 2000; Abbott/DND Conference 2002).

Meanwhile, TRIPs and the WTO have done nothing to facilitate technology transfer or development of any kind in poorer countries. On the contrary, their main effect for many countries (especially the small-island and sub-Saharan African regions) seems to have been to impede exports, inflate the prices of imported goods and medicines, and thus exacerbate trade deficits and inhibit growth – in other words, to *constrict* development (Correa 2000).[6] This has extremely negative implications for poor people's access to life-prolonging medicines. Studies done in the 1990s in India, Egypt and Argentina indicate that the introduction of patent protection for medicines increases prices by a multiple ranging from 3 to 41 times while resulting in greatly reduced local use of (modern, or non-traditional) medicines (Correa 2000, Box 1). And under TRIPs, the patents last for 20 years. As Shiva puts it, 'the patent system "regulates" competition. It does not necessarily stimulate technology generation, much less diffusion', since its main purpose is to ensure exclusive markets (2001: 4).

What of the mantra that patents provide drug companies in the US and Europe (those with the resources and capacity) the necessary incentive to engage in 'innovation'? To make the case that patents serve not only corporate profits but also the public good, industry spokesmen often cite gross figures reflecting the huge sums ($27 billion, $500 million per new product) they invest per year in R & D. What they fail to specify is the large part of this investment that goes to marketing research and the development of products aimed primarily at the North American, Japanese and West European markets – products to cure the endemic plagues of late capitalism, including not only heart disease and stress but also baldness, sexual dysfunction (Pfizer's Viagra) and body fat. Developing countries as a whole comprise 72 per cent of the world's population but only 13 per cent of the world's drug market. Since Africa accounts for only 1 per cent of world drug sales, it is not surprising that a Médecins sans Frontières (MSF) study found that, of the 1,400 new drugs patented between 1975 and 1997, only 1 per cent were for the tropical diseases that kill millions of Africans each year. As one spokesman for a French–German company conceded, 'We can't deny that we try to focus on top markets.... But we're an industry in a competitive environment – we have a commitment to deliver performance for shareholders' (McNeil 2000b: 6; Rosenberg 2001). The bottom line is the bottom line.

Nor do corporate representatives acknowledge that most of the pre-clinical research for many of the medicines they market and profit from (especially those for HIV/AIDS and tuberculosis) is conducted at public expense by universities and government agencies.[7] These institutions hold the original patents but often license them to private corporations.[8] In a study submitted as an affidavit in the 2001 South Africa case (see below), James Love, Executive Director of the Consumer Project on Technology (CPT), convincingly argues that markets are *inherently* unreliable as generators of 'scientific and technological research and development (R & D) to meet health care needs'. There are many reasons for this besides venal motives: the risks involved; the inability to recover all the benefits (many of which are non-excludable); the aversion of profit-oriented companies to doing research on 'adverse effects'; the lack of interest of such companies in poor people and their (unprofitable, hence neglected) diseases. Moreover, the patent system itself 'undermines scientific progress', since it encourages secrecy, competition and the hording of information; whereas scientific inquiry – contrary to the myths of capitalist entrepreneurship – requires openness, collaboration and information sharing (Love 2002: 177–8). Indeed, this is precisely why corporate IPR claims must inevitably rest on a bottomless but hidden reservoir of public sector and Third World intellectual labour; why, like corporate audits, patents conceal more than they reveal.[9]

On the whole, then, the 'advantages' of TRIPs seem overwhelmingly one-sided in favour of existing power imbalances in the global capitalist economy – profits, not people, and certainly not people's health. Patents are a market-based system whose aim is to protect profits and property, not to stimulate R & D. At the same time, Amy Kapczynski observes that 'TRIPs is a baseline' rather than a set of rigid, clearly enforceable rules (2002). In other words, its meanings will be determined by political realities more than by lawyers. Within the TRIPs regime itself, certain flexible provisions leave developing countries a 'margin of manoeuvre' – provisions that no doubt were won through hard negotiation. These include references in Article 7 to the 'transfer and dissemination of technology' as one of the treaty's 'objectives'; and in Article 8 ('Principles') to the right of member states to 'adopt measures necessary to protect public health and nutrition and to promote the public interest in sectors of vital importance to their socio-economic and techno-logical development'. Critical for the issue of access to medicines, they also include (1) the admissibility, under the doctrine of the international exhaustion of IPRs, of *parallel imports* – such as imports of cheaper versions of patented drugs from third countries (Article 6); (2) allowable *exceptions to patentability* in the case of 'diagnostic, therapeutic and surgical methods of treatment for humans or animals' in order 'to protect human, animal or plant life or health or … the environment' (Article 27);[10] and (3) provisions for granting *compulsory licences* (for example, to domestic companies to manufacture generic versions of patented drugs) 'in the case of a national emergency' such as an epidemic or other exceptional circumstances (Article 31 and Correa 2000). Moreover, the agreement's arrangements contain a transitional period pertinent to pharmaceutical products that allows developing countries to postpone the costly and difficult process of implementation for up to eleven years.[11] By 2005, however, these extensions will expire for all affected countries (see below).

Southern countries such as Brazil, India, Thailand and South Africa have used these soft spots in the TRIPs armour to defend policies that authorize the manufacture and/or importation of affordable generic drugs to treat HIV/AIDS – the antiretroviral and combination therapies that have transformed AIDS into a manageable chronic disease in the North. In the cases of Brazil and South Africa, they have done so in defiance of a continual barrage of threats by successive US governments and by cartels of multinational drug companies to bring lawsuits or economic sanctions against those countries for violating patent rights.[12] In fact, these threats themselves could be construed as violations of the TRIPs regime, in so far as they abrogate the multilateral dispute settlement process intended to avoid the kind of unilateral actions and intimidation tactics that the US executive and its Trade Representative have deployed with such fervour on behalf of Big PhRMA. Here as elsewhere, the US applies international law selectively to suit its own interests – even when the rules are ones it and its corporate clients initiated! For the many developing countries that rely on the US for much of their foreign trade, such threats can have undeniable 'chilling effects' on the production or importation of life-saving generic drugs (Barker and Mander 1999: 35).

Nonetheless, for all its muscle, the corporate agenda for TRIPs and ironclad patent protection has met extraordinary resistance – especially in regard to the issue of access to life-prolonging medicines for poor people with HIV/AIDS. By early 2001, the global campaign against 'Big PhRMA' on behalf of lower prices and Southern governments' right to procure affordable generic or patented drugs would become the most dynamic catalyst of efforts to fight AIDS in poor countries. A review of the chronology of events from early 1998 through the fall of 2001 (see **Box 3.1**) shows a spiral of resistance, counter-offence and renewed resistance, in which transnational health and human rights NGOs play a pivotal role in putting global capital on the defensive.[13] With drums, photogenic banners ('AIDS PROFITEER – DEADLIER THAN THE VIRUS', 'STOP MEDICAL APARTHEID!'), and a sharp sense of

Chronology of the global campaign for access to essential medicines

1994	**TRIPs agreement adopted** as part of Uruguay Round of GATT.
1997	**South Africa passes Medicines and Related Substances Control Amendment Act**, containing measures to make medicines more affordable and accessible.
Feb. 1998	**Pharmaceutical Manufacturers' Association (PMA) of South Africa and 39 drug companies file lawsuit against South African government** to interdict sections of the Act.
1998–early 1999	Clinton administration, US Congress and Trade Representative (USTR) pressure South Africa to drop law, threatening aid and trade sanctions.
Dec. 1998	**Treatment Action Campaign (TAC) forms in South Africa.**
Jan.–Mar. 1999	**MSF announces global campaign for access to essential medicines for poor countries**, joined by ACT UP and CPT. Health GAP forms in US.
July 1999	Health GAP and ACT UP (New York and Philadelphia) stage protests at kick-off of Vice-President Gore's presidential campaign: 'Gore lets Africans die for pharmaceuticals' profits!'
Sept. 1999	PMA suspends suit against South Africa; USTR announces cessation of sanctions.
Nov. 1999	UN Committee on Economic, Social and Cultural Rights issues statement on human rights obligations of WTO and trade liberalization.
Dec. 1999	**WTO meeting in Seattle; tens of thousands of protesters shut down the meeting.** Clinton administration ends opposition to Third World government policies regarding access to medicines providing they abide by WTO rules.
Jan. 2000	Vice-President Gore presides over special session of UN Security Council to declare AIDS a global 'security threat'.
April 2000	Women's Caucus introduces language on TRIPS, medicines and human rights at Prep Com for WSSD+5, United Nations, New York. World Bank pledges 'unlimited money' to combat AIDS in poor countries after Health GAP lobbying. ACT UP and Health GAP picket Pfizer headquarters in New York.
May 2000	Clinton issues executive order saying the US executive will no longer threaten trade sanctions against African countries seeking to procure cheaper AIDS drugs. Five major US and European drug companies – in conjunction with WHO, UNAIDS, World Bank, UNICEF and UNFPA – offer to cut prices for AIDS drugs in South Africa by 80 per cent. Brazil reintroduces amendment before World Health Assembly in Geneva asking WHO to establish a database listing prices for all

anti-AIDs drugs, including generics.

June 2000 **WSSD+5 UNGASS in Geneva adopts final document with Paragraph 80 on health as a human right, IPRs and 'access to life-saving, essential medicines'.**

July 2000 **Thirteenth International AIDS Conference in Durban, South Africa**; TAC organizes first global march for treatment access; Behringer offers to supply nevirapine free to developing countries for 5 years to prevent mother-to-child transmission (MTCT).

US Export–Import Bank offers sub-Saharan African nations $1 billion a year in loans (at commercial interest rates) to finance purchase of AIDS drugs.

After closing of Durban conference, PMA reopens its lawsuit.

Aug. 2000 African governments reject loans in favour of 'making drugs affordable'.

Oct. 2000 TAC launches campaign against Pfizer to lower price for fluconazole, transports generic version from Thailand into South Africa, holds press conference.

Jan. 2001 TAC announces intention to file *amicus curiae* brief in PMA case.

Feb. 2001 Cipla, generic drug manufacturer in India, offers to supply AIDS 'cocktail' drugs to MSF for $350 a year per patient and to Southern governments for $600.

TAC leads march of 1,000 people in Cape Town and produces 'AIDS profiteer' poster.

CPT's and Health GAP lobby new Bush administration to continue Clinton policy on access to medicines and no sanctions; Bush agrees.

Global treatment access coalition works with development, human rights and AIDS NGOs to make campaign a central focus of preparations for UNGASS in June.

Oxfam announces it will join global campaign for access and take it to Wall Street.

Mar. 2001 **PMA case against South African law is heard in Pretoria High Court; thousands demonstrate in 30 cities worldwide on 'Global Day of Action'**; TAC, MSF, Oxfam and Congress of COSATU call international press conference; TAC and COSATU hold all-night vigil and picket outside court.

MSF initiates worldwide petition campaign that gets 250,000 signatures and EU endorsement in support of South Africa.

Cipla asks SA government for licence to sell eight generic AIDS drugs.

Bristol-Myers Squibb says it will no longer challenge companies that want to sell generic versions of its AIDS drugs in Africa.

Brazilian government threatens to utilize compulsory licensing on AIDS medications produced by Merck and Hoffmann–La Roche; Merck agrees to cut prices on two drugs.

US files formal complaint with WTO against Brazil for violating TRIPs.

Apr. 2001   WHO, EU, French National AIDS Council, Kofi Annan and Nelson
            Mandela call on PMA to withdraw its suit.
            UN Commission on Human Rights issues resolution on 'Access to
            Medication in the Context of Pandemics such as HIV/AIDS'.
            PMA announces it is unconditionally withdrawing the suit (19 April).
            Two-day summit of 53 African governments adopts pledge to aim for
            15 per cent budgetary expenditure on health, with large amount going
            to AIDS prevention and treatment.

May 2001   Kofi Annan goes to Washington to seek commitment for $7–10 billion
            annual AIDS Fund; Bush pledges $200 million.
            Novartis, Swiss drug company, agrees to lower price of malaria drug in
            Africa.
            Pfizer offers anti-fungal drug for AIDS treatment free to 50 poorest
            countries.

June 2001   **UNGASS on AIDS at UN**; General Assembly agrees on Declaration of
            Commitment with targets, timetables, and gender-sensitive human
            rights approach.
            **Secretary-General promotes Global Fund to Fight AIDS, Malaria and TB,
            urges governments to raise $7–10 billion.**
            US drops WTO complaint against Brazil, agrees on settlement.

July 2001   MSF brokers deal with major drug companies and WHO to cut prices
            of five anti-tuberculosis drugs for resistant strains by 90 per cent.
            G-8 Summit in Genoa; thousands of demonstrators are back on the
            streets; one is killed by police.

Aug. 2001   Brazil moves to grant compulsory licence for generic version of
            patented AIDS drug; La Roche agrees to cut price another 40 per cent.
            Brazilian government withdraws threat.

Nov. 2001   **WTO Ministerial Meeting in Doha, Qatar; adopts Declaration on TRIPs,
            public health, and 'access to medicines for all'.**

timing, activists from South Africa's Treatment Access Campaign (TAC), US and European branches of AIDS Coalition to Unleash Power (ACT UP) and other groups used the streets to indict the greed and inhumanity of drug companies – publicly naming them and their CEOs. Meanwhile, TAC, MSF, Oxfam, Health GAP (Global Health Access Project) and CPT simultaneously utilized lobbying and legal strategies, in the media eye and behind the scenes, to expose government–corporate collusion and to secure agreements for lower prices, bulk purchasing and access to generics. This combination of strategies and their application at multiple levels – grassroots, national and international – have had a powerful and irreversible effect on global health politics.

I want to stress again the mutual reinforcement of activists working inside mainstream power arenas and institutions and those working outside, on the streets (see Chapter 2). There is no doubting the effective role that demonstrations and other forms of direct action have played in pressuring the US government and transnational drug companies to make significant concessions and in creating a broad public awareness of access to treatment as a human rights issue. Here are just a few examples that leap out of the chronology:

- June and July 1999: ACT UP (Philadelphia and New York) and Health GAP members picket Gore's 2000 presidential campaign kick-off in Tennessee, shouting 'GORE'S GREED KILLS'; while back in Washington CPT and Health GAP lobby the Clinton–Gore administration on the issue of access to treatment. Within a month, the administration has reversed its policy on HIV/AIDS drugs and patents.

- April 2000: AIDS activists from TAC and ACT UP, along with labour and religious groups, conduct a demonstration and sit-in against Pfizer in New York, denouncing the company as an 'AIDS profiteer'. October 2000: TAC chairperson Zackie Achmat returns from Thailand to South Africa carrying 5,000 tablets of generic fluconazole and conducts a press conference announcing TAC's 'patent abuse defiance campaign'.[14] By May of the next year, Pfizer – the world's largest drug company – announces it will provide its patented drug free to any South African who cannot afford it (Heywood 2001; McNeil 2000c).

- March–April 2001: As the PMA case against South Africa opens in the Pretoria High Court, thousands march in the streets of Pretoria, Johannesburg, Cape Town and cities around the world, capturing wide media attention; Nelson Mandela and Kofi Annan speak out; and MSF collects 250,000 signatures and endorsements from the EU and Dutch governments as well as world-famous pop musicians in support of South Africa and against the drug companies. PMA suddenly decides to withdraw the suit.

Yet there is no simple linear trajectory in this story, nor is local direct action successful in the long run except when it is conjoined with legal, political and media strategies involving meticulous in-depth research and transnational coordination. To understand the complex power relations in the campaign for access to treatment – relations that foreshadow future struggles of civil society groups against corporate globalization – we need to look more closely at three signifying moments in the chronology: the South African case, the Brazilian case, and the Declaration on TRIPs from the 2001 WTO meeting in Doha. Then we need to ask, what do these cases tell us about how gender and race figure in the politics of global health and how health in turn complicates the relations of global capitalism and trade?

South Africa. The racialized/gendered vital statistics on HIV/AIDS in Africa are the familiar, sobering drumbeat behind the chronology of events in **Box 3.1**.[15] Of the 40 million people estimated to be living with HIV/AIDS in the world in 2001, 95 per cent were in developing countries and close to 70 per cent (or 28 million adults and children) in sub-Saharan Africa. Of the 3 million who died worldwide that year, 2.3 million were in that region. Ninety per cent of all children worldwide born HIV+ are born in sub-Saharan Africa, where HIV prevalence among pregnant women can be as high as 36 per cent. And a recent World Bank report warns that the epidemic is undermining efforts to improve African children's access to education because of the very high rate of infections among schoolteachers as well as the children themselves (Schemo 2002). This is what Ronald Bayer (2002) calls 'the two worlds of AIDS', but it is really three worlds. Although HIV/AIDS may have been a gender-neutral killer in its earlier phases, particularly in the North, in more recent years it is becoming increasingly gender-biased. This is especially true in sub-Saharan Africa, where infection spreads mainly through heterosexual sex and mother-to-child transmission (MTCT). Fifty-eight per cent of infected adults in the region (as opposed to 50 per cent globally and 25 per cent in Western Europe) are women; women are a higher proportion than men of those who die each year; and infection rates among women are growing more rapidly. The differentials are even worse for young women and girls (ages 15–24), who in some countries (such as Zambia) have rates of infection three times higher than those of young men.

This gender-differentiated pattern is only partly the result of biology (higher 'viral load' of male secretions, larger surface area of female genitalia exposed, lesions caused by STDs and FGM). As numerous feminist analyses have revealed, it is even more the result of age-old social and cultural practices of gender subordination that intersect with the legacies of colonialism and apartheid. We have to reinterpret the frequently cited patterns of men's migration, working in mines, having sex with commercial sex workers and infecting wives and partners in the light of cultural norms dictating that women must comply with sexual demands of husbands or partners and that men must 'show their masculinity by having sex at a young age and with many women' (Klugman 2000: 166); or myths that having sex with a virgin will cure AIDS or avert infection. Such cultural myths and norms result in greater vulnerability of women and girls to sexual violence, shame, ostracism, loss of livelihood, prostitution – and hence infection. Barbara Klugman writes of the 'complex interaction of economic subordination and cultural subordination' in Southern Africa that results in women's and girls' compliance with men's sexual demands as well as the common practice of 'transactional' or 'survival sex' – sex in exchange for money, clothing, food, or other essential needs that women are unable to provide for themselves or their children (Klugman 2000: 146–7).[16] She also calls attention to another cultural practice common in the region: that of vaginal drying agents used to increase men's sexual pleasure but in the process causing women not only pain during sex but abrasions that (like FGM) increase their vulnerability to HIV and other STIs. In other words, 'sexual power relations' take many forms, both intimate and structural, all of which contribute to women's higher rate of death and illness from AIDS (Klugman 2000: 166).

Later in this chapter I will look more broadly at HIV/AIDS as one form of bodily mapping of 'global apartheid' and gender injustice. My concern here is to situate South Africa within the larger demographic picture of HIV/AIDS in the region in order to evaluate the importance of the legal and political victory there in April 2001. While South Africa does not have the highest rates of infection in sub-Saharan Africa (Botswana and Zimbabwe take the lead), it has the *greatest number* of people infected of any country in the world – an estimated 4.6 million, or 20 per cent of all adults and nearly 25 per cent of all pregnant women in 2000. In that same year, 250,000 people died of the epidemic in South Africa alone. A stunning photograph by João Silva of a woman in KwaZulu–Natal walking resolutely down the road past a row of caskets on display, including small ones for children, illustrates how death overtakes daily life in today's South Africa (Swarns 2001a, 2001b; *NY Times*, 31 December 2001, p. 9).

So when the PMA lawsuit against the South African government finally came to trial in the spring of 2001,[17] it naturally became the high point of the global campaign for access to essential medicines launched two years before. Initially PMA's suit contended that South Africa's 1997 Medicines Act (see **Box 3.1**), authorizing parallel imports or compulsory licensing to obtain affordable generic drugs, violated the sanctity of patent rights inscribed in

TRIPs. Mark Heywood, head of the AIDS Law Project (ALP) and National Secretary of TAC in South Africa, describes the aims of this corporate action as an attempt 'to annex additional powers and safeguards for intellectual property that are not part of TRIPs; to fill in some of the ambiguities in TRIPs, particularly its vagueness around "parallel importation"; and to warn other developing countries off a similar path' (2001: 4). But the drug conglomerates did not count on facing an alignment of forces that included not only the South African government but also high-profile humanitarian NGOs like MSF and Oxfam and world leaders like Kofi Annan and Nelson Mandela; all the UN agencies responsible for HIV/AIDS and health, and even the WTO; and an array of demonstrators outside the courtroom and in cities throughout South Africa, Europe and North America representing trade unionists, women's groups, religious groups, and people with AIDS as well as the major groups of AIDS activists. They did not anticipate that this trial would cast them in a media spotlight and become a truly globalized event.[18] Above all, they did not expect to encounter a powerful, highly knowledgeable adversary *inside* the courtroom in the person of TAC as an *amicus curiae* intervener.

Heywood's assessment of TAC's role and purposes in intervening as a 'friend of the court' is worth reviewing in some detail because it exemplifies a model for organizing around health as a human right that can be applied to many other human rights campaigns.[19] The heart of this model, taken from the anti-apartheid struggles of the 1960s–1980s, is a symbiosis between law and direct action, in which litigation becomes 'an instrument for progressive and people-driven advocacy and mobilization' (2001: 1). Indeed, one is struck in Heywood's account by the extent to which TAC played a leadership role in a two-pronged strategy that was simultaneously aimed at the court and at global public opinion. This 'proactive use of law' was grounded in a number of conceptual and strategic elements along with the traditions of anti-apartheid organizing. Conceptually, it never drifted from a solid human rights framework, one that exposes the subterfuges of conservative groups (such as TNCs) attempting to coopt human rights discourse for their own ends (as in claims based on intellectual property rights) – what Heywood calls 'dressing rights incursions in the language of rights protection' (2001: 2). On the contrary, in its *amicus* brief TAC argued '*that access to health is a human right that trumps rights to private property*' (my italics) and that the South African government had 'a positive duty', under both its own constitution and its international obligations, to 'progressively realize' rights of access to health care services and to protect rights such as dignity, life, equality and the duty to act in the best interests of the child – rights which are dependent on measures to improve socioeconomic conditions. (Heywood 2001: 6, 8)

Second, and absolutely pivotal to the TAC model, are close collaborations in every strategic action and aspect of the case with all the key players among civil society groups, both international and local. Throughout the treatment access campaign, and specifically in regard to the PMA lawsuit, these included not only MSF, Oxfam, CPT and Health GAP but also COSATU, whose leaders TAC briefed on the key legal and political issues in the case during a jointly sponsored all-night vigil. This is just one example of TAC's efforts throughout the case to carefully articulate its legal strategies inside the courtroom with the coalition activities outside, in which its own members and many other groups were engaged – marches, picketing, media outreach, MSF's petition campaign, and enlisting support from celebrities like the Rolling Stones and John Le Carré. Another striking example is TAC's use of the *amicus curiae* process itself as both an organizing and an advocacy tool. It did this by directly involving grassroots people from COSATU and doctors from MSF in affidavits about how the issues in the case impacted on their own lives and work (personal testimony) – a method, again, that followed the example of anti-apartheid lawyers. In this way, allied organizations were given 'a sense of ownership in the Court battle', which in turn helped to motivate their efforts as picketers and advocates outside the court (Heywood 2001: 7–8).

Finally, TAC's attitude toward the African National Congress (ANC) government during the trial remained one of distance and clear independence, even though technically – and in many respects substantively – TAC's arguments as *amicus curiae* supported the government and probably were pivotal in provoking PMA to withdraw its case. This was necessitated by Mbeki's stubborn opposition to antiretroviral therapy, which meant that 'the *amicus* intervention was but a stage in TAC's campaign for treatment access that would lay the foundations for intensified criticism of the government's policy concerning access to treatments for HIV' (Heywood 2001: 6 and below). Moreover, among the most important facts to be revealed in the trial was a series of offers by the drug companies to the government to lower their prices on triple-combination antiretroviral medicines in South Africa and what those offers were – facts the government had kept hidden. This paved the way for a post-trial advocacy campaign led by TAC resulting in further price reductions of around 50 per cent; though still at levels unaffordable to the masses of poor, these reductions nonetheless opened a wedge towards 'significant expansion of drug access in South Africa' (Heywood 2001: 11). Whether the drug companies were 'shamed and humiliated' over the loss of moral cover for property, as the *Guardian* in England announced, or retreated out of fear that a public trial would bare the deeper mysteries of property is uncertain. Thanks to the prodding of the TAC brief, however, 'the companies faced having to reveal some of their most closely guarded business secrets, including pricing policies, profit levels and the source of funding for research into key anti-AIDS drugs'. They chose to back out of the suit instead, but the advocates of corporate accountability had already won a significant victory (McGreal 2001).

From a strictly legal standpoint, because PMA dropped the suit, no decision, thus 'no binding legal precedent', emerged from the South Africa case. Yet, as Heywood's summing-up stresses, the political achievements of TAC's multi-layered strategy were tremendous. They no doubt helped to secure the Declaration on TRIPs adopted in Doha the following November (see below) and, above all, contributed immeasurably toward strengthening the transnational movement for health as a human right:

> Internationally, the intense focus on medicines, prices, patents and rights to health greatly broadened the support-base of an incipient movement that seeks to treat health as a human right and to promote the idea that commodities such as medicines, that are essential for health, should be treated differently under patent law to commodities that do not have any intrinsic link to human dignity and well-being.... On another level, it provided proof that the world's most powerful multinational companies are not invincible and can be brought to account by well researched, well argued mobilizations. This lesson will undoubtedly inspire other social struggles. (2001: 13)

It is important to note what is being challenged in this statement, as in TAC's legal arguments throughout the case: neither TRIPs nor the existence of patents but rather their *distorted interpretation* to aggrandize capital at the expense of human rights. Issuing a compulsory licence is not the same as 'patent breaking' but rather 'part of the patent system itself', a way of defining its lawful limits and one explicitly provided in Article 31 of TRIPs. In fact, compulsory licensing, rather than 'a concession made to developing countries', is a common mechanism used routinely by the US, Canada and other developed countries (Kapczynski, pers. comm. 2002; 't Hoen and Chirac

2002). Even though the pharmaceutical giants had initiated and embraced TRIPs as the embodiment of 'corporate rights' – an interpretation that some opponents of global capital all too readily join – the outcome of the South African case shows that TRIPs has become a contested terrain in the struggle to define and redirect globalization. As with any international or legal document, its meanings are nowhere written in stone; they evolve in the wake of political struggle. From the spring of 1999 to the spring of 2001, steadily mounting support for the idea that access to life-saving medicines is a human right and denial of such access to the poorest, most affected countries a gross injustice cast the 'exceptions' clauses of TRIPs in a new light. Then, after three years of strenuous objections that the South African law violated the sanctity of patents inscribed in TRIPs, the PMA retracted this argument even before the trial opened, resting its case on constitutional arguments instead. By this time even WTO officials had informally conceded the South African law was valid within the framework of international trade agreements. From a bastion of property rights, TRIPs had morphed into a potential enabler of national sovereignty over public health.

But subsequent events would raise serious questions about how much or what kind of a victory social justice forces won in the South African case. Already, during the year preceding the trial, the Mbeki government had cast doubts on its willingness to exert leadership in the matter of access to medicines for treating HIV/AIDS or even to take the epidemic seriously. First there were Mbeki's baffling public statements agreeing with a fringe group of AIDS 'dissidents' that HIV does not cause AIDS and that the cause of the African epidemic is poverty alone – a view thoroughly discredited by most researchers, including those in Africa. This controversy surrounded the Thirteenth World AIDS Conference, held in Durban in July 2000, where local AIDS groups protested government policies more vociferously than those of the giant pharmaceuticals. Then there was the government's questioning of antiretroviral treatment (ARV) on 'safety' grounds and its footdragging on the drugs' distribution – even after Behringer-Ingelheim had offered nevirapine free for five years to reduce MTCT (Schoofs 2000; Swarns 2000a, 2000b; Swarns and Altman 2000).[20]

In the months following the trial, controversy over the government's refusal to make ARV available throughout the country grew clamorous. As COSATU put it, 'the prevarication by the Minister of Health amounts to snatching defeat from the jaws of victory' (COSATU 2001b). By the fall of 2001 the Department of Health was only offering nevirapine to pregnant

HIV+ women in 18 pilot sites and had finally accepted Behringer's offer of free supplies – well over a year after it was made (Swarns 2001d; RHM 2001). Frustrated and angry at what it considered an irrational and arbitrary denial of life-saving treatment, TAC sued the government; and in mid-December the Pretoria High Court ruled that the state had 'an ineluctable obligation' to expand access to nevirapine to all pregnant HIV+ women under its care. As he left the courtroom surrounded by jubilant activists after the High Court's decision, Mark Heywood declared, 'We've made history today.' But in the same breath he commented more soberly: 'This judgment … doesn't solve the problem of AIDS in South Africa by any means' (Cauvin 2001).

Heywood's double-edged statement after the December ruling could be applied to the outcome in the PMA lawsuit as well and points to the limits of both victories. First, ARV for pregnant HIV+ women fails to address longer-term treatment for the women themselves or for non-pregnant women and men with AIDS. Focusing only on babies whose mothers will die, leaving them orphans, seems extremely shortsighted if not unethical.[21] Moreover, treatment is just one response to a much larger, more complex set of conditions the epidemic both reflects and exacerbates. On some level, Mbeki is right that poverty – intertwined with gender subordination, which he fails to acknowledge – is the ultimate culprit that allows the virus to thrive. From the beginning of the debate over access to medicines for HIV/AIDS, there have been those who argue that too much focus on treatment in a resource-poor environment draws resources from prevention as well as palliative care for those who are already dying and their families. Others urge that more study is needed to cope with the problem of viral resistance; that prioritizing HIV/AIDS will sap the ability of public health budgets to tackle other health crises, such as malaria, TB, and lack of clean water; and that, even if the drugs for ARV are free of cost, South Africa lacks a health infrastructure adequate to deliver them on a large scale along with the necessary monitoring, laboratory tests, counselling and follow-up (Houston 2001; Flanders 2001). Beyond all these complexities, a *gender-sensitive* programme of ARV should take into account the cultural constraints, alluded to earlier, that many women face. 'Learning their HIV positive status' may involve serious problems for women, including 'stigma and discrimination, violence against women blamed for infecting partners, shame, anxiety and other psychological sequelae' (Hankins 2000: 59). Without serious educational and political interventions to change the old, gender-biased attitudes of sexual shame and stigma, some women will reject ARV and the testing it requires.

Other health and AIDS activists, however, argue persuasively that providing ARV 'would put strong pressure on improving primary health care services' and 'could be an entry point for a radical reversal in the world's prioritization of resources for health' (Jackson 2001). From an ethical standpoint, they insist it is wrong to let people – including pregnant and non-pregnant women – die when an effective, life-prolonging treatment is available. From a practical standpoint, they note the success with which the South African Department of Health has managed and monitored on a national scale such treatments as those for cholera and high blood pressure; and point to the impressive record that countries with even weaker health systems and poorer resources than South Africa – especially Uganda and Senegal – have had in containing or reducing HIV infection rates.[22] Above all, they look at the example of Brazil, with its commitment to provide ARV and other AIDS drugs free to all who need them and its widely praised success in cutting the AIDS death rate in half in just a few years (see below). The message here is clearly that *political will*, even more than resources or an advanced health infrastructure, is the solution to AIDS in South Africa (COSATU 2001a; Altman 2000). But political will can rarely overcome the cultural climate in which it operates; it makes a tremendous difference whether that climate is one that affirms gender equality, sexual plurality and sexual pleasure or one that cloaks sexuality in punishment and shame.[23]

In the early years of the epidemic in South Africa – that is, prior to liberation and the 1994 elections – the Department of National Health and Population Development (DNHPD) as well as the ANC and a wide range of civil society organizations made strong commitments of principle to a National AIDS Strategy that would be 'holistic and multisectoral … including education and prevention, counselling, health care, welfare, and research' (Heywood and Cornell 1998: 66). Then, following elections and in the welter of the challenges facing the new ANC government, both popular opinion and national leaders retreated into silence, denial, or worse – a cruel stigmatization of people living with HIV and AIDS. AIDS was dismissed, even by progressive organizations like COSATU, as an 'imperialist plot' designed to reduce African population growth, or associated with gay, white, wealthy men and prostitutes.

Mark Heywood and Morna Cornell, writing in the late 1990s, offer a number of reasons (though not justifications) for this retreat. In part these were political, the ironic underside of democratic victory. First, the very climate of euphoria as well as high expectations from the new ANC government meant that concerns like HIV/AIDS got swept into the wings as drafting a new constitution, establishing new institutions, and addressing poverty and development took centre stage. In addition, 'political enfranchisement has been accompanied by a weakening – even paralysis – of many of the popular organizations that had started to consider AIDS as an urgent issue in the early 1990s', as many of their leaders became part of, or ceded power to, the new administration (1998: 68). The TAC-led campaign against the PMA and for treatment access as a human right has revitalized this movement, though the government continues to prevaricate.

But to understand the deeper roots of silence and shame we have to look at history and culture. Recalling the liberalism of the new South African constitution and the early National AIDS Strategy endorsed by the ANC, Heywood and Cornell soberly observe that 'principles are not always sufficient' and 'cultural practices that deny fundamental human rights cannot be wiped away by a constitution created by lawyers, academics, and politicians' (1998: 70–1). Like Klugman, they invoke the complex weave of social conditions with local cultural prejudices and practices involving the subordination of women, the sexual privileging of men, and, above all, a deep-seated homophobia that has infected even some ANC leaders and generated at best a silence on the subject of gay sexuality.[24] In turn, we should put these attitudes into the context of twentieth-century colonialism and apartheid; of centuries of European stigmatization of black Africans as sexually promiscuous, deviant and carriers of disease; and of documented scandals of Western and corporate medicine using Africans as 'guinea pigs'.[25] While this racist history surely does not excuse denial in the face of the epidemic or the evasive policies of Mbeki, it does place in a context and make more understandable the fears surrounding a sexually transmitted and deadly virus in South Africa.

Brazil. On 18 June 2001, at the beginning of the United Nations Special Session on AIDS, the Brazilian Ministry of Health (MoH), along with six Brazilian and Latin American AIDS-related NGOs, sponsored a half-page advertisement in the *New York Times* that read:

AIDS is not a business. The Brazilian Ministry of Health distributes the anti-AIDS cocktail free in Brazil to anyone who needs it. The United Nations has called this the best AIDS prevention programme in the developing world....

Local manufacturing of many of the drugs used in the anti-AIDS cocktail is not a declaration of war against the drugs industry. It is simply a fight for life.

As South Africa's government wavered in its AIDS treatment policies, Brazil assumed the undisputed leadership among Southern countries in the campaign to assert public health needs and human rights over intellectual property claims and corporate profits. This leadership manifests itself in multiple arenas – in negotiations with the US government and corporations; in UN forums such as the 2001 UNGASS on HIV/AIDS and the World Health Assembly (where Brazil successfully urged the publication of a WHO price index for AIDS drugs); in the global campaign against corporate biopiracy of the medicinal knowledge of indigenous groups; and above all in the national realm, in its creation of a model HIV/AIDS programme based in part on a viable domestic industry for producing ARV drugs that is predominantly public and non-profit.[26]

The success of Brazil's programme for preventing and treating HIV/ AIDS is evidenced first and foremost in its outcomes: 'It has halved the death rate from AIDS, prevented hundreds of thousands of new hospitalizations, cut the transmission rate, helped to stabilize the epidemic and improved the overall state of public health in Brazil' (Rosenberg 2001: 28). According to the national MoH, the overall 50 per cent reduction in AIDS-related mortality in Brazil since 1995 is exceeded in the large urban centres, which account for nearly one-third of all AIDS cases and where AIDS deaths have been reduced by nearly 75 per cent (Brazil MoH 2002; Teixeira 2002). Although the country's AIDS programme began in 1985, these exemplary outcomes date mainly from the mid-1990s, when it matched large World Bank loans with significant national budget allocations to create a $250 million AIDS funding package. It was also in 1996 that Brazil passed its law mandating universal access to drugs for treatment of AIDS – not, however, under any encouragement from the World Bank. On the contrary, Vera Paiva suggests that the Bank's restrictions on using its funds for anything but 'educational and prevention activities (since we were a "developing country")' may have served as a kind of negative incentive to Brazil's independent drug policy and its resistance to the US and Big PhRMA (Paiva 2002: 4).

Without question, the drugs component of this programme – relying heavily on the manufacture of generic versions of essential ARV drugs by the government's own research laboratory and factory, Far-Manguinhos – has been critical in making the programme cost-effective as well as in saving lives.

Rather than exacting trade-offs from other segments of the health system, the policy of treatment provision 'pays for itself' by having reduced hospitalizations by 85 per cent, decreased opportunistic infections and increased productivity among people with AIDS (Brazil MoH 2002; Teixeira 2002; Brazil MoH 1999; Rosenberg 2001: 28).[27] Moreover, through a combination of strategies – manufacturing its own drugs through the public sector being the most important but also negotiating with multinational manufacturers to reduce prices in the private market – Brazil has managed to reduce its budgetary expenditures on drugs for AIDS since 1999, both in total dollars spent and as a percentage of its overall health budget. And it has done this even as the total number of patients served by the universal access programme and the complexity of their regimens have increased annually.[28] According to a MoH study, by increasing the proportion of its ARV drugs obtained from domestic (mainly public) producers of generics rather than multinational producers of brand-name drugs (63 and 37 per cent respectively in 2001), the government saved an estimated $80 million in 2000 – or $540 million if compared to the cost of comparable drugs in the US (Brazil MoH 2002). And it has created an efficient as well as effective system of R & D to promote new drugs through a system of cost sharing between the public and private sectors during expensive later-stage trials (Macedo 2002).[29]

Combining universal treatment access with innovative outreach and education methods, Brazil's AIDS/STD programme disproves the view of pharmaceutical and medical élites that poor, illiterate people in developing countries are incompetent to handle the complex regimens of triple-therapy drugs. As sterile debates persist about whether treatment or prevention is more critical to combating the epidemic in the long run, Brazil's programme demonstrates conclusively that treatment and prevention, far from being in competition, are interdependent. In fact, the principle of their integral linkage is built into Brazil's 1988 constitution (Paiva 2002). When people know treatment is available, they are more likely to submit to testing and thus to be exposed to counselling on preventive and safer sex behaviour. In Brazil as in the US and Europe, availability of treatment has meant a decline not only in AIDS mortality but also in its prevalence; in the one year from 2001 to 2002, new infections dropped from 20,000 to 15,000, or by 25 per cent (CMH/WHO 2001; Bayer 2002). At the same time, the Brazilian government's commitment to making AIDS a number one public health priority has helped to upgrade and expand the country's primary health care system generally by creating a national network of AIDS clinics, trained health workers, counselling and diagnostic services, preventive outreach – including free condoms and clean needles – and epidemiological surveillance along with treatment access (Brazil MoH 1999; Rosenberg 2001). It has thus contributed to strengthening Brazil's public health infrastructure rather than depleting it.

Of course, Brazil's resources and capacity are enormous relative to most other Southern countries, especially in sub-Saharan Africa, giving it the ranking of a middle-income country.[30] But its success in developing a domestic pharmaceutical industry for ARV drugs and an effective HIV/AIDS programme is due not only to size and relative GNP but also to a constellation of mutually reinforcing political assets that have intersected with the AIDS epidemic. These include the historical context of democratization since 1984, with its strong emphasis on citizen participation; political commitment to a comprehensive national public health system (SUS) based on principles of social solidarity, multisectoral integration, decentralization and civil society involvement; and vibrant, well-organized gay and women's rights movements that have played a critical role in pushing for the broadest possible access to services and treatment without discrimination (Galvão 2001; Paiva 2000, 2002; Terto 2000; and Chapter 5, below).

Yet all of these political ingredients are to a large degree present in South Africa as well. South Africa has also undergone a profound political transformation and democratization process with the historic defeat of apartheid and election of a non-racist ANC government in 1994. Its urban-based civil society organizations – including those for women's health and HIV/AIDS – are likewise dynamic, skilled and well mobilized. And its new constitution is one of the most liberal in the world, one of only a few national constitutions that explicitly outlaw discrimination based on sexual orientation. In order to understand the differences between the two country contexts and their consequences for public policy, we have to consider differences in *sexual cultures*; for the HIV/AIDS pandemic is always and inescapably as much about sexuality as it is about health and social condition.

When I speak of sexual cultures here I am not referring to the enormous variety of sexual practices and sub-cultures that exist in many if not all societies.[31] Rather, I am concerned with the hegemonic cultural discourses of sexuality that capture policy makers and inform or constrain their public speech and action, especially regarding HIV/AIDS. Numerous studies suggest that Brazilian society is more open about sexuality than many, therefore lessening the stigma and denial surrounding AIDS and easing cultural receptivity to such projects as condom distribution, sexual education of youth, and discussion of diverse sexual practices (Parker 1991; Parker and Barbosa 1996; Paiva 2000, 2002; Rosenberg 2001; Diniz et al. 1998). But this openness is apparently selective and complex. As embracing as the hegemonic, 'Brazilianized' sexual culture may be of a strong STD/HIV/AIDS programme, it is equally hostile to the legalization of abortion – a struggle in which Brazilian feminists remain engaged to this day. Nor is it exempt from the sexual and gender subordination of women and a high degree of male sexual violence, especially against wives and partners.[32] And, as Veriano Terto Jr (2000) reminds us, Brazilian society is certainly no stranger to homophobia. So what makes the difference?

Through his ethnographic studies of sexualities in Brazil, Richard Parker offers us rich insight into the specificities of its cultural landscape. Parker's unravelling of the myth of a separate and freer, more passionate, less sin-tainted sexual world 'beneath the equator' reminds us that such mappings of sexual 'worlds' are not merely the fantasies of Western travellers but also become the prevailing images and stories that societies re-enact about themselves. For Brazilians, *carnaval* – with all its erotic and extravagant pageantry and its bacchanalian revelry – becomes a kind of utopia embodying 'the sensual nature of Brazilian life ... the chaotic mixture of races and cultures that has given rise to a new world in the tropics'. In its re-enactment for a brief time every year, *carnaval* offers 'a metaphor for Brazil itself – or, at the very least, for those qualities that are taken as most essentially Brazilian', including affirmation of the body and the erotic (Parker 1999: 363, 375–6). Within this cultural–sexual panorama, the widespread practice and acceptance of men having sex with men is alive and well. This traditional homoerotic model, though typically structured by rigid gender roles, cuts across all classes and sectors. Above all, the celebration of desire and eroticism as an essential part of the national ethos means that a public health programme affirming sexual differences and rights becomes not only possible but in some sense 'natural' (Parker 2000; Paiva 2002).[33]

At the level of social institutions, the onset of the epidemic in the early 1980s in Brazil coincided, in a critical historical conjuncture, with the end of dictatorship and the flurry of civil society and democratization movements: 'The emerging Homosexual Movement (*Movimento Homossexual*) grew parallel to, and attempted to form alliances with, other minority organizations and movements of the period (the women's, Afro-Brazilian and ecology movements, among others) that shared a concern with democracy, acceptance, and social justice.' Thus the epidemic itself was transformative in helping to galvanize segments of a pre-existing homoerotic culture into gay rights organizations and a self-defined gay community (Terto 2000: 62). AIDS NGOs such as ABIA (Brazilian Interdisciplinary AIDS Association), which has targeted men having sex with men, became focal points for homosexual Brazilian men. Such groups, with their strong civil and human rights perspective, 'opened a new field of activism, mobilized decisive community responses to the epidemic, and gave new dimensions to the visibility of homosexuality' (Terto 2000: 67–8; Parker 2000).

Brazil's successful HIV/AIDS programme is thus the product of a unique enabling environment formed out of the intersection between a prevailing sexual culture celebrating freedom and pleasure (including homoeroticism) and a strong political culture of active civil society mobilization empowering many social movements simultaneously. The gay movement has played a crucial part in advocating for services and prevention since the beginning of the epidemic, when it was predominantly a homosexually transmitted disease. As the male:female ratio in seroprevalence rates shifted rapidly in the late 1980s and 1990s, with women in poverty and heterosexual transmission accounting for the majority of all new cases,[34] the feminist, lesbian and popular health movements also became involved in activism around the disease. Quoting a former head of the national AIDS programme, Rosenberg notes the effect of AIDS activism on health care advocacy more broadly: 'There are now 600 non-governmental groups that work on AIDS. They demonstrated in the street for a higher budget for all diseases, not just for AIDS, and these protests were covered in the press' (2001: 29).

What also makes the Brazilian context unique, however, is the responsiveness of government officials, particularly in the national, state and municipal health departments, to popular and NGO demands. This is not an accident, since many of these officials, especially at middle-bureaucratic and municipal levels, have come out of the gay, lesbian and feminist movements.[35] The 1999 official MoH report to the Twelfth World AIDS Conference is entitled, significantly, *AIDS in Brazil: a Joint Government and Society Endeavour*. The report recognizes that current government policies concerning HIV/AIDS would not exist without the 'initiative from civil society' and social movements, particularly of people with AIDS. And it repeatedly and expressly links those policies to human rights: 'The most important fact in this period [early 1990s] was that the people living with AIDS started to get organized for their legal and human rights, questioning the epidemic not only as a technical challenge in the health arena but also as a political issue involving the whole of Brazilian society' (Brazil MoH 1999: 28–9).

In contrast to the economistic discourse of many UN and government advocates for access of the poor to life-prolonging medicines, official Brazilian policy firmly situates this issue in a human rights framework (see discussion of health sector reforms in Chapter 4, below). *AIDS in Brazil* proudly describes Brazil's law instituting universal access to AIDS drugs as 'one of the principal achievements in human rights in the recent history of the epidemic' (Brazil MoH 1999: 43). This strong human rights perspective, and the pivotal role in Brazilian politics of the social movements and sexual cultures that reinforce it, are key to understanding Brazil's outspoken stand on behalf of people's right to treatment and against the sanctity of patent monopolies.

Among all Southern countries, Brazil has been the most defiant in response to pressures from the US government and the multinational pharmaceutical lobby to uphold patents and accede to a narrow interpretation of TRIPs. During 2001 the temperature of the dispute rose considerably, as the MoH engaged in a series of threats and parries with two pharmaceutical giants, Merck and Hoffmann–La Roche, over the prices and availability of their ARV drugs. Under its own patent law, Brazil can manufacture generic forms of most of the drugs it needs to treat AIDS, including nevirapine and several of the protease inhibitors, because these either are not patented in Brazil or were commercialized before the law went into effect.[36] With regard to drugs patented since 1996, the law requires the patent-owning companies either to manufacture the drug in Brazil (to avoid expensive foreign exchange and importing costs) or to issue a licence to a local company to do so within three years of securing the patent. In March of 2001 – just as the South African case was coming to trial – Brazil's health minister, José Serra, threatened to produce cheaper copies of two patented drugs produced by Merck and one by Hoffmann–La Roche in order to meet the country's AIDS crisis. In other words, he threatened to utilize the compulsory licensing exception of TRIPs. The USTR immediately filed a formal complaint against Brazil with the WTO, following expressions of 'serious concern' by the US Commerce Department Secretary and imposition of heavy tariff duties on Brazilian exports to the US during the previous year (Bermudez *et al.* 2002).[37]

In his statement resisting pressures from the USTR and protesting its WTO action, Serra accused the US of hypocrisy, citing US protectionist policies that 'obstruct Latin American exports from entering its markets'. 'It is of course well known,' he remarked, 'that the USTR specializes in the defence of the interests of the American economy and not in global free trade.' And he warned, 'There is no way that the Brazilian government will retreat on this issue' (DAWN 2001a: 8). Two months later Dr Paulo Roberto Teixeira, head of Brazil's STD/AIDS programme, took a similarly tough stand against US policies at a press conference in New York. All efforts to combat the AIDS crisis would 'be lost', he suggested, 'if at the global level or in talking about international relations, the USTR [is allowed to dictate] what is good and what is not good for AIDS prevention and control' (Crossette 2001a). Signifying the importance of health in Brazil's national agenda, President Fernando Henrique Cardoso used the occasion of a visit to Washington in March 2001 to back up his health minister and Brazilian civil society in their commitment to access for all to life-saving medicines:

> Brazil has raised this banner because it is a cause that has to do with the very survival of some countries, especially the poor ones in Africa.... This is a political and moral issue, a truly dramatic situation that has to be viewed realistically and *can't be solved just by the market.* (Quoted in Petersen and Rohter 2001, italics added)

In June, on the eve of the UN Special Session (UNGASS) on HIV/AIDS, the US dropped its WTO complaint against Brazil.

One way to look at this story is to see compulsory licensing, and Brazil's deployment of it, simply as an effective 'negotiating tool to pressure companies to reduce the high price of imported medicines' (Oxfam 2001: 17). Both companies, first Merck and several months later Hoffmann-La Roche, ultimately agreed to lower their prices substantially, and in both instances the Brazilian government accepted the offer and backed down from its threats.[38] Yet the discourse through which this tense negotiation took place makes it clear that the real stakes are not so much the level of prices, or even equity in pricing, but *who shall have the power to establish prices of a life-saving good and on what ethical grounds.* The stakes are also whether Southern countries will be able to own the processes of research and development that directly affect their people's lives. For in the long run, as even a *New York Times* editorial admitted, importing cheap generic versions of essential medicines or, better still, getting the necessary technology transfers so they can manufacture their own is 'a more sustainable solution' for countries in Africa, Asia and Latin America than depending on corporate or donor largesse or shrewd negotiating tactics (*NY Times* 2000: 20; 't Hoen and Moon 2002). But this puts the right to treatment on a collision course with corporate global capitalism, and at this point in time it appears that no governments in the South, including Brazil, are willing to face such a collision.

In August of 2001, many anticipated that Brazil would be the first actually to issue a compulsory licence on AIDS drugs and thus test the limits of TRIPs with regard to life-prolonging medicines. But in the end that did not happen; instead the Brazilian government entered an informal agreement with the US to notify officials in the USTR beforehand whenever it contemplated challenging a patent. 'In other words,' as Sonia Corrêa remarks, 'we remain somehow hostage of the US' (personal communication). Other Brazilian activists have made similar comments, indicating that the country's laws and policies regarding patents fall short of the ideal 'model' some would wish. It should be remembered that only in the area of drugs for AIDS has Brazil developed a semi-autonomous, state-sponsored pharmaceutical industry. With regard to many other drugs, it remains reliant on patented imports from multinationals, with which its own very small private manufacturing sector can hardly compete. Thus the multinationals benefit the most from the patent protections that Brazil's 1996 law introduced, maintaining the monopolies and high prices that abound everywhere (Bermudez *et al.* 2002).[39]

Transnational AIDS and health NGOs were initially elated at Brazil's apparent defiance of the US over patents, seeing it 'as a moratorium on TRIPs in areas related to public health' and a model for Third World countries (DAWN 2001a: 6). Their disappointment at the retreat on compulsory licensing was compounded when the MoH issued a statement in January of 2002 clarifying that it 'definitely had no policy of exporting generic AIDS drugs' to other countries. NGOs were alarmed at this announcement, complaining that Brazil, with its unique capacity and political example in the global South, was now 'turning its back on its Latin American neighbours' and Africa.[40] The government's position, however, seems to be that its first responsibility is to provide AIDS drugs free to the hundreds of thousands of Brazilians who need them; and that its solidarity with Latin America and Africa should take the form, not of commercial exports, but of cooperative agreements for technology transfers (technical support and training in all aspects of production) to countries with potential capacity (such as Chile, South Africa, Cuba, China, Uganda, and Morocco); as well as donations or exchanges of government-produced generic drugs to countries in need (Brazil MoH 2002; Eloan Pinheiro and Maria Fernanda Macedo, interviews). Behind this policy, however, lurks the global politics of trade: the Brazilian government's fear of being perceived as using the TRIPs exemptions to compete in the global drug market, at least before such activity receives the imprimatur of the WTO (see discussion of Doha below) (S. Corrêa, personal communication).

Despite these complexities, I would still argue that the terms in which the conflict over drugs and patents evolved between Brazil and the US government/Big PhRMA suggest a significant and irrevocable shift in power. By June 2001 the US no longer felt it had sufficient support in the court of world opinion to sustain an action in the WTO based on TRIPs – although the WTO and TRIPs were supposedly created to protect its interests. By August the world's leading pharmaceutical companies had shown their inability to control prices for their AIDS drugs, even in a middle-income country like Brazil. And by December of that year, Brazil had initiated an offensive against corporate biopiracy of medicinal plants in the Amazon. In the latter action, the Brazilian government joined with indigenous groups to build towards a domestic biotechnology industry that will protect biodiversity and the intellectual property of Brazil's indigenous peoples. Seeking royalties for their traditional knowledge and a system of equitable sharing, representatives of Amazon tribal groups assert: 'We want to be part of the whole process, from research to the economic results' (Rohter 2001). With this statement, indigenous Brazilians challenge the underlying imperialist presumption that inspired TRIPs: that countries of the North have all the 'knowers' and 'innovators' while countries of the South remain forever the suppliers of raw goods and markets.[41]

Whatever Brazil's achievements in building an effective and sustainable STDs/AIDS treatment and prevention programme, Paiva insists that it is a mistake to hold Brazil up as a 'best practices' model to be imitated by others. To do so, she implies, is fatally to ignore differences in context-specific conditions and cultures: 'We may *inspire* other context-based initiatives, we may share common values and an idea of human rights', but there is no one-size-fits-all solution to the plague (Paiva 2002: 2, 16).

Dr Eloan Pinheiro, director of Far-Manguinhos until early 2003, argues on the contrary that Brazil can and must be a model for developing countries in this arena of pharmaceutical R & D, as well as in developing creative mechanisms for South–South technology sharing. Above all, she insists there should be no patent barriers, no exclusivity, but rather a principle of universal access to all essential medicines everywhere (personal interview, January 2003).

Yet, short of abolishing patent regimes altogether, many potential strategies exist whereby governments can implement the principle that even the poorest people have a human right to life-saving and life-prolonging medicines, and even the poorest countries a duty to provide 'the highest available standard' of public health. These include not only compulsory licensing and parallel importation but also North–South and South–South technology transfers to improve production capacity, rational drug use and use of generics, creating government-controlled funds for investment in R & D in which private donors would have a share, and 'patent pools' or public licensing systems that would require patent holders to freely share scientific and technological information and not horde these as 'business secrets' (Bermudez *et al.* 2002: 217; Love 2002b). All are mechanisms that respect the concept of intellectual property rights yet see such rights not only as subordinate to the right to health but also as entailing definite obligations of sharing and public access. So where does such an expansive approach to IPRs and patents leave the meanings of TRIPs?

Doha. The success of Brazil and South Africa in challenging US and corporate rigidities on patents, along with persistent encouragement from transnational health and human rights NGOs, gave a green light to developing country coalitions to move aggressively on the matter of access to essential medicines. In June of 2001, the WTO's TRIPs Council convened a special meeting on TRIPs and Public Health to address mounting concerns over the conflict between patent monopolies and health rights. There, a group of 47 developing countries submitted a joint paper asking that the upcoming WTO Ministerial Conference, to be held in Doha, Qatar, in November, 'take steps to ensure that "the TRIPs Agreement does not in any way undermine the legitimate right of WTO Members to formulate their own public health policies and implement them by adopting measures to protect public health"' (DAWN 2001a: 20). The same language was used in the 'Kochi Declaration' on 'Facilitating Access to Essential Health Commodities through South-to-South Collaboration', issued a week before the Council meeting by 16 African, Asian and Latin American countries who make up Partners in Population and Development.[42] The Kochi Declaration urged 'the importance of appropriate Southern representation in the governance of global health funds and initiatives'; and an interpretation or amendment of TRIPs consistent with '[increasing] self-reliance among developing countries on an equitable basis, with respect to availability, production, affordability, accessibility, use of essential health commodities, research and development', all of which it categorized as 'intrinsic components of [the] human right to health' (Partners in Population and Development 2001: 176–7).

The WTO's conference in Qatar – an inaccessible and tightly secure Middle Eastern potentate chosen expressly to avoid the massive demonstrations that shut down the 1999 conference in Seattle – was mostly a great disappointment, from the standpoint of advancing trade equity, gender justice or democratic processes within the WTO. It occurred in the shadow of 11 September and the US 'war on terrorism', and there was little room for dissent or creative debate (Williams and Francisco/DAWN 2002; Williams 2001a). Yet, pushed by a large bloc of Southern countries, the conference did adopt a Declaration on the TRIPs Agreement and Public Health that has helped to reinforce and clarify TRIPs's safeguard provisions (for full text, see *http://www.wto.org*). Though not a binding treaty under international law, the Declaration nonetheless has considerable political importance and could carry weight in any future controversy over access to essential medicines. Its crucial Paragraph 4 adopts the language of the Kochi Declaration:

> We agree that the TRIPs Agreement does not and should not prevent Members from taking measures to protect public health. Accordingly … we affirm that the Agreement can and should be interpreted and implemented in a manner supportive of WTO Members' right to protect public health and, in particular, to promote access to medicines for all. In this connection, we reaffirm the right of WTO Members to use, to the full, the provisions in the TRIPs Agreement, which provide flexibility for this purpose.

These flexibilities are defined more precisely than in Article 31 of TRIPs and include:

> 5(b) Each Member has the right to grant compulsory licences and the freedom to determine the grounds upon which such licences are granted.

> 5(c) Each Member has the right to determine what constitutes a national emergency or other circumstances of extreme urgency, it being understood that public health crises, including those relating to HIV/AIDS, tuberculosis, malaria and other epidemics, can represent a national emergency or other circumstances of extreme urgency.

In addition, for the least developed countries the Declaration extends the transitional period after which the patents section of TRIPs must come into effect for 10 more years, until 2016.

Assessments of the Doha Declaration were divided, including among transnational health and development NGOs. Members of MSF praised it as 'an unambiguous road map to all the key flexibilities the TRIPs offers', while Third World Network and International Gender and Trade Network leaders disparaged it as 'inadequate' for failing to amend TRIPs itself or to address issues concerning the patenting of life forms (Williams 2001a; Bello and Mittal 2001). Other commentators pointed out that, while the Declaration affirms TRIPs's compulsory licensing provision, compulsory licensing is only useful for the middle-income countries that 'have factories capable of producing these medicines'. And with regard to parallel imports of cheaper generic versions, 'even the rock-bottom prices charged by generic manufacturers ... are still far out of reach for most people in African nations ravaged by AIDS' (Dugger 2001).

Nonetheless, seen within the context of the entire global campaign around access to essential medicines, the Doha Declaration has to be understood as a step towards recognition of such access as part of the human right to health. As two MSF activists have written:

> For the first time since its creation, the WTO recognizes a hierarchy of values, the primacy of public health over free trade, and more specifically that medicines are not like any other commercial product. ('t Hoen and Chirac 2002, at *www.msf.org*)

Surprisingly, the USTR supported the Doha Declaration on TRIPs. One reason was that even the wealthy, powerful US had just come face to face with its own potential health 'emergency' during the anthrax scare the previous month, prompting the Bush administration to consider issuing a compulsory licence for generic forms of the drug Cipro, an antidote to anthrax under patent to Bayer. The whole world was aware of this irony (Dugger 2001; 't Hoen and Chirac 2002).[43] Another reason was that, in the context of needing international support for its 'war on terrorism' and having other controversial priorities in Doha – for example, guarding protective tariffs for US textiles, steel and agriculture – the Bush administration decided to sacrifice the interests of the pharmaceutical industry. The multinational drug companies must have seen this retreat on the sanctity of patents as a blow to their command over the large potential markets in AIDS drugs in countries like Brazil, India and China and a boon to generic competitors. But the moment of multilateral cooperation was short-lived.

With Doha, it thus seemed that Southern countries had achieved the subversion of corporate interpretations of intellectual property rules and their replacement with a more expansive interpretation, one that puts national sovereignty over public health and health as a human right above the inviolability of patents. By the late spring of 2002, only one country in the world – Zimbabwe, where adult HIV infection rates are around 25 per cent – had actually utilized Article 31 of TRIPs and the Doha Declaration to declare a 'national emergency' and import generic substitutes for AIDS drugs patented in that country. Moreover, at the WTO TRIPs Council meeting and subsequently in late 2002–early 2003, the US and other Northern countries embarked on a systematic campaign to sabotage any consensus on implementation of the Doha Declaration, insisting on numerous crippling limitations (*www.accessmed-msf.org*; Oxfam 2002; Russell 2002). Without a liberal implementation of the declaration, when TRIPs comes into force in all countries in 2005 it will be impossible to use compulsory licensing or to export generic versions of patented drugs. This will severely limit affordable supplies for countries unable to manufacture their own – that is, the countries that need the TRIPs safeguards most desperately. MSF has proposed an amendment to TRIPs that would allow such exports and has questioned the fairness of requiring developing countries to declare a 'national emergency' in order to utilize TRIPs safeguards when wealthy countries do not have to do so (*www.accessmed-msf.org*). But all this may be beside the point. As it escalated its unilateralist mission in military and security policy in 2002, so the US has pursued a staunchly unilateralist position with regard to international health. Increasingly relying on bilateral and regional trade agreements outside the WTO (particularly the 'Free Trade Agreement of the Americas', or FTAA), its aim is clearly to pressure its trading partners, bypass TRIPs, annihilate the Doha Declaration, and even lengthen the duration of patents (Oxfam 2002).

And so the struggle continues – through a process of negotiation that reveals the relations between global trade and access to health care to be a political terrain whose meanings change with shifts in the balance of forces. Currently the global dynamics of AIDS have made TRIPs a tenuous but potentially enabling field for the right to drug treatment in health crises. But in a world of US corporate and military domination, that field is rapidly shrinking. And beyond TRIPs looms GATS – the General Agreement on Trade in Services, also adopted in 1994 as part of the Uruguay Round but still under negotiation as to specifics. Feminist health care advocates warn that GATS is likely to usher in further privatization, corporate globalization, higher costs and diminished access for the poor in the area of vital health services (Williams 2001b; WGNRR 2002). If so, then a new and more difficult struggle will complicate the already busy agenda of transnational health activists. Perhaps one day it will become possible to remove essential medicines and health services from the domain of trade and patent regimes altogether and secure them as part of the global 'commons'. But that day seems a long way off.

'Equity pricing' or the human right to health?

The struggle over access to essential medicines is a case study in the fluidity and porousness of corporate global power structures, as well as their tenacity. I want to understand how and why this issue allowed transnational NGOs to advance the principle of health rights over property rights and thus make some dents in corporate power, and how and why a *human rights* perspective on health still meets formidable obstacles in a market-driven world. As Brazilian health policy recognizes, markets cannot solve the problem of AIDS. The question is, can they solve any health problems anywhere for anyone but the affluent and advantaged?

From the perspective of the giant pharmaceuticals, one of the most damaging aspects of the global campaign around medicines and its symbiosis with the global crisis of AIDS has been the public disclosure of alarming disparities in drug prices. Studies by MSF and UNAIDS in 2000 revealed that Pfizer was selling Diflucan for (US)$18 per pill in Kenya – a country 'that averages $5 per citizen per year' in its national health budget – whereas the generic version of fluconazole produced in Thailand cost 60 cents. Pfizer's wholesale prices for the same drug ranged from $8.52 in Kenya to $9.78 in the US, $11 in France, and $27 in Guatemala – all for a gross yield of around $1 billion a year for the company. The pattern of higher prices in some developing countries than in Europe and North America is not unusual; nevirapine was found in these studies to cost $430 per 100 units in Norway compared with $874 in Kenya (McNeil 2000a, 2000b). Alongside these prices – adding up to many thousands of dollars per year per patient for ARV 'cocktails' – the cost of generic versions is miniscule. Cipla can sell the active ingredient in combivir, an antiretroviral that GlaxoSmithKline sells wholesale for over $7,000, for under $240 and the finished generic version for just $275. Brazil can make its generic zidovudine combination drug for $1.44 a dose, compared with $18.78 for the brand-name version in the US (Petersen 2001; McNeil 2000a).

Why should there be such enormous and seemingly illogical disparities? Because drug prices are determined not by costs of production but by managerial estimates of market characteristics; or, as the pharmacist who oversaw the MSF study put it, by the logic of profit maximization. Applying this logic ruthlessly throughout the 1990s, the pharmaceutical industry in the US maintained profit rates three times higher than those of any other corporate sector (McNeil 2000a; Thom 2001). But differentials in prices and markets and how they are arrived at are part of 'business secrets', to be guarded closely and defended along with other corporate privacy rights. When, following Brazil's initiative, UNICEF, WHO, UNAIDS and MSF began to publish comparative price and source lists for safe AIDS drugs, including many from generic manufacturers, they effectively pierced the corporate veil covering pricing mysteries (McNeil 2002; CMH/WHO 2001; UNICEF/UNAIDS/WHO/MSF 2000).[44] The EU governments, who have long regulated drug prices in their countries, supported this move against the vociferous opposition of the US and the drug lobby. But the cat was out of the bag; like discrimination in wages, once disclosed, price discrimination in HIV/AIDS drugs was revealed to the world in all its stark reality, as a manifestation of global apartheid in the dispensation of life and death.

In this context, the giant pharmaceuticals adopted a new defensive manoeuvre that some of their more pragmatic critics defend as the best approach to AIDS treatment: 'preferential pricing lists' for Africa, or 'humanitarian' differential pricing. As Rosenberg puts it, 'The price cuts the drug companies fought until last year have now become their solution to the world's AIDS crisis' (2001: 58). In this strategy, discounts of 80–90 per cent on drugs for the poorest countries would show that 'we're doing our part' and thus address the industry's PR problem, while still yielding ample corporate profits. For the sale of drugs to poor countries at *any* price above cost is still profitable, since the alternative is no sale or ceding the market to the generic companies (Stolberg 2001).[45] What Big PhRMA is clearly counting on to offset generic competitors, whose prices are still one-half to one-third of corporate discounted prices, is the lure of brand names – the anchor of corporate globalization. The assumption is, who would buy a product made by Aurobindo when they can get the original made by Merck? (Like, who would buy Nike knock-offs when they can get the real thing for a little bit more?) Behind this assumption, of course, is the imperialist imaginary's first premise: that technological 'know-how' resides in the West; generics produced in the Third World can only be flawed, 'impure' imitations.[46]

But the deepest fear of the giant pharmaceuticals is not about African or Third World markets, which generate a tiny fraction of their total profits, but about the potential effects of lower prices on their markets in rich nations:

'They worry that publicity about generic prices will fuel the American demand for cheap imports or price controls' (Rosenberg 2001: 58). As the US health care system spun more deeply into fiscal crisis in 2002, spurred mainly by escalating drug and hospital costs as well as the diversion of funds to the 'war on terrorism', the chickens started coming home to roost.[47] Why should only people living in poverty in sub-Saharan Africa benefit from fairer prices on drugs, many were starting to ask. What about the millions of elderly for whom Medicare does not cover prescription drugs, to say nothing of the 42 million adults and children in the US who have lost or cannot afford health insurance? By the summer of 2002, access to medicines was looming as a major issue in the upcoming congressional elections. Members of Congress were submitting bills that would prohibit drug companies from securing automatic delays in the expiration of their patents and allow imports of cheaper drugs from Canada, thus expanding access to generic drugs in the US (Pear 2002b).[48] What if equity pricing were 'a truly global system' applied in all countries, not just the poorest ('t Hoen and Moon 2002: 222)?

The WHO Commission on Macroeconomics and Health (CMH) considers 'differential pricing in low-income markets' (which it equates with 'equity pricing') 'the best solution' to the crisis of HIV/AIDS and other epidemic diseases in Africa.[49] This approach gives drug companies a mantle of legitimacy through the veneer of 'public–private partnerships'. For example, in the Accelerated Access Initiative of May 2000, five UN agencies (WHO, UNAIDS, World Bank, UNICEF and UNFPA) backed a consortium of five major drug companies in announcing 80 per cent price reductions for their AIDS drugs in Africa. The understanding here is that many low-income countries in sub-Saharan Africa and elsewhere cannot afford these drugs even at generic prices, thus 'any large-scale access to the medicines by those that need them will require large-scale donor financing'. Corporate price differentials will make such financing – by a combination of private foundations, wealthy governments and multilateral institutions – economically feasible, 'while allowing the patent system to continue to play its role of providing incentives for research and development' (CMH/WHO 2001: 88, 125–6; Sachs 2001). WHO officials laud the value of bringing the private sector (that is, Big PhRMA) 'to the table' with international organizations and are uncritical of the way in which 'differential pricing' and 'public–private partnership' arrangements work to preserve the system of patents, pre-empt compulsory licensing, construct price reductions as a voluntary or 'charitable' response, and thus protect the entire system of markets and capitalist profits.[50]

In response to WHO's and CMH's conciliatory approach to the industry, members of MSF distinguish the concept of 'equity pricing' – 'the principle that the poor should pay less for and have access to essential medicines' – from 'commercial terms' like 'differential' or 'tiered' pricing, a marketing strategy whose central aim is profits. This strategy is 'dangerous' and 'extremely vulnerable ... on its own', since it relies mainly 'on the will of companies'. It needs to be supported by a range of other strategies, including the incorporation into national laws of TRIPs safeguards for compulsory licensing and parallel importation; bulk procurement, making it easier for international organizations and NGOs to negotiate prices and providing 'patent exceptions for globally procured medicines'; technology transfer; and generic competition ('t Hoen and Moon 2002: 219–20). We need to go deeper, however, to understand the inherent weaknesses of approaches to treatment access that rely principally on humanitarianism and bargaining with the private sector.

Humanitarian gestures by drug companies and donor agencies to create 'equitable' responses to health crises are inadequate because they fail to address the systemic roots of those crises or to require reliable mechanisms of enforcement and accountability, much less democratic participation in defining solutions by the people most affected (like pregnant women and all people with AIDS). They continue to treat health as a commodity and to assume that markets – albeit 'tiered' and adjusted for the poorest – are sufficient to meet basic health needs.[51] Focusing on AIDS or other epidemic diseases and defining these as 'national emergencies' or 'security risks' creates an aura of exceptionalism that ultimately serves to normalize the arbitrary pricing of medical goods and services and their unequal distribution in nearly all other areas of preventive and curative health, including reproductive and sexual health. Such exceptionalist approaches – including that of the 'global burden of disease' that I shall review in Chapter 4 – thus effectively reinforce the preservation of the vast majority of health-related interventions as the domain of 'private rights' (those of corporate owners of property) whose only normative underpinning remains profit maximization. Aggressive global campaigns to raise funds and awareness in the fight against HIV/AIDS and other diseases that are decimating poor populations in sub-Saharan Africa may certainly succeed in saving lives. Cooperation among private donor organizations, UN agencies and commercial suppliers have succeeded in the recent past in negotiating bulk procurement and delivery of such medical commodities as vaccines and contraceptives to millions of poor people throughout the world in an efficient, 'targeted' fashion. But these *ad hoc* and voluntarist strategies for solving health crises contain serious limitations that undermine both their ability to address gender and racial injustice and their long-term viability. Let me mention just two.

First, humanitarianism and 'public–private partnerships' inherently rely on good will, kindness, or, more likely, appeals to self-interest and public image. They involve no long-term, sustainable *mechanisms of accountability and enforcement*, another way of saying they are not institutionalized in any kind of formal democratic process. Consequently, they must perpetually depend on the kinds of *ad hoc* campaigns and pressure tactics that brought the issue of access to essential medicines for HIV/AIDS into the global spotlight in the first place ('t Hoen and Moon 2002). When international organizations like WHO and UNAIDS or NGOs like MSF undertake to negotiate 'equity pricing' or bulk purchasing on behalf of low-income countries, they still must do this on an *ad hoc*, drug-by-drug basis. The bargaining process itself remains a market transaction based on the assumption of corporate prerogatives rather than a legal decision based on corporate responsibility to uphold human rights. At the national level, the result of 'differential pricing' is that 'each price cut for each drug in each country is negotiated separately', or that countries must defend their right to seek cheaper alternatives in lengthy litigations in the national courts. Meanwhile, months and years go by and millions more die needlessly (Rosenberg 2001: 58; Terto, Jr 2002).[52]

In the area of research for new drugs, dozens of 'public–private partnership' arrangements have been created during the past several years, for example, to develop an AIDS vaccine and non-resistant drugs for malaria and TB. Like bulk procurement and negotiations for equitable prices, these arrangements may result in effective treatments or vaccines in the short term, and are certainly more likely to do so than relying on the market alone. But multinational corporate participants in such 'partnerships', while the first to impugn the public sector's competence and efficiency in drug research, are the last to admit the ways they and their shareholders become primary beneficiaries of 'public–private partnerships', even acquiring large donor funds that might have gone to government research institutions.[53] It remains to be determined whether the ultimate products of public–private joint research ventures (such as an AIDS vaccine) will be patented and, if so, who will own the patent. Will governments or, more appropriately, some international agency (WHO?) or a non-profit NGO like MSF have the authority and the political will to assert control over intellectual property rights – in the public interest – for such publicly subsidized and vital medicines? James Orbinski, who chairs MSF's Drugs for Neglected Diseases Initiative (DNDi), suggests that the concept of 'public–private partnership' evades these issues of owner-ship and accountability, for it blurs the lines of responsibility between the public, private and non-profit/NGO sectors and replaces duty with charity. A more ethically acceptable alternative framework would be one that regards all the parties in such an arrangement as 'public institutional actors' and holds them publicly accountable (Orbinski 2002).[54] Yes, but accountable to whom?

With regard to global health crises, rights and initiatives, the void in democratic governance is the most serious neglected disease. By using a combination of behind-the-scenes pressures, litigation and militant public action, well-organized NGOs were able to win many tactical victories against the US government and drug cartels in 2000–1 and to trigger an important shift in the terms of debate and the power dynamics concerning global trade and health priorities. But these efforts have still not culminated in a permanent mechanism that goes beyond negotiated price reductions or charitable donations, whether by the private sector or governments. In other words, transnational health and human rights movements have still not achieved an institutionalized process at the global level – a kind of international civil court comparable to the International Criminal Court – that could enforce the principle of health as a human right superior to corporate property rights over life-saving medicines (or services). Tina Rosenberg says that what is necessary in order to make essential drugs available to all who need them is 'an alteration of the basic social contract the pharmaceutical companies have enjoyed until now' (2001: 28). But surely this implies a whole new normative and governance system that would enforce corporate obligations and subordinate unlimited profits to health rights and social development – a different social contract altogether.

We have seen how effective voluntarism is in the case of the UN's Global Fund to Fight AIDS, Malaria and TB. Almost a year from the time Kofi Annan announced the fund and said it would require at minimum $7–10 billion a year, countries had pledged less than $2 billion and the US under the Bush administration a paltry $500 million over the next three years (Stolberg 2002). Yet, in the aftermath of the 11 September attacks, a crisis affecting Americans, Congress was able to come up with an immediate $40 billion for 'anti-terrorism' activities and a 20-year contract with Lockheed to produce military aircraft for $200 billion – enough to erase contagious diseases from the face of the earth. Sonia Ehrlich Sachs and Jeffrey Sachs (2002), reporting from the dying fields of a Malawi village, begin to question the utility of 'good faith' pledges:

Why aren't US leaders visiting the hospitals, villages, and health ministries in Africa to ensure that the United States is doing all it can do to stop the deaths?... We are spending tens of billions of dollars to fight a war on terrorism that tragically claimed a few thousand American lives. Yet we are spending perhaps one-thousandth of that in a war against AIDS that kills more than 5,000 Africans each day.... [A] tiny share of rich-country income – one penny of every $10 of GNP – would translate into 8 million lives saved each year in the poor countries.

Waiting for the US to 'do all it can do' recalls the second major defect of the voluntary 'equity pricing' approach: like many forms of foreign aid, it lacks long-term sustainability and is inconsistent with the right to development. After the PMA dropped its lawsuit against South Africa, the South African government stated that 'its primary interest is not in copying patented drugs but in importing generics from other countries or manufacturing them' (McGreal 2001). Yet the entire structure of TRIPs, compulsory licensing, and the tango between Southern governments and Northern-based drug companies over prices rests on an assumption I have continually questioned: that countries in the South lack the capacity to develop viable drug manufacturing and research facilities of their own, or at least to rely more on South–South and intra-regional cooperation rather than waiting either for the largesse of donors (especially the US) or the concessions of multinational companies.

In fact, a growing number of capacity-building and technology-sharing initiatives in Africa, Asia and Latin America belie this racist and imperialist assumption, as well as the assumption that the public sector is inefficient as both a producer and a researcher. Brazil of course stands out as an example of government efficiency in researching, developing, producing and distributing AIDS drugs. But Brazil is also leading initiatives in intra-regional solidarity by, for example, exchanging drug 'donations' with other MERCOSUR countries like Argentina, thus perhaps beating the US at its own game of bypassing trade rules and TRIPs altogether. Brazil has also initiated South–South agreements to transfer technology, thus helping countries in Africa and Asia to develop their own production facilities (Macedo 2002; Brazil MoH 2002). Other countries have begun to develop similar South– South technology-sharing collaborations – for example, networks between Thailand and Malaysia and among Thailand, Zimbabwe and Ghana; while quite a few Southern countries have developed various levels of R & D, and in some cases manufacturing, capability in the pharmaceutical field – including India, China, South Africa and Algeria along with Malaysia, Thailand and Brazil

(Navaratnam 2002; Olliaro and Navaratnam 2002). Several Northern government research institutions have also embarked on collaborative scientific training and research partnerships with countries in the South. The Malaria Research and Training Centre in Bamako, a project of the US National Institutes of Health, and the Multilateral Initiative on Malaria, involving a number of African countries and located in Dakar, are two examples (Varmus 2002).

Sustainability is not only about infusions of donor funds and affordable drugs but even more about development of infrastructure, organization, and coordination. What stands in the way of self-sufficient generic drug capacity in many countries in the South is not any inherent lack of ability nor even patent rules, but the need for better management systems within countries and better coordination across countries, those that have developed a generic drug industry (such as India and China) as well as those that have not (Navaratnam 2002; Torreele 2002). In addition there is the need for sufficient will and imagination, especially in US and European research centres, to maximize the Internet, universalize e-access and make all scientific publications and data electronically available free of cost – in other words, to create a global community of science and information sharing (Varmus 2002; Roberts 2002). But these are conditions that depend on an ethic of openness and collaboration. They must seem alien and subversive in the intellectual and philosophical climate that dominates not only Western-style capitalism but also Western corporatist science: the conviction that knowledge and ideas are private property and greed is the sole force driving the human quest for knowledge. Yet even the 'West' is full of models that prove how fallacious is this thinking. A scientist from the Human Genome Project, based in the UK, points out that that immensely successful, complex and large-scale research enterprise is organized entirely in the public and not-for-profit domain, its findings immediately available on the WorldWideWeb. Innovation and even competition (in Nietzsche's agonistic sense) thrive in an open, non-corporate, non-profit-driven culture (Roberts 2002).

If we took seriously the right to development codified in numerous international documents as well as the principle of 'transfer and dissemination of technology' contained in Article 7 of TRIPs, what would this mean for the potential capacity of many Southern countries to provide essential, life-prolonging medicines for their own people? What would it mean for the responsibility of Northern governments and multilateral organizations to tax exorbitant profits, cut military budgets and cancel debt in order to generate development resources for the South? Or to foster an ethic of global sharing rather than private acquisition concerning intellectual property? How would it challenge Southern governments to make good on their promises to reprioritize their budgets and expand national health spending to 15 per cent, 'including a significant proportion on AIDS' ('Africans Unite...'/*NY Times* 2001)? The Jamaican economist Mariama Williams (2001a) criticizes governments of the South for 'trade-offs and deal-making' with Northern governments and for letting themselves 'be trapped into [a] pervasive market access framework that pushes [them] to sacrifice everything for very minor entry into the markets of the North'. In the end, sustainable solutions to the problems of health and disease that plague Southern countries and poor people everywhere may be ones that go outside capitalist markets altogether and return to old-fashioned concepts of the public domain, or the common good, including essential medicines and health services as a 'global public good' (see Chapter 4). But the ability to make individual or group claims based on such concepts would still require a normative framework and a set of procedures grounded in human rights. It would also require much greater attention to the intersections of gender, race and poverty than the 'access to medicines' campaign has exhibited until now.

Specifying the human right to health in the era of HIV/AIDS

'Health is the human right that in practice most visibly marks distinctions of race, [gender] ... economic and social condition' because health, or its lack, directly inscribes the body and intensifies the race, gender, class and age distinctions that already mark it. Although it may be argued that other infectious diseases as well as non-infectious diseases cause more preventable deaths in today's world, HIV/AIDS figures so prominently in the battle for health as a human right because it most starkly locates the body at the crossroads of gender, race, class, sexuality and geography (Booker and Minter 2001: 12).

It is no accident that human rights agencies grasp this reality more fully than any other global institutions and provide a perspective on solutions to the epidemic that is more encompassing of all its complex social dimensions than do either macroeconomists or public health experts. That is because the UN human rights bodies have increasingly relied on regular consultations with women's human rights and other civil society groups, for the reasons I discussed in Chapter 2, and such groups persistently have pushed these bodies to apply the principles of indivisibility and intersectionality in their interpretive statements. In 1998 a series of joint consultations organized by the UN High Commissioner for Human Rights, Mary Robinson, and UNAIDS, with significant input from civil society groups, produced a set of International Guidelines on HIV/AIDS and Human Rights. These guidelines and their holistic view of human rights aspects of the epidemic were elaborated in a roundtable statement during the UNGASS on HIV/AIDS in 2001 as follows:

> responses to HIV/AIDS should explicitly take into account such factors as gender relations, religious beliefs, homophobia and racism, which individually or in combination influence the extent to which individuals and communities are protected from discrimination, inequality and exclusion and have the ability to access services and to make and carry out free and informed decisions about their lives. (UN/CHR and UNAIDS 1998; UN/General Assembly 2001a)

In addition, the guidelines enumerate a very inclusive list of human rights that directly affect HIV/AIDs risk, vulnerability and impact – rights to education, information in a language one understands, access to health care and preventive services, to travel and freedom of movement, to 'an adequate standard of living', and against discrimination. And they point out the documented fact that 'where individuals and communities are able to realize their rights, the incidence of HIV infection declines' (UN/General Assembly 2001a: 2–3). In a subsequent *Irish Times* article on globalization and human rights, Commissioner Robinson indicated her own strong commitment to heightening public awareness and action on these linkages. Challenging the assumption that trade is 'truly free and fair' in today's global economy, she asked, 'Are intellectual property rules conducive to ensuring access to drugs under the World Health Organization essential drug list?' And she linked 'a lack of respect for human rights ... to virtually every aspect of the AIDS epidemic, from the factors that cause or increase vulnerability to HIV infection, to discrimination based on stigma attached to people living with HIV/AIDS, to the factors that limit the ability of individuals and communities to respond effectively to the epidemic'. Among these factors, she noted that:

> Lack of adequate nutrition, of basic medicines, of clean water, of elementary education, of suitable employment, of equality for women, among a multitude of other privations, increase the vulnerability of ... poor people to HIV and AIDS. The poverty deprives them in turn of the means of treatment and care which are available to the wealthy. (Robinson 2002)[55]

This comprehensive understanding of the human rights dimensions of HIV/AIDS and appropriate responses to it builds on a 25-year history in which UN bodies and committees have attempted to define the right to health, contained in both the WHO Constitution and the ICESCR, in an inclusive, holistic manner. In the late 1970s, the World Health Assembly launched its 'Health for All' strategy (supposed to be achieved by the year 2000!) with a central focus on primary health care. In 1978 the International Conference on Primary Health Care issued what is known as the Alma Ata Declaration, emphasizing 'health for all people of the world' and adopting the WHO definition of health as 'a fundamental human right' and 'a state of complete physical, mental and social well-being, and not merely the absence of infirmity'. The Alma Ata Declaration also asserted that primary health care:

> Includes at least: education concerning prevailing health problems and the methods of preventing and controlling them; promotion of food supply and proper nutrition; an adequate supply of safe water and basic sanitation; maternal and child health care, including family planning; immunization against the major infectious diseases; prevention and control of locally endemic diseases; appropriate treatment of common diseases and injuries; and provision of essential drugs.... (quoted in Koivusalo and Ollila 1997: 7, 111–13)

As Koivusalo and Ollila remark, these initiatives suffered 'right from the beginning from a lack of resources and from competing viewpoints on health policies' (1997: 114). Today, as I shall discuss in the next chapter, there is a concerted effort within WHO and the World Bank to repudiate them in favour of narrower, more 'cost-effective' approaches to health care. Yet the human rights agencies of the UN persist in asserting a bold and visionary interpretation of the right to health. In May of 2000, the Committee on Economic, Social and Cultural Rights (CESCR) – the treaty body responsible for interpreting and enforcing the ICESCR – issued a General Comment clarifying 'the right to the highest attainable standard of health' contained in Article 12 of the Covenant. This right, it said, 'is not confined to the right to health care ... [but] embraces a wide range of socio-economic factors ... [extending] to the underlying determinants of health, such as food and nutrition, housing, access to safe and potable water and adequate sanitation, safe and healthy working conditions, and a healthy environment'. And not only material conditions but also a wide range of civil and political rights, such as 'education, human dignity, life, non-discrimination, equality, the prohibition against torture, privacy, access to information, and the freedoms of association, assembly and movement' are also 'integral components of the right to health' (UN/CESCR 2000). What this means in practice is that implementation of the right to health requires multisectoral approaches like those called for in the old Alma Ata Declaration (those that global health economists today wish to shelve); and that it can only be addressed effectively through a vision of gender equality, anti-racism, and human development.

In its May 2000 Comment, the CESCR also presents a view of the right to health, like human rights generally, as historically situated and evolving over time. Since 1966, it notes, when the International Covenants were originally adopted, the meaning of health has come to embrace such 'socially related concerns' as 'resource distribution', 'gender differences' and 'violence and armed conflict'. Also in tune with changing times, a paragraph on 'prevention, treatment and control of epidemic, endemic, occupational and other diseases' now 'requires

> the establishment of prevention and education programmes for behaviour-related health concerns such as sexually transmitted diseases, in particular HIV/AIDS, and those adversely affecting sexual and reproductive health, and the promotion of social determinants of good health, such as environmental safety, education, economic development and gender equity. The right to treatment includes the creation of a system of urgent medical care in cases of accidents, epidemics and similar health hazards.... (UN/CESCR 2000: 5)

Both the CESCR and the UN Commission on Human Rights have issued statements directly relating 'the right of everyone to the enjoyment of the highest attainable standard of physical and mental health' under international law to the obligation of states to ensure the accessibility and affordability 'to all without discrimination' of 'pharmaceuticals and medical technologies' for treatment of HIV/AIDS and its 'most common opportunistic infections' (UN/CHR 2001). In a statement delivered in late 1999 to the historic Seattle WTO Conference, the CESCR made its boldest assertion to date that human rights norms supersede trade rules in international law and that the WTO itself (whose founding instrument postdates the human rights treaties) must adhere to human rights principles, including respect for the right to health:

> It is the Committee's view that WTO contributes significantly to and is part of the process of global governance reform. This reform must be driven by a concern for the individual and not purely macroeconomic

considerations alone. Human rights norms must shape the process of international economic policy formulation so that the benefits for human development of the evolving international trade regime will be shared equitably by all, in particular the most vulnerable sectors. The Committee recognizes the wealth-generating potential of trade liberalization, but it is also aware that liberalization in trade, investment and finance does not necessarily create and lead to a favourable environment for the realization of economic, social and cultural rights. Trade liberalization must be understood as a means, not an end. The end which trade liberalization should serve is the objective of human well-being to which the international human rights instruments give legal expression. (UN/CESCR 1999: 2)

In its only Special Session on HIV/AIDS, the UN General Assembly fully incorporated this human rights perspective, as well as language from the Cairo, Beijing, Cairo+5 and Beijing+5 documents, into its 'Declaration of Commitment' (UN/General Assembly 2001b). The Declaration defines HIV/AIDS as not only a 'security risk' (as the Security Council had in January 2000) but also 'a global emergency and one of the most formidable challenges to human life and dignity, as well as to the effective enjoyment of human rights' (Paragraph 2). It devotes an entire section to the topic 'HIV/AIDS and Human Rights', reaffirming the link between 'respect for human rights and fundamental freedoms' and reduction of infection rates. Moreover, 'three of the four goals that are stated in the section on Human Rights explicitly address the rights of women and girls'; and many of the document's deadlines and targets are gender-related (SHAAN Online 2002).[56]

Given 'that globally women and girls are disproportionately affected by HIV/AIDS', the 2001 Declaration urges that by 2005 countries shall have taken actions to 'promote the advancement of women and women's full enjoyment of all human rights' and 'shared responsibility of men and women to ensure safe sex'; to 'empower women to have control over and decide freely and responsibly on matters related to their sexuality'; 'to increase capacities of women and adolescent girls to protect themselves from the risk of HIV infection', among other things by providing sexual and reproductive health services; and to promote women's and girls' empowerment by eliminating all forms of discrimination and violence against them, including harmful traditional practices, 'rape and other forms of sexual violence', and sexual trafficking (Paragraphs 59–61). With regard to MTCT, the Declaration urges that by 2005 the proportion of HIV+ infants shall have been reduced by 20 per cent and by 2010 by 50 per cent, and that '80 per cent of pregnant women accessing prenatal care' should have access to effective treatment, along with full information and counselling, to reduce prenatal and perinatal transmission (Paragraph 54).

The document's section on 'Reducing Vulnerability' is particularly attentive to the many forms of long-standing cultural practices and social conditions that make women, girls and boys vulnerable to infection and urges that countries identify and address these and provide accurate sexual health education, counselling and services for adolescents as part of their prevention programmes by the year 2003 (Paragraphs 62–4). By 2005, 'at least 90 per cent and by 2010 at least 95 per cent of young men and women aged 15 to 24 [should] have access to' preventive programmes and services.[57] Paragraph 68 recognizes the 'impact of HIV/AIDS … especially on women and the elderly … in their role as caregivers and in families affected by HIV/AIDS' and gives a deadline of 2003 for governments to evaluate and address this impact. Paragraph 70 on prevention urges increased investments in research not only on development of HIV vaccines but on 'female-controlled methods and microbicides'.

The June 2001 UNGASS on HIV/AIDS was the first meeting of the General Assembly ever devoted entirely to an issue of public health and health rights, and, significantly, it was a meeting in which 'leaders of Africa' dominated (Crossette 2001b). Moreover, in sharp contrast to the World AIDS Conference just one year earlier, where gender and 'reproductive and sexual health issues [of women] were by and large not visible on the main conference agenda' (Berer 2000b), this Declaration fully recognizes 'that gender equality and women's empowerment are a prerequisite to stemming the tide of the epidemic' (SHAAN Online 2002). This is no accident but rather a testament to the cumulative impact of transnational women's health and rights organizations on the deliberations of the General Assembly and their strong participation in the HIV/AIDS UNGASS (Freitas 2001). It also puts in sharp relief the absence of explicit gender analysis in the politics, slogans, and advocacy materials of the transnational movement for access to essential medicines and the vexing fact that this movement and the transnational women's health movement have so far been running along separate but parallel paths.

With regard to access to essential medicines, the Declaration of Commitment adopts intact the human rights language of the Commission on Human Rights and the CESCR, recognizing 'access to medication in the context of pandemics such as HIV/AIDS' as 'one of the fundamental elements' in achieving the human right to health (Paragraph 15). The substantive paragraphs on this issue, however, are disappointingly vague and obfuscating, avoiding specific deadlines and targets for actually making affordable drugs available to all who need them or specific methods and resource-generating strategies for assuring that low-income countries have the capacity to do so. Throwing a bone to every side in the debate over TRIPs and patents, they incoherently patch together language calculated to offend nobody and therefore to achieve nothing in the way of concrete guidelines for implementing access to treatment in national AIDS programmes.[58] This suggests a last-ditch effort by the US delegation to support patent rights and save face at the very moment when the US was dropping its case in the WTO against Brazil.

Nonetheless, the 2001 UNGASS Declaration may be seen as an important step toward the Doha Declaration on TRIPs, in so far as the General Assembly firmly proclaimed access to life-saving medicines as part of the human right to the highest attainable standard of health. When read together, and in the light of the CESCR's strong statement about the priority of international human rights and human well-being over 'trade liberalization', these documents provide useful weapons for civil society groups to call governments, TNCs and IFIs to account for their health policies and practices. But these formal and still weak mechanisms of global governance – UN conference documents, committee statements, human rights complaints – are only one small tactic in the larger struggle for a massive readjustment of power and resources in the world.

The story of the struggle for access to HIV/AIDS medicines illuminates the ways in which human rights discourse, as deployed by transnational women's and health movements to fend off corporate globalization, has become a discourse of social and economic justice:

> To date, access to life-saving medicines and care for people living with HIV and AIDS have been largely determined by race, class, gender and geography. AIDS thus points to more fundamental global inequalities than those involving a single disease, illuminating centuries-old patterns of injustice. Indeed, today's international political economy – in which undemocratic institutions systematically generate economic inequality – should be described as 'global apartheid'. (Booker and Minter 2001: 11)

The world's resources for HIV/AIDS treatment still evade those who need them most: 'of the 25 million HIV-infected Africans and the roughly 4 million each year with advanced HIV-related disease, only around 10,000 to 30,000 Africans receive antiretroviral therapy' (CMH/WHO 2001: 51). Likewise with prevention efforts: in 2000, with 95 per cent of those infected living in the global South, '95 per cent of all the AIDS prevention money [was] being spent in the industrialized countries' (Editorial/NY *Times* 2000: 10). The pledging of a $7–10 billion annual expenditure on combating HIV/AIDS is thus a gesture of implicit reparation towards the immense imbalance in resources and power that both global apartheid and global gender injustice perpetuate.[59] But the failure to realize even this inadequate goal clearly indicates that, to those who command global power, it still represents 'an optional charitable response' rather than a fundamental human right and therefore 'an obligation' (Booker and Minter 2001: 16). None of the health advocates or neo-Keynesian economists who advocate 'equity pricing' are saying that colossal corporate greed and massive militarization are wrong in themselves and incompatible with good health for the world's people and the planet. Yet, as I was completing this writing, the US 'war on terrorism' was spending over $2 billion a month on military and surveillance activities in Central Asia; the Bush administration was asking Congress for a $27 billion 'emergency fund' to fortify 'homeland security' and to fight the war in Afghanistan (decimated by two decades of war and untold civilian deaths from continued US bombing 'errors'); and the Global Fund to Fight AIDS, TB and Malaria was a tiny blip on the radar screen of global finance (Dao 2002a; Stevenson 2002).[60]

Yet even in this highly militarism context, the campaign for treatment access had opened up a window on global health inequalities that could no longer be shut. The pursuit of global militarism will only, in the long run, make the obscenities[61] – including in the heart of the Empire, as Americans find health care increasingly out of reach – all the more glaring. And the growing injustices will raise awareness that war and global capitalism are themselves contributors to disease. The 2001 UNGASS on HIV/AIDS was steeped in controversy over whether a focus on this epidemic was justified given the huge toll in human life from other infectious diseases, from lack of safe water and from war (Flanders 2001; Houston 2001; Jackson 2001). But clearly the problem is not one of ranking what is most deadly but of scrutinizing the ways in which all these preventable conditions are 'part of an interactive system' (Parker 1999: 7). In part this goes back to the issue of sustainability and capacity-building – the need to generate resources not only to provide drugs but to improve systems of health distribution and management. But it also refers to the systemic social and economic inequalities that exacerbate poor health – the patterns of joblessness, anomie, migration, and 'survival sex' that in turn are the product of armed conflict, export-oriented economic policies, the cannibalization of local markets by multinationals, and, of course, persistent traditions of gender subordination (Epstein 2001; Preston-Whyte *et al.* 2000; Klugman 2000).[62]

Examining the social roots of HIV/AIDS brings us to what physician and ethnographer Paul Farmer calls the 'political economy of risk', the complex grids through which 'social forces ... come to be embodied as individual pathology' (1999: 13). Farmer looks at the intersections of class, poverty and race with gender realities, particularly in the large parts of the world where poor women and girls are the most likely victims of the epidemic. Whether the wife of an intravenous drug user in Harlem, a single mother who has sex with a casual labourer in Haiti, or a trader in sex for survival in Durban's informal sexual economy, the women who face the highest risks of HIV infection, says Farmer, cannot be diagnosed in terms of 'medical issues narrowly construed'. Rather,

> their attempts to escape poverty were long bets that failed – and AIDS was the ultimate form their failure took.... Their sickness is a result of structural violence ... [which] is visited upon all those whose social status denies them access to the fruits of scientific and social progress.... Structural violence means that some women are, from the outset, at high risk of HIV infection, while other women are shielded from risk. (1999: 78)

Clearly these social realities have important implications for public health interventions, suggesting that 'economic and personal empowerment' of women and girls, as much as 'education and peer counselling', must be the object of programmes and policies (Preston-Whyte *et al.* 2000: 168). But they also have sobering political implications: racial and gender equality and health care for all will never flourish in a climate of corporate and military globalization. We need, then, to turn to this larger macroeconomic and political context.

Notes

1 See Altman 1995, 2001; Parker, Barbosa and Aggleton 2000; Klugman 2000. This chapter focuses on health care as a human right; for a broader discussion of human rights issues affecting people with AIDS, see Altman 2001; Bayer 2002; Heywood and Cornell 1998; Kalarathy *et al.* 2000; and the outstanding journal, *Health and Human Rights*, published by the Francois-Xavier Bagnoud Center for Health and Human Rights at Harvard University.

2 This phrase is from DAWN 2001a: 1 – an excellent source that this chapter relies on extensively.

3 Barker and Mander (1999) list the members of the corporate Intellectual Property Committee as consisting of three major pharmaceutical companies: Bristol Myers, Merck and Pfizer, along with DuPont, General Electric, General Motors, Hewlett Packard, IBM, Johnson and Johnson, Monsanto, Rockwell and Warner – that is, the largest biotech and infotech conglomerates. Carlos Correa contends that the US pharmaceutical industry was the strongest advocate of the patent provisions of TRIPs and 'a major beneficiary of the outcome of the Uruguay Round' (2000: 15).

4 Vandana Shiva puts this initiative in a larger historical frame, reminding us that patents have, from their debut in the fifteenth- and sixteenth-century European monarchies, been 'associated with colonization', discovery and conquest; from the time of Locke, their underlying ideology was always to ratify 'the enclosure of the commons' (2001: 11–13, 16–18).

5 PhRMA stands for the Pharmaceutical Research and Manufacturers of America, the powerful lobbying group for big US pharmaceutical companies, who have also been principal campaign contributors to both Democratic and Republican parties in US national elections.

6 Correa (2000: 34) suggests that the TRIPs agreement would actually have to be amended to allow for technology transfers (for example, environmentally sound technologies), and, presumably, the same would be true for the protection of local and indigenous knowledges. The application of compulsory licensing by developing-country governments (see further on in this chapter) does not, he says, require a patent holder to share technologies or methods of production.

7 Heywood (2001: 11) gives the examples of Yale University and the University of Minnesota, where 'compounds for two important anti-retroviral drugs ... were discovered and developed with public funds'.

8 Professor Harold Edgar notes that the third stage of medical research – large-scale clinical trials – is by far the most costly, and probably only giant corporations have the funds to support it (personal conversation). This fact, however, does not obviate the *social* dimensions of such research, that corporate profits rely on public inputs to the research process; and that lack of public funds to support clinical trials (rather than, say, missile defence) is a political choice.

9 Shiva likewise argues that the myth that patents are necessary to stimulate innovation is based on a faulty (and, by implication, Eurocentric) epistemology, one that conceives of science and technology as individual and isolated acts and ignores their indebtedness to diverse generations and non-European cultures (2001: 21–3, 50; also Shohat and Stam 1994).

10 This was a clear concession to India's 1970 Patent Act, which contains these exceptions; see Shiva 2001, Appendix.

11 Developing countries paid a heavy price for this postponement, however, since the trade-off was that the US and other industrialized countries also secured a long transitional period in which to continue protecting their agricultural and textile markets from developing-country competition (Correa 2000).

12 Besides the legal actions brought by the Pharmaceutical Manufacturers' Association (PMA) against South Africa and by the US against Brazil (see below), these tactics have included not so veiled threats by the US Trade Representative (USTR) and companies to engage in trade sanctions against countries that even consider undertaking parallel imports or compulsory licensing of drugs. In response to South Africa's Medicines Act in 1997 (see Box 3.1), the PMA 'closed factories, cancelled investments and took out scare ads suggesting that babies could be hurt by counterfeit generic drugs. Its chief lobbyist … threatened to cut off all new drug discoveries to South Africa if the law passed, including AIDS drugs, cancer drugs and antibiotics. Asked in a March 1998 interview if she was literally threatening to let thousands of South Africans die, she reluctantly conceded: "In so many words, yes"' (McNeil 2000b). Rosenberg (2001: 52) notes that just appearing on the USTR's 'Watch List', an official precursor to sanctions, 'is a form of sanction because it discourages investment'. There is little doubt that the USTR in the late 1990s became 'a virtual appendage of the drug industry' (Silverstein 1999: 16).

13 Most important among these groups have been Médecins sans Frontières (Doctors without Borders); TAC (Treatment Action Campaign) in South Africa; ACT UP (AIDS Coalition to Unleash Power, especially branches in Philadelphia, New York and Paris); Oxfam in the UK; the Health GAP Coalition (a network of AIDS and trade activists formed in early 1999); GTAC (Global Treatment Action Campaign – a coalition of Health Gap and TAC); and the Consumer Project on Technology (CPT), based in Washington, DC. See Gevisser 2001; Heywood 2001; TAC 2001a, 2001b; McNeil 2001; *www.CPTech.org*; *www.healthgap.org*; *www.globaltreatment access.org*; *www.msf.org*; *www.tac.org*. For a more detailed chronology of events, 1999–2002, see Health GAP Timeline, at *www.healthgap.org/hgap/accomplish.html*.

14 Fluconazole is the generic name of an anti-fungal medicine that can cure one of the deadliest complications of AIDS; its patented form is produced by Pfizer as Diflucan.

15 Statistics in this and the following paragraphs come from UNAIDS/WHO 2001; CMH/WHO 2001: 47–8; UN/The World's Women 2000: 67–9; Altman 2000 and 2002; McNeil 2001b; Cauvin 2001. I am relying on statistics from UN sources with the caution that vital statistics from Africa may be rough approximations due to the problems of data gathering in poor countries as well as the issue of co-morbidities that complicates mortality statistics anywhere.

16 For a sobering in-depth study of 'survival sex' in Durban, see Preston-Whyte et al. 2000. For further analysis of the gender and sexual dimensions of HIV/AIDS, especially in Asia and sub-Saharan Africa, see also Aka-Dago-Akribi et al. 1999; Heywood and Cornell 1998; Weiss and Rao Gupta 1998; Ahlberg et al., 2001; Baylies and Bujra 2000; Paiva 2000; UNAIDS 1999.

17 See the chronology in Box 3.1 for the odd zig-zags of this suit. Amy Kapczynski (pers. comm. March 2002) notes 'the cynicism' of the PMA and affiliated 39 companies party to the suit, illustrated in their suspending the suit under public pressure in 1999 and then reinstating it only two days after the July 2001 AIDS

conference in Durban had closed – 'once the press [and global activists] had left town'. After realizing the weakness of their position concerning TRIPs, PMA's lawyers shifted their arguments to focus on the South African constitution.

18 See Heywood 2001; TAC 2001a, 2001b; COSATU 2001a; Gevisser 2001; Swarns 2001c; Thom 2001.

19 The following summary is based on Heywood's December 2001 article, 'Debunking "Conglomo-talk": a Case Study of the *Amicus Curiae* as an Instrument for Advocacy, Investigation and Mobilisation'. Many thanks to Jonathan Berger of ALP for sending me this invaluable source in its final draft.

20 Nevirapine has been found to lower the risk of MTCT to 13 per cent by age 14–16 weeks with only one oral dose given to the mother during labour and another to the infant within 72 hours after birth. However, the very characteristics that make it so effective also create the risk that HIV+ women who receive this treatment will subsequently develop nevirapine-resistant forms of the virus (Hankins 2000). Thus the South African government's decision to go slowly and study the drug's effects may have had some medical basis.

21 It is disturbing that advocates as well as researchers and drug companies are more willing to take a strong stand on this issue in relation to 'saving babies' than in relation to prolonging the lives of women. Research on effects of ARV in preventing MTCT has virtually ignored the effects on pregnant women themselves of short-term ARV without other treatment. Behringer-Ingelheim's offer of free nevirapine to LDCs was designated 'only for MTCT and not to be used for combination therapy to suppress the replication of HIV' (UNICEF/UNAIDS/WHO 2000: 11). Although TAC's long-term political programme clearly embraces the reproductive and sexual rights of all women – 'Give Women a Choice, Give Children a Chance' proclaim the TAC T-shirts – its lawsuit against the government was confined to provision of ARV in obstetric settings only. Moreover, TAC apparently formed no working alliances with women's anti-violence or reproductive and sexual rights groups during these years; nor did its members have any time for women's movement speakers who suggested in large public meetings that a strategy focused on babies whose mothers will die, to the exclusion of women themselves, was highly problematic (B. Klugman, pers. comm. December 2002).

22 Senegal's infection rate has remained below 2 per cent, thanks mainly to the aggressive, outspoken policy of its president to educate people about AIDS, legalize prostitution, and set up free clinics to treat STDs (Altman 2000).

23 Displaying its lack of political will, the Mbeki government refused for months to comply with the High Court's ruling (upheld in July 2002 by the Constitutional Court). Meanwhile, leaders in Gauteng and KwaZulu–Natal began to defy the national government's policy, ordering that nevirapine be provided to pregnant women in public hospitals in their provinces. Finally in April 2002, after 'gentle arm-twisting' by Nelson Mandela, Mbeki reversed his AIDS policy, announcing that the government would provide universal access to nevirapine in public hospitals, not only for all pregnant HIV+ women, but also for rape victims (Swarns 2002; Lamont and Innocenti 2002).

24 They note, 'The ANC has always had an ambiguous position on the question of gay rights, adopting a politically correct position in its resolutions, but doing nothing to counter homophobia that has been encouraged by leaders like Winnie Madikizela-

Mandela who have argued that homosexuality is "unAfrican"' (1998: 79, n. 7). Compare Klugman, who states that 'South African HIV/AIDS [educational] materials make no effort to explicitly address gay people or to promote acceptance of gay relations' (2000: 159–60).

25 For documentation of this history and more recent episodes of medical and scientific racism imposed on Africa, see Jordan 1968, Schiebinger 1993, Butchart 1998, Shah 2002 and Le Carré 2001.

26 It is disheartening to contrast Brazil's policies on access to AIDS drugs with those of India, which was able to develop a vigorous generic pharmaceutical industry (though private rather than public) because of a 1970 law exempting drugs from patentability. Companies like Cipla in Bombay produce good-quality, generic antiretroviral drugs for $350–700 per patient per year, cheap enough for the Indian government feasibly to provide universal free ARV for all those who need it within the country, as does Brazil. Yet, succumbing to 'overt and covert resistance' from the transnational and local drug industries, the Indian government has systematically deregulated prices on nearly all drugs and refused to adopt a policy of public support for new drug research and generic provision (Sen et al. 2002: 428–9). For a summary of the numerous exceptions to patentability for food, medicine and drugs in India's 1970 Patent Act, see Shiva 2001: Appendix. Presumably to assure compliance with TRIPs, however, a 1999 amendment to this Act annuls most of these exceptions, ignoring even the TRIPs safeguards.

27 Rosenberg (2001: 29) notes that while Brazil spent $444 million on AIDS drugs in 2000, including purchasing raw materials as well as manufacturing and distribution, it saved $422 million on hospitalizations averted in 1997–9; and to this one must add the amount saved from drugs to treat opportunistic infections and from increased productivity among AIDS patients. Among other things, 'the incidence of tuberculosis in HIV+ patients has dropped by half' in Brazil. See also Oxfam and Galvão, in DAWN 2001a.

28 In 2001 there were 113,000 HIV+ Brazilians receiving ARV treatment (95 per cent adults and adolescents, 5 per cent children), compared with 23,000 in 1997 (Brazil MoH 2002: 13).

29 Maria Fernanda Macedo, who is patent manager of Brazil's publicly owned Far-Manguinhos plant, explains that in this arrangement the government remains the primary patent holder and the private company a non-exclusive licensee (personal interview, March 2002).

30 According to the Commission on Macroeconomics and Health, only one-third of developing countries have the capacity to produce medicines, while another one-third 'import 100 per cent of the medicines they consume' (CMH/WHO 2001: 127, n. 122).

31 For a sampling of the enormous recent literature documenting this variety, see Altman 1995, 2001; Blasius 2001; Lancaster and Di Leonardo 1997; Parker and Gagnon 1995; Parker, Barbosa and Aggleton 2000.

32 Thanks to Sonia Corrêa for reminding me of these realities. For vivid examples of pervasive male violence against women in everyday Brazilian life, especially in the rural North-east, see Diniz et al. 1998.

33 Paiva (2002) describes how this open and festive sexual culture translates into AIDS and STD prevention programmes – like the one in Amazon State, training

female sex workers, men who have sex with men and transvestites as peer educators and utilizing street theatre, festivals and an International Women's Day march.

34 According to MoH figures, the male:female ratio in reported AIDS cases nation-wide dropped sharply from 28:1 in 1985 to 7:1 in 1988, and then to only 2:1 in 1998. In 1996, there were 284,000 HIV-infected men compared with 200,000 infected women, and women accounted for 70 per cent of all new cases in the country's South-east region, where most HIV prevalence is concentrated (Brazil MoH 1999: 14, 16–17).

35 Two examples are Richard Parker, who served for a brief time as chief of the Prevention Unit for the Brazilian MoH's National AIDS Programme; and Maria José Araújo, who has directed the Women's Health Programme of the municipality of São Paulo. In the national MoH, three senior staff in the Women's Health Programme come from the National Feminist Network on Health and Reproductive Rights. (Thanks to Simone Diniz for this information.)

36 Bermudez et al. relate that this law was submitted in 1991, in the shadow of the GATT negotiation process, but only passed in the Brazilian Congress in 1996, after a period of intense controversy and opposition by those who protested that it would have severe effects on the national economy and compromise Brazil's con-stitutional commitment to health care as a right for all (2002: 212).

37 For more detailed accounts of this negotiating process, see Rosenberg 2001; Oxfam and Galvão in DAWN 2001a; Crossette 2001a.

38 Merck agreed to lower the Brazilian price of its brands of efavirenz and indinavir to 20 and 17 per cent of their US prices, respectively; Hoffmann–La Roche ultimately reduced its price for Viracept (nelfinavir) to around 30 per cent of the US market price (Petersen and Rohter 2001).

39 Even with regard to production of ARV drugs, Brazilian researchers indicate the system has serious problems – such as dependence on other countries for its raw materials; time lags between when new drugs are licensed and their availability to public health providers; and lack of both incentives and toxicology research centres to develop new combinations of drugs that are under patent by different laboratories (Bermudez et al. 2002; Terto, Jr 2002; interview with Eloan Pinheiro, January 2003).

40 Letter from Richard Stern in Costa Rica, transmitted on Health GAP's listserve (healthgap@Crit.Path.Org), 31 January 2002. The incident provoking this statement was an action by members of MSF and TAC, who had transported to South Africa quantities of generic drugs manufactured in Brazil and obtained by MSF through an agreement with the Oswaldo Cruz Foundation (the MoH's research branch). The NGOs' purpose was to begin testing the limits of the Doha Declaration (see below).

41 It is important to note that South African researchers with the University of Cape Town's Medical Research Council have already implemented such a benefit-sharing arrangement with traditional healers in indigenous communities. The goal is to ensure that these healers and communities are equal partners in both the material and the non-material benefits of biotechnology research on traditional medicines (Matsabisa 2002).

42 The 16 countries are Bangladesh, China, Colombia, Egypt, Gambia, India, Indonesia, Kenya, Mali, Mexico, Morocco, Pakistan, Thailand, Tunisia, Uganda and Zimbabwe.

43 The US has used compulsory licensing before for a variety of technologies (though

not pharmaceuticals), and Canada in the 1970s and 1980s developed a thriving generic drug business through a compulsory licensing system, making its drugs far more affordable to Canadians (Pollack 2001; Abbott 2002).

44 In March and April 2002, WHO published new lists of ARV drugs, including triple-therapy combinations, certified safe based on the organization's factory inspections, and added 12 new ARV drugs to its essential drugs list. These lists include generic manufacturers from India, relative prices, and treatment guidelines for health providers (McNeil 2002).

45 Even outright gifts, like Behringer-Ingelheim's donation of nevirapine and Pfizer's of Diflucan, are profitable for large drug companies, since they gain from them not only a kind-hearted public image but, more importantly, lucrative tax write-offs against their US and European sales (thanks to Harold Edgar for this useful point).

46 Typifying this prejudice, the International Federation of Pharmaceutical Manufacturers in Geneva, a big PhRMA lobbyist, railed against 'the current plague of substandard and counterfeit medicines' when WHO released its new list in March 2002 (McNeil 2002).

47 A series of reports by health journalist Robert Pear in the *New York Times* described health care as the 'new darling of pork barrel spending' and attributed most of the inflated government spending to (a) the mushrooming of private hospitals, hospital complexes, nursing homes and other medical facilities; and (b) the rise in drug prices and insurance premiums (which reflect increases in hospital and drug costs). These increases translate into enormous profits for drug and insurance companies, not necessarily into better or more accessible health care (Pear 2001b, 2002a; Pear and Toner 2002).

48 Senator Debbie Stabenow – a feminist health care expert and leader of this effort in the Congress – told reporter Pear: 'We have an industry that is the most profitable in the world.... when an industry is allowed to make 18 to 20 per cent a year, at the same time it's raising prices three times the rate of inflation, and people who need life-saving medicine cannot afford it, I think it's time to ask where the corporate responsibility is' (Pear 2002b).

49 CMH, which published its 200-page final report in December 2001, is a WHO-sponsored project chaired by Harvard economist Jeffrey Sachs. The report, *Macroeconomics and Health: Investing in Health for Economic Development*, is the outcome of dozens of preliminary reports, six working groups, and over 100 collaborators.

50 This became evident at a three-day conference in New York City on 'The Crisis of Neglected Diseases' organized by MSF's Drugs for Neglected Diseases Working Group, especially in the remarks of a WHO representative (Brandling-Bennet 2002; *www.accessmed-msf.org*).

51 Even competition from generic manufacturers, while effective at the moment in challenging the patent and market monopolies of giant multinationals, is an unreliable strategy in the long run. Generic producers are also businesses interested in maximizing profits and may raise their prices in the future.

52 James Love (2002: 181) points out another reason why differential pricing and bulk procurement are not an adequate answer to the problems the current patent system poses to universal treatment access, since these approaches 'deal with the inventions after IP rights are in hand. By not directly funding the pre-discovery R & D, there

are no mechanisms [for public agencies] to assert property rights post-invention.'

53 This kind of arrogance was well displayed in remarks by the CEO of Glaxo-SmithKline-UK at the Conference on the Crisis in Neglected Diseases in March 2002. GlaxoSmithKline, the second-largest drug company globally after Pfizer, apparently received substantial funding from the Gates Foundation, WHO and the UK's DFD to conduct large-scale trials on a new malaria drug – a 'not-for-profit' joint venture (see conference report at *www.accessmed-msf.org*).

54 The mission of the Drugs for Neglected Diseases Initiative is 'to lead research and development for new drugs for the *most* neglected diseases' through North–South and South–South collaborations that treat such drugs as global public goods, so that private sector involvement and intellectual property considerations become secondary to the primary aim of 'equitable access to new drugs'. See 'DNDi, the Drugs for Neglected Diseases Initiative, Concept and Preliminary Proposal' at *www.accessmed-msf.org*. According to some speakers at the DND/MSF conference in 2002, certain public–private partnerships for research – for example, GAVI (the Global AIDS Vaccine Initiative) and the Medicines for Malaria Venture – are based on agreements that exclude private sector partners from rights over drugs for people in developing countries. The issue of whether or not MSF's new DNDi, which will launch its own research projects to find drugs for tropical diseases the corporate sector ignores, might become a patent holder has been the subject of much debate within the organization. See *www.accessmed-msf.org* and MSF/DND 2002.

55 After four harried years of trying to use her UN post to implement a broad, global justice approach to human rights and working closely with women's and other human rights NGOs, it was sad but not surprising that Commissioner Robinson 'resigned' in 2002, under relentless pressure from the US government.

56 Paragraph 58 states that by 2003 all countries shall have put into place 'appropriate legislation … to eliminate all forms of discrimination against and to ensure the full enjoyment of all human rights and fundamental freedoms [including access to health care] by people living with HIV/AIDS and members of vulnerable groups'. Unfortunately, the careful attention the Declaration pays to gender as well as adolescence is marred by the refusal of some delegations to allow the specification of gays, lesbians or sex workers in the paragraphs designating 'vulnerable groups'; thus the naming of these groups was omitted (Steinhauer 2001).

57 These provisions contain the by-now-standard UN trade-offs in language on adolescent sexuality. Thus 'expanded access to essential commodities, including male and female condoms and sterile injecting equipment' is 'balanced' with 'encouraging responsible sexual behaviour, including abstinence and fidelity' (Paragraphs 52–3).

58 Paragraph 55 gives a deadline of 2003 for the development of 'national strategies' to 'address factors affecting the provision of HIV-related drugs', including 'affordability and pricing', 'differential pricing', and 'health care systems capacity'. It urges efforts to provide 'the highest attainable standard of treatment for HIV/AIDS' through 'strengthening pharmaceutical policies and practices, including those applicable to generic drugs and intellectual property regimes, in order further to promote innovation and the development of domestic industries consistent with international law'. Paragraph 103 blandly proposes, at the global level, to 'Explore, with

a view to improving equity in access to essential drugs, the feasibility of developing and implementing ... systems for voluntary monitoring and reporting of global drug prices.' This is puzzling, since such a system has already begun under the joint auspices of WHO, UNAIDS and MSF.

59 The June 2001 Declaration of Commitment urges countries to 'ensure that the resources provided for the global response to address HIV/AIDS are substantial, sustained and geared towards achieving results' (Paragraph 79). It lays out as the goal to reach 'by 2005 ... an overall target of annual expenditure on the epidemic of between US$7 billion and US$10 billion in low- and middle-income countries and those countries experiencing or at risk of experiencing rapid expansion for prevention, care, treatment, support and mitigation of the impact of HIV/AIDS, and take measures to ensure that needed resources are made available, particularly from donor countries and also from national budgets, bearing in mind that resources of the most affected countries are seriously limited'.

60 In his state of the union address in January 2003, President Bush paired the expected announcement of a unilateral, preemptive military invasion of Iraq with the unexpected announcement of a plan to triple US spending on global AIDS. He was asking Congress, he said, 'to commit $15 billion over the next five years, including $10 billion in new money, to turn the tide against AIDS in the most afflicted nations of Africa and the Caribbean' (*New York Times*, 29 January 2003). A transparent effort to mute the world's outrage over an illegal, aggressive war, Bush's proposed increase in AIDS spending nonetheless dovetailed neatly with concerns about the destabilizing effects of AIDS in the region with regard to its prized oil production (Dao 2002b; Cauvin 2002). Subsequent developments, however, have revealed an apparently 'humanitarian' gesture to be just another foray of neoconservatism and global unilateralism. As this book was going to press, administration extremists were threatening to link the supposed 'new money' for AIDS (yet to materialize) to the 'global gag rule', to make funds conditional on acceptance of its anti-abortion, abstinence-only policies. It was looking more and more like a manoeuvre to deploy the US assault on sexual and reproductive rights while simultaneously subverting the multilateral and more liberal approach of the UN-sponsored Global AIDS Fund (Stolberg 2003).

61 I borrow the term from Zillah Eisenstein's powerful 1998 book, *Global Obscenities*.

62 'Throughout sub-Saharan Africa, HIV infection is most common in places like the mines and plantations and urban squatter camps where these young people live and work, and where the wealth of the globalized economy meets extreme poverty' (Epstein 2001: 38).

4 Managing Health Under Global Capitalism
Equity vs Productivity

Poor people have few assets in part because they live in poor countries or in poor areas within countries. They also lack assets because of stark inequalities in the distribution of wealth and the benefits of public action. (The World Bank 2000/2001: 77)

In the end, it may very well be that global business rules, while governments and international organizations are left to manage people and soften the harshest consequences of globalization, especially for marginalized groups, including women. (Meyer and Prügl 1999: 16)

'Globalization' = global capitalism

In the previous chapter, I situated the lags in South Africa's recent policies regarding access to treatment for HIV/AIDS, and specifically the policies of its current President, Thabo Mbeki, within a historically specific sexual and gender culture. But Mbeki's reluctance to adopt a strong and aggressive stance *vis-à-vis* the Northern pharmaceutical companies and on behalf of South African people's right to the highest attainable standard of treatment has other motives as well: winning South Africa's acceptance as a first-string team player within the existing power structure of the global economy.

Timed to coincide (and gain favour) with the G-8 meeting in Canada in June 2002, Mbeki announced the plan of African heads of state across the political spectrum to form a new regional governance entity called the African Union (AU), linked to a 'New Economic Partnership for Africa's Development' (NEPAD). This entity would be based on principles of democracy, free elections, human rights, self-reliance and open markets. It would maintain the right of collective intervention to stop genocide and war crimes in the region. Above all, it would seek to secure debt relief and 'increased access to Western markets and foreign aid and investment' in African countries 'that embrace democracy'. Replaying the historical game of imitating the colonizers, its leaders boast that the new African Union will be 'modelled on the European Union', including a regional parliament, a central bank and a standing army to handle disputes (Swarns 2002a, 2002b; Mbeki 2002). Mbeki – as the AU's foremost spokesman – remains conspicuously silent on the subject of HIV/AIDS as he courts the masters of global capitalism to be recognized as a 'partner' (if a junior partner) in their club. An opposition statement by African civil society organizations contends that, behind its rhetorical homage to 'democracy', the AU/NEPAD is 'a top-down programme driven by African élites and drawn up with the corporate forces and institutional instruments of globalization, rather than being based on African peoples' experiences, knowledge and demands' ('Declaration on NEPAD' 2002). It thus becomes just one more sign of the hold that global capitalism, or 'globalization', has on nearly all governments in the South.

Critics of the macroeconomic and cultural trends commonly referred to as globalization disagree about the extent to which those trends represent deep-rooted continuities with previous forms of capitalism and imperialism or a fundamentally new historical era.[1] Some recent analysts even raise unsettling questions of nomenclature, suggesting that the very term is an obfuscation that means everything and hence nothing; in Bauman's words, 'a fad word fast turning into a shibboleth, a magic incantation, a pass-key meant to unlock the gates to all present and future mysteries' (1998: 1). Others make a more radical structural critique, arguing that this catch-all term is really a euphemism meant to cover over the enormous inequities, power imbalances, and forms of capitalist exploitation now centred in a US-based empire and a new form of international sovereignty: 'a unitary power' that purveys 'a new notion of right'; that centrally regulates 'both the world market and global power relations'; and that treats every imperial war as 'a civil war, a police action' (Hardt and Negri 2000: 9, 11).

The term 'globalization' certainly obscures more than it reveals, lending an aura of inevitable progress and irreversibility to very diverse phenomena that are often both regressive and changeable. At the same time, without denying the vastly disproportionate power and imperialist aims wielded by the US state and US-based corporations within this matrix, I find the concept of 'empire' both fatalistic and not particularly useful to describe a historical period of capitalist hegemony that is still more porous, fluid, contradictory, and multi-centred than that concept implies. So throughout this discussion I shall substitute the term *global capitalism* for globalization, while sympathizing with those who see in the recent anti-globalization movement, with all its polyglot fragments and perspectives, a vibrant force for positive change.[2] Wherever they stand on terminology, the various critiques of global macroeconomic and cultural patterns in the twenty-first century seem to unite around several common themes:

- *'hypermobility of capital'* (Smith 1997: 175) ('capitalist markets penetrate and exploit every pocket of available space' – Eisenstein 1998: 121), along with the *commodification* of everything and the *integration of capitalist markets and financial transactions* everywhere;

- *'liberalization' of trade*, abetted by international organizations like the WTO and the IMF, whose role is to administer structural adjustments, tariff reductions, the transition to export-oriented economies, and the opening of markets (Barker and Mander 1999);

- *a unipolar world*, since the fall of the former Soviet Union has left the US as the single superpower and self-appointed commercial, military and ideological centre of global capitalism;

- explosion in the use of *electronic communications and information technology*, contributing to the acceleration of financial flows, cultural flows and transnational organizing;

- *loosening of national and regional boundaries*, so that people, goods, money, information and ideas – but also viruses, pollutants and arms – move more rapidly and fluidly around the globe (Appadurai 1996; Smith 1997);

- *weakening of the modern nation-state*, which has ceded much of its power to both transnational corporate and international financial actors (O'Neill 1995; Appadurai 1996; Eisenstein 1998; Sassen 1998); and

- *centrality of privatization* to the entire process, involving abdication by the state of its public welfare and social service functions to the private sector and transformation of the state into primarily a conduit and increasingly a police and military apparatus to ease the transnational flow of capital and goods (Taylor 2002).

Rather than an 'empire,' which still connotes an overarching structure whose shape is hierarchical and whose centre is clearly visible, this panorama suggests an amorphous but all-encompassing network – Hardt and Negri analogize it to a rhizome – in which the staple distinctions and boundaries of modernity dissolve. As Richard Parker (1999) puts it,

> notions of North and South, the developed as opposed to the developing world, center and periphery, the first world and the third world, and so on … fail to describe the ways in which the world is in fact experienced today…. [T]he contemporary globalized or globalizing, late-modern or postmodern world … is marked by processes of social, cultural, economic and political change that ultimately link both the West and the Rest as part of an interacting system.

Along with this erosion of boundaries across societies, regions and cultures comes an evaporation within societies of the distinction between public and private spaces, between 'the social' and 'the individual' or 'personal', that was modernism's principal way of understanding itself. And with the demise of that distinction comes, not only the vulnerability of individuals and communities to constant (commercial, sexual, ideological, military) invasion and scrutiny, but also the converse: the disappearance of what Eisenstein calls the 'idea of publicness', that is, a sense of public obligations and social rights concerning the health and well-being of people and their environments (Eisenstein 1998; Hardt and Negri 2000). Approximating a form of neo-feudalism, public obligation and social right devolve into charity.

Like modern industrial capitalism, global capitalism is not just a series of inexorable historical trends; it is also a set of neoliberal doctrines and precepts – called by some economic or 'market fundamentalism' – intended to legitimate and consolidate those trends. The most orthodox among these is a belief – indeed a kind of blind faith – that 'free, unfettered, "liberal" markets work perfectly' (Stiglitz 2002: 74). Enfolded within this belief are several unproven assumptions: that, in the long run, markets and competition are the best solution to nearly all human needs; that the *sine qua non* of a good life for all societies is economic growth; and that there is 'an automatic and inherently positive link between trade, growth and development'. In other words, trade and trade liberalization constitute the engine that will drive growth and therefore bring prosperity, magically creating the apocryphal 'level playing field' while assuming it already exists (Williams 2001a). As for the state, it shrinks to its irreducible function of maintaining public order, national security and a hospitable environment in which markets will prosper (including itself serving as a lucrative market for the private sector, in its military procurement and sub-contracting capacities). Even in the realm of social service provision, the state does not disappear entirely. Rather, it becomes just one more vendor in a marketplace of competing providers; it loses its 'public' character.[3]

During the 1990s, many feminist transnational groups – such as DAWN, the International Gender and Trade Network, the Women's International Coalition for Economic Justice and WEDO – joined other global justice organizations in challenging this neoliberal dogma on empirical as well as ethical grounds. In statements confirmed by volumes of UN data as well as the protests of poor people throughout Latin America, Asia and Africa, they have pointed out that, under conditions of corporate globalization, world poverty and the gaps between rich and poor both within and among countries continue to increase.[4] At the upper end of this divide, 'the 15 richest people in the world enjoy combined assets that exceed the total annual GDP of all of sub-Saharan Africa. At the end of the 1990s, the wealth of the three richest individuals on earth surpassed the combined annual GDP of the 48 least developed countries' (Yong Kim *et al.* 2000: 14; UNDP 1998). Even more significant than individual wealth at the macroeconomic level is the increasing concentration of capital in private corporations. Reflecting this trend, the *Human Development Report* for 2000 states that 'transnational corporations and their foreign affiliates produced 25 per cent of global output in 1998, and the top 100 … had sales totalling $4 trillion'. Put another way, more than half of the world's 100 largest economies are corporate conglomerates, not nation-states (Barker and Mander 1999). Meanwhile, small, low-income countries in Africa and the Caribbean find that their products – especially textiles, clothing, and agricultural goods – are still shut out of lucrative markets by Northern governments trying to protect their own farmers and industry ('free trade' for us but not for you). The 'benefits' of global market integration and liberalization accrue disproportionately to the most powerful countries and people, and these inequities receive tacit approval from the multilateral trade regime of the WTO (UNDP 2000a; Williams 2001a & b; Social Watch 2001).

How does all this translate into privatization? Citing World Bank figures, the UNDP also reports that 'private investment as a share of gross domestic investment in low- and middle-income developing countries' rose during the 1980s and 1990s 'from 54 to 72 per cent in South Asia, 70 to 84 per cent in Latin America and the Caribbean, 52 to 68 per cent in sub-Saharan Africa and 51 to 55 per cent in East Asia and the Pacific'. The result is 'a shortfall in public spending of up to $80 billion a year' relative to what would be needed for 'universal provision of basic services'. This is made worse by 'serious discrimination', so that public subsidies for health care, education, sanitation and water in many countries overwhelmingly benefit the rich rather than the poor (UNDP 2000a: 79, Box 4.5 and Figure 4.1).

Numerous writers and UN reports have commented on the adverse snowball effects of these trends, which are now well known. National governments in both poor and middle-income countries, fearing capital flight and denial of IMF loans, give way to pressures to enact structural adjustments, deregulate business, cut taxes as well as social spending, stabilize local currencies, and clamp down on trade unions (see Stiglitz 2002). The result – compounded by huge burdens of national debt[5] – is (1) the reduction of public sector programmes, on which working people and people in poverty depend; (2) rising unemployment, as the anticipated economic growth fails to 'trickle down' or keep pace with the loss of public sector jobs, and local small producers (many of them women) become displaced by export production and foreign goods; and (3) the inability of the state even to provide 'safety nets' any longer, due to the shrinkage of public revenues from lowering of tariffs on imports and taxes on capital.[6] It may seem obvious that poverty exacerbates ill health, but it is less frequently recognized that privatization directly exacerbates poverty: 'In India, the increased cost of medical care is the second most common cause of rural indebtedness' (Sadasivam 1999: 11). Privatization, in turn, means commodification – including commodification of the most basic elements of life. The World Commission on Water for the Twenty-first Century reports that 'the poorest people in the world are paying many times more than their richer compatriots for the water they need to live, and are getting more than their share of deadly diseases because supplies are dangerously contaminated' (Crossette 1999: 15).

While 'the super-rich get richer', they also get healthier and live longer relative to the super-poor and even the not-so-poor (UNDP 2000a: 82). Researchers and international agencies have accumulated data that map the deleterious health impacts of global capitalism in its recent ascendancy. A study by the Center for Economic and Policy Research (CEPR) in Washington presents a 'Scorecard on Globalization' comparing the 1960–1980 decades with the hyper-globalizing period between 1980 and 2000. Overall, it finds 'no evidence in these data that the policies associated with globalization have improved outcomes for most low to middle-income countries'. In fact, the CEPR study finds a 'very clear decline in progress' since 1980 in nearly all countries in both *per capita* income growth and such standard public health indicators as life expectancy and infant, child and adult mortality. And on all the indicators, the CEPR report tells us, women are 'harder hit by this deterioration than men' (Weisbrot *et al.* 2001: 2–3, 11). Its findings are echoed in the widely publicized CMH report, which speaks of 'incipient backsliding' in public health outcomes worldwide, including a slowing and, in some of the poorest countries, a reversal in infant and child mortality rates and the percentage of women whose births were assisted by skilled attendants (CMH 2001: 46).

These declines are especially severe in sub-Saharan Africa – not only because of the AIDS pandemic, civil wars and corrupt governments, but also because of development policies that stress growth and exports over human well-being, and foreign direct investment and loan policies that virtually redline much of Africa.[7] In Sierra Leone and Malawi the life expectancy is now below 40 years (compared to nearly 80 in Japan, Europe and North America). In Africa's poorest countries, 10 per cent of all newborns will die before they reach one year old (UNDP 2000a: HDI 1). In Zimbabwe, the imposition of user fees for public health services has been linked to the doubling of maternal mortality in that country, while structural adjustments have entailed lay-offs of thousands of nurses and doctors (Epstein 2001, citing Gaidzanwa 1999). Severe shortages of public sector health workers from both layoffs and the AIDS epidemic's devastation contribute in turn to higher rates of death from AIDS and other infectious diseases (including ones that are curable, such as tuberculosis and malaria) as well as infant mortality and maternal mortality and morbidity. And, to complete the vicious circles, unaffordable charges for health care also result in greater malnutrition, hence worse health and greater poverty – especially, under conditions of gender subordination, for women and girls (Farmer 1999; Stillwaggon 2001).

The uneven impact of global capitalism's harsher side is thus not only geographical but also distinctly racialized and gendered. Those who languish in the shadows outside the glitter of the global shopping mall (or the closed-down hospital) are overwhelmingly Africans and dark-skinned and indigenous peoples in Asia, Latin America and the urban ghettos of the North. And they are disproportionately women. As many feminist economists note, women are surely over-represented among the world's absolute poor, although indicators to measure precise trends in the 'feminization of poverty' are still lacking (UNIFEM 2000). Women are also those whose caretaking burdens multiply when public health and other social services are cut; who, because they are more likely than men to be employed in the state sector, suffer higher unemployment rates due to privatization; and who are most vulnerable to prostitution and sexual trafficking under these conditions (Wichterich 2000; UN/General Assembly 1999; Sassen 1998; Elson 1995, 2001). A recent UNICEF report on 27 countries in Eastern Europe and the former Soviet Union found that free markets have an adverse impact on gender equality, leaving women and girls 'worse off'. Rising female unemployment and loss of income bring reduced life expectancy due to 'increased smoking, alcohol consumption, drug abuse and unsafe sexual activity', and consequently high rates of HIV/AIDS (UNICEF 1999; Olson 1999).[8] Moreover, as young women become the workers of choice in globalized electronics, food and clothing factories, they confront the growing health hazards that come with trade liberalization and unregulated working conditions – including exposure to toxins, long hours, lack of any health benefits, and sexual abuse (Wichterich 2000; Sadasivam 1999; Williams 2001b).

Women pay for the cumulative social deficits of global capitalism and privatization in another way as well, in so far as these trends undermine the very international instruments that were designed to promote gender equality. O'Neill, referring mainly to the Women's Convention and the ICESCR, points out that these international conventions, with their provisions for 'better social protection through social security programs, health and safety regulations, day care centers and accessible health care', were written with the model of a strong, interventionist state in mind, based on principles of solidarity and social rights. One could make the same observation about the UN conference documents of the 1990s, despite their unbinding legal status, in so far as they continually call upon signatory governments to take positive actions to implement gender equality, women's empowerment, eradication of poverty and access to health care, including comprehensive reproductive and sexual health services. O'Neill's point is that there is a fundamental incompatibility between such provisions and global economic trends, contributing to the failure of states to carry out their commitments (1995: 62–3). With the best will in the world, the privatized state, caught between debt and the global marketplace, may simply shrug its overburdened shoulders and say, 'Fine, but who is going to pay for these human rights?'

Yet it is important to realize that global capitalism is far from inexorable and states are far from powerless. Global capitalism is a complicated mix of real social processes and multinational corporate dreamworks, giving both the illusion and the promise of a better life and greater communion among peoples.[9] One has only to look at the waves of mass protests – in Tanzania,

Bolivia and Paraguay as well as Seattle, Prague and Genoa; the successful resistance of a country like Malaysia to IMF strictures against capital regulation;[10] or the insistence by Southern governments on putting public health before patents in TRIPs, to see the fissures in the global market and that states and popular movements still have power to contest it. Of course, deficient economic resources can become a convenient excuse for lack of political will. 'The vagueness of international instruments and rights to health' and loopholes regarding 'available economic resources' too easily let governments off the hook: 'It is left to governments and their economic advisers (usually from the World Bank or the International Monetary Fund) to set the benchmarks for what is the "highest attainable standard of physical and mental health" within the constraints of resources' (Heywood and Cornell 1998: 75). But the global campaign for access to medicines has shown that 'benchmarks' are a matter of political struggle, and civil society groups must take the lead.

Some months after the 2002 World Social Forum in Porto Alegre had gathered together tens of thousands of community activists from all over Latin America, mass protests in Paraguay blocked the President's attempt to privatize the state telephone company; similar resistance in Ecuador and Peru stopped the governments there from selling off the state-owned electricity facilities to private foreign companies; and Bolivians came close to electing an anti-privatization indigenous leader as President. The mayor of the Peruvian city of Arequipa commented: 'We privatized and we do not have less poverty, less unemployment. On the contrary, we have more poverty and unemployment.' His words echoed the findings of a survey conducted throughout the region by the Inter-American Development Bank in which 63 per cent of respondents said the effects of privatization had been negative (Forero 2002).

Feminist writers have stressed the double-edged character of globalizing processes in regard to the expansion of women's movements for equality, health and empowerment. Lene Sjørup reminds us that 'women may be victims in one respect, while being global actors in other respects', and that 'the economic landscapes are not just exterior forces which crash upon women' but that 'women also participate in [them]' – as family and community members, as workers, and also as transnational feminist activists (1997: 95–6). Family planning clinics may still be driven by population-reduction goals and remain oblivious to reproductive rights and 'choice', but women in developing countries everywhere use their services in order to realize their own aspirations for fewer children (Petchesky and Judd 1998). The ubiquitous 'free trade zones' dotting border towns in Central America and cities in Asia are definitely means for transnational corporations to exploit women and girls as cheap, tractable labour; but in some places they also become the best available alternative for young women seeking a modicum of independence from impoverished, tradition-bound rural families (Wichterich 2000). In Nigeria, in what even the media called a 'peaceful protest', 150 unarmed village women managed to shut down the operations of the giant multinational oil company ChevronTexaco, occupying the plant and holding 700 employees hostage for over a week. They threatened to remove their clothes and stand naked – a traditional method African women use to shame those in power – unless the company met their demands: jobs for villagers, schools, clinics, electrical and water systems, and fish and chicken farms so the women could make their own livelihoods. And ChevronTexaco complied (*NY Times* 2002).

Ruptures in the hegemonic surface of global capitalism may have destabilizing consequences, unleashing religious fanaticism and terrorist violence. But they also open up spaces for alternative visions and liberatory social action – action that moves back and forth between the local and the global. *Political* globalization – of which the UN conferences in the 1990s were a kind of microcosm – has provided a medium through which transnational women's movements have come together across their many cultural, regional and class differences to develop common goals and strategies. Eisenstein, citing the Beijing conference as the hallmark of such movement, remarks on its potential power:

> Many women across the globe are building dialogues that contribute to a deliberative public discourse that deploys public-mindedness in the fight against violence, hunger, poverty, the destruction of the environment, and sexual/racial oppression.... Such dialogue – which both mutes and invites conflict – can build a transnational public of women's and girls' voices that creates the very same liberatory democratic process it imagines. (1998: 163)

Global capitalism reforming itself: the World Bank on poverty and health

Already in the late 1990s, serious cracks began to show in the global capitalist veneer. The failure of the 'Asian tigers' in 1997; chronic economic and health crises in Russia and other transitional economies; and the onset of recessions and widespread bankruptcies, downsizing, lay-offs and plunging stock markets in many of the leading capitalist countries sent shock waves through the central institutions that manage the global economy. These unanticipated economic downturns, along with the mounting size and visibility of mass protests, muffled the optimism of many of global capitalism's champions and triggered a period of self-searching and ideological revision. Even the unipolar configuration of global power seemed fractured and unstable. By late summer 2001, the US – still the world's single most powerful country economically and militarily – had also become its chief outlaw and rogue nation: refusing to comply with evolving international legal and normative standards on just about any issue; isolated from its closest allies in Europe and Japan; derelict in paying its large backlog of UN dues; voted off the UN Human Rights Commission in Geneva; rudely walking out of the World Conference Against Racism (WCAR) in South Africa; and widely distrusted for its cowboy, go-it-alone political leadership.

Although the 11 September 2001 terrorist attacks on the US seemed to inspire a moment of sympathy for Americans and of enlightened multilateralism in the Bush administration as it sought allies for its 'war on terrorism', that moment quickly dissipated. In the months following the attacks, the US administration had forged ahead declaring a 'with-us-or-against-us' crusade of permanent war and unilateral right (Petchesky 2001/2002): bombing scores of innocent civilians in Afghanistan; 'unsigning' the International Criminal Court (ICC) statute; withdrawing from the Anti-ballistic Missile Treaty with Russia; supporting the Israeli government's ruthless policies against Palestinians and threatening to overthrow the government of Iraq at whatever cost, despite almost universal condemnation from the rest of the world; rounding up hundreds of Middle Eastern immigrants and curtailing domestic civil liberties while mouthing the rhetoric of 'freedom'; guarding protections for its steel and agriculture while mouthing the rhetoric of 'open markets'; and meanly withholding adequate funding for the Global AIDS Fund, or any funding for the UN's work in reproductive health and family planning.[11] Abandoning health needs and rights became a major part of the collateral damage wrought by US globalomania.

In the face of economic crisis and political and military arrogance, many people across the globe – defenders of democracy as well as potential terrorists – were starting to question the invincibility and rightness of global capitalism. In response, some global managers themselves began to rethink the neoliberal agenda.[12] By the turn of the millennium the volley of critiques of neoliberal dogma, even from within the World Bank, and the undeniable evidence of its failures had induced international organizations to reframe their growth-oriented policies and to address issues of systemic poverty and ill health – at least in rhetoric. A shift to a kind of 'neo-Keynesian moment' seemed particularly evident in the position of the World Bank. Bank leaders began openly to question the orthodoxy of the past two decades, to some extent separating themselves from both the IMF and the US Treasury on global economic priorities. Many commentators, including *Business Week*, started talking about a 'breakdown in the Washington consensus' (see Stiglitz 1998; Sanger 1998; Wolfensohn 1998; *Business Week* 2000; Houtart and Polet 2001). Joseph Stiglitz, the Bank's chief economic adviser from 1997 to the middle of 2000, was particularly outspoken in his critique of the 'devastating effect that globalization can have on developing countries, and especially the poor within those countries', and the blame he levelled at IMF lending policies and conditionalities in particular, and the 'anti-democratic' and non-transparent procedures of the IFIs more generally in contributing to this devastation (Stiglitz 2002: ix, xiv). 'Fiscal austerity, privatization, and market liberalization', Stiglitz argued, had become not only 'the three pillars of Washington consensus advice throughout the 1980s and 1990s' but also 'ends in themselves' – that is, fundamentalist dogma (2002: 53).

Capitalist self-regulation is a very old story, with precedents in many eras of state and international economic intervention (including the establishment of the Bretton Woods institutions and the Marshall Plan after the Second World War). My concern is to understand the effects of this most recent episode on health care and health sector reform, including the implications for sexual and reproductive health. Thus my focus is on the World Bank because of the Bank's central importance in setting global health policy, financing international health reforms, and exemplifying the neo-Keynesian factor in global financial and development policies.

In their revised approach to poverty and development, Bank publications stress four key elements: (1) a new look at the relationship between economic growth, poverty and inequality; (2) a Comprehensive Development Framework (CDF) that not only places poverty reduction at the centre but also seeks support from 'the poor themselves'; (3) effective state policies – and therefore stronger, more effective state institutions – to redistribute resources in order to create 'pro-poor' public goods; and (4) greater consultation and 'partnerships' with civil society and the private sector in the implementation of such policies (Wolfensohn 1998; World Bank 2000). Of course, this new emphasis on the role of the state and civil society is intended not to replace markets but to supplement them in areas where markets have been found to fail – that is, precisely in alleviating poverty, ensuring health and well-being, and fostering equality, especially of women. The CDF is, in other words, *a variation of welfare state capitalism at the global level* and in that sense signifies a kind of revisionist or *neo*-neoliberalism. James Wolfensohn, the Bank's director since 1995, explains this 'new development framework' as one going beyond adjustment and growth to emphasize social sector investments, especially in health and education, and 'a policy of inclusion' aimed above all at empowering women and girls (Wolfensohn 1998). The Bank's *Annual Report* for 1999 describes its mission as 'to work with countries to help protect public expenditures in crucial areas in the social sectors; protect access to basic social services, especially for the poor; improve social insurance … and increase project and program impact on health, nutrition, population and education indicators' (1999a). And the Bank's Poverty Reduction Strategy Paper (PRSP) of 2000 seeks 'to strengthen country ownership of poverty reduction strategies' and 'to broaden the representation of civil society – particularly the poor ("the true experts on poverty") – in the design of such strategies' (p. 1).

Though vaguely worded and devoid of any operationalizing mechanisms, the World Bank's new emphasis on 'consultation' and civil society participation seems to have stirred up controversy among some of its more high-placed advisers, for whom even token democracy in any aspect of macro-economic decision making still remains unacceptable.[13] Clearly the efforts of global capitalism to reform itself are fraught with divisions and discord at the highest levels. More important, the 'cracks within the neoliberal consensus' seemed an encouraging sign that years of criticisms of SAPs and Bank-sponsored projects by development, environment, and women's NGOs had had some impact (G. Sen 1998).[14] Even the Bank's focus on creating more effective governance institutions was in part prompted no doubt by criticisms from NGOs and angry protests by popular movements – not only against Bank policies but against the corruption and authoritarianism of many governments (for example, in Mexico, Nigeria, and Indonesia).[15] And it is surely no coincidence that the World Bank and IMF chose their annual ministerial meeting just prior to the Seattle WTO, where tens of thousands of demonstrators were anticipated, to announce the new, more 'participatory' poverty reduction strategies. Every such meeting since 1999 has made some kind of 'pro-poor' or anti-HIV/AIDS gesture.

Yet I would argue that the World Bank's new Poverty Reduction Strategy (PRSP) and Poverty and Health programme are not just the old SAPS 'differently packaged', although they definitely are still 'predicated on a market and trade liberalization model' (Williams 2001b: 4). Revisionist neo-liberalism is not just an attempt to stave off criticism by giving capitalism a more human public face but also reflects intense debate within the Bank over economic analysis and perhaps philosophy. Most influential on the neo-Keynesian side of this debate have been Joseph Stiglitz, the Bank's former chief economist, and Amartya Sen (both Nobel laureates), both of whom call into question the reliability of markets and economic growth alone to guarantee poverty reduction or, by implication, social equality and better health. Stiglitz's theoretical work (for which he shared a Nobel prize) demonstrated that markets acting by themselves will always be imperfect and inefficient due to 'asymmetries of information' between employers and workers, lenders and borrowers, etcetera. Markets are especially unreliable, he argued, when it comes to providing 'goods that are essentially public in nature' – such as prevention of public health and environmental hazards (see Stiglitz 2002: xi, 222 and below, on 'global public goods').

More directly relevant to health, Amartya Sen's work in the 1990s emphasized the lack of any demonstrable correlation between economic growth and either the proportion of government spending on health or actual improvements in health outcomes. 'Despite their very low levels of income,' he pointed out, 'the people of Kerala, or China, or Sri Lanka enjoy enormously higher levels of life expectancy than do the much richer populations of Brazil, South Africa, and Namibia' – or, for that matter, African American men in the US (Sen 2001: 336, 339). Much of Sen's work, moreover, has been devoted to demonstrating empirically and ethically that development requires political freedom and the opportunity to fulfil one's 'capabilities' as much as it does higher incomes or growth in the economy (Sen 1993, 1994, 1999).

Following Sen's lead and under Stiglitz's supervision, the World Bank, in its 2000/2001 World Development Report (WDR), *Attacking Poverty*, moved more forthrightly than ever to reject the hallowed assumption that economic growth alone will eliminate poverty or that markets can be relied on to ensure health, education and gender equality – especially for the poor. In fact, cross-country variations in poverty reduction and inequality, the report stated, 'show no systematic association with growth'. Why not? Because (unsurprisingly) 'how growth affects poverty depends on how the additional income generated by growth is distributed within a country' (World Bank 2000/2001: 52–3). This kind of thinking almost begins to sound like the UNDP's *Human Development Reports*, which for some years have argued that 'economic growth … is not an end in itself'; that growth must be supplemented, not only by safety nets for the poor, but by economic policies that are themselves 'pro-poor' as well as governance institutions that give the poor more political power (UNDP 2000a: 38–9; UNDP 2000b: 80–1) While the World Bank avoids the strong indictment of growth-oriented policies evidenced in the UNDP's recent publications, the approach reflected in the 2000/2001 WDR is very much focused on redistribution – or 'redistribution with growth'.[16]

Of course, the idea of the laissez-faire state that moves aside to let the market solve all problems has always been a fiction of capitalist ideology, since capitalist growth itself depends on the state, not only to buffer society against its ruthlessness, but also to create the conditions of stability, predictability and *controlled* competition under which markets can thrive (Field, Kotz and Bukhman 2000; Block 1987; Miliband 1969). Even before the 1997 crisis, World Bank publications had begun to challenge the 'minimalist state' favoured by neoclassical economics and proved such a disaster in post-Soviet Russia, calling instead for more effective and powerful states that are better adapted to global market conditions.[17] As Stiglitz and other neo-Keynesians had argued, contrary to the image of the 'invisible hand', markets are neither perfect nor self-regulating. Because of 'information asymmetries' they require 'prudential regulation' in order to create stability and minimize risk. This means clear systems of formal and informal rules in the financial, legal, judicial, and educational realms and strong enforcement machinery; 'a rule-based culture in public institutions'; and the political will and capacity on the part of states to focus on the priority tasks of protecting private property rights and ending corruption.[18]

Under its 'new development framework', the Bank gives primary weight to the state's active role in reducing poverty and inequality by helping poor people increase their assets. To implement this role, it recommends three methods: (1) *redistributing resources* through tax reforms and budgetary reallocations; (2) *improving delivery of services*; and (3) *involving communities in decision making.* Conceding that 'markets do not work well for poor people', the Bank urges redistributive policies targeted especially to health, education and infrastructure (2000/2001: 79) Arguing that redistribution and efficiency, human capital and physical capital, are complementary, it praises countries such as Costa Rica, Morocco and Mauritius that have chosen to spend more on improving rural roads, sanitation, health and education and *less* on 'debt service, subsidies to the nonpoor, loss-making or inefficient public enterprises, and the military' (2000/2001: 82). Military spending and paying off foreign debt receive particularly strong censure as 'regressive' and 'unsustainable' fiscal policies in this revised outlook: 'Mauritius cut its military budget and invested heavily in health and education. Today all Mauritians have access to sanitation, 98 per cent to safe water, and 97 per cent of births are attended by skilled health staff' (2000/2001: 5, Box 2). At least on paper, the World Bank has travelled a long way from the 1980s generation of structural adjustment programmes (SAPs).

The Bank's interest in NGOs and 'NGO involvement' is not new, going back at least to the establishment of an NGO–World Bank Committee in 1982. But that interest has intensified in recent years, particularly in relation to health and human development policy, as a result of NGO activism and the impact of the UN conferences. At the international level the Bank has set up a number of consultative groups 'to strengthen Bank–NGO dialogue'. These include the External Gender Consultative Group established right after the Beijing conference 'to provide guidance in mainstreaming gender issues in the Bank's work' and to act as a bridge to secure greater input from civil society organizations into its research and policies (World Bank 1998b, 1998c and 1999a). At the national level, the emphasis is more on the participation of NGOs and other civil society organizations in service provision and policy-making processes, including (1) *decentralization* of numerous state functions and services, through greater responsibility of local governments and/or 'horizontal relationships' among local governments, NGOs, citizen groups, and private businesses; and (2) other '*participatory mechanisms*' for 'bringing the state closer to people', such as involvement of community-based organizations (CBOs), trade unions and NGOs in performing public tasks and in local decision making (World Bank 1997: Chapter 7).

Undoubtedly the call to bring in NGOs and other groups as decision makers and service providers has a variety of motives. Koivusalo and Ollila ask 'how much the "civil society" discourse and donor infatuation with NGOs has to do with democracy and human rights, and how much it has to do with finding cheaper and more efficient alternatives to faltering governmental delivery systems' (1997: 102). In Chapter 5 I look more critically at the dilemmas facing women's health NGOs who try to fill the gap left by state abandonment of health services. Nonetheless, it is certain that Bank administrators view NGOs and civil society as playing an essential role in the liberalization of societies and markets and – like many UN agencies and treaty bodies – look to NGO consultants for expertise in gender-related matters.

Specifically with regard to health, the 2000/2001 WDR echoes Amartya Sen in emphasizing the absence of any predictable correlation between economic growth and improvements in health indicators (see Table 5.2).[19] It follows Sen also in citing Kerala for having 'life expectancies greater than those in Washington, DC, despite vastly lower income levels' (World Bank 2000/2001: 34). The message here is not that growth does not matter, but rather that state interventions to improve the health and longevity of their populations can be 'growth-mediated' or 'pro-growth' (Sen 2001: 340; World Bank 2000/2001: 96). The same message reverberates from the CMH 2001 report, which makes a strong appeal for greater spending on health, both by donor countries in the Third World and by national governments in their own budgets, as an investment in greater productivity and stronger economies. The CMH argues 'that investments in health should be a central part of an overall development and poverty reduction strategy' and praises the World Bank's moves in this direction (CMH/WHO 2001: 6).[20]

But the purpose of state interventions under global capitalism, in providing health benefits for the poor as in anything else, is to complement and buttress markets, not to compete with them. Thus, while urging Third World governments to invest in health, the Bank simultaneously warns them of 'clear bounds to state action. In today's globally integrated world intrusive state action can *undercut the functioning of markets and the incentives for private investment* – killing job opportunities, not creating them' (2000/2001: 80, italics added). This is a far cry from the UNDP's admission that growth and markets in many cases destroy jobs and livelihoods and that income (including corporate profits) 'does not trickle down' (UNDP 2000: 43). As the Bank sees the global-capitalist welfare state, its role is to step in with subsidies and/or services only in those areas where 'market incentives' (that is, opportunities for high profits) are lacking. In the health field, this would mean social insurance schemes that do not provide universal coverage – since this would drive up 'demand and prices' for private care and benefit wealthy people – but instead focus on 'catastrophic health incidents' (World Bank 2000/2001: 85) It would mean public investments, not in curative care (that is, hospitals), but rather in preventive care such as controlling infectious diseases. Prime examples of the latter are international cooperation in the successful campaign against river blindness and the Global AIDS Vaccine Initiative (GAVI). In these cases, 'few market incentives' exist to motivate the private sector since the sub-Saharan African countries where these diseases prevail are so poor and unprofitable; thus public sector activity becomes both appropriate and efficient (2000/2001: 182–3; see also Chapter 3 above). The profit motive remains the overdetermining principle constructing 'win–win policies in the health sector' (2000/2001: 79).

While eloquent about protecting access to social services and including the marginalized, the World Bank statements and reports examined above make major concessions to neoliberal doctrine and are clearly aimed at protecting and even expanding, rather than questioning, the centrality of the private sector.[21] 'Ensuring universal access to basic health services' can best be achieved through privatization measures, complemented by subsidies or vouchers ('safety nets') for poor people. Thus 'universal access' is not intended to imply universal *rights* or universal *coverage*, since it is assumed that all people but the very poorest will be able to pay for these services in the market, either through insurance plans or user fees. In the Bank's conceptual model, preventive health care is a 'pure public good' (that is, not profitable); thus the state should invest in controlling infectious diseases through immunization and sanitation programmes. In contrast, curative health care is a 'pure private good': 'if government does not foot the bill, all but the poorest will find ways to pay for care themselves'. Thus the state should get out of the business of operating public hospitals and clinics – to say nothing of manufacturing generic AIDS drugs – and let the private sector take over (World Bank 1997: 27, 51–4).[22]

By 2000, Bank analysts had decided that this approach to health care was not only economically sound but also equitable, since most poor people, they assumed, live in remote rural areas and have no access to hospitals anyway (World Bank 2000/2001: 79). But this assumption ignores both the impact of global capitalism on rural migration and urban poverty and the Bank's own qualitative data. In its earlier, much-touted study, *Voices of the Poor* (Narayan and Petesch 2000), Bank researchers cite testimony from 'the poor themselves' that 'illness was the most frequent trigger of a slide into deeper poverty' and 'the greatest fear for poor people is the risk of large hospital fees' (World Bank 2000/2001: 83). So much for listening to 'the true experts on poverty'; so much for community participation in designing strategies.

In the end, the World Bank's new strategies on poverty and health, though an advance beyond past generations of SAPs as well as the policies of the other IFIs and the US government, are riddled with contradictions. The Bank wants participation and empowerment of NGOs and the poor, but not social movements that challenge 'free markets' and privatization as *systemically* unjust, nor the responsibility of incorporating the 'voices of the poor' into its own health policies. It wants strong, reliable state institutions but fails to support the kinds of global redistributive measures (debt cancellation, 'Tobin taxes', TNC regulation, protective tariffs on key industries) that would be needed to provide the resource base and revenues for such institutions to be sustainable. It wants public (state) commitments to investments in health and education with participation by communities and NGOs, yet advocates financing and delivery schemes that give the biggest share to the private sector. The immediate cause of these contradictions is the internal doctrinal and political struggle I alluded to earlier. Before the 2000/2001 WDR was even completed, Stiglitz had resigned his World Bank post because of pressures concerning his criticisms of the IMF; Ravi Kanbur, the report's lead author, also subsequently resigned under 'pressure to tone down the emphasis on poverty reduction', while US Treasury Secretary Lawrence Summers was reported to have had a hand in rewriting the report's sections on globalization. Even though the WDR is not considered an official policy document, evidently it requires oversight from global capitalism's Chief Financial Officer (Press 2002: 14; Kahn 2001; Wilks 2000). Apparently the World Bank's 'neo-Keynesian moment' was just that – a fleeting moment.

In sum, global capitalism's prescription for health provision is a two-tiered system in which the market becomes the source of most services for most people, while those who cannot afford to pay ('the most vulnerable') are left to the mercy of (often non-existent) 'safety nets'. As the US system with its millions of uninsured painfully illustrates, health care becomes a commodity for many ('health consumers') and a form of 'public assistance', or an unattainable luxury, for the rest. The very concept of 'safety nets' is problematically vague, failing to specify timetables, beneficiaries, mechanisms of enforcement, or basic minimums that must be met *as a matter of human right*; it generally assumes different standards and benefits for the poor and for the affluent.[23] Putting so much social need into the hands of the private sector not only creates two classes of social citizenship. It also omits any institutionalized, democratic mechanisms of accountability regarding standards of quality and access. Supply and demand, profits or their absence, become the ethic governing distribution, rather than principles of human rights and social inclusion. All these macroeconomic assumptions hover around the current trend toward health sector reform – one of the most interesting strategies global administrators are deploying to help ease the pain their own adjustment and market-protection policies have inflicted.

Health sector reforms: Where is gender? Where is justice?

In the final 'Key Actions' document for ICPD+5, a subtle change of language from the Cairo document appears in which reproductive and sexual health, placed 'within the context of primary health care' in the POA, has now been placed 'in the broader context of health sector reform' (Paragraph 52). This small change in wording signifies a major shift in the global politics and discourses of health, a shift in which the older (1970s) framework of 'basic health care for all' has been replaced by a cost-effectiveness approach focused on 'reducing the burden of disease' and maximizing results – including access and equity as well as health outcomes – relative to the resources invested. This approach has acquired the shorthand rubric of 'health sector reform' (HSR), although that rubric represents a wide range of disparate strategies (WHO 2000: 53).[24] The government delegates and mainly feminist NGOs who participated in ICPD+5 were quite aware that reproductive and sexual health and rights will have to engage with HSRs, since they encapsulate the major international and national policy initiatives that will affect all of health provision in the next decade within the larger context of global capitalism. The extraordinary thing, however, is that the relationship to date is so non-reciprocal. Within the HSR framework and methodology, the ICPD agenda, with its emphasis on gender equality and women's empowerment and its broad conceptualization of sexual and reproductive health, is conspicuous only by its gaping absence.

In a study of HSRs in Zambia, one of the few countries where such reforms have actually taken off in a full-scale way, Priya Nanda argues that the divergence between these 'two overarching global agendas' is not inevitable, since, in theory at least, they share certain common goals: greater equity, better access and quality, integration of services and decentralization of decision making. Hardee and Smith (2000) make a similar argument, stressing that better and more efficient use of existing resources can be an important way of improving access, equity and equality. In practice, however, HSRs and ICPD proceed along different paths in part because 'different stakeholders dominate the two movements' – in one case, ministries of health, ministries of finance, health planners and economists; in the other, women's health movements and NGOs and, to a growing extent, international population and reproductive/ sexual health agencies. Therefore they have 'different perceptions of priority health problems' and how to solve them (Nanda 2000: 5–8).[25]

Beneath these different perceptions, I would argue, lie more fundamental conceptual and philosophical differences that demarcate two different worlds of discourse. In theory, there is no reason why the goals of efficiency and cost-effectiveness should be incompatible with either better health outcomes or gender/race/class equality and human rights; inefficient and wasteful health systems can hardly be socially just. It is also true that the Cairo and Beijing frameworks, and the women's groups who remain their principal advocates, have been vague at best when it comes to spelling out what 'integration of services' would mean at the level of health systems, changes in their budgetary and administrative arrangements, and cross-sectoral coordination between health systems and other health-related sectors. That said, however, for the global health reformers who continually recite the mantra of 'equity, equality and efficiency', the balance seems overwhelmingly on the side of efficiency. The terrain where they feel at home is that of cost–benefit calculations and 'managerial/technical concerns', their comfort level sharply dropping when it comes to apparently abstract and 'unmeasurable' concepts like equity, equality and above all human rights (Evers and Juárez 2002; Standing 2002a; Berer 2002; Ravindran 2002).

Underneath a pretence of objectivity and neutrality, this managerial/ technical bias sits upon a deeply entrenched ideology that favours quantification, commodification, privatization and the rule of experts – the dominant worldview of market economism and corporate governance that characterizes today's global capitalism. And this worldview is very difficult to reconcile with such goals as broadening access to services and decentralizing (or democratizing?) decisions over priorities. The tensions become clearer if we look at the three primary objectives of HSRs: *changes in priority-setting mechanisms, changes in organizational/managerial systems,* and *changes in financing mechanisms* (Ravindran 2002). Women's health advocates and global health reformers might agree on the importance of reforms in all three areas, but their different philosophical and political standpoints would result in very different choices. With regard to priority setting, the tendency among health reformers has been to focus on objectives and 'indicators' that are easily measurable and quantifiable, hence to prefer formulae like 'the burden of disease' (see below) and targets that fall within vertically organized health categories. In contrast, the most frequent problems of sexual and reproductive health, rather than being discrete incidents or disease entities, 'are interconnected and often cumulative' and typically do not even involve illness or disability except when the services have failed on some level. Moreover, sexual and reproductive health cuts across the categories of 'preventive' and 'curative' and 'primary/ secondary/tertiary' that ordinarily divide health programmes. Hence it is not surprising that sexual and reproductive health has had a low priority in the 'basic service packages' of HSR (Berer 2002; Merrick 2002).

In regard to managerial changes, how one evaluates a reform such as 'integration of services' will be very different depending on the question one is asking. 'How much will it cost?' (relative to old-style vertical programmes) will generate a very different answer from, 'How much will it cost in the long run?' much less, 'How will it affect the quality of care and the right of access to services from the standpoint of potential users?' Likewise, decentralization can take many forms. Devolving health decisions to a more local but equally élitist level of public administration, privatizing those decisions within the corporate sector, or redirecting health priority setting to democratic bodies representing civil society are very different strategies, with different implications for equity and equality (Hardee and Smith 2000).

Finally, with regard to financing mechanisms, the World Bank and WHO economists responsible for inventing and disseminating HSRs start from the basic premise of needing to allocate scarce resources within fixed budgetary parameters. In contrast, transnational feminists and other critics of global capitalism, whose focus is on implementing human rights and social and gender justice, question the existing global and national distribution of resources and the assumption of scarcity itself. This difference reflects not only a false splitting between 'economic justice' and 'gender justice' (Sen and Corrêa 2000) but also a basic disagreement about what justice even means and how to generate the resources to make it possible. It is no accident that these contradictions are the very fault lines I discussed in Chapter 2 that weaken the Cairo framework and that underline the health policies and reports of the World Bank.

In assessing the current directions of HSRs for women's health and reproductive and sexual rights, it is important to pay attention to the key role of the World Bank, whose 1993 World Development Report, *Investing in Health*, laid out the original HSR goals and methods.[26] The Bank has become the most powerful institution now setting global and national policy agendas in regard to health care, having 'replaced WHO as the major donor in the health field' (DAWN 1999: 39). To a large extent, this shift in global leadership coincides with not only a decline in bilateral aid for health, but also command over colossal resources. An organization that can decide to lend $27 billion to the 22 designated 'heavily indebted poor countries' (HIPC), $7.3 billion to new social sector spending in its 1999 financial year, and $700 million to Brazil alone for unspecified health allocations, almost by definition comes to control the direction of policies in the health and human development field. By its own estimate,

The World Bank is the largest single source of external funding in developing countries for human development – which includes health, nutrition and population (HNP), education, and social protection. These sectors are also the fastest growing areas of Bank lending, accounting for 20 per cent of lending for the last three fiscal years, as compared with 3 per cent a decade ago. (World Bank/HNP 1999: 14; see also Forman and Ghosh 2000; Parker 2000)[27]

At least in its official statements, the Bank seems to be taking the lead among international organizations in promoting multisectoral, equitable approaches to health care provision and responding to criticisms from women's and development groups. It has embraced the ICPD framework by 'linking population policy more closely to poverty reduction and human development, and adopting a reproductive health approach that integrates family planning, maternal health, and the prevention of sexually transmitted infections, including HIV/AIDS' (Epp 2001: 1). Its 1999 annual report calls for gender-sensitive and multisectoral approaches to human development and poverty reduction generally, and health care in particular, emphasizing the inter-linkages between better health, 'reproductive choices', nutrition, greater education, income security and 'more active participation in local and national decision making'. The CMH has endorsed the Bank's broad parameters for HSR in these respects, putting multisectoral integration, non-discrimination and democratic participation in an even broader political context:

> Countries in violent conflict, or that repress ethnic or racial minorities, or that discriminate against girls and women, will find it difficult or impossible to make sustained improvements in health sector capacity. Countries that centralize power in authoritarian institutions and deprive local communities of power and participation in their own affairs, including health, will also fall far short of the potential gains. (CMH/ WHO 2001: 73)

In no area of its work has the World Bank been more responsive to the views of transnational women's NGOs than in its Health, Nutrition and Population (HNP) division.[28] Confirming the anxieties of old-line population groups, a recent HNP report describes its projects as '[addressing] a broad range of objectives' that 'serve not merely reproductive health but a wide range of health needs'. Lowering fertility and population growth rates is only one small piece of its human development agenda. HNP urges 'broad, multi-sectoral approaches' to 'population issues' and, in marked contrast to other World Bank reports and statements, explicitly links such approaches to the Cairo and Beijing conferences and to a human rights framework. Placing women's empowerment at the centre of its strategies, the HNP report recognizes that effective reproductive health projects are inseparable from efforts to end poverty, malnutrition and domestic violence; prevent HIV/ AIDS and other STDs; and expand girls' and women's access to education, good jobs and incomes. Appealing to its economists, it argues that the Bank has a 'comparative advantage' enabling it to create 'synergistic policies that link investments in different sectors, including health, education, and gender, to achieve optimum impact' (World Bank/HNP 1999: 13–15, 19 and Figure 3). [29]

If global HSR policies were governed by HNP (the Bank's most 'feminist' section), and if their guiding principles were primarily those of decentralization, multisectoral coordination, and community and women's empowerment, women's health movements would have little reason for concern. But in practice these aims are in tension with those that thus far have dominated the HSR literature – cost containment, cost-effectiveness and investment of the most resources in the 'highest cost' diseases and in basic packages of services. In their narrower (and more prevalent) version, HSRs have two main purposes: (1) restructuring state systems of health financing and delivery to facilitate private investment, greater efficiency and access; and (2) providing health care resources in areas where 'market incentives' are absent – that is, where the market clearly fails. These goals dovetail with what I have called the revisionist neoliberal approach to macroeconomic policies: free markets stabilized by moderate (and globally centralized) regulations; and privatization softened by minimal (and locally decentralized) 'safety nets' for the very poorest. Generally speaking, then, HSRs embody most of the basic components I have attributed to the World Bank's development policies, along with their inherent contradictions. As Hilary Standing describes it,

> HSR can ... be seen as an amalgamation of the economic efficiency and public sector/good governance international agendas. Elements of it, particularly those concerned with controlling health sector expenditure, relate to economic crisis and structural adjustment policies. Other elements, particularly those connected to public sector and institutional reform, are related to governance issues and the role of the state as the overall regulatory body.... HSR is not one agenda, but multiple agendas which are tied to different political economies, including the level of state capacity and the role played by external agents such as donors. (Standing 1999: 1, 8)

In other words, we might say that HSRs lack any conceptual coherence as a single unifying rubric. Standing observes that national and international efforts to address crises in the financing and delivery of health care have

Major components of health sector reforms

Cost-effectiveness – defining more efficient ways of structuring, financing, and planning health systems, including health ministry reorganization, particularly through sector-wide approaches (SWAPs).

Basic packages of essential services tailored to particular country priorities and needs and targeting the burden of disease.

Decentralization – devolving management and service provision (as opposed to overall policy and allocations) to district and local levels.[30]

New financing and cost recovery options - including user fees, community financing schemes, insurance programmes, and vouchers.

Managerial reform - improving the human resource component by, for example, reducing personnel and/or monitoring performance.

Private and non-profit/NGO sector involvement and *'improved stakeholder participation'* in service delivery, management and accountability processes.

Sources: Standing 1999: 8–10; Evers and Juárez 2002: 23.

emphasized different goals in different geographical contexts. Thus in Latin America, where both state agencies and civil society organizations, particularly women's health groups, are relatively strong, the priorities have been reform of social security systems, decentralization, and a major role for both the private sector and NGOs. In sub-Saharan Africa, where countries are heavily donor-dependent, face 'severe crisis in health sector budgets', and have 'weak state capacity to manage and regulate the health sector', attention has gone more to 'financing mechanisms and improvement of human resource management' (1999: 16). Despite regional and national variations, certain common elements emerge – many of them reflecting the Bank's influence (see **Box 4.1**). Several of these merit fuller discussion because of their implications for sexual and reproductive rights.

Sector-wide approaches. Recent HSR proposals have emphasized what are known as 'sector-wide approaches' (SWAPs), aimed at establishing common policy, budget and procedures across the sector and 'ownership' by the national government in dialogue with donors and other stakeholders. SWAPs are 'multi-donor supported sector-investment programmes' for poor and middle-income countries that locate most of the responsibility for planning, budgeting, procurement and monitoring in national ministries of health (MOH). They represent a shift from the array of disparate, uncoordinated and sometimes overlapping projects financed by separate donors 'to a more integrated sector-based approach'. The goal is to build institutional capacity and sustainability in the health sector, especially for delivering primary care, rather than just to contain costs (Evers and Juárez 2002: 19–21; WHO 2000: 123; Standing 2002a). In this respect, SWAPs are an advance over the more scattershot, fragmentary approaches to health services that have prevailed in previous decades and an effort to move away from the bias toward secondary and tertiary care 'accessible only to the well-to-do in urban areas'. They are also an attempt to correct the heavy-handed conditionalities for public sector policy laid down by the World Bank and IMF in their earlier SAPs (Salm 2000: 18; UNDP 2000b: 33).

Nonetheless, the most common standard of evaluation for SWAPs remains the economic one of *cost-effectiveness*, and the principal methods of implementation are those of (1) tightening rather than expanding the services provided through the public sector to a 'basic package of core services' for the poorest and most vulnerable; and (2) imposition of fees for some public-sector services along with privatization of many others (Elson and Evers 1998; Standing 1999; DAWN 1999). From a gender perspective and one that seeks to implement sexual and reproductive rights for women and girls, these methods seem highly problematic. With regard to 'basic packages of services', Evers and Juárez present contrasting tables showing that the typical 'core services' likely to be available through a sector-based reform represent a considerably narrower agenda relative to the elements of sexual and reproductive health contained in the Cairo POA. The former consist of 'family planning and reproductive health' (including prevention and treatment of HIV/AIDS and other STDs); 'child health'; 'communicable disease control'; and 'some curative service provision'. The Cairo Programme, on the other hand, includes not only the full range of all these services but also services for infertility and the prevention and treatment of gynaecological cancers. Above all, it includes the *enabling conditions* for gender equality and women's empowerment, without which girls and women are all too often unable to benefit from these services even when they exist –

conditions such as literacy, education, access to livelihoods, and the elimination of harmful practices (female genital mutilation, domestic violence, sexual trafficking) that undermine a 'satisfying, safe sexual life' (see Evers and Juárez 2002: 23–4; Cairo POA, Paragraph 7.3; and Chapters 1 and 2, above).[31]

It is unimaginable that such conditions could ever be achieved without cooperation of all sectors and ministries related to social development as well as civil society, along with the MOH. As Evers and Juárez note, 'Because the Ministry of Health drives the process and financial flows and reforms are ministry-specific, the importance of water, sanitation, transport and education for women's reproductive health and rights cannot easily be institutionalised in a SWAP' (2002: 22). Even the most basic components of vertical family planning programmes are often made inaccessible to women and girls, especially unmarried adolescents – even if they have financial means – because of cultural norms perpetuated by religious institutions, the media, conservative groups or family members (Petchesky and Judd 1998). Where in the arsenal of health sector officials and health economists are the tools to confront these problems, much less such health-related and socio-culturally embedded matters as sexual trafficking and FGM?

In other words, the implementation of sexual and reproductive health rights requires *multisectoral*, not sector-based, approaches and can only be addressed effectively through a broad gender and development lens (Elson and Evers 1998). Within countries, it requires the intervention of ministries responsible for education, culture, child welfare, public works, and immigration at least as much as the MOH, and effective mechanisms for coordinating all of these. If we are serious about the holistic vision of Cairo and Beijing, and more broadly the 'right to the enjoyment of the highest attainable standard of physical and mental health', only multisectoral or cross-sectoral strategies can ultimately translate those rights into public policies and programmes. And this is true not only for sexual and reproductive health (particularly HIV/AIDS prevention and treatment) but also for many other health problems such as malaria and tuberculosis, as both the World Bank and the UNDP acknowledge (UNDP 2000a; World Bank 1999a; World Bank/HNP 1999b). In fact, sexual and reproductive health could be seen as an excellent model or entry point for introducing multisectoral arrangements in service delivery and management to address other health problems. But thus far global health reformers have failed to see this potential, since for them 'reproductive health as envisioned at the ICPD is just another vertical programme' (Hardee and Smith 2000: 6, citing Tom Merrick) – which is to say that 'reproductive health' is still translated narrowly as family planning + HIV/AIDS prevention.

Evers and Juárez argue that it may be better for the health and well-being of women and girls in the long run to make investments in infrastructural improvements like clean water and sanitation rather than in the health sector (2002).[32] But this way of putting the issue remains within the economistic framework of trade-offs and scarcity rather than that of human rights. Where is the justice (or sense) in having to choose between clean water and sanitation and, say, condoms or emergency obstetric care? And what assurance is there, using the economies of SWAPs and calculations of the 'burden of disease', that vital components of sexual and reproductive health will not be bartered away in return for water and sanitation?

In this respect it is interesting to go back to the 1978 Alma Ata Declaration (see Chapter 3, above), whose definition of 'primary health care' states in part:

> Involves, in addition to the health sector, *all related sectors and aspects of national and community development*, in particular agriculture, animal husbandry, food, industry, education, housing, public works, communications and other sectors; and demands *the coordinated efforts of all those sectors*. (italics added)

Alma Ata's emphasis on 'social justice, universal access and intersectoral action' is repeated in both the Cairo POA and the Beijing Platform. The Copenhagen Declaration's Commitment 6 also invokes Alma Ata and calls for 'an integrated and intersectoral approach … to provide for the protection and promotion of health for all in economic and social development'. Yet many current proponents of HSRs and SWAPs seem to be going in the opposite direction – backward in fact, to 'vertical, disease-oriented programmes' that prevailed in the 1950s and 1960s; to 'limited public expenditures' focused on a narrowly defined 'package of services'; and to privatized care, financing and user fees (Paalman *et al.* 1998: 24; Koivusalo and Ollila 1997: 113–14).

Financing methods. The trend toward increasing privatization of health care has meant that even poor people in many low- and middle-income countries find themselves relying more on private health providers.[33] At the same time, beleaguered public health systems – under pressure from foreign debt, declining revenues, and IFI loan conditionalities – have begun introducing 'cost recovery' or 'cost sharing' mechanisms for public sector services. The result of this double squeeze has been that households are sustaining more and more of the burden of paying for health services, including many related to sexual and reproductive health – services the poor cannot afford. In other words, 'cost recovery' is a handy piece of techno-managerial jargon that means shifting from public to private responsibility for costs. Specifically, 'evidence suggests (a) that health costs are rising as a proportion of household expenditure in many countries [and] (b) that poor people pay disproportionately more than the better off for health care which is often of worse quality' (Standing 2002a: 17). Sen, Iyer and George found that in India, out-of-pocket payments constitute over three-quarters of total health expenditure and, owing to rising costs in both private and public health facilities, 'the poor are being squeezed out'. They also note the negative gender implications of these increased costs, since women and girls are likely to be the least favoured in distribution of household resources for health (Sen *et al.* 2002: 431).

Not only women's health advocates but Jubilee South, trade union federations and other social justice groups supporting debt moratorium have objected to the imposition of out-of-pocket user fees for services that were previously provided free of cost, particularly as a condition of debt relief.[34] Gender disaggregated data on the impact of user charges on access to health services, as well as on actual health outcomes, are sparse and contradictory, but a general pattern does begin to emerge. One study in South Africa indicates that withdrawing user fees may not lead to higher utilization of maternal health services, since women continue to opt for traditional healers or may have other problems (transport, child care) that prevent utilization (Schneider and Gilson 1999). In Uganda, on the other hand, lowering or abolishing user fees did contribute to greater use of services but also demoralized health workers, who lost income as a result (Mackintosh and Tibandebage 2001). The burdens to poor women of introducing user fees for health services need to be balanced against the *informal costs* they often bear (transport, child care, providing their own bed linens, food and medicines) in utilizing supposedly 'free' public services as well as the frequent practice by public health providers of extracting illicit cash payments under the table (Evers and Juárez 2002; Nanda 2002; Standing 2002b). It may be that 'a fixed, transparent user charge set below the level of current informal costs and with a clear exemption regime' would be fairer and more beneficial for poor women than free services accompanied by onerous hidden costs. But even World

Bank studies have found that attempts to set up fee waivers for the poor have lacked fair methods of means testing and monitoring – in Zimbabwe, for example, most of the poor did not receive the waivers – and have often been 'too low ... to protect vulnerable populations' (Standing 2002b: 18; Sadasivam 1999: 11).

We need more empirical data to document how and whether women are hurt by the introduction of user charges for health services; more specifically, we need data comparing different country and local contexts and different types of provider (public, private non-profit, for-profit, NGO, etc.) regarding informal as well as formal costs and broken down by rural/urban location, class and ethnicity as well as gender. Yet the fact remains that 'in most countries out-of-pocket payments are an especially regressive means of raising health care revenues' (Koivusalo and Ollila 1997:159). Ability to pay such charges depends on 'access to an independent cash income and control over its use', or to jobs with health insurance, which many women lack (Standing 1999: 9–10). A study in Bangladesh seeking to relate low utilization of maternity services to ability to pay found:

> The mean cost of a normal delivery was 25 per cent of average monthly household income; the cost of a caesarean section was 95 per cent ... 51 per cent of the families did not have enough money to pay for maternity care. Among these families, 79 per cent had to borrow from a relative or money lender. A quarter of families were spending two to eight times their monthly income for maternity care. (RHM 1999: 179; Nahar and Costello 1998)

Further,

> Studies in Kenya, the former Zaïre, Nigeria, Zimbabwe, and other countries have shown that attendance at health facilities by the poor dropped sharply within days after the introduction of user fees. In Zimbabwe a doubling of deaths in childbirth has been attributed to the introduction of user fees in public maternity wards. (Epstein 2001: 35)

Evers and Juárez arrive at 'very negative conclusions' based on the existing empirical evidence about how user fees impact on service utilization and access as well as efficiency and cost-recovery (2002: 27). Likewise, in her study of the Zambia case, Nanda reports that user fees vary greatly from one district to another and do not yield sufficient revenues to cover as much as '5 per cent of total recurrent costs (including salaries and drugs)'. Although they are 'nominal', user fees in Zambia are highly resented in a context where health services were previously free and where now centres cannot even provide medicines. For rural subsistence farmers who lack cash, they are simply impossible (Nanda 2000: 31–2).

Health insurance plans are a logical alternative to user fees for financing health care, but here too a gender analysis discloses a very discouraging picture. Private insurance exists only in high and middle-income countries and is inaccessible to the poor (Musgrove *et al.* 2002). Moreover, since most private insurance is employment-related, the majority of women are excluded altogether because of their confinement to the lowest-paying, least secure, and generally uninsured segments of the labour market (Standing 2002a; Jecker 1994; Sadasivam 1999). In this sense, private and employment-based insurance is inherently gender discriminatory. Moreover, it would seem (again, on the basis of insufficient cross-country data) that, even when they do cover women either on their own or through husbands, private insurance schemes in both developing and developed countries discriminate on the basis of gender, often failing to cover such reproductive health needs as contraception, prenatal and maternity care, and childbirth (Evers and Juárez 2000). As Standing observes, the increasing reliance on 'insurance solutions' to fund health care signals 'greater emphasis on curative services than on basic public health and preventive care' (2002a: 20).

We need to know much more about how women fare under social health insurance programmes and the extent to which such programmes are more or less likely than private insurance to cover the full range of sexual and reproductive health services. Yet if World Bank proposals are any indication, once again the prevalent thinking on financing of HSRs is not promising. Public or universal health insurance plans, the 2000/2001 WDR urges, should focus on 'catastrophic' illnesses and disabilities since they 'create much greater problems for poor people than frequent, minor illnesses' (2000/2001: 85, 152). But this conclusion would probably exclude coverage of most reproductive and sexual health needs, other than emergency obstetric care for the most serious maternity complications and prevention and treatment of HIV/AIDS. It is also flawed by gender blindness, ignoring the extent to which poor households are able to endure 'frequent, minor [and chronic] illnesses' only because of women's constant caretaking activity and their willingness to absorb pain and suffering in their own bodies as a fact of daily life. This is just another reflection of the Bank's refusal, like most governments, to take seriously into account women's unpaid labour and its hidden costs, despite the Bank's rhetorical emphasis on integrating gender into its 'new development framework' (Elson and Cagatay 2000).

Finally, the argument about insufficient data cuts two ways; the impulse toward cost recovery and market solutions to resource deficits has proceeded 'despite an almost total lack of knowledge' about their real impact on poor women or other marginalized groups (Koivusalo and Ollila 1997: 159). At best, HSRs constitute a 'giant experiment' that moves forward without any solid evidence that it can deliver the equity and access it promises (Marge Berer, informal comment, 2002). The evidence that exists – for example, in India – suggests that privatization and deregulation have resulted in higher costs and decreased access for nearly all medical commodities and services, with especially adverse consequences for the poor and women (Sen *et al.* 2002). As Schrecker argues with regard to Canada, 'supporters of privatization do not explain how additional revenues made available through the private purchase of health care, or of health insurance, would generate benefits to anyone other than the purchasers'. Nor do they give counter-evidence to the increasingly grim scenario of a 'destructive downward spiral in which reduced spending leads to declining quality, deteriorating access, and accelerated secession or exit by those healthy and wealthy enough to have the option' (Schrecker 1998: 143).

DALYs and the 'burden of disease'. The goal of achieving cost-effectiveness through 'cost-recovery' schemes and limiting health services to a 'basic package' has inevitably generated economic tools for setting priorities. In all the debate among health economists and public health researchers that has surrounded the most influential of these tools – the 'global burden of disease' (GBD) and the DALY (Disability-Adjusted Life Years) – one of the most interesting and least noted problems is the ways in which they undermine other major goals that HSR proponents theoretically embrace. Whereas SWAPs, integration of services, decentralization and 'improved stakeholder participation' were intended to transform older vertical arrangements in management and financing and to expand equity in access, in practice (though not in theory or intention) GBD and the DALY have the opposite result. Yet all of these contradictory methods and approaches arose out of studies sponsored by the World Bank.[35]

The concept of a 'global burden of disease' was intended to make resource allocations in the health sector more efficient by selectively targeting for prevention or treatment 'the few diseases that are responsible for the greatest

mortality and morbidity in less-developed areas and for which there are me
of control in terms of the efficacy and cost of interventions' (Koivusalo and
Ollila 1997: 114). The Global Fund against AIDS, TB and Malaria is a
policy outcome of this kind of thinking, just as the DALY is a technical and
methodological outcome. First introduced in the Bank's 1993 WDR,
Investing in Health, the DALY is a mathematical measure of the GBD that for
the first time combines information on both mortality and morbidity in a
single computation. It is intended to provide governments and health
researchers with 'an "evidence-based" approach to health resource allocation'
and priority selection (Reidpath *et al.* 2001: viii). While the DALY has
undergone a number of refinements in response to criticisms, its most basic
methodological assumptions have remained fairly constant: (1) that it is
both possible and necessary to compute a single number that aggregates 'loss
of healthy years caused by all diseases and deaths in a population' (Nygaard
2000: 118); and (2) that this calculation can be applied to prioritize health
care interventions in a way that is both cost-effective and 'disentangled from
advocacy' – that is, separable from all contextual factors but adaptable to
different country contexts by varying the 'essential national package of
health services' (WHO 1997; Murray 1994; Murray and Acharya 1997;
Reidpath *et al.* 2001).[36]

One positive byproduct of this quantitative, utilitarian approach has been
a coordinated and more aggressive effort by UN agencies such as the World
Bank, WHO, UNAIDS, UNDP and UNICEF to attack such deadly or
disabling but preventable diseases as malaria, tuberculosis, river blindness and
AIDS. The devastating impact of these diseases on sub-Saharan African
countries means that a concerted mobilization of resources to prevent or cure
them becomes one important step against global medical apartheid. Indeed,
the campaign for access to essential medicines as a human right, which I have
praised as a kind of model for women's health activists, as well as MSF's Drugs
for Neglected Diseases campaign, have obvious affinities with the GBD
approach.[37] That said, the approach is highly problematic and has come under
a volley of criticism from feminist and other public health advocates and
researchers. Whether arrogant or merely naïve, the belief of economists that
they can devise formulae for assessing the impact of health conditions that are
so technically unimpeachable and objective as to be 'disentangled from
advocacy' – that is, immune from social values and political scrutiny – seems
patently mistaken. Precisely because health conditions of all sorts – especially
sexual and reproductive health conditions – are inseparable from a wide range

of social and contextual conditions that directly affect both their incidence and their severity, political advocacy is intrinsic to decision making about priorities in allocating resources to health.[38]

Major criticisms focus on the kinds of exclusions, 'flawed ... assumptions and value judgments' built into the DALYs/GBD methodology, but most of these come back to the questionable notion that it is possible to standardize a single measurement for comparing the 'disease burden' in all countries. Its originator Christopher Murray and other DALY proponents argue that such a single, global measurement is absolutely necessary to assure comparability across countries and contexts as well as fairness (so that health resource allocations are not skewed by particular social values). As Elizabeth Nygaard (2000) elegantly demonstrates, however, the GBD/DALY project contains an inherent contradiction: To calculate the 'disability weight' of a particular disease in any country requires assessments of its 'severity'; but such assessments cannot be made without taking into account a wide range of 'contextual factors' whose inclusion then skews the 'objectivity' and reliability of the measurement. In fact DALYs do not compute the *burden* of disease at all, because the varied social and personal meanings of that burden are impossible to quantify. At best they calculate 'time lived with a disability and time lost due to premature mortality ... adjusted for age, sex and time of illness', and only for certain well-defined illnesses (Anand and Hanson 1997: 686–7; Murray 1994). In the end, no purely objective assessment tool is possible; value choices have to be made, or else a whole series of value judgments and biases will remain buried under the pretence of objectivity.[39]

In an attempt to provide empirical support for the argument that measurements of disease burden have to be *context-specific*, a recent study by Reidpath and his associates at the University of Melbourne looked at two different diseases – paraplegia and epilepsy – in two very different country contexts (Australia and Cameroon), factoring in a variety of key social and contextual differences, particularly urban versus rural environment, gender, and class. A critical aspect of this study is its reliance on not only quantitative but also qualitative data, including self-reporting, in order to obtain 'rich and detailed descriptions' of how people actually experience a particular health condition under diverse social circumstances (2001: 60). Acknowledging that self-reporting may be an inaccurate reflection of actual health status, Reidpath and his associates point out that information about both health status (population-based and clinical measurements) and lived experience is critical to health policy and priority setting.

Utilizing this multi-factorial methodology led the Melbourne researchers to a finding of 'enormous differences' in both the nature and the magnitude of the disease conditions in the two country and diverse local contexts selected, and among different social groups (such as women and men) within those contexts. Thus, access to wheelchairs, often motorized, makes paraplegia a totally different condition in the more developed setting of urban Australia than it is in (mostly rural) Cameroon, where paraplegics are isolated and immobile. And for women who are single mothers and also paraplegics in Cameroon, their isolation and social stigmatization compounds the burden. (In the area of sexual and reproductive health, we could compare the difference in the 'severity' of RTIs for women who have sanitary facilities in developed countries or in urban middle-class settings with those Mukherjee studied who lack such facilities – see Chapter 2, above.) Thus, they argue,

> It is important that one measure the burden, as much as possible, as it truly occurs, not in an arbitrarily distorted reality. The experience of a health condition is an interaction between a person and their social, cultural, and environmental contexts.... (2001: 63)

This emphasis on 'disability' or 'disease burden' as a *lived reality* leads to the conclusion that any 'meaningful' study of the burden of disease must take into account 'the effect of social, cultural, and environmental factors', which the application of a single, abstractly computed measurement like the DALY is unable to do (2001: xi).

Other critics have pointed out that the hidden biases of the DALYs approach discriminate not only against 'those who are different along dimensions *not* included in the DALY information set' but also against some who are included. Age-weighting, for example, assigns lower value to years of life or time lost during childhood and old age; likewise, illness of an able-bodied person counts more towards the burden of disease (for purposes of claiming public resources) than does that of a person with a pre-existing disability (Anand and Hanson 1997: 688). Even more problematic is the method's determination to cancel out class and poverty levels, especially given the World Bank's recent programmatic focus on attacking poverty and HSR's stated purpose of redirecting more health resources to the poor. Ignoring such differences as class, race and ethnicity in effect denies substantial empirical data showing their significant impact on health outcomes, not only in developing but also in highly developed countries.[40] Consequently, applying the DALY to determine health priorities is likely to worsen social inequalities (Paalman *et al.* 1998; Reidpath *et al.* 2001).

In the light of all this, it should not be surprising that DALYs are also an inadequate way of evaluating health policies and programmes from a gender perspective. Feminist critics have faulted the ways in which the narrow, vertical focus of the DALY on discrete disease entities leaves out of account many burdens suffered by women that depreciate their health and well-being if not their longevity. On the positive side, AbouZahr points out that 'the DALY methodology in the 1993 WDR ... brought reproductive health issues onto the health and development agenda more prominently than ever before', since, unlike earlier quantification methods, it considers morbidity as well as mortality (AbouZahr 1999: 119). Illustrating this, the WHO's recent listing of 'cost-effective' health interventions considered desirable under the DALYs/ GBD method would include, along with treatment of tuberculosis, malaria, immunization and tobacco control, 'maternal health and safe motherhood interventions', family planning and HIV/AIDS prevention. Significantly, however, this listing and the entire WHO 2000 report avoid any mention of the Cairo agenda, including the actual burdens and inequalities women experience and the broad, multisectoral interventions that would be needed to alleviate them. As AbouZahr emphasizes, some of the most pressing conditions that are endemic in many women's lives, especially in developing countries, and cause them the most pain and suffering – menstrual disorders, reproductive and urinary tract infections, genital mutilation, obstetric fistulae, domestic violence – are completely absent from the DALY's radar screen:

> The loss of a limb or of one of the senses is intuitively easy to understand. The loss of a clitoris may be a little harder to quantify. And how does one ascribe a disability weighting to a continuous vaginal itching or unpleasant vaginal discharge? Such conditions are not even necessarily painful, nor do they prevent a woman from exercising her daily activities. They do, however, make life extremely unpleasant, which is not easy to quantify in health terms. And what disability weight should be attached to regular beating by a partner when its consequences may not be evident? (AbouZahr 1999: 123)

The reasons why the quantitative, narrow methods presently being used by global health economists to determine health priorities are 'fundamentally problematic' come back to their underlying assumptions about what matters for a healthy life (AbouZahr 1999: 124). The assumptions of the DALY/GBD framework rest entirely on a capitalist patriarchal ideology that privileges *productivity* (or what Murray and Acharya [1997] call 'functioning achieve-ments') above all else. This means that the framework ignores the kinds of suffering and ill health that women, especially the poorest and most vulnerable women, have been socialized to endure without stopping their normal work and (devalued) domestic tasks – such as chronic backache and RTIs (G. Sen *et al.* 2002). It also provides no means to evaluate the *quality* of health care services as women experience them.[41] Yet that experience may have a direct bearing on the 'burden of disease', since we know that practices such as disrespectful or abusive treatment, lack of confidentiality, and cultural insensi-tivity discourage many women from returning to clinics and therefore function as *de facto* barriers to access (Diniz *et al.* 1998; Raj *et al.* 1998; Seif El Dawla *et al.* 1998; Nanda 2000).

'Priority setting depends upon the notions of justice which are the point of departure for decisions on the allocation of health care resources' (Nygaard 2000: 123). *Justice*, in turn, has to do with the normative prescription that social and material necessities of life (including health care) ought to be distributed fairly among individuals, communities, countries and regions of the globe, without discrimination based on arbitrary categories of exclusion. But 'non-discrimination' is only one dimension of justice and must always be balanced with *equity* – which is the ethical requirement that we pay close attention to the *differences* in needs, conditions, perspectives and experiences that characterize differently situated social groups. It is not the case that global capitalism lacks any concept of justice; rather, its principles of distribution – what counts as 'fair' and what is alleged to create the most well-being in the long run – are those associated with protection of private property, 'expansion and preservation of open world markets', and increasing a population's (and the global economy's) economic productivity (World Bank 1997: 141). For these purposes, it is most convenient to treat all individuals and groups as presumptively the same, not different – consumers in a global health commodity market. The technocrats who command the HSR field – whose role is to palliate the sore spots in global capitalism, not to critique it – accordingly treat justice as a kind of Rawlsian 'original position' in which basic health needs can be aggregated into a global mathematical formula plus a package of 'essentials' and all extraneous differences set aside.[42] By making the DALY 'colour-blind' (and class- and gender-blind as well), they avoid the complex and challenging methodological problems of multi-factorial and contextual analysis; they also assume an 'equality' that exists neither in any society nor in the real-life burdens of disease.

As suggested earlier, despite the challenge from neo-Keynesians in its midst, the World Bank's overall health policy is still primarily market-driven. Following the Bank's lead, the WHO has opted to discard the principles of social solidarity and universal coverage in its recent critique of Alma Ata and its uncritical embrace of 'private finance and provision', tempered presumably by 'safety nets' (WHO 2000: 15). A cost-effectiveness approach that conceptualizes health care recipients as both 'human capital' and consumers has become the express policy of Director-General Gro Harlem Brundtland, who sees it as a useful strategy for 'moving health up the agenda of governments and politicians' (Leon and Walt 2001: 6).[43] The *World Health Report 2000* is saturated with this approach. 'To require the health system to obtain the greatest possible level of health from the resources devoted to it', it states, 'is to ask that it be as cost-effective as it can be. This is the basis for emphasizing those interventions that give the most value for money, and giving less priority to those that, much as they may help individuals, contribute little per dollar spent to the improvement of the population's health' (2000: 52). In circular fashion, the values packed into the word 'improvement' in this statement are those of cost-effectiveness as determined by the DALY/GBD methodology – that is, selective investment in health based on estimated contributions to economic productivity.

It is striking that the lengthy index to the 2000 *World Health Report* does not contain a single entry for human rights – nor, for that matter, for abortion, contraception, gender, reproductive health, sexual health, sexuality or women! Avoiding the ICPD framework altogether, the report's main reference to 'rights' throughout its pages has to do with patients' rights understood from the standpoint of national legislation and consumer protection (2000: 130, Box 6.7).[44] The CMH report, aimed at an audience of global policy makers and advocates steeped in economistic discourse, does acknowledge the idea of health as one of 'the basic human rights enshrined in international law'. For most of its 200 pages, however, that report also grounds its case for global and multilateral health investments, including to combat HIV/AIDS, on arguments derived from human capital theory concerning the wasted resources and losses in productivity and GNP resulting from widespread disease and poor health indicators. The corollary, of course, is that making such investments will 'pay off' in terms of poverty reduction and enhanced growth (CMH/WHO 2001: 1–4). But growth of what and for whom?

We have seen the downside of reliance on 'private finance and provision' at the national level. At the global level, bilateral aid for health generally and for reproductive health specifically (especially USAID funds) has declined since the ICPD in 1994. Its replacement by targeted funds and private philanthropic donors like the Gates Foundation not only has resulted in diminished funds for sexual and reproductive health but also has signalled 'a *de facto* return to vertical interventions'. And this return, signifying the influence of the DALY/GBD approach to deciding health priorities, has devastating consequences for the integrative, multisectoral requirements of sexual and reproductive health and rights (Standing 2002a: 8; Forman and Ghosh 2000).[45] Nowhere is this clearer than in the most important UN initiative to date attempting to mobilize governments towards a firm agenda of timetables and targets for health, education and poverty eradication – the 2001 Millennium Development Goals (MDGs), which omitted the ICPD and ICPD+5 targets for reproductive health provision (see Chapter 2).

Perhaps sobered by the backlash against sexual and reproductive health and rights under the Bush administration, the World Health Assembly passed an important resolution at its Ninth Plenary Session in May 2002 on 'WHO's contribution to achievement of the development goals of the United Nations Millennium Declaration'. That resolution reinvokes the commitments undertaken in the ICPD POA, Copenhagen Social Summit, Beijing Women's Conference and World Summit on Children as well as the Declaration on the Elimination of Violence against Women and their follow-up reports, thus implicitly linking these documents to the MDGs. It further makes a strong statement recalling that the WHO constitution defines 'enjoyment of the highest attainable standard of health' as a 'fundamental right of every human being without distinction of race, religion, political belief, economic or social condition [or gender]' and noting that this includes 'access to good-quality reproductive-health care, including family planning services that are effective, affordable and acceptable'. And the resolution 'urges Member States ... to strengthen and scale up' their commitments under the MDGs by, among other things, increasing development assistance as well as national investments in the health sector; generating greater resources for research into cures for neglected diseases; and '[encouraging] the pharmaceutical industry and other relevant partners ... to make essential drugs more widely available and affordable by all who need them in developing countries' (WHO 2002).

This resolution deserves recognition in so far as it puts the WHO officially on record as urging an expansion of the MDGs to include an explicit and more comprehensive commitment to reproductive health and health as a human right. At the same time, I would suggest two notes of caution. First, a

WHA resolution, directed at the actions of member states, may have little to do with the working policies, programmes and perspectives of the organization itself. And those, by all available evidence, have not only cast Alma Ata into the dustbin but also strongly favour a GBD/cost-effectiveness approach over one based on human rights. Second, even when international organizations (like national governments) espouse human rights principles at the level of rhetoric, they do not always understand or accept what those principles mean in practice, including for their own policies. We need to go beyond rhetoric to probe meanings.

Alternative ethics of health provision

Social justice in the provision of health care services involves three basic components: *access, quality* and *resources*. In no country in the world where the deregulated market has overridden principles of universality, social rights and public responsibility have these three components been achieved. Experience shows we cannot rely on markets to organize low-cost, accessible and multisectoral approaches or to assure the conditions for health across gender, race–ethnicity, class, national and other lines of social exclusion. The World Bank concedes, 'Markets do not work well for poor people' (2000/1: 79). But we need to go further and recognize that 'the market does not necessarily work for health sector services', not for *anyone* except the rich (Evers and Juárez 2000: 27). Clearly, innovative thinking is needed – not to adapt sexual and reproductive health to the narrow, technical formulae of HSRs, but to move health reform efforts in a more complex and holistic direction.

The ethical vocabulary currently favoured by macroeconomists and health reformers seeking to reconcile market systems with principles of social justice and inclusion is that of 'global public goods'. The concept of 'global public goods' was originated by economists in the US in the second half of the twentieth century but was brought into a larger frame of attention by a group of policy analysts at the UNDP in the late 1990s. Its purpose is to develop a macroeconomic framework for valuing and financing 'goods whose benefits reach across borders, generations and population groups' and are thus 'under-provided by local and national governments'. Unlike ordinary commodities, such goods are ones that the market does not handle well or has no interest in because they are, in economists' terms, 'non-excludable' and 'non-rivalrous in consumption', meaning that their ownership and use cannot be packaged, transferred, and privately appropriated. Examples might be safe airways and oceans, an intact ozone layer, universal access to essential medicines and condoms, or a world free of infectious diseases (Kaul, Grunberg and Stern 1999: ix–xxi; CMH/WHO 2001; Stiglitz 2002).[46]

From an economic standpoint public goods are problematic because there are not only few market incentives to provide them but also very weak mechanisms of international cooperation to make sure they do get provided. Moreover, most global public goods are not 'pure', or universal, but 'impure', meaning their immediate benefit may accrue to private individuals but in the long run has important social consequences. It is thus presumably more difficult to develop common understandings and funding mechanisms that define these as global public goods and enforce their provision (Kaul, Grunberg and Stern 1999). The World Bank has attempted to address the problem of market failure and national government incapacity to provide basic needs by promoting the creation of 'pro-poor international public goods' based on bilateral, multilateral and private donations (World Bank 2000/1: 181). With regard to health, the Bank, as we have seen, defines most preventive care – including sanitation and combating infectious diseases – as public goods. It assumes, for example, that the corporate sector will never produce a vaccine for AIDS (because the African market is too unlucrative to justify the costs). Since the AIDS epidemic has been defined as a 'security risk' for the globe, however, it becomes an area of health need that deserves international cooperation and funding; hence the establishment in 1996 of GAVI represents international recognition of a 'pure global public good' (World Bank 2000/1).

The impetus to name global public goods in the first place naturally comes from economists who, like Stiglitz, understand that markets are imperfect and inefficient and that 'goods that are essentially public in nature' do exist (Stiglitz 2002: 222). In this sense, the concept brings us closer to a perspective of social justice than do those of human capital or supply and demand. Moreover, in the prevailing social context, where markets normally determine choices and values, where any ethos of collective need or common good has been lost, it is useful to have a language for seeking common ends that is intelligible to macroeconomists, the chief arbiters of value in the regime of global capitalism. Unfortunately, however, the global public goods framework has certain weaknesses. First, as I understand the notion of 'non-excludable' and 'non-rivalrous,' it comes down to lacking the properties of a commodity (a good capable of being appropriated or exchanged). But a cursory survey of the contemporary capitalist horizon makes clear that *anything* is potentially commodifiable – clean air, clean water, virtual sex, public safety, gene lines – as long as capitalists can create a market for it, including in the state (Taylor 2000).[47] More important, that framework does not depart from classical liberal or neoliberal economic theory in so far as it rests on the ethically empty norm of 'satisfaction of wants', or utility. In other words, it conceptualizes 'goods', like commodities, in abstraction from the conditions and needs of the people who use them, providing no intrinsic standards for distinguishing between a 'piece of cake' and an injection of nevirapine (Durano 2001). As even its promoters concede, the global public goods perspective gives us no way to define priorities – *which* health investments should be designated global public goods – apart from the vagaries of 'policy debate' (Kaul, Grunberg and Stern 1999: 16). We may easily agree that R & D for drugs and vaccines to combat neglected diseases should qualify, but then why not also adequate food, education and health care for all those whom market prices exclude?

A more satisfying ethical framework for determining health priorities is the idea of 'capability' as developed by Amartya Sen. This framework gives less importance to subjectively defined (and ethically neutral) values of utility and more to indices of 'well-being' that will allow individuals 'to lead the kind of lives they value' – that is, to enjoy human freedom (Sen 1999: 18). It goes beyond human capital theory's narrow focus on 'functioning' in economic productivity terms to incorporate both individual aspirations and potential and the social conditions to make those aspirations and that potential realizable. Thus the capability framework embraces not only health, education and nutrition but also 'achieving self-respect', 'taking part in the life of the community' and 'appearing in public without shame' as ends in themselves and as indispensable enabling conditions for people's capabilities to be realized (Sen 1993: 36–7). Indeed, Sen's focus on capabilities and freedom would shift the whole vantage point of mainstream economic theory to one more in tune with feminist concepts of gender equality and women's empowerment. Yet, while the capability framework is helpful in pointing towards ethical criteria for setting health priorities, both it and the global public goods framework lack any criteria or mechanisms for implementing and enforcing those priorities – that is, for transforming institutional power relations. To give global public goods ethical content; to specify principles of social, racial and gender justice; and to provide clear standards and procedures of accountability and enforcement, we need a human rights approach.

Human rights as the framework for determining the priorities of health care systems requires entirely different criteria from those of market-based or cost-effectiveness approaches – criteria closer to those contained in the Alma Ata Declaration and confirmed in Cairo, Copenhagen and Beijing; or to the feminist ethical principles outlined in Chapter 1. The perspective of human rights allows us to raise some basic questions about three problems that the other approaches do not adequately address: first, the assumptions embedded in the language of commodification and consumerism; second, the absence of reliable mechanisms for democratic participation and public accountability; and third, the credo of market models that limited resources and scarcity are an irrevocable fact of life.

At bottom, the current debate about health care reform resolves into a distinction between whether health should be treated as a private commodity or as a public good and a human right. The differences go deeper than language – or rather, language matters, it *signifies*. When we call the women who rely on reproductive health services 'consumers' or 'users', we reinforce the marketization of health care rather than challenging it. Moreover, the language used to describe 'stakeholders' has a subtle but significant bearing on the form their 'consultation' takes and whether or not, or how effectively, they are involved in priority setting. Individual health 'consumers' or 'users' may be subjects of marketing research to find out about their product preferences or may be surveyed for their evaluation of provider practices. But this is very different from a model of health provision that treats the recipient of services as a citizen with rights, that encourages her 'to feel that she has "the right to have rights and to create rights"' and 'to regard herself as the agent and subject of her own actions' (Paiva 2002: 12). And it is not at all the same as communities mobilized on the basis of claims for social justice and human rights and organized to participate directly in the design and evaluation of services.

Rachel Kumar, critiquing the ideologies surrounding the Reproductive and Child Health Programme (RCH) in India (see Chapter 5), argues that, in the thinking of the health and family planning bureaucrats and service providers she interviewed, a market discourse of 'clients' or 'consumers' of services and a rights discourse of 'citizens' have in effect been collapsed:

> The notion of *'rights'* in this context marks a fluid terrain that portrays users as consumers/clients *and* citizens; as citizens, they have the right to reproductive health, and as consumer/clients within a market paradigm, they have the right to the services they demand [and pay for]. The public space of citizen rights, therefore, becomes merged with the marketplace of consumer tastes. (2000: 117)

My point is that this sort of conflation of rights and consumerism, freedom and shopping – as endemic as it is to capitalist ideology historically and across the globe – reflects a deep ethical confusion that we need to resist and expose.

The biggest problem with relying on cost-effectiveness and privatization to meet basic health care needs is that the market has no built-in mechanism of public accountability to assure that standards of quality, universal access and non-discrimination are in fact met. 'Free market' systems are thus inherently antithetical to health care as a human right, since human rights enforcement depends on reliable systems of public regulation and accountability – which is not the same thing as *ad hoc* consulting of community 'stakeholders', much less allowing individual consumers to 'shop around' (the regulatory solution of market-fundamentalist economics). A human rights approach differs at its core from either a market-oriented or a welfare-state model because it provides (a) general norms through which the potential beneficiaries of programmes and services can feel entitled to make social justice claims; (b) public standards for evaluating programmes and services from the standpoint of the needs and well-being of those whom they are designed to benefit; and (c) mechanisms of accountability for enforcing those standards. Market-based and cost-effectiveness approaches cannot do this because they are ethically closed systems; that is, they measure 'value' only by private preferences, with the market as its own reference point; or by price, with the lowest costs having highest value (cf. Schrecker 1998). And welfare state solutions cannot do this either, in so far as they treat the recipients of services as passive victims or clients rather than as rights-bearing agents and equal participants in decision making.

Effective and genuinely democratic community participation, especially women's participation, in designing and monitoring HSRs and sexual and reproductive health services will happen neither as an accident of the market nor as a beneficent gift of the welfare state. Such participation can only come about as an *achievement* by robust, politically conscious social movements. In turn, the logic of such movements – especially in non-democratic societies or democratic societies in which corporate interests dominate public decision making – arises out of radical oppositional ideologies and practices, not 'consultations' or 'partnerships' with the managing institutions of global capitalism.[48] Its goal is strong democratic institutions with ongoing processes for oversight and accountability. These should (1) engage civil society at all levels – local, national and international – and (2) include in their purview all centres of power whose activities affect health: TNCs, IFIs, the WTO and religious organizations as well as health providers, governments and IGOs. A few embryonic models already exist: for example, the Citizens' Health Councils in Brazil, the people's and women's participatory budgeting experiments in South Africa and elsewhere, and the slowly emerging openings towards using UN human rights machinery to hold the IFIs and TNCs responsible for violations of international law and human rights, including the right to health care (see Chapters 5 and 6).

Yet conceptualizing the recipients of health services and other social programmes as rights-bearing 'citizens' presents other problems of exclusion, especially under conditions of globalization. To the extent that health entitlements are tied to national citizenship and limited by restrictive definitions of citizenship, they may neglect or deliberately exclude the massively growing numbers of globalized bodies, many of whom are women and girls: internal and transnational migrants (especially undocumented immigrants and 'guest workers'), refugees, prison and detention camp populations, and the victims of trafficking.[49] Most discussions of the implications of HSRs and SWAPs for sexual and reproductive health or women's health care generally show a surprising lack of attention to the situation of women migrants and refugees in both developed and developing countries. In so far as HSR projects assume a bias toward citizen-based entitlements to health subsidies, such projects will not address the health needs of migrant, refugee and incarcerated women, men and children. This problem points to the necessity always, from an economic justice and human rights standpoint, of looking at gender oppression, not in isolation, but as it intersects with other forms of discrimination such as those based on race, ethnicity, class or immigrant status. It also underlines the importance of standards of health provision that are grounded in *human* rights, as well as effective global mechanisms of accountability, enforcement and financing.

On the matter of finances, human rights-based approaches give us a more expansive and hopeful perspective than do the pessimistic constraints of markets or the indeterminate parameters of 'global public goods'. As moral and legal principles, they supersede the assumption that reforms and national budgets must operate within existing limits of scarce resources and that policies to expand public resources must never threaten the sanctity of private property, markets or economic growth. As a terrain of continuing political struggle, they make it possible – as we saw in the example of TRIPs – to assert the priority of human health and well-being over the rights of property. A good case can be made that social and economic rights, as embodied in the

ICESCR, contain an implicit recognition that playing fields are not level and that inequalities must be redressed through explicit redistributional rules and enforcement mechanisms.[50] This is not naïvely to dismiss the problem of resources but rather to point to the simple fact that the twenty-first-century world of global capitalism is packed with resources, only they have been stolen from the 'global public' by the private few.

Ultimately, solutions to the problem of resources will have to engage with the need for mechanisms to fundamentally redistribute the world's wealth – among and within countries, from wealthy countries to UN agencies, and from the private sector to publicly accountable bodies. Without effective redistributive strategies, health reforms in most countries will continue to focus on efficiency rather than human rights, and sexual and reproductive health will continue to be the loser in the process of budgetary and sectoral triage. Alternative approaches to the prevailing conceptual framework of HSRs – and a return to the principle of 'health care for all' *with* gender equality – must identify alternative sources of revenue that will tap into the huge stores of wealth that global capital has concentrated in a few countries, transnational corporations and individuals. They must refute the dogma of scarcity by challenging the injustice of such obscene concentrations of wealth and waste of existing public resources on military violence and corruption. This means abandoning the very concept of 'aid', as groups like the Association for the Taxation of Financial Transactions for the Benefit of Citizens (ATTAC) and others have proposed, in favour of concepts of reparation and global taxation:

> For a real partnership [between Africa and the G8], the concept of 'aid' should be replaced by a common obligation to finance international public investment for common needs. Rich countries should pay their fair share based on their privileged place in the world economy.... Transfers from rich to poor should be institutionalized within what should ultimately be a redistributive tax system that functions across national boundaries.... (Booker and Minter 2002: 5–6)

If women's health groups became more adept in 'broader systems level thinking' and if they were somehow in charge of reorganizing health systems, they too would surely have to face problems of resource allocation and setting budgetary priorities (Evers and Juárez 2000: 57). But transnational women's groups have for years been engaged, in coalition with development and anti-poverty organizations, in advocating a variety of strategies to achieve a more just distribution of global resources. These include: debt cancellation (not just 'relief,' and not just for the handful of countries who meet donor 'conditionalities'); both national and global taxes on international capital flows (so-called Tobin or currency transaction taxes); national taxes on foreign direct investments, linked to labour rights; outlawing of corporate tax havens; demilitarization; a global development fund or Marshall Plan for poor countries; and participatory mechanisms to assure that the revenues acquired from such measures are channelled into health, education and poverty eradication (Francisco 2002; *DAWN Informs* 2002).[51] Susan George of ATTAC says, 'as Bush himself has proven, it's possible to identify, target and close down accounts belonging to anyone the United States identifies as a terrorist – so why not the accounts of drug barons and traffickers in women, children, endangered species and armaments?' (George 2002: 13) In addition, applying the combined concepts of 'global public goods' and basic human rights to such health necessities as clean water, essential medicines, condoms and microbicides might effectively create more resources by taking these goods out of the constrictive domain of market pricing and placing them under public regulatory agencies.

Such strategies are the result of an incipient international civil society participating in UN proceedings like Copenhagen+5 and the Financing for Development Conference and in the World Social Forums in Porto Alegre. Obviously their implementation would require a radical restructuring and realignment of power within existing global governance institutions, including the subordination of the IMF, World Bank and WTO to a much stronger UN system than currently exists. Some have proposed a 'world tax organization' or a new Bretton Woods conference to construct a global financial system that is truly democratic and representative of the world's peoples rather than the privileged site of the wealthiest countries (see Kapstein 1999; Houtart and Polet 2001; and Chapter 6, below). Not surprisingly, within UN forums ideas like a Tobin or currency transaction tax or accountability mechanisms for the IFIs and TNCs have met a wall of opposition led by the US government and joined by its allies in the EU, Japan, Australia, and the corporate sector. Transnational NGOs themselves disagree on a number of issues regarding how to transform the 'international financial architecture' – whether measures for capital regulation are most appropriate at the national or global level; whether FDI is always or ever beneficial for local populations in developing countries; whether the dominant institutions of global capitalism, especially the IMF and the World Bank, can or should be reformed at all or whether they should be abolished altogether.[52]

But proposals for a global Marshall Plan, Tobin-type taxes, or other forms of global capital regulation and accountability come at a historically opportune moment. It is a moment when the heads of the wealthiest US-based corporations are being indicted for high crimes and corruption; when even the mainstream US media openly acknowledge that a $30 billion IMF bailout loan for Brazil is aimed rather at protecting US banking firms than Brazilians; and when millions of working people in the global North are finding themselves closer than ever to the plight of those in places like Argentina, with pensions, life savings and jobs dissolving in air. The time of global capitalism's greatest crisis is a time that invites the most radical public expressions of resistance and transnational solidarity. Whether economic justice *and* gender justice become integral to these expressions will depend on the commitments and strategic insights of women's movements, acting at both global and national levels.

Notes

1 For different versions of the continuity argument, see Petras and Veltmeyer 2001; Smith 1997. For variations of the 'newness' position, see Appadurai 1996; Bauman 1998; Hardt and Negri 2000; Sassen 1998; and Barker and Mander 1999: 1, who characterize globalization as 'the most fundamental redesign and centralization of the world's political and economic arrangements since the Industrial Revolution'. Of course, the neoliberal and mainstream media everywhere tout globalization as a bountiful and inevitable era of closer ties among nations, markets and peoples, though the more liberal among them (such as former US President Bill Clinton and multi-billionaire philanthropists like George Soros and William Gates) recognize and want to correct its inequities (see below).

2 Eisenstein 1998 makes a similar move; see also Brecher, Costello and Smith 2000 and Houtart and Polet 2001, who apply a nearly classical Marxist dialectic to celebrate 'a very different globalization' or 'globalization from below', which they contrast to 'neoliberal globalization'.

3 DAWN calls this the 'marketization of the state'; see Taylor 2000.

4 See World Income Inequality Database at *www.wider.unu.edu/wiid/wiiddoc.htm*.

5 'Nigeria's external debt exceeds a full year's GNP'; Tanzania spends nine times as much on debt servicing as on health care and Ecuador eleven times as much (Sadasivam 1999: 10; UNDP 2000a, Table 5.3). It is still unclear how much of this burden will be lifted by agreements of the G-8 countries to extend debt relief to certain heavily indebted poor countries (HIPCs), since qualifying for such relief is in most cases linked to future economic reforms and other conditionalities. Nor can we know how much, if any, of the resources made available through debt relief will be used to finance health care.

6 Compare a 1999 UN General Assembly report on 'The Role of Women in Development': 'Under the conditions of globalization and market liberalization, it appears that the state's ability to provide social protection and human capital

investment ... has diminished' (UN/General Assembly 1999: 91).

7 The pattern of current global financial flows continues the uneven development of the past. 'Red-lining in the global financial markets' means that whole continents (sub-Saharan Africa) and entire communities (from the slums of Bombay to the migrant worker camps of California) are left out of the flow (Smith 1997). In 1998, 80 per cent of foreign direct investment went to just ten countries, most of them in East Asia and Latin America, while sub-Saharan Africa and South Asia remained 'bad investment risks' (*Business Week* 2000).

8 The gendered impact of global capitalism may in some settings fall more heavily on men. Field, Kotz and Bukhman show that declining life expectancy among young and middle-aged Russian men took a sharply worsening course in the years following imposition of neoliberal market 'reforms' and was directly caused by premature deaths from alcohol abuse, murder, and infectious diseases. They persuasively link this trend to the psychosocial and behavioural impacts of the abrupt transition to capitalism, including high rates of crime, suicide, unemployment and despair. Life expectancy has declined much more sharply for men than for women (58.3 years vs 71.7 years in 1995): 'Russia is on its way to becoming a country of widows and fatherless children. At present rates, about half of all males now aged 16 will not reach the official retirement age of 60' (2000: 159, 167, Table 7.2). However, in these same years, the *increase* in 'loss of working potential' from suicides and alcohol-related deaths (though not from murders) has been much higher for women than for men (see p. 170, Table 7.4).

9 See Eisenstein 1998 for a penetrating analysis of the 'virtual', the 'real' and the just plain mystified in global capitalism; see also Marx and Engels, *The Communist Manifesto*.

10 Stiglitz points out that, after risking 'the wrath of the IMF' by imposing curbs on foreign capital speculation, Malaysia recovered more quickly and successfully from the 1997 crisis than any other Asian country (2002: 93).

11 At this writing, the US was: the only industrialized country to refuse signing the Kyoto Protocol on Global Climate Change, despite compromises designed to meet US objections; one among only a couple of dozen countries that has failed to ratify the Women's Convention and the *only* country that hasn't ratified the Children's Convention; persistent defender of protectionist policies for its farmers and steel industry despite constant trumpeting of 'free-trade' rhetoric; active opponent of the new International Criminal Court and the treaties banning landmines and germ warfare; subverter of a new multilateral treaty to combat illegal small arms trafficking; sole country in the world to threaten an unprecedented space-based defence system and one of a dozen (including Iran, North Korea and China) that has failed to ratify the Comprehensive Nuclear Test Ban Treaty; and proponent of a new doctrine of 'permanent military supremacy' over all the world (Klare 2002). The Bush administration also refused to pay an approved $34 million in aid to UNFPA on the alleged grounds – refuted by its own State Department – that such aid would assist 'forced abortions' and involuntary sterilizations in China. This was on top of imposing the 'global gag rule' on NGOs and health services receiving US aid – see Chapter 2.

12 The two most widely known examples are Joseph Stiglitz, former chief economist for the World Bank and Nobel Prize winner in economics in 2001; and George Soros, the multibillionaire financier and philanthropist (see Stiglitz 2002; Soros

2000, Press 2002). The cascade of US bankruptcies and accounting scandals in 2001–2 – beginning with the fall of the giant conglomerate Enron and extending thereafter to a host of US-based telecommunications and other firms – stimulated a period of public outcry and gestures toward some sort of reform and re-regulation. But at this writing it appeared that the most that might emerge from these scandals would be yet another set of inquiries, government rules and industry self-regulation bodies intended to salvage Big Business's public image and market predictability more than transparency and justice.

13 In a speech to the World Bank Country Directors' Retreat in May of 2001, former US Secretary of the Treasury Lawrence Summers, now president of Harvard University, sharply criticized the idea 'that there would be a generalized improvement in decision making processes by giving more weight to local community [sic]'. Summers cites 'the success of the Asian countries' in 'achieving economic growth' as evidence that 'the move toward empowerment rather than an economic approach' is misconceived. (A copy of this speech was circulated over a large international NGO e-mail network in June of 2001.) Elson and Çağatay (1999) remark that the Bank's mantra about 'national ownership' seems more geared to government finance ministers than to civil society organizations.

14 Successful NGO pressure on Bank policies resulted in its decision to pull out of several dam projects, such as the proposed Narmada Dam in India, which community and environmental groups warn will destroy local livelihoods and ecology. A transnational coalition of development NGOs, also working mainly over the Internet, defeated OECD negotiations for a Multilateral Agreement on Investment (MAI) (G. Sen 1998). Other influential transnational campaigns to influence World Bank policies are the '50 Years Is Enough' network and 'Women's Eyes on the World Bank'. In the case of the highly publicized Narmada Dam, however, the Indian government decided – against advice from the World Commission on Dams and the Bank – to go ahead with its construction.

15 In early 1999, a Bank report delivered 'a blistering evaluation of its own operations in Indonesia', confessing 'that its officials turned a blind eye to corruption, growing repression and a collapsing financial system in the final years of President Suharto's 33-year rule' (Sanger 1998 and 1999).

16 The UNDP goes much further towards radical critique and reform than anything coming from the World Bank. In its *Human Development Report 2000*, it not only insists on a 'human rights approach' to development and poverty reduction – which the Bank almost never does – but even states: '[Growth] can be *ruthless*, leaving losers to abject poverty. *Jobless*, creating little employment. *Voiceless*, failing to ensure participation of people. *Futureless*, destroying the environment for future generations. And *rootless*, destroying cultural traditions and history' (2000a: 81). In its report, *Overcoming Human Poverty* (2000b), after condemning old-style policies of 'supplementing rapid growth with social spending and safety nets' as inadequate (2000b: 38), the UNDP asserts boldly: 'Economic growth cannot be accelerated enough to overcome the handicap of too much income directed to the rich. Income does not trickle down; it only circulates among élite groups' (2000b: 43). Unfortunately, the UNDP's influence and resources *vis-à-vis* global capitalism are miniscule compared to those of any of the IFIs.

17 The most important documents are the 1996 World Development Report, *From Plan to Market*, focusing on the transitional economies of Central and Eastern

Europe and East Asia; the 1998 publication, *Beyond the Washington Consensus: Institutions Matter*, which focuses on the democratizing states of Latin America and the Caribbean and their relation to civil society; and above all the 1997 World Development Report, *The State in a Changing World*.

18 See World Bank 1997: 41–2, 51; World Bank 1998b: 11–13, 44–5, 99, 135; World Bank 1999a: 99; and Stiglitz 1986, 1996. These were the years of Stiglitz's tenure at the Bank and reflect the strong impact of his thinking.

19 The WHO table ranking countries by 'fairness of financial contribution to health systems' ranks Colombia first, followed by mostly European countries and Japan along with Djibouti and Libya and, somewhat less high, Canada, Cuba and the United Arab Emirates. The USA in this ranking is 54–55, along with Fiji; and Vietnam, China and Brazil are very near the bottom, followed only by Myanmar and Sierra Leone (WHO 2000, Annex Table 7).

20 In fact, WHO figures indicate the absence of any positive relationship between the proportion of government spending on health and good health outcomes (see WHO 2000, Annex Table 7). Merely looking at the gross percentage of a country's national budget or GDP that goes toward health tells us nothing about programme priorities, allocation patterns or who benefits – as the coexistence of high spending and inequalities in the US system attests.

21 In its 1999 financial year, the Bank's lending in the Human Development sector totalled $7.3 billion, with 49 per cent going to 'social protection' (pensions, labour market reforms, social funds such as unemployment insurance); 27 per cent going to education; and 24 per cent going to HNP. This contrasts with the total of $12.8 billion that went to Private Sector Development, mainly in finance, transportation and manufacturing. See *Annual Report 1999*, Figures 3.3, 3.4.

22 Apparently this World Bank position, as presented in WDR 1993, gave the green light to the Indian government in its decision in the mid-1990s to abandon curative care, especially hospitals, to the private sector. See Kumar 2000: 35, 102; Sen *et al.* 2002: 425–6.

23 In fact, the Bank's commitment to protecting 'basic social services' and encouraging social sector investments is premised on the assumption of not only a two-tier system but also a trilateralization of social sector financing itself: *public investments* in health, education and infrastructure that concentrate on infectious diseases, clean water and primary and secondary education; *social insurance* programmes (pensions, unemployment) financed by participant payments; and *social assistance* programmes targeted at the very poorest. 'Social insurance programmes', such as pensions and unemployment insurance, may involve a mandatory savings component or regular payments by the insured, while 'social assistance programmes' are subsidies to the poor and may involve *quid pro quos* such as work requirements (World Bank 1997: 55–8). On 'safety nets', see also Elson and Çağatay 2000; UNDP 2000b.

24 In what follows, I will be addressing some of the underlying ideological and political assumptions of approaches to HSR as they have been formulated at a global level, rather than their applications in particular country contexts. Reports at a recent meeting convened by the journal *Reproductive Health Matters* to examine the relationship between HSRs and sexual and reproductive health/rights in some 15 country contexts and internationally suggested, in fact, not only a wide disparity in country-level applications, but also that the highly technical methodologies of

HSR such as DALYs (see below) are mostly being ignored at the country and local levels. Accordingly, I shall pluralize 'HSRs' to reflect the disparities between academic models being produced by international health economists and the apparently wide variations in reforms that are actually taking place within different countries.

25 In the past few years, several efforts to generate dialogue between health reformers and sexual and reproductive health advocates have taken place, sponsored variously by the Center for Health and Gender Equity (see CHANGE 1998), the Ford Foundation (see Ford Foundation 2000 and 2002), *Reproductive Health Matters* (see previous note) and the World Bank (see 'Adapting to Change: a Learning Programme on Population, Reproductive Health and Health Sector Reform', at *www.reprohealth.org*). It is still too soon to know the impact of such efforts on policy. Tangcharoensathien (2002) charts the correspondence between the goals and targets adopted at ICPD+5 and 17 indicators for monitoring sexual and reproductive health developed by WHO, further suggesting the potential for synergy.

26 This publication is no longer in print and can only be accessed through libraries or on CD-ROM. Its original premises have undergone substantial revision, as indicated in various issues of the *WHO Bulletin*. The funding figures that follow come from a presentation by Tom Merrick, former Senior Population Adviser at the World Bank's HNP Department, at a meeting held by the Rockefeller Foundation in October 1999; and *The World Bank Annual Report 1999*, available on the Bank's website (*www.worldbank.org*).

27 Within its total HNP lending, the Bank had committed about 30 per cent, or $780 million, to some 36 reproductive health related projects as well as '$690 million to 46 countries for HIV/AIDS prevention and care' by the end of 2000. It had also pledged an additional $600 million to improving existing HIV/AIDS prevention, care and treatment programmes on a region-wide basis in Africa and the Caribbean (Epp 2001: 2).

28 Two factors have shaped the HNP agenda: the strength of NGO advocacy and research, and the unusual commitment to gender and integrative perspectives of the sector's former Senior Population Adviser, Tom Merrick.

29 As an outstanding example of this 'multisectoral approach', it cites the Bank-funded Malawi Social Action Fund, which supports schools, reproductive/ maternal and child health facilities, community water sources, women's employment opportunities and rural/urban markets, plus requiring that at least one-third of Community Project Committee members be local women. See World Bank/HNP 1999, Annex 5.

30 I will address the issues of decentralization in Chapter 5, in the context of evaluating national-level efforts by women's health groups to provide services, implement ICPD, and monitor sexual and reproductive health programmes.

31 Standing (2002a: 10) cites the Health and Population Sector Programme of Bangladesh as a new SWAP that not only includes many elements of the ICPD agenda in its Essential Services Package but also integrates these with 'child health care, communicable diseases, limited curative care', and a focus on 'improving the health status of poor rural women and girls'. Thus far, however, little improvement is evident – in part because of a lack of 'political commitment' among national and local officials but also, I suggest, because of the absence of the enabling conditions

contained in a broader interpretation of the ICPD POA. Such conditions would include politically empowering women as citizens, NGOs and public officials to influence health policy and implementation.

32 The argument echoes an ongoing debate among public health scholars about the relation between health sector spending and actual improvements in health. Many find evidence 'that the health sector and medical advances have played very little part in explaining the improvements of health of populations in the long term' (Leon and Walt 2001: 7; see also WHO 2000, Annex Table 7). In the Zambian experience with HSRs, on the other hand, the 'essential health package' does include water and sanitation as well as MCH, family planning, malaria, tuberculosis, and HIV/AIDS/STDs. But there are insufficient resources to pay for the package. See Nanda 2000: 18.

33 The TAC brief in the South Africa–PMA case (see Chapter 3) emphasized 'the interconnectedness of the private and public health services' in South Africa, in so far as poor people increasingly utilize both (Heywood 2001: 10). In India people below the poverty line receive 80 per cent of outpatient care, 40 per cent of hospitalizations, over 30 per cent of institutional deliveries and 27 per cent of antenatal care through private sector providers (Ravindran 2002; Sen *et al.* 2002: Table 11.6).

34 Under heavy lobbying from such groups, the US Congress in its 2000 foreign aid appropriations bill attached a requirement that the US would not fund debt relief in HIPCs if user fee requirements were attached (Dunne 2000; Epstein 2001).

35 Many thanks to David Peters of the Johns Hopkins School of Public Health who first called my attention to the fact that some proponents of HSR within both WHO and the World Bank, who are focused more on health systems, reorganization and financing, consider themselves in an opposite camp to the 'disease lobbies', focused on developing objective and value-neutral measures to identify the most costly diseases. But this only reinforces my contention that HSR – and the Bank's health policies – are inherently riddled with contradictions.

36 Reidpath *et al.* (2001) give an excellent summary of the various evolutions of the DALY, particularly the ambiguous vacillations between the concepts of 'disability' and 'handicap' and the equally confusing stance of Harvard University's Christopher Murray – the DALY method's principal author – regarding the omission of any contextual factors versus the estimation of an 'average social milieu' (2001: 61–2). Regardless of these shifts, however, the underlying assumptions seem the same. What is much less clear is the influence of this kind of measurement at the level of national and local health departments. Anecdotal evidence at the RHM Bellagio meeting in February 2002 concerning experiences in some two dozen countries would seem to suggest that the DALY has had little or no impact at these levels. Reidpath *et al.*, on the other hand, assert (without offering specific evidence) that it 'has been adopted by governments, multilateral agencies and researchers' at a 'staggering' rate (2001: viii).

37 These NGO-initiated campaigns are also very different conceptually, in so far as they make human rights rather than utility and cost-effectiveness the centre of their approach (see my discussion later in this chapter).

38 Compare Reidpath *et al.* 2001: 9, 65–6, who also point out the relentless advocacy of the DALY proponents and the self-justifying premise in their claim to be context-free and value-neutral.

39 Reidpath *et al.*, noting the later shift by DALY proponents from a 'disability weight' free of any context to an estimate of an 'average social milieu' applicable globally, point out similarly that such an estimate would be valid only 'if the average social milieu within each region [or country or locale] were the same as the global average milieu' (2001: 7) – in other words, reducing all social milieux to a global norm amounts to decontextualization. See also Allotey and Reidpath 2002.

40 For example, black women of all classes in the US are nearly four times more likely than white women to suffer preventable maternal deaths (Stolberg 1999a, 1999b; see also A. Sen 2001 and Breen 2000).

41 WHO criticizes 'the primary health care movement … for giving too little attention to people's *demand* for health care, which is greatly influenced by perceived quality and responsiveness, and instead concentrating almost exclusively on their presumed *needs*' (WHO 2000: 15). But the DALY/GBD framework, developed and applied religiously by the WHO, leaves even less room for assessing user perspectives on the quality of care.

42 Christopher Murray has embraced this gender, race and class-neutral 'fairness principle' explicitly as the ethical foundation of the DALY (see Murray 1994; Murray and Acharya 1997; see also Rawls 1971).

43 Leon and Walt define the difference between a 'human capital' approach and a 'capabilities' approach: 'while in the former everything is ultimately measured against the yardstick of economic activity, [the latter] places at the centre the individual and their [sic] capacity to achieve their own goals' (2001: 15, n. 4; A. Sen 1999: 74–5).

44 As Brundtland's time as Director-General of WHO came to an end, in 2002–2003, the organization seems to have taken a stronger turn towards a human rights approach in its public presentations. See the entry on 'Health and Human Rights' on its website, at *www.who.int/hhr/en/*; the Director-General's fervent (but unsuccessful) appeal to the UN Commission on Human Rights to undertake formal consideration of possible violations of the human right to health of Iraqi citizens – especially women, children, the elderly and the disabled – subjected to US military invasion; and her pledge to incorporate a human rights framework 'as a useful guide for analysis and action' across WHO's activities (*www.who.int/dg/speeches/2003/ commissionhumanrights/en/*).

45 Standing reports that the Gates Foundation in 2000 alone devoted 15 per cent of its budget ($212 million) to reproductive and child health and 26 per cent ($367 million) to 'conditions associated with poverty' (HIV/AIDS, malaria and tuberculosis).

46 Theoretically, if essential medicines were categorized as a 'public good', then governments might retain the patents (along with control over pricing and distribution to facilitate universal access); or as a 'global public good', then the WHO might become the patent holder; or the patent system might be dispensed with altogether. This is the thinking of MSF's Drugs for Neglected Diseases Initiative (DNDi), which seeks to foster 'a paradigm shift from market-driven to needs-driven drug development, with public responsibility and leadership in both developing and developed countries' (see 'DNDi, the Drugs for Neglected Diseases Initiative, Concept and Preliminary Proposal', at *www.msf.org*, and Chapter 3 above).

47 Examples abound: exclusive real estate in 'fresh air' sites, bottled water, Internet

commerce, privately run prisons, patent battles over the genetic code, and increasing subcontracting of state activities to private firms. The argument I am making here may sound like a cynical version of market fundamentalism, but the premise I have in mind is the converse: that *no* process of commodity production and *no* market transaction is 'essentially private' – that is, immune from social or public consequences.

48 I shall address the problems of such 'partnerships' in greater depth in Chapter 5.

49 The paragraph of the ICESCR allowing 'developing countries' to exclude 'non-nationals' from economic rights (Articles 2–3) is very unfortunate in this regard.

50 Only in one paragraph, concerning the right to 'an adequate standard of living' and 'adequate food' (Article 11), does the ICESCR explicitly require states 'to ensure an equitable distribution … in relation to need'. Nonetheless, the formulation of all these rights – to work, food, housing, health care, etcetera – as human rights in the first place creates a presumptive obligation to generate the necessary resources to make them real.

51 Organizations like DAWN and WEDO were proposing such solutions to the problem of resources as early as 1995, in the context of the Beijing Women's Conference and the WSSD (see Chapter 2). ATTAC, based in Europe, leads the effort at present.

52 See *DAWN Informs*, March 2002 for a cogent summary of debates that took place in a session on Controlling Capital Finance at the 2002 World Social Forum.

5 Implementing International Norms at the National Level

Women's Health NGOs in the Firing Line

The global environment in which transnational and national women's health movements are trying to turn the promises of Cairo and Beijing into practical realities is an increasingly discouraging one. As the previous chapter described, that environment consists of (1) macroeconomic policies aimed at growth, 'free trade' and minimal 'safety nets' rather than eradicating poverty, creating conditions of social justice and increasing human well-being; (2) weakened capacity of national institutions responsible for health and development relative to those responsible for policing and security; and (3) a dominant approach to health reform that emphasizes cost-effectiveness and aggregate statistics about 'life years' over better lives for women and girls. Since 11 September 2001, a right-wing US regime has channelled colossal resources into its 'war against terrorism' and assumed a posture of arrogant unilateralism; this, combined with economic declines everywhere, has made already disabling conditions dismal. In a global climate fraught with danger and backlash, access to the highest attainable standard of health care, including sexual and reproductive rights, becomes part of the collateral damage.

And yet this larger, grimmer picture is not the whole picture. As we saw earlier, advocates for access to medicines did achieve some important victories even after 11 September. The idea of health as a human right has won major constituencies in countries like South Africa, Brazil, and even to some extent the US, as more and more people are seeing their health security disappear in the debris of corporate bankruptcies and downsizing. And popular movements in Latin America, Africa and Asia – often with women at the forefront – are challenging corporate power holders over the right to a decent life and livelihood. A synergy between transnational struggles for health and other social and economic rights and national and local movements for justice occurred in the aftermath of Cairo and Beijing. Perhaps the most useful outcome of women's participation in the UN conferences of the 1990s was that it provided focus and coordination for advocacy and social change efforts at the national level. With so much stake in the documents they themselves helped to shape, transnational women's NGOs went back to their countries during the 1990s armed with guidelines to help them evaluate existing reproductive and sexual health services and rights and to advocate for improvements in quality and access. The human rights framework of the documents as well as their emphasis on NGO and civil society participation strengthened the authority of women's groups to inform and empower

Local organizing to bring Cairo and Beijing alive: the Asmita Resource Centre for Women

The Asmita Resource Centre for Women in Hyderabad works mainly among *dalit*, tribal and other marginalized groups. Its networks extend throughout the state of Andhra Pradesh and provide an integrated programme linking campaigns and popular education in many areas: gender violence, economic development and workers' rights, legal and cultural literacy, bridging communal and language divisions, promoting the work of women writers and artists from both Muslim and Hindu communities, and strengthening the access of women and girls to health services, including reproductive and sexual health. Asmita's 'Self-Help in Health' programme culminated in the publication of *Nâ Shariram Nâdhi* (India's version of *Our Bodies, Ourselves*) and a programme to train rural traditional birth attendants; and the group's campaign against sexual harassment in the workplace helped to influence an important judgment and guidelines for employers on sexual harassment issued by the Indian Supreme Court in 1997.[1]

In so many of its projects, Asmita connects the principle of 'my body is mine' to a critique of dominant population and macroeconomic policies and a vision of a more equitable distribution of power, resources and information across genders, castes, classes and age groups. Asmita's core team teaches the provisions of the Beijing Platform, the Cairo POA and the Women's Convention in its work with grassroots urban and rural women, as sources of legitimacy for a women's empowerment agenda. As the principal NGO responsible for disseminating the Beijing Platform in South India, Asmita has distributed thousands of posters and documents and created a cloth scroll emphasizing the intersections among women's rights to livelihoods, literacy, control over their bodies, political participation and health; and of all these with such macroeconomic necessities as debt cancellation, full employment, minimum and equal wages, enhanced social sector budgets and land reforms.[2]

grassroots women about their rights and to hold their governments to account. This is true despite the severe external constraints imposed in nearly every country by the disabling environment I have summarized. Whether it can remain true in an era of endless 'war on terrorism' and the global security colossus is something I will ponder in the final chapter.

NGOs as country-level implementers and monitors

Cross-country surveys conducted by transnational coordinating groups such as DAWN and WEDO reveal that the Cairo POA and the Beijing Platform are alive and well at the country level – thanks largely to the efforts of women's NGOs like Asmita who have become their *de facto* caretakers and implementers on the ground. But the extent to which these efforts thus far have resulted in any concrete policy changes or improvements in health services and enabling conditions varies greatly from one country context to another. The surveys also show that actual applications of HSR, as opposed to technocratic theories, are highly context-specific; their direction in practice depends as much on the political will and ideology of government agencies and the skill and commitment of feminist advocates as on the availability of resources. Moreover, although virtually all sources report major expansion of private financing and provision of health relative to public,[3] when we look more closely at the national setting it would appear that the very concept of 'privatization' is too abstract and over-generalized. We need to deconstruct this concept in the light of actual practices to know what we are talking about even when we refer to the 'private sector'. For-profit corporations? Non-profit NGOs? Religious institutions? Grassroots CBOs, either religious or secular? Or some hybrid arrangement of these and public sector agencies? And in each case, there are issues of scale and power. It makes a big difference whether the NGO in question is an international giant like CARE International or IPPF or a locally based and always under-resourced, overextended group like SOS-Corpo in Brazil or Asmita in Hyderabad.

DAWN's survey of post-Cairo implementation efforts involved 23 countries in five geographical regions (see DAWN 1999). With regard to concrete outcomes of implementation, DAWN's assessment is decidedly mixed but with a cautiously optimistic tone overall. Primary among its findings is the 'effective impact' the ICPD process – helped very much by the momentum and energy of Beijing – has had 'across the South'. This impact is evident in both 'a semantic revolution', incorporating the language of reproductive and sexual health and rights, and a number of positive long-term developments towards reformed policies and services. These include:

1   Official abandonment of demographic targets in some countries (such as India, Indonesia and Thailand) where abuses have been rampant in the past;

2   Integration and cross-sectoral coordination of women's health, MCH and family planning services in some countries (such as Brazil, Uruguay, Nicaragua, Philippines and Ghana);

3   A broader definition of reproductive health since Cairo to now include components such as interventions against domestic violence (South Africa), breast and cervical cancer treatment and prevention (Brazil, Mexico, Philippines), and HIV/STD treatment and prevention (virtually everywhere); and

4   A number of reforms expanding women's access to legal abortion, trained providers and follow-up treatment for post-abortion complications (liberalized laws in Guyana, Cambodia, Ghana, Mexico and South Africa; more modest reforms in Brazil, Bolivia and Namibia).

On the negative side, however, DAWN found as many disturbing trends in most of the countries surveyed. These include the persistence of verticality and resistance to 'integrative efforts' in many health programmes; a continued imbalance in resources, with programmes renamed 'reproductive health' but family planning still receiving 'much bigger' allocations than other components; the constraints of 'health reform', including the proliferation of privatization and cost-recovery schemes that 'keep the poorer populations (rural, women, old persons) away from hospitals and health centres'; and the prevailing inadequacy of financial resources and dependency on international donor assistance. DAWN's analysis observes that not only is there an absolute scarcity of resources at the country level but '*quality* of expenditure is as critical as the amount of resources invested'. Thus, for example, while 'reduction of maternal mortality … requires investments in primary health programmes to be combined with improvement in referral systems and obstetric assistance … in the current scenario, donors are reluctant to fund infrastructure, and structural adjustment requirements curtail domestic investment' (DAWN 1999: 37–40). Again, the macroeconomic disabling environment looms large.

The WEDO survey – encompassing 50 countries represented by nearly 100 NGO and 18 government respondents – confirms DAWN's findings but with an even more pessimistic set of conclusions. 'All respondents to this survey', it notes, 'cite economic reforms as paramount constraints in implementing the ICPD Programme. Health sector reform in particular is emerging in most countries as a challenge to expansion of reproductive health services' (Sadasivam 1999: 10). As documented in the previous chapter, nearly every-where that user fees and commercialization of services have been introduced, the results have been detrimental for women as health service clients, health workers and household managers. The decline in public spending and the commodification of health care have resulted in hospital closures in Peru and Russia. In Ukraine and Bulgaria they have led to a disproportionate and risky reliance on repeat abortions because women cannot afford contraceptives at market prices. At the same time, trends in public spending on health reflect a pattern of widespread unevenness, even among low-income countries. In sub-Saharan Africa alone, based on WHO estimates for 1997, public health expenditure as a proportion of general government expenditure ranged from 2.2 per cent for Guinea-Bissau to 15.4 per cent for Zimbabwe, with most countries ranging somewhere in between (Musgrove et al. 2002: Table 1; Standing 2002a). While per capita spending on health in most HIPC countries is under $10, in India it is $21 and in Sri Lanka $18. In some countries (such as Egypt, South Africa, Nigeria and Bangladesh) total health – including reproductive and primary health – expenditures since the mid-1990s have actually increased significantly (Standing 2002a: 13; Forman and Ghosh 2000; Sadasivam 1999). Yet there are few systems in place to determine precisely where and how additional funds are being spent and no evidence that larger gross expenditures have translated into actual improvements in access to or quality of primary and sexual and reproductive health care for poor women in these countries.

Decentralization of services and decision making, a common aspect of health reform, was also a strong objective of the Cairo and Beijing frameworks and their emphasis on empowering women and increasing civil society participation. But all reports suggest 'the jury is still out on the benefits of decentralization in health'. Whether or not it succeeds in empowering women's groups and local communities or 'simply [shedding] responsibilities from the central government' depends on the extent to which devolution of responsibility is accompanied by devolution of capacity and resources (World Bank 2000/2001: 86). In certain countries, decentralization has in fact meant an increase in efficiency and in access for poor and rural women. Yet the devolution of services from the central government to district or local governments – or to NGOs – also frequently entails the transfer of greater authority and responsibility without adequate finances, equipment and staff. The WEDO survey and case studies by HERA members have uncovered troubling signs that locally based women's health and other NGOs are being pulled into a global privatization strategy that 'empowers' them with too few resources to do too much – what Standing calls 'unfunded mandates' (2002a: 16). Especially in countries that are most dependent on international donor aid and where governments have enacted structural adjustment policies that reduce their own commitments in the social sector, women's NGOs have been recruited to take up the slack in service provision – just as individual women have been expected to take on added caretaking burdens within households. Moreover, women are unlikely to benefit from decentralization as long as traditional patterns of gender, class and caste subordination prevail within local communities: 'unless the question of who constitutes the community is understood and addressed upfront, men and local élites may dominate decision making and capture project benefits' (World Bank 2000/ 2001: 90). Yet the objective behind decentralization of health programmes and services – to create participatory, democratic models of health care management and decision making – remains absolutely vital.

One manifestation of NGO involvement in national and local-level implementation efforts is what UN and neoliberal jargon has come to call 'partnerships', that is, working relations between private sector or civil society groups and governments, IGOs or international donor agencies. The political implications of such partnerships are ambiguous at best. On one hand, women's and other transnational NGOs have consistently demanded that their voices and views be heard and that they be given an equal 'place at the table' in all policy-making arenas. Hence the repeated statements in all the 1990s UN conference documents, that governments and international organizations should strengthen 'partnerships with the NGO sector' and integrate civil society groups into the policy-making process, are clearly a hard-won NGO achievement (ICPD POA, Chapter 15). Recognition as serious participants in the implementation and monitoring of international agreements is an important step in the development of an international civil society and democratization of the UN system. On the other hand, under existing conditions the concept of partnership between NGOs and most governing institutions, whether at the national or the international level, raises many troubling concerns. Often, more than coopting women's NGOs, national governments and UN agencies seek partnerships with NGOs when their own control over resources and implementation mechanisms is in decline; women's groups find they are 'empowered' within increasingly powerless and bankrupt institutions. Or else, as in the case of the World Bank and most governments, the balance of power remains very one-sided.

Analysing the contradictions in the World Bank's approach to NGO and community participation helps to illuminate the pitfalls for women's health groups in 'consultation' or 'partnership' arrangements. First, there is a tension between the Bank's advocacy of strong governing institutions and its cultivation of relations with local NGOs as a buffer against government corruption or incompetence. By working directly with communities and NGOs, the Bank may perpetuate the weakening of the state's role in providing social services, especially in those countries where states are already weak. By gingerly deferring to the sovereignty of states, on the other hand, it may undermine the participatory involvement and capacity of NGOs. Second, the Bank's purpose of forming partnerships with NGOs and CBOs at the international and country levels is severely limited by the fact that such involvement is ultimately on the Bank's terms. The handful of NGO members of World Bank consultative groups are appointed as individual experts, not as representatives of social movements or even organizations. Within countries, Bank project administrators can decide which NGOs and CBOs will participate or be 'consulted'; there is nothing in the Bank's mandate to assure that community or NGO representatives are democratically selected or that all groups affected by a project are included. Above all, there is still no international mechanism within the UN system to assure Bank accountability and transparency either to citizens within countries undergoing 'restructuring' or to an embryonic global civil society.

In the best of scenarios, will NGOs – particularly women's NGOs – find themselves doing public sector work without public sector authority and with inadequate resources? Will they unwittingly help to further the process of privatization, relieving the state (or IGOs) of responsibility for providing universally accessible social services and for enforcing private sector compliance with human rights standards? The vast inequality of power and resources between large institutions and NGOs not only undermines the possibility of real partnership but creates a Catch-22 situation in which, to 'build capacity' among NGOs so that they can 'come to the table' with dignity and respect, the dominant party in the partnership must play the role of donor.

Herein lies the danger of cooptation and NGOs becoming distanced from social movements and their critical, transformative visions (Häusler 1994).

In order to make a more accurate assessment of the role women's NGOs have played in promoting implementation of reproductive and sexual health and rights at the national level, I will look at a number of country-based case studies. Some of these involve NGOs as monitors and critics of government practices with regard to the ICPD POA – in other words, acting as advocates of women's rights from the vantage point of civil society and sometimes in opposition to the state. Others involve NGOs as subcontractors of government or large donor agencies, acting as direct service providers or implementers of Cairo commitments and therefore in some sense within or *in the place of* the state. Still others represent new kinds of policy-making and executing partnerships that may – or may not – signal alternative models of governance. In no way does this small and rather arbitrarily selected group of cases represent a scientific sampling of what women's health movement activists are doing in so many countries across the globe. The cases were selected only to illustrate the complexities of trying to situate reproductive and sexual rights in the context of social development and the variety of strategies that women's groups in very diverse settings are using to link those rights to a broader set of issues.[4]

Women's groups in India probably have the longest experience of dealing with state policies related to population, family planning and reproductive health, since the Indian state was one of the first to adopt an official family planning programme as part of its first Five Year Plan in 1951. (Ram 1999; see also Health Watch 1998; Visaria and Visaria 1999; Rishyasringa 2000). For most of its history India's family planning programme epitomized the kind of demographically driven, target-based approach that has tended to create so many abuses and to alienate women's groups in many countries. Under the pretext of development and even redistribution of resources, the programme has aimed above all to reduce fertility by promoting provider-controlled methods (mainly sterilization, but also IUDs and hormonal implants); using a system of positive and negative incentives; and imposing family size quotas on lower-level workers through an administrative apparatus controlled from the top.[5]

Despite protests and criticisms by women's health groups and other NGOs, and despite several attempts in the 1980s to integrate family planning with family welfare and child health programmes, the official focus until the mid-1990s continued to be raising the 'number of accepters' and reducing the number of births. But this narrowly defined policy, oblivious to women's health needs, had already begun to shift even prior to the ICPD, due in large part to pressures from organized women's groups in India but also to concerns within the government that the programme as it existed simply was not working. 'Obsession with contraceptive targets had become an end in itself ... decoupled from its original goal of fertility reduction' (Health Watch 1999: 69). Birth rates in most states were falling very slowly if at all, clinic workers were feeling harassed, and clients were dissatisfied with the low quality of care. Thus the Cairo conference was timed perfectly to reinforce calls for reform and recommendations by a government-appointed expert group in 1993 for a new national population policy that would have a 'pro-nature, pro-poor, pro-women and pro-democratic choice approach' (Mallik 2002: 9).

The result of all of these pressures for change before and during ICPD was two government/World Bank sponsored programmes, introduced in 1996, for a new direction in service delivery: the 'Target-Free Approach' (TFA) and a more integrated reproductive and child health programme (RCH). Major elements of the new policy included: (1) eliminating method-specific demographic targets; (2) moving to 'client-centred programme management', including an emphasis on 'gender sensitivity' and quality of care; (3) expanding the range of contraceptive choice; (4) providing an 'essential package of reproductive and child health services' that would include prevention and treatment of STIs and RTIs as well as family planning services and MCH; (5) male participation in family planning; and (6) involving both NGOs and *panchayats* in implementing and monitoring the new policy.[6] NGOs specifically are supposed to have a complementary role to that of government, including involvement in community-level advocacy, counselling, screening, funding and monitoring (Health Watch 1998; Nayyar 1999; Pachauri 1999; Mukherjee 2002). In addition, the new RCH programme was supposed to be organized on a multisectoral basis – coordinated by the Ministry of Health and Family Welfare but also involving ministries such as Welfare, Urban Development, Rural Development and Education (Kumar 2000).

India's new post-ICPD population policy was hailed by many observers as marking a welcome 'shift in paradigm' on the part of the government, 'from a top-down, male-dominated, bureaucratic, target-driven programme, to client-friendly, gender-sensitive services that respond to people's needs' (Pachauri 1999: xv, xliii; Health Watch 1998: 73). No one questions that such a shift is difficult and will take time, given India's enormous poverty and entrenched

Health Watch in India: monitoring the 'Target-Free Approach'
(excerpted from A. Nayyar 1999)

In 1994, a network of voluntary organizations, researchers, activists and concerned individuals formed a civil society organization, Health Watch. This organization is committed to monitoring post-ICPD action in the country. This was a significant development because, for the first time, researchers worked together with activists on health matters, particularly those who had been working at the grassroots level with no access to research data. Along with other civil society organizations and individual activists, Health Watch continued to put pressure on the government to remove method-specific targets and adopt a holistic reproductive health approach. By establishing a dialogue with the highest level of government, it provided inputs to health and related policy matters.

Health Watch organized a regional consultation on the preparation of a manual and facilitating feedback to the government. In addition, Health Watch discussed the proposed reproductive and child health programme [RCH] during these consultations. It lobbied government officials, facilitated and organized orientation and training programmes, and accessed and disseminated information. These consultations led to several recommendations to strengthen reproductive and child health service delivery.

The experience of Health Watch demonstrates how, through advocacy, a network of NGOs can provide feedback to the government. Though NGOs in India provide a small proportion of health services, they are more concerned with improving the quality and outreach of public services. The government has been wary of activist NGOs and the relationship between the two has not always been smooth. By initiating a dialogue and using alternative advocacy strategies, Health Watch has shown that there are several areas of mutual collaboration.

gender, class and caste hierarchies. Yet assessments thus far by observers close to the mainstream HSR perspective are strikingly more sanguine than those of women's health groups, especially Health Watch (see **Box 5.2**). Evaluators associated with the Population Council in India describe the new programme's 'essential package of services' design in terms that uncritically replicate the DALYs/'burden of disease' framework and associate 'programme performance' with the old counting of births and contraceptive/sterilization 'accepters' (Pachauri 1999: xvi, xxi–xxii; Khan and Townsend 1999). A World Bank consultant and management specialist in India notes that health workers in some states appear happier with the new decentralized management scheme, since it involves them directly in a 'community needs assessment' exercise involving their own 'guesstimates' about contraceptive needs and targets. He agrees with programme managers that the notion of gearing services to clients' expectations is not very useful, since 'in terms of health care, clients do not have clear expectations and are not able to evaluate service quality' (Murthy 1999: 131, 134–5). Apparently forgotten are the new criteria of eliminating targets altogether and adopting 'client-friendly,' 'gender-sensitive' and participatory practices.

In sharp contrast with these evaluations, reports by Health Watch and its associates find many 'weaknesses and anomalies' in the TFA as it is currently being implemented. They remark that in most cases, while the rhetoric is progressive, attitudes of service providers and programme administrators remain fundamentally unchanged (Health Watch 1998). Their review confirms that numerical targets and quantitative methods of evaluating performance are still firmly in place, only now determined at the local or district rather than the national level. The reforms seem to empower, not clients, but auxiliary nurse-midwives, whose entire training is geared towards 'quantitative achievements': 'Client segmentation [by existing number of children] and target-setting are still of primary importance to the government…. [W]e have still not shaken off the old regime' (Health Watch 1999: 9, 15). Moreover, while abortion has been legal in India since 1972, public abortion services remain virtually unavailable to poor women because of the lack of trained doctors in small towns and rural areas. Nor have services been set up for treatment of RTIs, so common among poor women in India,[7] or to address 'the needs of adolescents, male sexual behaviour, issues of violence, and the gender relations that shape sexual and reproductive behaviour. The underlying assumption, once again, is that only women who are married and in the reproductive age group will have services focused towards them' (Health Watch 1998: 71–2).

How the TFA has worked in practice, however, seems to vary across different Indian states. Visaria and Visaria found health workers in Tamil Nadu pleased that 'the pressure is off' (for meeting family planning quotas) because they 'are able to inquire about women's health, their children's health' and are 'better accepted in the community' when people identify them not just 'as family planning workers' but as general family care providers. Clients in Tamil Nadu also perceive 'that the pressure to accept sterilization has lessened, and that the health workers inform and encourage couples [at least, those with fewer than two children] to accept reversible methods' (Visaria and Visaria 1999: 92–5, 99). Kumar (2000) found a similar sense of relief among health workers in neighbouring Kerala. It would thus seem that implementation of the programme on the ground depends very much on the local culture of health provision and awareness, which is very different in different regions and states.

Overall, the policies of India's central government since ICPD seem to involve a complex veneer of 'women's empowerment' and gender/social justice rhetoric over old attitudes and practices (Mukherjee 2002). In February of 2000 the central Indian government introduced a new National Population Policy (NPP) that incorporates many of the more progressive and expansive elements of the RCH and adds attention to 'drinking water, fuel, fodder, child care centres, access to primary health care' and nutrition. But the same policy also recodifies traditional gender roles and returns to a narrow focus on the 'reproductive years', neglecting the needs of adolescents and post-menopausal women (Mukherjee 2002: 7). Most disturbing of all, both the NPP and new independent population policies adopted in six states seem to be leaning 'toward active promotion of a two-child norm [and] rejection of the ... TFA' (Mallik 2002: 11). In particular, some states (especially Rajasthan, Andhra Pradesh and Uttar Pradesh) have adopted policies that officially reinstitute some of the most abusive practices of the past: numerical targets for sterilization and long-acting hormonal contraceptives, and incentives and disincentives intended to curtail births among the poorest and most marginalized groups. These include such blatantly unethical policies as promising health insurance to 'couples below the poverty line who undergo sterilization with not more than two living children' (and thus withholding it from those who do not); giving preference for land allotments to 'accepters of sterilization with two or less children' and cash awards to couples who adopt permanent methods of contraception; denying access to government jobs, *panchayat* seats and education in government schools to those who fail to adhere to the two-child norm; and rewarding (or punishing) local governments and *panchayats* with more (or less) funding and development resources based on their 'performance' (Mallik 2002: 12–15; Mukherjee 2002: 8–9).

Both Mukherjee and Mallik stress the egregious (and unconstitutional) ways in which such policies linking social welfare benefits and democratic rights to fewer children are certain to worsen the conditions of the most disadvantaged groups in India – Scheduled Castes and Scheduled Tribes, who already are the poorest of the poor; Muslims, who tend to have higher fertility rates than Hindus; and the women of all these groups, who have the least power and receive the fewest resources within their households and communities. Health Watch has pointed out that women rather than men within couples will bear the brunt of punitive fertility policies, since many men will abandon wives and children rather than be disqualified from local elections or government jobs (Mukherjee 2002). At the same time, the resurgent fixation on numerical targets and negative and positive incentives is illogical, since a number of the states that have imposed draconian policies (such as Andhra Pradesh) have experienced 'a sharp fertility decline' in recent years, and 'a significant fertility transition is under way in large parts of India' (Mallik 2002: 14; Mukherjee 2002: 10).

So how should we understand this retreat and the perversion of 'women's empowerment' and 'decentralization' into old-style coercion, gender bias and racism (only shifted this time to the state and local level)? Mukherjee wonders 'if the NPP 2000 is just a "showpiece" to the rest of the world to display India's attempts to incorporate the Cairo mandate' while retaining targets and human rights abuses 'at the ground level under state supervision' (2002: 10). It would also seem that decades of enforcing numerical targets have become a deeply ingrained habit in provider, official and community cultures; that 'obsession with contraceptive targets' has indeed become 'an end in itself' (Health Watch 1998, 1999).[8] On a larger scale, however, we might ask whether India's most recent population policies represent a back-lash against the ICPD framework and the transnational and national women's movements that have so strongly – and with apparently limited success in India – advocated policies that promote women's equality and their reproductive and sexual rights. Indeed, they may mark a backlash against women's participation in the policy-making process altogether.

On the matter of *panchayat* and NGO involvement in decision making in India's 'new' approach to reproductive health, recent experience does not encourage optimism. A survey by Mukhopadhyay and Sivaramayya suggests caution about romanticizing women's role in the *panchayats*. They point out that women's election to these local councils is still a far cry from their empowerment and that they are still reluctant to speak out in public settings, especially on issues as taboo as reproductive and sexual rights. Actual empowerment of women in local decision-making bodies, they observe, requires their involvement in 'a support structure' of women, such as feminist NGOs with strong ties to the local community (1999: 344–7). As for government intentions to involve women's NGOs in implementing and monitoring the RCH programme, there too progress seems very limited. Health Watch reports a reluctance of national and state government officials to dialogue seriously with the women's groups whose participation the new policies were supposed to bring about, or to hold themselves accountable in any real way:

> Shortly after the ICPD, the government invited a number of NGOs to a workshop to discuss 'partnership' in the post-ICPD era. It became clear at this meeting that the government and many NGOs have rather different conceptions of partnership.... Although the government is now more willing than before to involve NGOs in service provision and support activities ... [it] is generally wary about (and some bureaucrats are openly hostile to) open debate and discussion about policies or programmes. NGOs in this view are seen as a tool rather than as partners who can play a valuable role through dialogue and advocacy.... Despite the existence of a strong women's health movement in India as evidenced by the number of dedicated NGOs and networks ... NGOs are rarely invited to any platform for dialogue with government, nor are they included in district-level RCH committees, nor do they participate anywhere in framing the health sub-centres' Action Plans. (Health Watch 1998: 73)

The Indian case is one in which the government, though formally democratic, distances itself from civil society organizations, and women's NGOs remain frustrated advocates and critics outside the public health system rather than genuine partners. What the work of Health Watch tells us is that the critical scrutiny and oppositional role of NGOs with regard to ICPD implementation, health reform initiatives and human rights enforcement in India – including insistence that the Indian state live up to its own democratic and constitutional principles – is both more vital and more contested than ever. The case of Egyptian NGOs involved in combating FGM in their country is somewhat different. There NGOs themselves maintain distrust and distance from an autocratic government that continues to play both sides between secular and Islamist groups and engages in harsh legal repression of NGO activity, especially in the area of human rights.[9] 'Partnership' with government under these authoritarian circumstances is out of the question; vigilant critique and external pressure, including broad coalitions among diverse NGOs, remain imperative, though also dangerous, for activists.

The FGM Task Force exemplifies this model and has been one of the most effective women's health advocacy groups in the Middle East, despite considerable political and economic constraints and a public focus on one of the most sensitive and controversial issues in the reproductive and sexual rights panorama. Its work is an important example both of how transnational interactions contribute to the strategies and conceptual frameworks of local campaigns and how national NGOs have attempted to link campaigns in the area of reproductive and sexual rights to broader issues of women's empowerment and development. Formed as an 'umbrella coalition' in late 1994 under the auspices of the National NGO Commission on Population and Development (organized to follow up ICPD implementation), the Task Force originated in conversations in 1993 between Nahid Toubia – a Sudanese doctor based in New York but educated in Egypt and founder of RAINBO[10] – and Egyptian leaders who had previously worked on the FGM issue. While the tendency of Egyptian NGOs 'to approach social issues in terms of rights rather than services' surely predated these exchanges, the RAINBO acronym conveyed an explicit emphasis on women's control over their bodies and the principle of bodily integrity that fits well with concerns of the Egyptian women's movement about violence against women and harmful traditional practices. The ICPD, with the world's eyes on Cairo, provided a catalysing and legitimizing context allowing Egyptian NGOs to come together from a variety of perspectives (health, human rights and feminist) to bring new vitality and public awareness to the FGM campaign (Helmy 1999; Seif El Dawla 1999).[11]

While the Egyptian Task Force is structured as an open, inclusive coalition, its ideas and strategies are strongly shaped by feminist perspectives. First, the group decided to retain the terminology of 'female genital mutilation' rather than the more neutral 'female circumcision' or 'genital surgery' and to advocate 'its unconditional denunciation, regardless of the name' (Helmy 1999: 2; Seif El Dawla 1999).[12] Second, its political and ethical stance puts key emphasis on issues of women's right to bodily self-determination and sexual pleasure in the context of their right to equality and full social development. This stance sees the practices grouped under the term 'FGM', whether or not they 'involve actual cutting', as intended to acculturate young girls to believe 'their bodies are sinful and dangerous, that they are social property and should ascribe to social norms and values in the way they relate as women to their bodies'. The campaign to ban FGM 'is about women's ownership of their own bodies and culture' and thus becomes inscribed within a much larger political struggle:

> Those who opposed our activism against FGM were not only motivated by a desire to preserve tradition or custom but were working hard to prevent any positive change in the balance of power between government and NGOs, religious and secular groups, and men and women. They sought to maintain existing patriarchal hegemony and deny women the right to self-determination. (Seif El Dawla 1999: 128, 133–4)

The strategic importance of taking an approach to the issue that emphasized women's human rights and bodily integrity rather than 'health hazards' became clear in the controversy over FGM that emerged in the aftermath of ICPD. During and immediately after the conference, Islamist organizations in the country mobilized in support of FGM (and against women's rights groups) 'as a tradition that constitutes part of Egyptian identity ... and morals, as opposed to the ethics and morals being "imposed" by the West' (Seif El Dawla 1999: 132). In response to this political pressure, the then Minister of Health issued an unprecedented decree permitting the

The Egyptian FGM Task Force: linking FGM to social and economic justice

(excerpted from Seif El Dawla 1999: 133–4)

[T]he political fight over FGM [waged by the Egyptian FGM Task Force] has become a matter of standing up for the status of women in Egypt. It concerns the winning of democratic rights by the young Egyptian women's movement, who need to express their own perspectives and present their own views on tradition and religion, instead of having their views dictated by other political forces and paying for this with their own flesh, whether through compliance or resistance.

•••

For us, the struggle against FGM involves promoting the welfare of women and their right to take full control of their lives, not conducting a battle against women who circumcise their daughters. Both those women who do circumcise their daughters and those who do not are the supporting armies in this battle. Every day, they make choices based on their own needs, on what permits them to maintain a respectable and accepted role in society, and on what they can afford socially and politically.

•••

[One] problem with certain international attempts at addressing FGM has to do with consistency in using a human rights discourse. Organizations who wish to support Egyptian efforts in combating FGM should have a comprehensive approach to the multiple human rights issues that exist in Egypt, and not be selective about what they support and what they are ready to turn a blind eye to. It is inconsistent, for example, to be troubled by the practice of FGM and ignore broader health policies that deprive poor women – who are the majority of women in Egypt – of the basic right of access to the minimum level of primary health care. An organization that supports the privatization of health care services in Egypt is hardly in a strong position to advocate the eradication of FGM on human rights grounds.

practice by medical doctors in public health institutions – ostensibly to avert the negative health consequences of 'back-street' FGMs. But a series of events resulted in the reversal of this decision in the courts and reaffirmation of the older law banning the practice. These included the deaths of several young women circumcised in hospitals; the appointment of a new and more sympathetic Minister of Health; a public declaration by the Sheikh of Al Azhar University, supreme religious authority in the region, that FGM has no religious or scientific basis; and vigorous organizing and advocacy by the FGM Task Force (Seif El Dawla 1999).

The Egyptian Task Force attributes its own effectiveness thus far not only to its strong grassroots base and inclusive, open organizing methods but also to the breadth of its analysis: 'we have pushed the debate further – FGM is no longer an isolated issue' but has been embedded firmly in a women's rights, human rights and 'development gender approach' (Helmy 1999: 1, 3). Such an approach signifies the integral links between a matter that, steeped in tradition, seems quintessentially 'cultural', and a broad range of other political, economic and social conditions indispensable to gender equality and development for women. In other words, it illustrates the *indivisibility* of rights discussed earlier. Yet the Task Force's integrated approach is fully aware of the deeply ingrained cultural and social influences that perpetuate the practice and that motivate women themselves to adhere to it despite the pain and humiliation it causes them. Both the 1995 Egyptian Demographic and Health Survey, which indicated that fully 97 per cent of ever-married women aged 15–49 had been circumcised, and the qualitative research of the IRRRAG team in Egypt show the pervasive acceptance of the practice and the insufficiency of legal action alone to eliminate it. Young women in the IRRRAG study saw circumcision as 'a passport into social acceptance and belonging', while their mothers viewed it as necessary to win their daughters suitable husbands (Seif El Dawla *et al.* 1998: 85; Egypt, National Population Council 1995). The campaign against FGM, as the Task Force fully realizes, has to be part of a long-term struggle for women's full empowerment (see **Box 5.3**).

An ironic dimension of the Egyptian case is that, while Cairo hosted the 1994 ICPD, five years later the holistic approach to reproductive and sexual health prescribed in the POA is still virtually non-existent in the host country. One significant step toward integration of services that did occur in Egypt shortly after the conference was the dissolution of the Ministry of Population and the transfer of its functions to the Ministry of Health (MOH). But this measure has not in the slightest deterred the strong trend begun in the 1980s towards privatization of health services in the context of SAPs, application of cost-recovery mechanisms, increasing prevalence of fee-for-service facilities, and the dominant role of external donors, especially USAID, in determining health priorities. The adverse consequences of these patterns for women's reproductive health include a disproportionate emphasis on family planning to the exclusion of other vital services; declining access of Egypt's huge impoverished population to increasingly expensive treatment (especially to drugs, which have soared in price); continued high maternal mortality due to high rates of anaemia and the fact that few births are attended by trained personnel; and exclusion of women, who are more often unemployed and generally not covered by their husbands, from employer-sponsored health care (Sadasivam 1999; Seif El Dawla 1999).[13]

Seif El Dawla demonstrates how the defeated effort to medicalize FGM reflected the trend towards privatization and user fees in health delivery. Most doctors in Egypt, she notes, are 'underqualified, underpaid and under-motivated'; doctors belong to one of the society's most hierarchical and conservative professions. Being able to perform FGM in public hospitals for a fee would have offered them 'a new source of income at women's expense' (1999: 132–3). Their alternative, of course, is to flee the public sector for private (and unregulated) practice – a trend encouraged by USAID and government loans to private practitioners. NGOs may also participate in the privatization process and become fee-for-service providers to 'fill the gaps left by the state's withdrawal of support for basic services'. But their participation in monitoring quality of care in either the public or the private sector is severely restrained by the harsh laws governing NGO activities in Egypt and the exclusion of NGOs or clients (as opposed to medical, insurance and donor groups) from limited government efforts to evaluate public health care (Sadasivam 1999). This larger context makes the success of the Egyptian FGM Task Force all the more remarkable. Indeed, recent research findings on FGM in Egypt show that girls who were 10–19 years old in the post-ICPD years are significantly less likely than their mothers' generation to have undergone FGM (El-Gibaly et al. 1999). While this is truer of girls in Lower Egypt and urban areas and daughters of more educated women, it does suggest that the coalition's advocacy campaign is beginning to have a real impact at the level of social norms and the empowerment of girls, as well as at the level of state policy.

In addition to the strategies of internal monitoring of government services and programmes (Health Watch) and national coalition building and popular

No to impunity: the case of Marina in Peru

(written by members of Movimiento Manuela Ramos, with special thanks to Frescia Carrasco)

Marina is a 23-year-old woman who lives in Puno, a city located 3,000 metres above sea level in southern Peru. Her native tongue is Quechua. In Puno she works as a street vendor, and it was during one of her trips to the town that she had an accident. As a consequence, she began to have headaches, so she decided to go to the doctor. On 15 January 1996, she went to the public hospital of Puno for medical help. That day the public hospital was on strike, and she was seen by the general practitioner, Salmón Horna, who, using the opportunity of a gynaecological examination, raped her. This sexual assault produced vaginal bleeding and a state of severe emotional suffering, leading her to consider suicide.

Marina's *via crucis* began after the rape, continuing to this date. In pain, sad and alone, she felt that this crime should not remain unpunished, so she reported it to the national police. They tried to persuade her to withdraw her accusations, telling her that a physician could not commit rape. When she persisted, they conducted the medical legal examination without the necessary sanitary conditions, such as using rubber gloves, risking her health and aggravating her vaginal bleeding. During the court proceedings, Marina faced humiliation and a gender-biased system, as demonstrated, for example, during the face-to-face confrontation, where her aggressor was allowed to humiliate her. The unfair, months-long and discriminatory court proceedings concluded in the Superior Court of Puno. The verdict, based on gender bias and an arbitrary evaluation of the evidence, declared the rapist innocent, and the crime was left unpunished. The terrible events experienced by Marina not only damaged her physically and emotionally; they also affected her family and her community.

Domestic channels having been exhausted, and considering that national public health officers and administrators of justice had violated Marina's human rights, the Latin American and Caribbean Committee for the Defence of Women's Rights (CLADEM) and the Center for Reproductive Law and Policy (CRLP) brought her case to the Inter-American Human Rights Commission in April 1998, charging the Peruvian state with violations of the Convention on the Elimination of All Forms of Discrimination Against Women (CEDAW) and the Inter-American Convention to Prevent, Sanction and Eradicate Violence Against Women. In March 1999 the Commission granted a hearing, attended by Marina. The Commission's mediation resulted in an amicable solution among the parties. CLADEM and CRLP (now CRR) are monitoring the implementation of the agreement.

education (Egyptian FGM Task Force), country-based NGOs are increasingly utilizing the jurisdiction of international treaty bodies to investigate and report national violations of women's reproductive and sexual rights. For example, the Polish Women's Federation for Family Planning produced an 'alternative report' that it presented to the UN Committee on Economic, Social and Cultural Rights (which monitors the ICESCR) documenting the damaging consequences for women's health of 1990s legislation severely restricting abortion in Poland and the failure to provide family planning services through the public health care system.[14] This generated an expression of concern and explicit recommendations from the committee (Stanchieri *et al.* 1999). Likewise, national and regional women's health NGOs in Mexico, Peru, Nigeria, Zimbabwe and elsewhere, acting in concert with the US-based CRLP, have produced detailed 'shadow reports' on reproductive rights violations in those countries to present to the semi-annual sessions of the Committee on the Elimination of All Forms of Discrimination Against Women (CEDAW, charged with monitoring the Women's Convention).[15]

In the case of Peru, CLADEM has been particularly vigilant in publicizing atrocities as well as bringing them to the attention of international human rights bodies. In 1996–7 CLADEM and other women's NGOs in Peru helped to document the rampant forced sterilization of poor, rural and indigenous women in some towns, where providers believed that fulfilment of quotas was a condition for job retention and promotion. The coercive tactics such women experienced ranged from 'tubal ligation festivals' promoting surgical sterilization (and no other methods) free of charge, to promised gifts of food and clothing, to 'aggression, intimidation and humiliation'. Ultimately, the unsanitary conditions under which the procedure was performed resulted in three women's deaths, and Peruvian women's NGOs called for the resignation of the Minister of Health (CRLP/CLADEM 1999: 63; Sadasivam 1999; Sims 1998). Women's NGOs in Peru have also worked to expose other forms of physical, psychological and sexual abuse of women in Peruvian hospitals and clinics. The particularly horrifying case of Marina, raped by a public health doctor in his private office under the pretext of a gynaecological examination, was the first sexual rights case to be brought before the Inter-American Human Rights Commission – thanks to the persistence of Peruvian women's health and rights groups (see **Box 5.4** and CRLP/CLADEM 1999).

The influence of women's health NGOs such as CLADEM and CRLP in refocusing and broadening the range of issues the treaty bodies address is clearly significant. In its report to the Peruvian government in August 1998,

CEDAW noted its 'concern that there is a close link between the number of abortions performed and the high maternal mortality rate' and stressed 'that criminalizing abortion did not discourage abortions but rather had the effect of making the procedure unsafe and dangerous for women'. In striking contrast to the US-imposed 'global gag rule' that would come just one year later, it thus recommended that the Peruvian government 'review its law on abortion and ensure that women have access to full and complete health services, which include safe abortion, and to emergency medical attention when complications arise from abortions'.[16] In addition, it expressed concern about lack of information and 'access to adequate contraception among poor women in urban and rural areas, indigenous women and teenage girls'; high maternal and infant mortality and teenage pregnancy rates; as well as the prevalence of 'malnutrition and preventable diseases' among poor women and girls. Finally, it made clear that addressing these serious deficiencies in the Peruvian health system would require attention to the problems of poverty: '[The Committee] notes that the main factor which affected women … in the most disadvantaged sectors was *lack of resources* to avail themselves of medical care when needed' (quoted in Stanchieri *et al.* 1999: 183–4, italics added; see also Center for Reproductive Rights 2002, Chapter 4).

It is too soon to know whether these human rights claims and reports to governments will have any positive effect on the actual quality of health services in the countries involved. Certainly there are limits to the strategy of appealing to international and regional human rights bodies that can only offer 'expressions of concern' and recommendations lacking any enforcement power. Yet such a strategy – especially if combined with a strong media campaign – can embarrass and create international moral pressure on governments and thus strengthen the influence of NGOs as advocacy groups in the national arena. Moreover, the determination to utilize existing human rights machinery as a vehicle for national-level advocacy both reflects and reinforces a commitment to building civil society and the role of NGOs as monitors of government compliance with international agreements. This is particularly true in most of the Latin American countries, where women's health groups are strong and emerged as part of broad movements for democratization and citizenship rights. Within such a politicized culture, the Latin American and Caribbean Women's Health Network sees monitoring as an expression of 'the belief that *this civil practice is essential to development*' (LACWHN 1998: 4).

NGOs as service providers in lieu of the state

Peru is a complex case, since its women's health NGOs operate simultaneously at all three levels analysed here – advocacy, service provision and partnership with government agencies. Yet this is the scenario in many countries where women's health movements with many years of experience operate in the context of (a) a strong, progressive civil society base and (b) a philosophy of community participation and empowerment. From such a perspective, the old family planning vocabulary of 'service delivery', 'provider' and 'client' no longer applies, connoting as it does a one-way flow (usually of contraceptives to 'accepters') rather than a reciprocal process of communication and learning. ReproSalud – the innovative project initiated in 1995 by USAID and Peru's Movimiento Manuela Ramos (Manuela) – is in no sense a 'service provider' in conventional terms. Its role is better understood as that of *facilitator* of women's empowerment to achieve better reproductive health services and outcomes; and its situation as *in between* the public (state), the local community, and the private (household, individual).

Initially funded for five years by a $25 million USAID grant (renewed for another five years in 1999), ReproSalud has been described as a 'rare example of a large-scale donor-funded project that truly seeks to fulfil the spirit of the ICPD Programme of Action' (Coe 2001: 7). Rather than 'delivering' products or counselling, its objective is to improve the reproductive health of periurban and rural women by empowering the women themselves and their CBOs to make their own decisions and demand improvements in health services. Emphasizing preventive and participatory methods, the project aims to 'actively [involve] women in identifying, prioritizing and resolving their own reproductive health problems' and to make sure women's perspectives are fully incorporated into all levels of health care design and delivery. Its process of participatory research (*autodiagnósticos*) and training of community women as educators, advocates and trainers of others is grounded in a theory of collective action, self-help and the rootedness of sexual and reproductive health in social conditions and life context (Rogow 2000). Thus, in addition to cultivating women's sense of entitlement, ReproSalud also seeks to address the 'socioeconomic, cultural and gender-based barriers that prevent them from making decisions' (Coe 2001: 7).[17] The income-generating projects, designed to give both the organizations and the individual women greater autonomy and sustainability, are obviously an important part of this agenda (see **Box 5.5**). More recently, '[establishing] dialogue with men at the

Creating grassroots participation in reproductive health services: the ReproSalud project in Peru
(excerpted from Galdos & Feringa 1998)

ReproSalud is comprised of three components that work together to facilitate women's involvement:

1. *Community-based reproductive health*: Manuela Ramos seeks to work with approximately 200 women's community-based organizations (CBOs) to serve as ReproSalud counterparts in almost 1,000 communities throughout Peru. For each CBO, the process begins with an a*utodiagnóstico*, a participatory qualitative research technique that creates a trusting environment for women to reflect on personal experiences and beliefs as they relate to reproductive health. Such reflection enables women to identify their reproductive health needs. Based on their understanding of the concepts of severity and frequency, women then prioritize their needs by voting for the most important problem.

Through another participatory process, each CBO develops and implements [small, sequential] subprojects to address the prioritized problem. ... After being trained by Manuela [promoters elected by each CBO] go out into their communities and conduct educational sessions with women. Promoters' efforts are supported by educational modules that Manuela has prepared. ...

In subsequent subprojects, popular education continues to be emphasized, but activities that complement the Ministry of Health's (MOH) service delivery are also included. ... Thus, in some areas where women have called for improved counseling in contraceptive methods, CBO promoters are being trained in counseling and referring women to health posts. In other areas where maternal mortality is a concern, CBO promoters are being trained to identify women with high-risk pregnancies, to educate them about their risk factors, and to refer them to the local health post. Throughout all subprojects, CBOs are encouraged to inform local authorities and MOH personnel about their activities and to use these encounters to voice concerns and demands.

2. *Advocacy*: This component builds on and strengthens the subprojects in the reproductive health component by encouraging women to channel their concerns to authorities and to hold them accountable for adequate responses. This is done at the community level by the presidents of the CBOs, gathered in Reproductive Rights Defence Committees, who negotiate directly with health authorities. At the regional and national levels, ReproSalud brings women from different communities together to share experiences, develop common solutions to common health problems ... and to hold government officials accountable for promises made the year before. ... Meanwhile, Manuela Ramos participates in the larger movement for the human right to health and human rights coalitions.

3. *Income-generation*: This component was incorporated to respond to the economic and gender barriers that rural women face to using existing health services. By increasing women's access to credit and markets, and by changing the control of resources within the household, women will be more able to direct financial resources to their reproductive health care. Two activities comprise this component. The first, village banks, increases women's access to microcredit. The second is the commercialization of handicrafts. [It] calls for first identifying market niches and then designing goods and training women to produce for those niches.

community level' has become another important part. Focused only on women at the outset, ReproSalud, when urged by the community women, later took on the task of involving men as trainers and workshop participants. Giving men an 'opportunity to learn about their bodies and about sexuality' and to discuss problems of alcoholism, violence and communication within families, has become one of the most vital aspects of ReproSalud's mission (Rogow 2000: 15–16).

Clearly the undertaking of ReproSalud in Peru was a highly risky and unprecedented venture for both Manuela and USAID. At the time of the initial grant, no autonomous NGO identified with the women's movement – in the region or perhaps in the world – had received such a large sum of money from any donor, much less USAID; and Manuela was subjected to considerable criticism from other feminist groups, suspicious of collaboration with an agency notorious for its hardline population control policies. For USAID also this was alien territory. The agency had never invested in a feminist project that had no interest in traditional family planning or delivering contraceptives and 16 per cent of whose total budget was devoted to empowerment and income-generation activities seemingly unrelated to population or health (Rogow 2000). Coe suggests that a sizeable core of officials within the agency remained sceptical about, if not altogether hostile to, funding such a heretical project. Further, ReproSalud's qualitative, participatory methods hardly meshed with the bureaucratic evaluation measures of cost-effectiveness and numeric indicators.

Meanwhile, the Peruvian government under Fujimori, despite having signed the ICPD POA, was anything but a 'partner' for ReproSalud. The stark contrast between the documented abuses of women's reproductive and sexual rights committed by government and private health providers in Peru and the participatory methods of the ReproSalud project point to an undeniable reality: in many national settings, the women's NGOs who originated the feminist values that permeate the ICPD POA are the organizations *best qualified to put those values into practice*. Often avoiding public health services because of the indignities they suffer there, rural and indigenous women no doubt find ReproSalud's approach more compatible with their needs and desires.

At the same time, such extensive NGO collaboration with a large inter- national donor and the national government creates hard dilemmas for previously autonomous NGOs like Manuela. One of the most perplexing, as Manuela's members fully recognize, is the tension inherent in '*the dual role of collaborating and critiquing*' (Galdos and Feringa 1998: 32). This tension arose in regard to both the coercive government sterilization campaigns and the medical rape case described in **Box 5.4**. In the former case, feminist NGOs found themselves caught between genuine atrocities in the public health services and the eagerness of right-wing religious forces to use these incidents to repudiate all public sector family planning programmes. The result was an ineffective period of attempting 'quiet diplomacy' before finally coming out publicly to oppose sterilization abuse. In the rape incident, Manuela referred the case to CLADEM-Peru 'because it did not want to jeopardize its tenuous relationship with the MOH' (Galdos and Feringa 1998: 29). That relationship was corroded from the outset by 'suspicion and jealousy toward the project', with MOH officials resenting the transfer of substantial funds and responsibility to a feminist group and CBOs rather than its own staff (Coe 2001: 31). Manuela's reliance on CLADEM shows the advantage of a large and unified feminist movement able to devise a kind of 'internal–external' division of labour *vis-à-vis* the state. But it also shows the delicacies of the 'internal' position and its potential for compromising a strong advocacy role.

The 'fine line' between seeking agency support and collaboration and 'advocating for changes in … reproductive health programmes' (Coe 2001: 31) became even more apparent at the international level, when Manuela's members found themselves faced with the US government's repressive 'global gag rule'. As Victoria Villanueva and Susana Galdos wrote in a letter to President Clinton protesting the violations of human rights and freedom of speech entailed in that law:

the Manuela Ramos Movement would not have signed an agreement with USAID if this law had been part of the original cooperative agreement. We are now in the difficult position of having to choose between needed funding for a historic project, on the one hand, and essential democratic participation on the other. Either way, there is a cost to women's reproductive health and to democracy in Peru. (Villanueva and Galdos 2000; Cohen 2000: 139)

The Peruvian example illustrates other problems that arise when women's health NGOs take on major functions as service providers or monitors. In the case of ReproSalud – expected to facilitate an alternative model of reproductive health care for much of the country – the administrative and managerial demands are staggering, and a budget that at first appears quite large for an NGO begins to seem meagre relative to the task. More serious than the problem of resources is the fact that Manuela, while performing major public health functions, is not part of the public sector and has neither the *authority* nor the *accountability* of a government agency. So it sits tenuously in between the public and the private – and relieves the public sector of responsibility. These limitations become particularly salient when we consider the issues of 'partnership' between NGOs and governments or multilateral agencies and the need to strengthen rather than replace public services, discussed below. Yet without the activities of Manuela Ramos through the ReproSalud project, it is highly doubtful whether feminist approaches to reproductive health would be available at all to impoverished and indigenous Peruvian women. This is even truer in countries where public health services are virtually non-existent because of the weakness or collapse of state institutions – in Tajikistan, for example.

In Tajikistan the NGO Ghamkhori's Khatlon Women's Health Project (KWHP) is making it possible for a highly impoverished and predominantly Muslim population to have access to basic reproductive health and nutritional knowledge and resources that public authorities – still unable to provide an adequate level of jobs and services after ten years of independence – have neither the means nor the will to provide (see **Box 5.6**). Like ReproSalud in Peru, Ghamkori eschews any notion of imposing a 'basic package of health services', relying instead on the felt needs of the local residents. Nor does it focus strictly on family planning but integrates contraceptive methods into a more comprehensive set of health and infrastructural needs that are both preventive and cost-effective – from education about physiology and nutrition to cleaning up drinking water sources. The emphasis of Ghamkori on

Involving men: the Khatlon Women's Health Project in Tajikistan

by Colette Harris, Virginia Tech University

The Khatlon Women's Health Project (KWHP), run by the Tajik NGO Ghamkhori and largely funded by Christian Aid of London, has been in existence since 1997, originating as a result of discussions between myself – then a researcher on gender issues in Tajikistan, CIS – and local women concerned about the position of poor, rural women in the post-Soviet period. KWHP grew out of Freirian principles of education as an empowering process as well as the international women's movement, with its emphasis on women's and girls' rights and the crucial role of reproductive and sexual health services. A vital part of the project's empowerment strategy is the inclusion of men and boys in educational activities.

KWHP works in the villages of southern Tajikistan most affected by the civil war of 1992–7, which exacerbated the severe economic downturn following the dissolution of the Soviet Union. The project's overarching goal is to support participants to increase control over their lives and environment. To this end it starts by encouraging each village to form management committees to take on responsibility for the project and 'contract' the services of Ghamkhori. The NGO then sends in a team of a midwife and four educators – one each for men, women, girls and boys – who will spend one day a week in a village over a six-month period. The educators facilitate group discussion sessions, with the participants choosing the topics and drawing up the timetables. To ensure that sessions prioritize the participants' knowledge and ideas, varied tools are used, including story telling, role playing, listing, sorting, ranking and visual aids such as picture cards. The chief role of the facilitators is to insert pertinent questions to aid in critical thinking, reflection and building problem-solving skills.

Subjects chosen for discussion include health issues such as malaria and typhoid, reproductive issues such as the working of the reproductive system, childbirth, contraception and STDs/AIDS. Teenagers receive sex education, and boys not only learn the function of the clitoris for satisfying their brides-to-be but are also helped to understand the positive effects of showing respect and affection. Additional themes emphasized include women's and children's rights, family violence, and the importance of the more powerful family members – men and elders – respecting the opinions and rights of the less powerful. In other words, the objective is gender training.

The midwife provides reproductive health services, including family planning, infertility clinics, well-baby clinics, and support for victims of domestic violence. She also trains village medics in improved diagnostic skills, minimal antibiotic use and communication skills. The educators help enhance the capacities of local schoolteachers and collaborate with religious leaders. Since traditional law and popular Islam are far more constraining on women than the *Qor'an*, the latter is frequently consulted on matters of rights. Young people, especially young women, are very empowered by learning about the freedoms granted in Islam and that traditional practices may be opposed without contravening religious laws.

In May 2000, with funding from the Swiss Development Organization and the Lombard Odier Bank, Ghamkhori opened a women's centre in the town of Kurgan Teppa, where their office is located. The purpose of this centre was in part to provide educational and medical support for urban women but mainly to provide psychosocial, legal, sexological and gynaecological support for victims of gender-based violence, who can be walk-ins or referrals from another project. Male staff also work with the police and other relevant bodies to sensitize them to women's issues through gender and rights training.

After the project ends in each village, the committees both serve as liaison between the community and Ghamkhori and help make the project sustainable by supporting the population in their adoption of new practices. While male committee members help organize bus services and clean drinking-water sources, women police problem families to provide support against domestic violence. The overall results of these projects have been reduced violence and increased warmth among family members and communities, where the inhabitants are restoring the infrastructure the state can no longer provide. Project participants have learned problem-solving and management skills that give them an increased sense of hope and well-being, enabling them to improve their lives despite the persistent problems of the post-Soviet period.

Ghamkhori's success stems from its commitment to participants taking joint responsibility for projects, setting the agenda and keeping control during educational sessions. For the first time people are getting together to exchange ideas and are learning to form their own independent opinions, which they find very empowering. Above all the emphasis on gender training has begun to produce real changes in male–female relationships. Inclusion of men and boys in the project has been critical, since their support is essential for the production of social transformation.

integrating both religion (used as a means of empowerment) and men and boys into its activities is not unique, as ReproSalud shows, but it is remarkable. Clearly this project illuminates the possibilities of transforming service provision into an educational and empowering experience and of making 'male involvement' an opportunity to bridge traditional gender divisions.[18]

In various country contexts feminist alternative models of reproductive and sexual health education are providing new information and learning experiences that reach out not only to women and men but also to youth – again, in ways that state-administered health programmes are unequipped and unprepared to do. In Nigeria – which embarked on the road to civilian democracy after decades of military dictatorship in 1999 – women's groups have made extraordinary recent advances in the area of sexuality education for adolescents. This achievement is all the more remarkable given the national political and economic context: a persistent colonial legacy of ethnic and sectoral divisions and government corruption and mismanagement; endemic rural and urban poverty alongside tremendous oil wealth that gets siphoned off by national élites and transnational corporations; a fledgling and fragile democratic state, in formation only since the 1999 elections; a history of containment of, if not disdain for, independent women's NGOs (those not officially sanctioned by the state); and a less than encouraging record when it comes to implementing international commitments regarding public health services and reproductive and sexual rights (Abdullah 1995; Ikeji 1996; Osakue and Martin Hilber 1998). While the Nigerian government endorsed the ICPD POA and the Beijing Platform, it has allocated very few resources to carrying out their provisions – owing in part to SAPs and the perceived necessity of public sector contraction, and in part to absence of political will. Nigerian women lack any access to emergency obstetric services, and abortion is illegal except in the case of life endangerment to the woman, resulting in high risk of maternal death. In addition, 'National health policy ... only emphasizes maternal and child health and family planning and focuses more on population numbers than on quality of life and well-being' (Sadasivam 1999: 47; see also Osakue and Martin Hilber 1998). Meanwhile, the government has decided to invest $283 million in a new soccer stadium (Onishi 2002).

The Nigerian government's obliviousness to reproductive and sexual health issues outside the reproductive years, and particularly to issues relevant to adolescents, has persisted until very recently despite the alarming statistics published in its own country report for ICPD. These include 'that 2 out of every 5 secondary school girls have had at least one previous pregnancy; 150 out of every 1,000 women who give birth are 19 years old and under; over 60 per cent of patients presenting at Nigerian hospitals with abortion complications are adolescent girls; abortion complications account for 72 per cent of all deaths among young girls under the age of 19 years; and 50 per cent of the deaths in Nigeria's high maternal mortality rate are adolescent girls, due to illegal abortion' – all of which contributes to very high school expulsion and drop-out rates and early marriages for girls. Most distressingly, officials readily admit 'that most of the cases of HIV positive persons known at present are in the age range of 15–24 years' (AHI 1999: v, 5).

Government inertia or complacency has never stopped women's NGOs in Nigeria from engaging in vigorous advocacy and service provision activities – usually the two combined – with whatever internal and external resources they have been able to muster. True to form, several national women's health NGOs who have been involved in transnational meetings and networks – especially Action Health Incorporated (AHI) and Girls' Power Initiative (GPI) – began working concertedly after the Cairo conference to fill the gap in implementation activities related to adolescent reproductive and sexual health. One part of this effort was to develop a national policy for adolescent sexuality education, the other to carry out that policy through concrete education and outreach services in local schools and communities. The *Guidelines for Comprehensive Sexuality Education in Nigeria* – endorsed by the country's National Council on Education and Federal Ministry of Education as well as over 80 national organizations – are being integrated into public school curricula at the local level. Funded by the US-based MacArthur Foundation and adapted to Nigeria's particular cultural and social needs from guidelines previously developed by the Sexuality Education and Information Council of the United States (SEICUS), the document's overall aim is to address issues of adolescent sexuality 'more proactively in order to substantially reduce unwanted pregnancies, unsafe abortions and STDs/HIV/AIDS' (AHI 1999: 13). The Guidelines are intended to provide a broad framework for schools and other institutions, not to be a curriculum in themselves, and thus to accommodate the very diverse religious and ethical perspectives that characterize the country.

A glimpse at the Guidelines' content reveals a degree of breadth and openness present in few societies in the world, including in so-called developed countries. The Nigerian Guidelines pay careful attention to: (a) *age-appropriateness* (four stages of development, beginning with ages 6–8 and ending with ages 18–24, or young adult); and (b) the *complexity of sexual experience* (six key concepts, including 'human development,' 'relationships', 'personal skills', 'sexual behaviour', 'sexual health' and 'society and culture'). Avoiding moralism or dogma, they encompass a wide range of diversity in sexual orientations, experiences and family forms. They attempt to inform young people thoroughly and accurately about the ways to avoid sexual abuse, disease and unwanted pregnancy, while emphasizing the pleasures and satisfactions that consenting human sexual relations (of diverse kinds) can bring when exercised wisely (AHI 1996).

As important as their content is the creative *process* by which Nigerian women's NGOs have nurtured the Guidelines from an idea all the way through to a national policy, and then taken major responsibility for implementing that policy at a grassroots level. Key to this process was the convening in 1995–6 of a National Guidelines Task Force consisting of relevant government ministers, representatives of IGOs such as UNICEF and WHO, academic researchers, and a very wide range of women's health, religious, media and professional (medical, teachers', family planning) organizations. The diversity of the Task Force helped to mobilize a broad base of support for the Guidelines despite considerable religious and conservative opposition. This, along with a focused media campaign and a high-profile national conference featuring dozens of youths speaking out on their own behalf ('Youths Speak, Adults Listen!'), succeeded in translating advocacy into official policy. Moreover, in addition to educating policy makers and working directly with youth to increase their knowledge, communication skills and self-esteem, GPI organizers have engaged in community outreach to parents, thereby gaining the support of parents and local communities for their work (Esiet and Madunagu 1999).

In some ways, the Nigerian sexuality education case study resembles that of the Egyptian FGM Task Force, in so far as it reflects the transnational travel and adaptation of feminist ideas and the formation of a broad-based national coalition to implement the ideas at home. In Nigeria, however, it has been left to the determination and skills of women's NGOs to administer and carry out the policy in local schools, teen and parent groups and community-based organizations. In contrast to the situation of ReproSalud in Peru, the Nigerian groups do not depend for their financing on either their own government or that of the US. Yet the negative side of this independence is that women once again – with insufficient resources, infrastructure and power – are doing all the work. Moreover, they must contend with a split between what political leaders say in international forums, especially in their eagerness to placate the conservative position of the US government on adolescents and sexual rights, and their much more supportive policy at home.[19] This variation of what Latin American feminists call a *doble discurso* is obviously preferable to that described by Barbara Klugman with regard to the Southern African countries, in which political leaders make public statements supporting the necessity of empowering women and youth in sexual decision making, yet in 'actual policy' restrict school-based sexuality education programmes to messages that emphasize abstinence only or the most technical and 'gender-blind' information (Klugman 2000; Shepard 2000). Yet the contradictions are nonetheless frustrating for the work of women's NGOs.

In the Caribbean, women's health NGOs have also been preoccupied with implementing Cairo by providing reproductive and sexual health services to adolescents in order to stem the tide of very high teenage birth and fertility rates in the region as well as the rapidly rising rate of heterosexual HIV transmission among young people. Similar to the Nigerian case, NGO activity in the Caribbean takes place in the context of moderately cooperative governments whose motivation and capacity as providers are severely constrained by macroeconomic pulls, shrinking resources and global trade inequities that put small island economies at a disadvantage. Thus women's health NGOs find themselves once again in the position of primary implementers and providers by default. Caribbean women's groups have focused specifically on projects to increase 'male responsibility and partici-' pation in meeting the ICPD goals', to address not only teenage pregnancy and HIV/STI infection rates but the alarming growth of male violence, child prostitution and sex tourism. They see these problems as directly related to growing poverty and the larger macroeconomic context:

> NGOs have ... challenged the chronic state of uneven development and inequity in the region, and reaffirmed the urgency of addressing the economic, social and political structures that reproduce inequities between men and women in their relationships within families and communities. ... With health expenditures shrinking, sexual and reproductive health information, education and services have become significantly inaccessible to the poor. The impact of shrinking resources is also linked to the increased vulnerability of women and children to sexual exploitation, HIV/AIDS and domestic violence. (Noel-De Bique 1998: 33)

In their effort to realize the Cairo agenda and to fill the gap of lagging or non-existent public services, Caribbean NGOs have not only sought funding from external donor organizations to carry out innovative projects but reached out to form 'partnerships' with private companies and trade unions as well as government agencies. An example is the 'male responsibility' pilot project initiated by the Family Planning Association of Trinidad and Tobago

Trinidad and Tobago: implementing a male responsibility strategy in sexual and reproductive health
(excerpted from Noel-De Bique 1998)

In 1996, the Family Planning Association of Trinidad and Tobago (FPATT) established the first health clinic to assist men in participating in their own health and that of their families. Reproductive health services are provided for men, including prostate examinations, vasectomies, family planning counselling and referrals for STD/HIV cases. This represented the operationalizing of the FPATT's policy to increase male participation in sexual and reproductive health and reproductive rights. The FPATT used core funding from IPPF to pilot the project. With the threat of reductions in international and national funding, the project was re-engineered to enhance its cost effectiveness and sustainability. Using an innovative resource development strategy, partnerships were formed with companies in the male-dominated sectors of the economy (such as oil and insurance) and with trade unions, [who agreed to help fund and facilitate] FPATT's provision of high-quality sexual and reproductive health services to employees in [their] workplaces. This enabled FPATT to expand its male clinic services to men who cannot afford them, and [to] their families, in poor communities throughout Trinidad and Tobago.

The response to this initiative has been tremendous. Reports are that it has increased FPATT's credibility in the community, enabling it to be a more effective advocate for gender equality in traditional spaces of male resistance. FPATT has also formed other partnerships with male grassroots organizations, women's organizations and the male advisory committee of the Ministry of Culture and Gender Affairs to build awareness of reproductive rights among men using popular art forms. It also assisted in the formulation of Trinidad and Tobago's National Population Policy.

In the case of its private sector support, not only did FPATT show that it had a track record of being effective in the delivery of reproductive health services; [but also] companies could see the benefits to their employees and themselves in financial and human terms from partnership with FPATT.... FPATT seized [another] window of opportunity during its 'Male Sexual and Reproductive Health Week'. Recognizing that little had been done to promote reproductive rights to men with men, [it] mobilized approximately 2,000 young men in five communities throughout Trinidad to express their perspectives on male violence and reproductive rights through interactive drama. The FPATT worked to enable the participation of other NGOs through its administrative abilities, technical skills and financial resources. Although FPATT maintained direct administrative control over the activities, it facilitated the role of stakeholders (the Ministry of Culture and Gender Affairs, male grassroots organizations, including Men Against Violence Against Women, and women's organizations) in defining how best to make the voices of young men heard within the framework of women's empowerment.

(**Box 5.7**). As small developing countries like those in the Caribbean start to lose international financial assistance for sexual and reproductive health, with the US government's punitive withholding of funds from organizations like UNFPA and IPPF on anti-abortion grounds, this kind of bridge building to private groups will become an increasingly necessary and vital means of project survival.

The case studies presented in this and the preceding sections reflect varying degrees of government relation to women's NGO activities, ranging from grudging tolerance, neglect or even hostility to public expressions of cooperation and support. In all the cases, however, NGOs find themselves bearing the chief responsibility for advocating, shaping, generating resources for and in many instances actually implementing a given reproductive and sexual health/rights policy. While this means a certain degree of autonomy from government scrutiny, since in none of the cases are government agencies funding or subcontracting for the services of NGOs, it also has more ambiguous implications, including 'significant issues of social and gender equity' (Noel-De Bique 1998: 36–7). These issues involve questions, not so much about NGO capacity – which in fact is often superior to that of public agencies – but rather about equitable allocation of resources and responsibility between predominantly female NGOs and male-dominated state authorities.

Again we return to the problem of whether increasing NGO involvement sometimes contributes to and reinforces the global trend toward decreasing public sector involvement in health care, particularly in the area of reproductive and sexual health. Are women's health NGOs – assisted and encouraged by international donor agencies – abetting the process of privatization, and with what long-range consequences? In a recent article focused on the vulnerability of women's human rights NGOs to fundamentalist attacks, Meredith Tax helps to put this problem back into the larger context of global capitalism and its nationalist and fundamentalist opponents. In this context, she recalls the many recent instances of national women's NGOs that have been 'called tools of the US or the World Bank' for having utilized concepts or received funds from abroad (one thinks immediately of the Egyptian FGM Task Force or the Nigerian coalition for comprehensive sexuality education): 'The World Bank has understood, in sub-Saharan Africa at least, that women keep some societies from falling apart completely, and for that reason it wishes to support their efforts at financial independence. But that does not mean it will intervene to protect them when things turn nasty' (Tax 1999: 26). (The same might be said about private foundations as donors.) More to the point, Tax quotes from a 1998 speech by feminist activist Patricia McFadden to the African Women's Leadership Institute:

[The African women's movement is] taking over the civic responsibilities which the state should be shouldering, and we are not critically asking ourselves whether this is our agenda or it is an imposed agenda.... If we continue to separate the private from the public, our movement will die, and we will be wrapped up in welfarism and catering for everyone else's needs, and we will never reach our political goals. (Tax 1999: 27)

NGOs as 'partners' in health reform

As if to illustrate McFadden's concerns, the Swaziland Schools HIV/ AIDS & Population Education Programme (SHAPE) is an example of an NGO activity that originally was a government (MOH) programme, funded by a large private donor (CARE International), which then only became registered as an NGO after the Ministry of Education declined to run the project.[20] Although it seems very different from NGOs that arise out of an independent women's movement, SHAPE presents many issues pertinent to other women's health NGOs that are attempting to provide health services in some kind of 'partnership' arrangement with both government agencies and the private sector. Begun well before the ICPD, in response to the mounting prevalence of HIV/AIDS among youth and young adults in Swaziland, SHAPE performs a large array of preventive activities, mostly based in the secondary schools. These include: curriculum reform that involves 'life skills education' and gender issues; in-service training workshops for guidance and counselling teachers; HIV/AIDS education training for students in teacher training colleges; adolescent reproductive health programmes run through school-based health clubs; training in reproductive health counselling and condom provision for health service providers; and the beginning of programmes for primary schools, parents and out-of-school youths.

It is interesting to note the institutional arrangements within which SHAPE performs this exhaustive range of *public* functions. Funded since 1990 by a combination of grants from Shell Oil–Swaziland, the EU, UNICEF and UNFPA, 'SHAPE works in collaboration with the Ministries of Health and Education', including 'a formal partnership agreement' with the latter and visible links to both. Clearly these ties give the organization's work a degree of legitimacy among donors, parents and the general public it might not have if perceived as a separate women's NGO. On the other hand, according to its programme manager, SHAPE has found itself caught in intersectoral rivalries between the two ministries with which it attempts to maintain this trilateral partnership; in other words, the impact of the failure of national health sector reform to institute multisectoral integration falls most heavily on the responsible NGO. What this has meant in the Swaziland situation is that both agencies slough off responsibility for virtually all HIV/AIDS education and outreach services, and their coordination, onto the NGO's shoulders. As Shongwe discreetly puts it, 'governments may come to rely on an NGO beyond the mandated partnership roles' (1998: 54). We might ask, however, whether once again women are playing the role of the partner who does all the public housework but with neither public power nor public accounta-bility. Meanwhile, a company like Shell Oil improves its image while helping to improve the survival of its next generation of workers; and the government guards its revenues for macroeconomic purposes it deems more urgent than the sexual and reproductive health of youth.

Noel-De Bique articulates some of the more troubling questions that such NGO–government partnerships raise. First, addressing the disparity in resources, she asks, 'To what extent will the work of NGOs be funded by government for the delivery of services? Have resources been committed for the institutional strengthening of such NGOs?' In most of the cases examined here, the answer is clearly no. Second, she cites the inherent conflict that NGOs like FPATT in Trinidad and Tobago and SHAPE in Swaziland are forced to contend with: the 'drive to professionalize' and 'to compete effectively in a privatized health environment' versus a deep-felt commitment 'to provide quality care for all, particularly for those who are unable to afford it'. This is the ambiguous and uncomfortable space – *between the hegemonic market and the moribund welfare state* – that women's health NGOs increasingly find themselves inhabiting. Finally, Noel-De Bique suggests a kind of reverse inequality whereby government officials responsible for policy formulation and implementation of UN conference agreements 'lag behind the work and experience of NGOs'. Yet 'NGO diversity is not reflected in government structures or in the institutions which are mandated to implement or monitor' such agreements. This is a failure not only to ensure greater *inclusion* of NGOs in government programme planning and review (the situation of Health Watch in India, for example) but also to ensure the *accountability* of NGOs themselves to a broader social movement. How can NGOs tied into formal government or donor partnerships 'continue to see their role as representing the interests of the broadest base of civil society'? (Noel-De Bique 1998: 38.)

Women's health NGOs in some countries have been experimenting with creative solutions to these kinds of problems, exploring the limits of what might be possible in the current globalized and privatized political economy. In Peru, for example, a Tripartite Commission for Monitoring the Implementation of the ICPD POA – made up of government representatives, IGO representatives and members of civil society, including women's organizations – was set up in 1997. The LACWHN regards Peru's Tripartite Commission as 'the most important achievement of the [Latin American and Caribbean] women's health movement concerning participation in population and development policies during the post-Cairo period' (LACWHN 1998: 24). With support of both the Ministry for the Promotion of Women and Human Development and the MOH, the Commission is intended to be a mechanism that will (a) operationalize cross-sectoral integration on reproductive and sexual health matters and (b) utilize the expertise and grassroots involvement of women's health NGOs to train and inform, rather than replace, public agencies. Thus the ReproSalud project serves as a kind of bridging mechanism to sensitize government clinicians and staff to the health needs and priorities of poor women. More recently, as Peru's MOH has become increasingly aligned with the religious far right, Manuela Ramos has geared its advocacy programme towards addressing attacks on gender equality and reproductive rights by building strategic coalitions with a range of local civil society groups. The long-range purpose is 'to involve the whole community in demanding their rights', so that enforcement of these rights and of innovative health proposals will be sustainable against a potential backlash and beyond the duration of the ReproSalud project.[21]

An even more integrative model of 'partnership' can be found in the relations between Brazil's women's health movement and government agencies responsible for implementing the ICPD POA. Though not embodied in a single formal structure like that in Peru, these relations have evolved over a decade and a half of measures to embed health policy in the broad processes of democratization and civil society engagement, and for that reason they are probably more developed than anywhere in the world (with the possible exception of Cuba, after which some elements of Brazil's health system are modelled). The result is an unparalleled degree of *institutionalization* of the Brazilian women's health movement, through representation on a wide array of commissions to oversee health policy at various levels – federal, state and municipal.

As early as 1983, long before the Cairo conference, the Brazilian women's movement pioneered a Comprehensive Women's Health Programme (PAISM), which was adopted by the MOH the following year and included the wide range of services encompassed in Cairo's concept of reproductive health (pre-natal, obstetric and post-natal care; gynaecological cancer and STI treatment and prevention; adolescent and menopausal care; and contraceptive provision and counselling). To ensure that this programme is fully implemented within the federal and local public health systems, the Brazilian women's health movement has been organized since 1991 into a national network of some 200 organizations and centres (the National Feminist Health and Reproductive Rights Network, or *Rede Saúde*). From the 1980s to the present, feminist health activists in Brazil have occupied key roles in some national, state and municipal agencies concerned with health (most notably in the city and state of São Paulo). Moreover, a strong rights perspective has consistently infused the work of Brazilian women's health NGOs, which have been in close alliance with the National Council of Women's Rights (CNDM) since its inception in 1985 and more recently with the women's National Health Council advisory board (see **Box 5.8**). Indeed, as Sonia Corrêa asserts, 'the Brazilian experience in the 1980s, both in advocacy and in policy formulation, must be interpreted as one of the relevant contributions to the paradigm change that occurred at the ICPD' (Corrêa 1999: 8; Brazil MOH 1999).

The political and social context in which the Brazilian women's health movement arose is a unique one and helps to explain the breadth of its vision as well as Brazil's expansive and participatory approach to public health. In addition to the country's large size, natural wealth and economic growth during the 1980s and 1990s, that context includes

1   a widely publicized and rapid demographic transition in which the society's overall fertility rate dropped from 5.8 to 2.7 in the two decades between 1970 and 1991;

2   a steeply rising female labour force participation rate, both reflecting and contributing to the decline in fertility;

3   a vibrant process of democratization in the post-dictator years, including the mobilization of civil society organizations, community and workers'

Achievements of the Brazilian health model through institutionalizing civil society participation
(excerpted from Corrêa 1998)

Between 1995 and 1999, significant progress was achieved in the realization of the sexual and reproductive health goals of PAISM and ICPD. This was due to the vigilant functioning of the National Commission on Population and Development (CNPD), its integration of NGO representatives and ten different ministries, and the mobilization of the various women's health and rights institutions – the Rede Saúde, the CNDM and a new Women's Health Cross-Sectoral Commission (CISMU) which began in 1996 to function as a National Health Council advisory board. During this period, the unrelenting work of women's and HIV/AIDS NGOs to influence public debate and their direct intersection with the official government monitoring bodies succeeded in securing a number of important legislative and policy reforms. These include major strides toward reduction and epidemiological tracking of maternal mortality; expansion of pre-natal care, coverage for home births and payments for both normal and high-risk births in hospitals; quotas on payments for surgical deliveries (to reduce the number of caesarean sections); launching of the Viva Mulher Cervical Cancer Prevention Programme, to reach millions of women who never before had pap smears; new protocols regulating surgical sterilization and expanding access to reversible contraceptive methods; defeat of a proposed constitutional amendment to ensure 'the right to life from the moment of conception'; and a protocol under the SUS to provide for pregnancy interruption and emergency contraception for women victims of sexual violence.

Achievements in the area of abortion are especially noteworthy, given that Brazil is a predominantly Catholic country with a growing evangelical Protestant movement. While abortion is still only legal in cases of rape and life endangerment, 14 hospitals are now providing full abortion services in the prescribed cases and thus carrying out the ICPD's Paragraph 8.25. The role of women's organizations has been particularly productive at decentralized levels in pressuring for and monitoring the implementation of abortion services as foreseen by law. In some states and municipalities, many programmes designed to involve and change the mindset of professionals, while not highly visible, were critical in this regard. In the area of HIV/AIDS prevention and treatment, advocacy initiatives by NGOs have also succeeded in expanding access to treatment of people living with HIV and AIDS, securing the HIV-AIDS Medication Law of 1996 and ensuring free universal access to all anti-retroviral medications, including protease inhibitors and AZT, for all infected people including pregnant women. Finally, the post-Cairo implementation process has achieved greater cross-sectoral interaction within the Brazilian public health system, with an ongoing initiative to systematically integrate the PAISM with the STD/AIDS and Adolescent Health Programmes (CNPD 1999).

movements throughout the country as well as 'a complex array of participatory and social accountability mechanisms';

4   a strong federal system involving a decentralized management and policy-
making structure, particularly in the arenas of education, social welfare
and health, with much responsibility devolving to municipalities and
states (for example, in the procurement and distribution of AIDS drugs),
thus enlarging the space for input by local civil society groups into policies
and programmes; and

5   a firm commitment of the society as a whole to a universal health system
(SUS) providing free coverage to the majority of Brazilians for many basic
treatments and services and giving high priority, especially since the mid-
1990s, to primary care, STI/HIV/AIDS prevention and treatment,
reproductive and sexual health, and cross-sectoral approaches (see Corrêa
1998; Brazil MOH 1999, 2002; and Chapter 3).[22]

Following the Cuban example, the Brazilian health system's emphasis on
decentralization and public sector responsibility is embodied in a system of
popular Health Councils representing local citizens (half lay people and half
health providers and government officials) that monitor expenditures and
policy implementation of municipal, state and federal health agencies. Moreover, along with direct delivery of primary and family health care by nurses
and doctors, tens of thousands of Community Health Agents, primarily
women, conduct household follow-up and health education activities at the
local level. Both the STD/AIDS prevention and treatment programme and
all other sexual and reproductive health care are fully integrated within this
comprehensive, community-oriented system. And both not only operate
within the health sector but also rely on cooperation across many sectors –
including ministries of education, justice, labour, planning and others (Brazil
MOH 1999; Corrêa 1998).

The strong commitment in principle of the Brazilian health system to
policies of redistribution, solidarity and poverty reduction is unquestionable.
In Chapter 3 we saw how the Brazilian government's policy of universal
access to free AIDS drugs has motivated it to defy the constraints imposed by
global capitalism on the human right to health. The drugs policy derives
from two basic sources integral to the Brazilian health system: the principles
of solidarity and constitutional and human rights, and the continual vigilance and public pressure of civil society organizations. Corrêa underscores

how these two factors have likewise steered the post-Cairo reforms in Brazil's sexual and reproductive health policy. While that policy predated Cairo and Beijing, the conferences and the national machinery set in place to implement them clearly propelled it forward, in the context of financial restructuring and a decentralization process that encouraged local and NGO initiatives. Brazil's National Commission on Population and Development (CNDP), set up in 1995 to monitor ICPD implementation, is not only headed by a leading figure of the women's health movement but also firmly committed to a politics of redistribution, solidarity, social accountability and human rights (CNDP 1999). In Corrêa's analysis, health reform in Brazil has substantially improved 'women's quality of life' in large part because of the active role of women's organizations 'in exerting pressure on the health system (convincing managers, sensitizing and training health professionals) and ... mobilizing public support, creating coalitions, stimulating public debate and systematically monitoring policies'. A statement by the Women's Health Coordinator of the Pernambuco State Health Department underlines the crucial importance of this work with local managers and health providers:

> The impact of Cairo will be strong or not depending on how its definitions are translated or not translated by the women's movement [to] network managers and professionals, since the latter are normally so detached from the international debate. If no one exists to provide the connection, nothing happens. (Corrêa 1998: 10)

These very positive dimensions of Brazil's health system coexist, however, with an enormous disparity between rich and poor that rivals that in the US, along with vast racial and regional inequalities in income, education, employment and access to health care. (Most poverty is concentrated in the black population and the North and North-east regions.) This continues to be true despite improvements in the Brazilian economy in the mid-1990s and a reduction, or stabilization, in the numbers of people living in poverty (Kerstenetzky 2001; CNDP 1999). What this means in regard to health is that 'policy guidelines do not always reach local levels' and the positive effects of decentralization and improved quality of primary and reproductive health care are unevenly distributed (Sadasivam 1999: 193). In the STD/AIDS programme, for example, decentralization has meant that availability of new drugs in the public health services often lags behind their production and licensing at the federal level and that the poorest regions still suffer deficits in treatment and care (Terto 2002).

As Corrêa states, the successes of the Brazilian model 'do not eliminate the challenges'. First, apart from budgetary constraints, 'the lack of systematic policies to correct inequalities' (social, racial and regional) in access to services and quality of care still plagues Brazil's SUS and needs to be given the highest priority both by the system and by its civil society partners (Corrêa 1999: 21). Second, even with the best of political will, challenges remain acute in the financial domain; for while investments in public health increased significantly during the mid-1990s and are larger than those in many other countries (nearly 15.5 per cent of the entire government budget in 1995), they lag behind increases in other sectors (Sadasivam 1999; CNPD 1999). One reason Brazil is able to sustain the unusual level of universal coverage and treatment it does through the SUS is the national financial transaction tax it adopted in 1996 (the same year as the law was passed assuring universal access to free drugs for AIDS). Health advocates successfully secured the new tax as a resource to guarantee stability and increases for financing of the SUS (especially primary health care, municipal level health provision, and HIV drugs) in the midst of the financial crisis of the late 1990s (Corrêa 2002).

Yet during the years of research and writing this study, the IMF, the US and other donor countries exerted huge pressures on the Brazilian government to introduce austerity measures that would involve serious cutbacks in social expenditures. This occurred in the wake of the 1998 financial crises, Russian loan defaults and the instability of Brazil's own currency and financial markets, and again in 2002, after the Argentine collapse began to reverberate in Brazilian and Uruguayan markets. The return of economic crisis on a regional scale in 2002 saw the IMF offering Brazil a $30 billion rescue loan with conditions that forbade any government coming to power after the next election from defaulting on its foreign debt, reducing the budget surplus below 3.75 per cent, or thus diverting from free-market policies by increasing public spending. This was clearly a move to try to influence Brazil's 2002 elections (which foreign lenders correctly feared would be won by the left-wing workers' party leader, Luiz Inácio Lula da Silva) in order to rescue the investments of US banks (Andrews 2002; Rohter 2002). If a relatively wealthy, middle-income economy like Brazil can be held hostage through global financial blackmail, what chance is there anywhere for meeting the challenge of full equality in access to sexual and reproductive health care or, in the long run, Brazil's commitment to a politics of social solidarity and universal provision?

On the other hand, what gives cause for hope in the Brazil case is not only the strength of 'civil society organizations and social accountability mechanisms', which help to sustain Brazil's independence against external political pressures (CNDP 1999: 89). It is also the multiple and interwoven roles played by civil society organizations, giving them a strong presence both inside and outside the state. Women's health groups like SOS-Corpo, Fala Preta, Coletivo Feminista Sexualidade e Saude and Cepea embody a 'partnership' model involving (a) strong representation on government–civil society monitoring bodies by (b) nationally coordinated networks of independent women's NGOs that in turn represent (c) major participation and leadership in transnational women's coalitions and caucuses (including in UN and alternative forums, like the World Social Forum) as well as (d) organic links with local CBOs *and* health professionals and managers. These organizations connect fully to the global while translating and implementing human rights principles into local and national policy. They effectively 'provide the connection', creating an organic model that links each level of decision making and interweaves transnational activism with government and civil society.

Although newer to the democratization process and struggling with far heavier political and economic burdens, post-apartheid South Africa reflects a context similar to that of Brazil: a political culture of rights; a strong commitment to principles of equality and universal provision of basic social needs; and a vibrant, mobilized civil society that works cooperatively with a progressive government leadership. As they did in the anti-apartheid struggle, women's groups have played a key role in shaping the ANC's health and social policies as well as the 1996 South African constitution. This, along with the egregious history of racist population control practices under the apartheid regime and the fact that the first democratic elections coincided with preparations for the Cairo conference, may help to explain why the new constitution explicitly enshrines not only the right to health but bodily integrity and reproductive and sexual choice.[23] The constitution also provides that 'Everyone has the right to (a) health care services, including reproductive health care; (b) sufficient food and water; and (c) social security, including, if they are unable to support themselves and their dependants, appropriate social assistance'; and that 'No one may be refused emergency medical treatment.' Moreover, the ANC's Reconstruction and Development Programme (RDP) stated that 'every woman must have the right to choose whether or not to have an early termination of pregnancy according to her own individual beliefs'. In 1996 South Africa's National Assembly, amidst tremendous debate (including within the ANC), passed the Choice on Termination of Pregnancy Act, which makes abortion legal for any reason at any point in the first trimester (Klugman *et al.* 1998; NPU 1999; Guttmacher *et al.* 1998).

Not only does the holistic, human rights-based framework of the South African government, including the right to health, extend back to the Freedom Charter of 1955, but, as in the Brazil case, the inclusion of reproductive and sexual rights in that framework predated – and no doubt contributed to – the ICPD. From the start the ANC's approach to health policy was to create 'a single health system, with equitable distribution of resources and delivery organized through district health authorities with a primary health care approach and community accountability'. Upon the ANC's coming to power in 1994, one of the first actions of the new health minister was to make free health care available to all pregnant women and to children under six years; in 1996 this was extended, as one of the Presidential Lead Projects under the RDP, to cover primary health care for all persons (Klugman *et al.* 1998: 5–6; NPU 1999). As the Women's Health Project (WHP), a leading South African NGO, observes, 'This reflects the socialist and human rights roots of the new government, which put equality and equity at the centre of its platform.' And, 'by asserting the right to health care for the majority of people, who are poor', it runs directly counter to the tenets of mainstream HSR and neoliberalism, with their emphasis on privatization and cost recovery (Klugman *et al.* 1998: 10).

As we saw in Chapter 3 with regard to treatment access, principles are not enough to guarantee practical implementation. Yet in South Africa's case the principles are firmly grounded. Its Population Policy puts health and well-being before numbers and includes the tasks of 'creating an enabling environment for poverty alleviation' as well as establishing the conditions for gender, racial and age equality. The centre of this policy is 'a strategy for reducing poverty and socioeconomic inequalities through meeting people's basic needs'; thus universal provision of adequate and affordable housing, safe water, sanitation, and vitamin and mineral supplements 'to curb nutritional anaemia' – while still very far from achieved – currently stand at the top of the government's implementation agenda. With regard to reproductive and sexual health, its first priority was to 'shift away from narrow and vertical family planning' to a system that fully integrates reproductive and sexual health services into primary health care across the life cycle. Moreover, South Africa's integrative health policy recognizes the need to promote 'the culture of male responsibility [and participation]' and that 'gender violence ... constitutes a significant threat to the health of women across all races, age groups and classes' that must be addressed (NPU 1999: 16, 22, 28). The alarmingly high HIV prevalence rate in South Africa, especially among young women and pregnant women, has led to an attempt to integrate relevant management structures and services. The Department of Health not only runs the HIV/AIDS and STD directorate but also coordinates an inter-ministerial committee on AIDS and a Partnership on AIDS Project to work with NGOs, who provide most of the available direct services, especially for adolescents. An emphasis on barrier methods in contraceptive distribution includes free provision of condoms and introduction of the female condom, and the HIV/AIDS/STD directorate now has a specialist who focuses on gender and AIDS (Sadasivam 1999; NPU 1999).

Thus far in free South Africa's young history, most of this exemplary framework for reproductive health care exists more in principle and policy than in practice, impeded by the staggering dimensions of poverty, racial inequality and insufficient resources inherited from the apartheid years. Critical assessments by NGO monitors and the government itself point to numerous shortcomings, not only in health outcomes and distribution of services but in conceptualization. For example, the 1997 White Paper on the Transformation of the Health System conflates 'women's health' and 'reproductive health'. As the WHP points out, this ignores that 'reproductive health is not the sole preserve of women' while 'women's health goes far beyond that of reproduction' (Klugman *et al.* 1998: 11). In regard to contraception, while utilization rates are high and fertility rates relatively low in South Africa, the old pattern of reliance on sterilization and injectables – with over 60 per cent of women using Depo Provera 'mainly for lack of other convenient methods' – indicates that the policy of disseminating barrier methods still has a long way to go (Sadasivam 1999: 54). While the policy recognizes the prevalence of domestic violence and its importance as a health problem, health workers are not sufficiently trained to deal with this problem, especially as it affects girl children; nor have strategies been developed to address gender power relations as they impact on health (NUP 1999; Klugman 2000). Further, for safe abortion to be accessible to all South African women under the new law requires implementation measures, such as a 'comprehensive outreach and educational campaign' to inform women of their rights and training of health care workers, who still may refuse either to perform abortions or to make referrals. (Guttmacher *et al.* 1998: 193).

South Africa's universal primary health care system suffers from many deficiencies: health workers who feel overloaded and are poorly trained; inadequate facilities and supplies, including drugs and essential equipment; lack of reliable transport; and the continued failure to meet the basic infra-structural needs (housing, safe water, toilets) of much of the poor African population (see Box 5.10 and Xaba 1998). Increasingly, pressures from inter-national donors as well as its own constituencies in the poor rural areas and townships are leading the government toward macroeconomic policies that may shift the balance more toward growth than redistribution. Thus, while free primary health care for all, including reproductive and sexual health care, remains the policy, the 1996 Growth, Employment and Redistribution (GEAR) programme aims at cutting budget deficits, avoiding tax increases, and lowering public expenditures on social services. Women's groups worry that this may signal a move toward greater reliance on private health practitioners; already it has meant the loss of paid maternity leaves for women workers in the 1997 Basic Conditions of Employment Act (Sadasivam 1999; NPU 1999). Such a move would be especially ominous, given the clear benefits that free primary and reproductive health care have meant for women, not the least of which is increased access to and utilization of public health services. Like the Brazilian health scenario, however, that in South Africa becomes more hopeful thanks to the relentless vigilance and critical stance of the civil society organizations upon which the government continues to rely for policy formulation and evaluation.

NGOs and CBOs, especially those of women, have played a key role in the planning and implementation of South Africa's new health and population policies and their strong adherence to a human rights perspective. This is the natural outgrowth of the ANC's historic ties to popular and feminist organi-zations (Kemp *et al.* in Basu 1995). Most South African NGOs are involved in local community development activities or in advocacy at the national and international levels; very few provide, or wish to provide, primary health care services, which is seen as a function of the state. While in many ways supporting the policies of the government (as in TAC's campaign and brief against the PMA lawsuit), these organizations have also challenged and critiqued government health policies at many turns, calling for resistance to donor pressures for reduced public expenditures and exposing gaps or contradictions in access to services (ARV treatment is a good example). In 1997 a civil society coalition called the National Progressive Primary Health Care Network mounted a 'Health Rights Are Human Rights' campaign and,

The Transformation of Reproductive Health Services Project in South Africa

(excerpted and synthesized from Xaba *et al.* 1998; and Fonn *et al.* 1998)

The TRHSP grew out of a process begun by the Women's Health Project in 1993 for women throughout South Africa to identify their health needs [in order] to inform the new South African government's policies on women's health. This process, carried out in partnership with other NGOs, produced 13 women's health policy proposals and a national conference in 1994 to develop them. Although the policies were not based on the ICPD, their spirit and essence are similar to those in the Cairo POA, and they have since been used country-wide to advocate for improvements in women's health. This process also fed into the ICPD: a WHP staff member was on the official government delegation and brought with her the human rights, equity and gender equality approach to health of WHP's grassroots project in South Africa.

South Africa's first democratic elections in April 1994 created a new political environment and opportunities to do things differently. The National Women's Health Conference and plans for the TRHSP were an outgrowth of that context. With funding from UNFPA and the UK DfID, WHP developed the project in partnership with the Departments of Health and Welfare of three provincial governments. (Provinces in South Africa are responsible for implementing policies developed at the national level.) The aims of the TRHSP were to strengthen reproductive health services in the three provinces; collect a body of information to inform health systems' achievement of reproductive health; identify barriers to quality of care and methods to overcome them; build the confidence and capacity of health providers at all levels of the health system; and increase understanding of the impact of social inequality, especially gender inequality, on health and health services.

In developing the TRHSP, WHP made a strategic decision to work to build the capacity of public sector health services, rather than offering alternative services, because the poorer sections of South African society – women and children – use government services. Such services are perceived by most of the public to be inadequate, with poor quality of care. A related goal of the TRHSP was to help public health services recognize their disregard for users and to remedy this through development of a greater commitment to improving access and quality.

The project's participatory methods included such tools as key informant interviews with managers, self-administered questionnaires with primary health care staff, facility checklists at primary health care clinics, focus group discussions with community women to assess currently available services, and 'Health Workers for Change' workshops designed to build gender awareness and empowerment among women health workers. A second phase reviewed nursing education and the nursing curriculum in seven nursing institutions, using similar methodologies to the first phase.

WHP's professionalism and clear vision made government and funders take the work seriously – as did the fact that they could see concrete, mutual benefits from the TRHSP. The perennial undervaluing of women's NGOs by many governments was turned on its head by this project.

using radio broadcasts, toll-free call-ins, community discussions, and other outreach methods to document popular views and experiences, developed a South African Health Rights Charter as a tool for users and health professionals to evaluate services (Klugman *et al.* 1998: 20). This campaign undoubtedly helped prepare the ground for TAC's treatment access campaign in 2000–1.

No group has been more central to developing health and population policies that integrate gender, human rights and social development concerns than the Women's Health Project (WHP), based at the University of the Witwatersrand in Johannesburg (see *www.wits.ac.za/whp*). Founded in 1991, the WHP is an independently funded NGO that focuses on health systems research and evaluation, policy development, advocacy and training in gender issues of health workers, managers and grassroots women, especially those in the most disadvantaged communities. Its members have been directly involved in transnational women's health movements, as well as participating in the South African delegation to Cairo, Beijing and the ICPD+5 activities; thus it merges local, national and international perspectives. Composed of white and black South African women from both university and community development backgrounds, WHP functions in a partnership relation to government, but from a standpoint of critical independence. Its Transformation of Reproductive Health Services Project (**Box 5.9**), begun in 1995, illustrates this complex role.

The WHP's positive assessment of the outcomes and potential impact of its work in the TRHSP emphasizes the contributions it was able to make towards changing the awareness of government health providers, thus improving health worker–client relations and ultimately the quality of care in South African health clinics. By functioning as a health systems monitor and trainer rather than direct service provider, and by receiving its funds directly from external donors rather than through the Health Ministry, it has been able to maintain its autonomy and at the same time help to strengthen the public sector in three of the poorest provinces. Nonetheless, this very positioning has a more dubious side to which the WHP authors refer in their evaluation. Since the provinces had no experience in administering donor funds, and the South African government had 'no mechanisms in place to handle such funds', it was left to WHP to channel monies to the province level. This put the organization in an odd position: 'an NGO effectively showing the government how to overcome its own systems problems. It also elevated WHP as a powerful NGO – something WHP neither planned nor desired' (Xaba *et al.* 1998: 59).

The discomfort WHP expresses here, while unusually self-aware, reflects a situation that is increasingly common in developing countries and one inherent in many of the case studies presented above: 'partnerships' between NGOs and governments are often in actuality partnerships between NGOs and international donor agencies, for whom NGOs become not only the conduits of health reform project funds but in effect the *administrators of health reform agendas over and above the state.* In the case of the WHP's work in South Africa, given the politics and vision of both the NGO and the government involved, the consequences of this arrangement are likely to be beneficial in the long run – to the state, the NGO, health workers and women clients. But will this be true in other country settings? Are there circumstances in which this positioning of NGOs *between* the state and external donors may serve to erode even further state responsibility for the quality of health care? Will this in turn lead to a shift in the balance of power from state institutions towards both donor and civil society organizations – organizations that, albeit non-profit, are nonetheless accountable only to themselves? Under what conditions, in other words, might this form of 'NGO privatization' either advance or retard the goals of gender equality, human rights *and* public accountability in health care provision?

The many faces of privatization

Recently many commentators in the international relations field have expressed concerns about what I earlier called the underside of NGO empowerment in both transnational and national political processes. Usually these critiques are made from the standpoint of less empowered groups – community-based and grassroots organizations representing poor and marginalized people – as well as scepticism toward the objectives and motives of powerful international donors. Summarizing this set of arguments, Koivusalo and Ollila ponder whether NGOs are being 'used as a vehicle for privatization and social sector restructuring' that meets the needs of donors more than those of poor people in developing countries. They worry that projects elevating NGOs as providers and implementers of social sector reform have as their aim the promotion of a 'neoliberal, market-based model of social provisioning' and the further shrinkage of the state's role. Likewise, Silliman (echoing Patricia McFadden) argues that, 'even when [NGOs] are given adequate resources to implement programmes ... [they] may well be performing services and providing forms of welfare that are the responsibility of governments'. Moreover, the increasing professionalization and donor dependency of many NGOs may not only diminish their capacity for effective advocacy and opposition. These trends may also tend 'to [undermine] grassroots organizations representing poor people' and to divert or disable excluded groups 'from demanding that the state agencies deliver the goods'. In other words, NGO empowerment replaces 'struggle politics', yet NGOs may be no more efficient, skilled or sensitive to community needs than government officials, while they lack the presumed accountability of those officials to local communities (Koivusalo and Ollila 1997: 100–1; Silliman 1999: 156–7).

While raising these concerns to some extent, the country case studies I have examined reveal a more complex picture. First, it is crucial to remember that NGOs are not a monolith; they vary tremendously in their size, power and resources, their relations to both donors and national governments, and above all the extent and quality of their connection with grassroots movements. Most of the women's NGOs involved in these case studies, though in no sense representative either of such movements or of NGOs as a genre, do make great efforts to both connect with the voices and needs of grassroots women and 'work with, rather than replace, the functions of the state' (Koivusalo and Ollila 1997: 101). This is definitely the case with the Repro-Salud project in Peru, in its emphasis on empowering its CBO members to negotiate directly with local health authorities and Manuela Ramos's persistent advocacy against regressive MOH policies. Those NGOs involved in direct provision of services are in some cases troubled about the state abdicating its functions and the burden this places on their own workload (SHAPE in Swaziland). In other cases they are finding creative ways to use their gender education and training skills to enhance the role of local and district public health providers, thus *bringing the state back in* (WHP in South Africa). In most cases, however, women's NGOs become involved in providing health services to meet an urgent and desperate need that would not be met otherwise. In situations where governments are debt-burdened, corrupt or disinterested or the state is in disarray (Tajikistan), the notion of popular demands and 'struggle politics' may seem a luxury in the face of survival.

Second, if NGOs represent a wide continuum of politics and practices, so too do international donor agencies. As any NGO that has received international funding knows, while donor dependence is a serious problem, it makes a huge difference in one's ability to carry out a project effectively and autonomously whether one's donor is the Ford Foundation, the Swedish International Development Agency (SIDA), USAID or UNFPA. Some donors are private foundations with a great deal of flexibility and freedom from red tape, and in a few cases very pro-women and pro-poor policies. Some are annexes of government ministries or UN agencies with tremendously onerous bureaucratic requirements they must both impose and fulfil, and vulnerability to sudden budget shrinkage due to US cuts in family planning aid (UNFPA, for example). Others are large and complex international financial institutions, like the World Bank, whose agendas and procedures may differ from one sectoral or regional office to another. Privatization may be less the cause than the consequence of a lack of capacity on the part of state agencies and the urgent need to 'deliver the goods' in whatever way possible. In the direst circumstances, it may be necessary to take a hard-nosed attitude to the motives of international donors in order to sustain projects that advance health and protect human rights: developing HIV/AIDS prevention programmes, creating alternative models of health education, setting up integrated, 'one-stop' health services for rural women, providing seed money to women's health groups in urban slums to make community improvements as they see fit.[24] Some of these projects are funded by the most powerful and suspect donors – the World Bank in Brazil and India, USAID in Peru – and yet they also appear to be among the projects doing the most to empower the poorest women in the communities where they live. Progressive critics have to deal with this contradiction and figure out what it means in the long run.

Concerning the issue of NGOs abetting privatization through their function as service providers, consider another complexity: the growing power of religious institutions as 'private' providers of health care, including reproductive health. Nowhere is this power more evident than in the social service functions of the Catholic Church world-wide.[25] As most of the world's states rush to divest themselves of responsibilities for social service and health care provision, ceding these to the private sector, the Church continues to expand its already vast activities and centuries of experience in this field. In some countries (especially in sub-Saharan Africa) it may be the single most important or reliable institutional provider of education and health care,[26] which partially accounts for the silence or conservatism in UN debates of countries such as Nigeria and the Philippines that depend on the Church for social and financial resources. At the same time as it gives the Vatican tremendous influence over both domestic politics in some countries and voting blocs within the UN, this command over health care provision undermines the practical implementation of women's reproductive and sexual rights (see **Box 5.10**).

A case in point is the United States, where not only have huge for-profit 'managed care' institutions (often insurance companies) virtually taken over control of most health care, raising many ethical issues of patients' access and freedom of choice, but the Catholic Church, with its vast network of hospitals and managed care plans, is rapidly becoming one of the most important health providers in the country. The US Catholic Church currently operates 48 HMOs (Health Management Organizations) throughout the country, many of them directed to the poor under the Medicaid (government reimbursement) programme. These organizations serve as primary care providers and managers for hundreds of thousands of people and, under congressional authorization since 1997, may refuse payment or even referral for family planning services (CFFC 2000). In thus denying vital reproductive health care to the women and girls most likely to experience unintended pregnancies and STIs, Church-operated health provision thus 'breaks the continuity of health care delivery, compromises the quality of care women receive, creates a disconcerting Church/state relationship, and undermines the stated goals of managed care to provide comprehensive health care services' (NARAL/NY 2001: 4).

In addition, as CFFC's ongoing survey of the trend toward Catholic–non-Catholic hospital mergers reveals, in some locales Catholic hospitals are now the only option available – at the cost of many essential reproductive health services that the Church considers immoral (see **Box 5.10**). This ominous trend for women's reproductive and sexual rights in the US suggests that women's health NGOs may feel compelled to get involved in both the delivery and the monitoring of health services to counter the rush by private companies and religious organizations to fill the gap left by the state. For example, the National Abortion Federation (NAF), a consortium of both non-profit and for-profit freestanding abortion clinics in the US, was formed in 1976 and continues to operate by default; for, although abortion is a constitutional right in the US, public hospitals and many private physicians refuse to provide abortions because of continued pressure and harassment by anti-abortion forces (Joffe, Anderson and Steinauer 1998; Joffe 1995; Petchesky 1990).

The Catholic Church and hospital mergers in the US
(excerpted from CFFC 1998)

Catholic hospitals must abide by the *Ethical and Religious Directives for Catholic Health Care Services*, which are issued by the US bishops. The *Directives* ... forbid services that contradict Church teachings.... Catholic teaching currently holds that many reproductive health services are immoral.... Many Americans are unaware that the Catholic health care *Directives* prohibit, among other things, tubal ligations, vasectomies, *in vitro* fertilization, and the prescribing or dispensing of contraceptive devices and drugs [in addition to abortions]. The *Directives* even restrict use of the morning-after pill for rape victims who go to Catholic hospitals or clinics.... In a merger of Catholic and non-Catholic hospitals, officials must negotiate how the new entity will honour women's consciences while satisfying the dictates of the Church hierarchy....

Catholic hospital networks have been expanding quickly of late. Forty-two Catholic systems participating in a *Modern Healthcare* survey grew by 12 per cent in 1996, acquiring outright 55 hospitals to bring their combined total to 527. Catholic Healthcare West acquired eight hospitals in 1996, for a total of 32. The Sisters of the Sorrowful Mother–US Health System added seven in 1996 to end the year with 22. This growth far outpaced those of large for-profit systems; Columbia/HCA Healthcare Corporation grew only 3 per cent that year. In 1995, only the Daughters of Charity National Health system was among the nation's ten largest health care systems, as measured by each system's number of hospitals. In 1996, Catholic Health Initiatives and Mercy Health Services joined the top-ten list. With 64 hospitals, Catholic Health Initiatives became the largest Catholic chain....

Catholic systems are financially strong as well.... [F]ive of the nation's ten largest health care systems, as measured by net patient revenues, are Catholic. The Daughters of Charity system, with net patient revenues of $3.6 billion in 1996, is the highest-earning Catholic system....

A growing number of Catholic hospitals face no competition for their business because no similar facility is readily accessible. Access to reproductive health services is likely to suffer in these areas, even as the Catholic hospital derives certain financial benefits from its status.... In 1994, CFFC identified 46 Catholic sole provider hospitals dispersed across 17 states. That number has now shot up to 76 Catholic sole provider hospitals, spread across 26 states.... Some of these hospitals serve counties (most of them rural) where Catholics make up less than 1 per cent of the population. These Catholic hospitals are essentially rewarded, through higher rates of Medicare reimbursement, while they deny reproductive health care to an entire county.

The increase in Catholic sole provider hospitals can be attributed to the growth of US Catholic health care for two reasons. First, as non-Catholic hospitals in rural areas have closed, Catholic facilities, supported by an ever-stronger Catholic health care network, have survived. Second, in some cases a merger or acquisition involving a Catholic and a non-Catholic hospital has resulted in one Catholic institution.... Administrators of failing non-Catholic hospitals are desperate for resources, and many Catholic hospitals and systems are in excellent financial condition. As Catholic coalitions continue to build their resources, more and more non-Catholic hospitals will be forced to make concessions to Catholic hospitals. As a result, CFFC fears future mergers could decimate reproductive health services.

Finally, as the case studies also illustrate, states too are tremendously varied, and the differences in their political cultures, ideologies and institutional structures are an important factor determining the potential impact of NGO activities. It is interesting in this respect to contrast the nature and limits of NGO–government 'partnership' in the Philippines and Brazil – two predominantly Catholic countries that have undergone recent transformation from dictatorship to democracy and are characterized by strong and vibrant civil society (including women's) groups. Indeed, the women's health movements in Brazil and the Philippines are among the strongest, best-coordinated and most organically linked to popular social movements of any in the world. Women's health NGOs in the Philippines – who, like the *Rede Saúde* in Brazil, generally operate through organized coalitions – have made important gains in implementing the principles of the ICPD. In the post-Cairo period – in part due to a sympathetic Minister of Health but even more to 'sustained advocacy by [women's NGOs] and feminist individuals in the government' – they managed to turn the country's population policy in a much more feminist direction. The old-style family planning programme (administered by the National Population Commission) and maternal health programme (administered by the Department of Health) were merged into a much broader Women's Health and Safe Motherhood Project, including a component designated 'gender and women's empowerment'. This shift to a reproductive health approach involved not only the elimination of targets but new programmes for the diagnosis and treatment of STIs, RTIs and cervical cancer (DAWN 1999; Francisco 1998).

Yet other aspects of the Philippines reproductive health policy have remained stubbornly hostile to women's and young people's sexual and reproductive rights. Despite a deeply pronatalist, pro-motherhood culture, women in the Philippines do not have access to quality pre-natal and obstetric care, and almost half of all pregnant women in the country, according to a 1997 World Bank study, suffer from anaemia and malnutrition. Most women, who work in the informal sector, have no access to health insurance, and for those who do have insurance, there is no coverage of normal (non-surgical) births (Sadasivam 1999). Since the Arroyo government came to power in January 2001, health needs have fallen even lower in the government's priorities, as it rushes to be the most obedient ally of the US in its 'war on terrorism'. Meanwhile, the DOH has become captive to 'fundamentalist elements inside and outside the Church' and impervious to the efforts of women's groups to initiate change (Women's Groups/Philippines 2001). Not only does the Philippines continue to have one of the most restrictive abortion policies in the world, but the reproductive health programme provides virtually no adolescent sexual and reproductive health services, no initiatives to promote male responsibility, and little in the way of services to address violence against women in a country where its occurrence is commonplace. Sexuality education is limited to the 'family life' curriculum approved by the Church, and the provision of contraceptives is heavily constrained by both Church resistance and dependence on donors such as USAID for imported supplies (Francisco 1998; DAWN 1999; Fabros *et al.* 1998). In 2001 the government quietly issued a memorandum withdrawing registration of an emergency contraceptive drug it had approved and made available just two years earlier. This was done without any prior notification of women's health advocacy organizations, NGO service providers, or even the DOH units originally authorized to distribute the drug (WOMENLEAD 2002).

And why is all this the case, despite the tireless efforts of a highly vocal and mobilized women's health movement? One has only to look at two major structural features of the Philippines state that democratization has left untouched: the enormous, entrenched political power of the Catholic Church in nearly every area of social policy – far greater than the Church wields in Brazil; and an economic system that has not only been drained by recent crises and IMF-imposed 'fiscal discipline' but is historically and ideologically committed to privatization and commercialism. Even before severe cuts diminished the already meagre health budget from 3.4 to a mere 2.2 per cent of total government spending, the vast majority of health care provision in the country was already privatized and subject to user fees – out of reach for much of the impoverished population (Sadasivam 1999). In the absence of any official recognition of health care, including reproductive and sexual health, as a social and human right, or of state responsibility to meet basic health needs, women's groups in the Philippines struggle on every front: to end poverty and debt service, to resist privatization and user fees in the health sector, to expose sexual exploitation and abuse of young migrant women in the 'free enterprise zones', and for universal access to safe contraception (Fabros 1999). Maintaining independence and an oppositional posture *vis-à-vis* the state is absolutely essential in this context, whereas something closer to an authentic partnership – with a solid base in grassroots movements and readiness to be critical when the need arises – seems more feasible in the Brazilian and South African contexts.

Comparing the Philippines situation with that in Brazil or South Africa suggests that *the state does matter*; that its effectiveness, investment policies and social philosophy help determine the limits of what civil society organizations will be able to achieve – short of social revolution – in the realm of human development. The WHP in South Africa puts the matter forthrightly: 'Development requires an effective state.... It is in relation to services for the most disadvantaged that the state must take up its responsibility to decrease inequality, one of the core public activities ... crucial to development' (Fonn *et al.* 1998: 30). Nowhere is this truer than in the area of health care, as Maureen Mackintosh and Paula Tibandebage have argued:

> To face exclusion and abuse when at one's most vulnerable is an important element of poverty as it is experienced. Conversely, effective claims on a health care system can be an important economic asset for the poor. Hence health care, because of its moral, economic and social significance, is a potential focus for organized political demands for inclusion, and health care provision has been seen by many governments as an important element of state building and of constructing a relationship between state and citizens. (2000: 4)

Both the Brazilian and South African scenarios suggest models in which active civil society organizations and socially committed state institutions can interact to create strong systems of accountability even where some services are provided by NGOs or the private sector. We must continue to press for strengthened state functions and the responsibility of the state to protect universal access to the full range of health care as a matter of human right. But we also have to recognize that *markets are not going to disappear*. It is not a question of states *versus* markets, public *versus* private, but rather of *which kinds of private entities* are going to be involved in providing basic social services and monitoring functions, with *what sorts of values and objectives*, and under *what kind of public scrutiny and accountability mechanisms*. In the twenty-first century, health as a human right, not a commodity, must come to prevail within or in spite of markets. The implementation of human rights norms will increasingly belong to hybrid institutions that cut across old boundaries of public and private space and local, national and international identities.

Notes

1 *Nâ Shariram Nâdhi* is Telegu for 'My Body Is Mine'. The book was written by Sabala and Kranti, two of Asmita's advisory group members, and published in 1995. See also National Alliance of Women (NAWO), *Supreme Court Judgment on Sexual Harassment at Workplace*, Landmark Judgment Series 1 (New Delhi: NAWO, 1997).
2 Interview with Kalpana and Vasanth Kannabiran, 26 March 2000; Asmita Resource Centre for Women, *Towards Building a Gender Just Society, Review of Activity, 1991–8* (Asmita, n.d.), pp. 23–4.
3 See Standing 2002: 14–15 and Table 4.2 for recent sources and estimates.
4 Two extremely useful collections of similar case studies are Haberland and Measham (2002) and Naples and Desai (2002). The former focuses explicitly on implementation of Cairo within countries and contains some cases that overlap with those presented below. Naples and Desai offer a much broader analysis of women's transnational activism across very diverse issues and regions.
5 Mukherjee (2002) notes that the programme's focus was mainly on men until the 1970s, when the public outcry over mass forced vasectomies led the government to change the now-tainted term 'family planning' to 'family welfare' and to adopt a strategy that targeted women.
6 In the mid-1990s, India passed two constitutional amendments providing that one-third of all seats in elected local councils, or *panchayati raj*, would be reserved for women. As a result, some '800,000 women, many of them from impoverished and socially depressed backgrounds', are now representing their communities on these councils (Mukhopadhyay and Sivaramayya 1999: 340–1; Jain/UNDP 1996).
7 In Rajasthan, women who seek abortions or complain of RTI or STI symptoms ('white discharge') are simply referred to private doctors, who charge fees they almost always cannot afford (Visaria and Visaria 1999). Bang et al. (1989) first reported the extremely high incidence of RTIs and STIs among rural Indian women; for a more recent and excellent discussion, see Ramasubban (1999).
8 Critics have blamed the TFA for declining 'performance' levels in sterilization acceptance (Mallik 2002).
9 Egyptian Law No. 32, regulating charity organizations, was amended in 1998 to allow extensive government intrusion in the work of NGOs, including imprisonment of activists. Human rights leaders in particular have found themselves 'under fierce attack' and their leaders arrested for criticizing the state (Sadasivam 1999).
10 Research, Action and Information Network for the Bodily Integrity of Women, based in New York City (*www.rainbo.org*). The FGM Task Force pulled out of the National NGO Commission in 2000.
11 The Task Force got an additional and unexpected boost when CNN in Egypt, during preparations for ICPD coverage, chose to broadcast a particularly graphic

documentary about the circumcision of a young Egyptian girl that created a public sensation.

12 For other discussions of this controversial issue of terminology, see Assaad 1999; Abd el Salam 1999; DeJong 1999; Obermeyer and Reynolds 1999.

13 A recent law passed in adherence to SAPs reduced both the length and number (from three to two) of employed women's maternity leaves, constituting a *de facto* antinatalist incentive contrary to the spirit if not the letter of the ICPD POA (see Seif El Dawla *et al.* 1998).

14 The 1993 Act on Family Planning, Human Embryo Protection and Conditions of Permissibility of Abortion made abortion illegal in Poland except in cases of threat to a woman's life, rape, incest or foetal impairment, thereby reversing the much more liberal law of the previous four decades. The more recent law has affected poor women most harshly and forced women with adverse medical conditions to carry their pregnancies to term, in at least one case resulting in a woman's death (Sadasivam 1999; Polish Federation for Women and Family Planning 1999).

15 As of January 2003, the CRLP officially changed its name to Center for Reproductive Rights.

16 At 270:100,000 live births, Peru has the highest maternal mortality ratio of any country in the Latin American and Caribbean region except Bolivia (UN 2000: Table 3A). On the 'global gag rule', see Chapter 2 above.

17 For a discussion of the concept 'sense of entitlement', see Petchesky and Judd 1998. For a much more thorough review and analysis of the work of ReproSalud, see the excellent monographs by Coe (2001) and Rogow (2000).

18 For a much fuller and fascinating discussion of gender and health in Tajikistan, see Harris 1998 and 1999.

19 At the UN Conference on Children in 2002, the Nigerian government publicly supported the abstinence-only, anti-sexual and reproductive rights position of the US-led conservative faction – despite the fact that that same government continues to sponsor the liberal Sexuality Education Guidelines in their domestic policy. (Interview with Bene Madunagu and Grace Osakue.)

20 All of the information on SHAPE that follows is based on Shongwe 1998.

21 Many thanks to Sandra Vallenas from ReproSalud for providing this information.

22 The SUS 'provides over 70 per cent of outpatient and hospital care, managing a vast network of public units and accredited private services. For approximately 120 million Brazilians [out of a total population of around 160 million], SUS is the sole source of medical care' and provides a free, all-inclusive benefits package (Corrêa 1998).

23 The 1996 constitution's equality clause prohibits discrimination on the basis of 'race, gender, sex, pregnancy, marital status, ethnic or social origin, colour, sexual orientation, [and] age'; and its 'freedom and security of the person' clause states: 'Everyone has the right to bodily and psychological integrity which includes the right to make decisions concerning reproduction; to security in and control over their body; and not to be subjected to medical or scientific experiments without their informed consent.' South Africa's is one of a tiny number of national constitutions in the world thus far that specifically guarantees freedom from discrimination based on sexual orientation.

24 See Gill/World Bank (1999) for an interesting account of Bank-supported health

and community development projects linking local NGOs and poor grassroots women in India. The Delivery of Improved Services for Health (DISH) project in Uganda (a partnership of the Johns Hopkins School of Public Health, the University of North Carolina, and the Uganda Ministry of Health) integrates the whole range of reproductive and sexual health services included in the Cairo POA, under the slogan, 'Care for Others, Care for Yourself' (see *http/:www.jhuccp.org*).

25 During ICPD+5, Vatican spokespeople used this as an argument supporting the Holy See's UN non-member-state status as well as a 'conscience clause' in the abortion paragraph. Of course, if providing social services were a condition of being a 'state', then many of the UN's member states would be disqualified.

26 According to the *Statistical Yearbook of the Church for 1997* (Libreria Editrice Vaticana: Città del Vaticano, 1999), the Catholic Church operates 5,188 hospitals, 17,157 ambulatory clinics, 825 leprosaria, and 12,209 nursing homes (for the elderly, chronically ill and disabled) throughout the world – a total of 35,379 health care institutions. The number of Church-run primary and secondary schools world-wide numbers nearly 2 million. (Thanks to Larissa Gray of the Permanent Observer Mission of the Holy See to the UN for this useful source.)

6

Conclusion

Reflections on Global Governance and Transnational Feminist Movements in an Era of Infinite War

A few years ago … it seemed as if there was a real promise of hope for the poor – both black and white – through the Poverty Program. There were experiments, hopes, new beginnings. Then came the buildup in Vietnam and I watched the program broken and eviscerated as if it were some idle political plaything of a society gone mad on war, and I knew that America would never invest the necessary funds or energies in rehabilitation of its poor so long as adventures like Vietnam continued to draw men and skills and money like some demonic destructive suction tube. So I was increasingly compelled to see the war as an enemy of the poor and to attack it as such. (Rev. Martin Luther King, Jr, 1967)

What is emerging is the need for globalization as an economic process to be subject to moral and ethical considerations and to respect international legal standards and principles. (Mary Robinson, 2002)

Prologue

My purpose throughout this book has been twofold: first, to explore the manifold ways in which reproductive and sexual rights intersect with, and are embraced within, a wide range of health, human rights, human development and social and gender justice issues; and, second, to use this inquiry to rethink the complex political dynamics in which transnational women's NGOs find themselves, as they manoeuvre within a globalizing yet deeply divided and grossly inequitable world. In the 1990s and early 2000s, transnational women's NGOs continued to play a central role in the creation and implementation of international norms and agreements related to reproductive and sexual rights. Feminist groups in the 1990s had a major impact at both international and national levels in shifting dominant discourses about reproduction, population and sexuality in a direction that puts the ends of women's health and empowerment above that of reducing population growth and that links sexual and reproductive rights to macroeconomic transformation and human development. This is a major historical achievement and a mark of the power of transnational women's NGOs and feminist ideas.

Yet in the new millennium an increasingly hostile economic, cultural and political climate has severely limited the translation of this discursive shift into effective policies and programmes. In the circumscribed world of UN conferences, women's groups have found themselves on the defensive even to retain the language achieved in the 1990s regarding sexual and reproductive health rights, much less to obtain the necessary accountability mechanisms and resources to make good on the promises. At the UN Special Session on Children in 2002, they managed – with extraordinary difficulty and skill – to defeat the agenda of conservative religious groups, led by the Bush administration, for 'abstinence-only' sex education, reproductive health services that explicitly preclude abortion, family planning without contraceptives, and a definition of 'the family' solely as marriage between a man and a woman. But the result was a mere two paragraphs on 'sexual and reproductive health' that basically cross-reference the previous conference documents and give most emphasis to the important but uncontroversial goal of reducing maternal and neonatal morbidity and mortality (Girard 2002). At the Millennium Summit in 2000 and the Financing for Development Conference in 2002 women's health groups were powerless to prevent the holistic vision of Cairo and Beijing being replaced by a handful of 'feasible', quantifiable, and presumably cost-effective targets (see Chapter 2). And in Johannesburg, at the World Summit on Sustainable Development in September 2002, the US-led conservative faction once again tried to subvert health as a human right by making it conditional upon 'national laws and cultural and religious values' and replacing every reference to human rights in the final Declaration with the nebulous phrase 'human dignity'.[1]

Meanwhile, women's and all progressive social justice groups have watched the UN itself – a political arena where it seemed to matter in the 1990s that we make 'women's voices' heard – become increasingly ineffectual and subservient to global corporate, military and fundamentalist forces. These forces, despite their patent moral and ethical corruption, wield institutional and material power far greater than any that feminist groups could possibly attain at this moment – especially after 11 September 2001.

Shortly after the horrific attacks on the World Trade Center and the

Pentagon, George W. Bush launched a 'war against terrorism' that would have no end in time or space. Deploying a classic imperialist manipulation of feminism, its rationale was not only to avenge and protect America but also to 'rescue' the women of Afghanistan, if not the entire Gulf and Central Asian regions. As I was revising this manuscript for publication, the US government was spending $2 billion a month to wage its 'war against terrorism' – a total of $37 billion one year after the 11 September attacks and projected to multiply by tenfold over the ensuing decade (Stevenson 2002). Its search-and-destroy missions in the mountains of Afghanistan, its relentless bombings there that killed more innocent civilians than all those lost in the World Trade Center, and its efforts to fortify 'homeland security' within the US had not succeeded in capturing Osama bin Laden or destroying the Al Qaeda network or making Afghanistan and Afghan women more secure or free from warlord violence.[2] Yet the Bush administration was proposing a $48 billion increase in its military spending for 2003, the largest increase in a generation (Dao 2002). It concluded a treaty on nuclear weapons with Russia that essentially abandoned the mutual protections of the old ABM treaty and preserved thousands of nuclear missiles for imminent use (Plesch 2002; Arkin 2002). And it proclaimed a new strategic doctrine of unprecedented bellicosity that would give the Imperial United States a unilateral right of pre-emptive attack and 'permanent military supremacy' over 'any imaginable adversary at any point in time' (Klare 2002: 12; Sanger 2002).[3] It thus prepared the way for a pre-emptive invasion of Iraq – against the opposition of the United Nations and most of the world, with only a single ally-in-arms, Britain – and the perpetuation of the bloody mimetic saga of Jihad vs Crusade.

Why was this happening? What was it all about? Some astute observers of US foreign policy surmised that the Great Game this time – the ultimate stakes over which some lives become valued much more than others – is not very different from what it was through most of the last two centuries: land, water and, above all, oil. A former member of Tony Blair's Cabinet writes in the *Guardian* that the movement of massive numbers of US troops, tanks and fighter planes back into the Gulf region under cover of ousting the evil Saddam Hussein has more to do with instability in neighbouring Saudi Arabia and the goal of seizing control over 'the world's largest oil reserves' before they fall 'into the hands of an anti-American, militant Islamist government' than it does with 'fighting the war on terrorism'. With an overwhelming military presence in the region, 'no longer would the US have to depend on [and protect] a corrupt and unpopular royal family to keep it supplied with cheap oil' (Mowlam 2002). *Corporate tribalism* – the allegiance to the oil, gas and military hardware industries based in the south-western and western US states – bears certain resemblances to ethnic and warlord tribalism. The Bush government, mirroring its jihadist enemies, thrives on war, a permanent state of war. But the war it seeks is not only against terrorism but for Unocal, the Carlyle Group, Aramco, Halliburton, cheap crude, unimpeded pipelines, unlimited SUVs, and a President whose image is manly (see Petchesky 2001/2002).

Amidst this grotesque explosion of masculinist militarism, feminist visions for social and gender justice embodied in UN documents come to seem utopian and futile, and the regime of international law and the UN agencies responsible for global health and conflict resolution are consigned to irrelevance. Human rights, multilateralism and international cooperation get buried beneath the wings of the phoenix superpower that issues ultimatums in return for rubber-stamp approvals. And lesser powers (Israel, India, Russia, China, Zimbabwe) follow the lead, declaring their own 'wars against terrorism' to justify repressive policies. In such a climate, ideas like 'health security', 'human security' and 'social security' become shadowy relics in the face of the prerogatives of 'national security' (or oil security); the welfare state and the democratic state become ghosts in the citadel of the total security state. Of course, the US, which can boast 40 per cent of the world's military spending, already has sufficient high-tech military power to overwhelm any and all countries (if not terrorists with box-cutters). But its unrivalled imperial might is not gaining Americans more actual security in everyday life, any more than it is Afghanis or Israelis or Europeans. The world has never been more dangerous.

Women's human rights groups have been at the forefront of efforts to seek non-violent, multilateral solutions to conflicts through international law. The new International Criminal Court's founding statute makes rape, sexual slavery, enforced pregnancy and other forms of sexual violence war crimes and crimes against humanity. Resolution 1325, adopted unanimously by the UN Security Council in October 2000, calls attention to the gender dimensions of armed conflict and ensures women's equal participation in peacekeeping and peace-building efforts (Rome Statute 1998; Hague Appeal *et al.* 2000). These are historic achievements that women's peace groups can claim: without their efforts none would have come about. But the US, having 'unsigned' the ICC treaty, threatens to subvert it; and Resolution 1325 remains a noble sentiment, unenforced in Afghanistan, the Middle East or anywhere else. 'National sovereignty', now enfolded within a US imperial order, is alive and well, as much a patriarchal construct as ever. The 'war against terror' becomes a pretext for power that claims immunity from international accountability, democracy and human rights.

A year before the fatal 11 September, leaders of 191 nations, including the US under Bush's watch, agreed to the following targets to be reached by 2015, as part of the Millennium Development Goals (MDGs): cut in half the proportion of people living in poverty and suffering from hunger; reduce by two-thirds the under-five mortality rate; reduce by three-quarters the maternal mortality ratio; halt and begin to reverse the spread of HIV/AIDS as well as the incidence of malaria and other major diseases; cut in half the proportion of people in the world without access to sustainable drinking water (then numbering over 1 billion but expected to reach 3 billion, or 40 per cent of the world's population, by 2015).[4] How sobering that only a year and a half later – in the shadow of the 'war on terrorism' and the perpetual security state – this agenda, which seemed paltry and reductive to many of us at the time, now seems a veritable utopia.

Even Americans, in the heartland of imperial power, suffer a social and health toll exacted by militarism and the boundless 'war on terrorism'. Ironically, the anthrax scare and the perceived threat of bioterrorism that rattled the United States in the fall and winter of 2001 exposed the gaping inadequacies in the US public health system, after 15 years of budgetary cutbacks and privatization. For a brief moment, US health advocates thought the bioterrorism threat might be a wake-up call that would result in restoring decent funding for public health in the US. Yet the $11 billion the Bush administration budgeted to defend America against bioterrorism turned out to be for expanded stockpiles of vaccines and antibiotics, construction of containment laboratories, research into new drugs and biodetectors – in other words, a new bioterrorism industry, not more public hospitals, clinics or sexual and reproductive health or primary health care services for the poor (Stolberg 2001, 2002). In fact, Bush's budget would *reduce* Medicaid payments to public hospitals in at least 31 states and clamp down on other mechanisms states have found to finance health care for the poor and disabled (Pear 2002a). It would do little or nothing to address the escalating costs of prescription drugs for the elderly – far be it from the capital of global capitalism to regulate drug prices as most European countries and Canada do. And it would do absolutely nothing for the 41.2 million men, women and children without health insurance in the country – unless they happen to be victims of a bioterrorist attack, or foetuses. The Bush administration cynically offers pre-natal care to 'unborn children', not to pregnant women, under the Children's Health Insurance Program – a cheap toss to right-wing anti-abortionists in the US but degrading to low-income women (Toner 2002; Pear 2002b). Losing one's job in America means losing health insurance; being uninsured in America is a low-grade, daily kind of terror.

This grim scenario brought me to a pessimistic train of questions that recalled Martin Luther King's ominous words in the midst of the Vietnam War, over thirty-five years ago. Can war – particularly a globalized state of permanent war and ubiquitous police surveillance – ever be compatible with the goal of assuring equity and justice in access to health care and a healthy life for all? Is the 'war against terrorism' ultimately a war against health and all forms of social justice – an 'enemy of the poor' and especially women? Will we allow human rights and women's empowerment to get buried in the ashes of 11 September? I believe a worse danger than terrorism now is that all the resources that might have been channelled toward reducing misery; eliminating maternal mortality; treating, preventing and curing AIDS; and promoting equality will be diverted into the waging and deflecting of violence. As the US military-corporate establishment careens from Iraq towards new adventures in North Korea, Syria, the Philippines, Uzbekistan, Kyrgyzstan, Yemen and Iran; as our borders become more patrolled and fortified and Muslim, Arab and South Asian immigrants increasingly become the targets of unconstitutional detentions and racist harassment, I have to wonder whether this endless war and all its ancillary security production will sap the energies and budgets for health, education, and racial and gender justice for years to come – meanwhile inflaming the global hostility and terror it was supposed to curtail.[5]

And yet … never was the need greater for those 'international legal standards and principles' Mary Robinson calls for, to challenge the violence of global capitalism and global militarism and subject them to an effective system of democratic and participatory governance. This book has focused on the matters of health provision, gender equality and human rights; yet there is no way to 'reform' or implement those areas of policy without a thorough restructuring of existing systems of global governance and how they involve both national governments and transnational civil society organizations. So let me think about what such transformation might mean.

The need for global governance

I ended the previous chapter by arguing, as many others have, that more than ever under conditions of global capitalism we need effective, responsive systems of national governance; the state is still important (Eisenstein 1998; Hardt and Negri 2000; Stiglitz 2002). It is not a question of national *or* global sovereignty, since the national is no longer able – technologically, economically, or politically – to function autonomously, and the global can only function through the national and the local. Nor is it a question for feminists and other social activists of engaging with the state *or not*, or with global institutions *or not*, since power works through these different levels simultaneously – in a complex, sometimes decentralized, sometimes concentrated network of pressure points – and we must be engaged with power wherever it is. Rather, the real questions have to do with how to advance democratization at all the levels while understanding that democratization is not an event but an ongoing and never-ending process. We must imagine how to construct a globalized world that reflects popular mandates and aspirations rather than trade liberalization agendas and the interests of warmongers and corporate élites; and how to revitalize state and local responsibility for social welfare without underwriting authoritarian regimes.

Clearly, the past decade of efforts in this regard has shown limited results at best. Critics have charged that the UN conferences of the 1990s – which, after all, produced documents that are not only flawed but have no binding legal force – amounted to a tremendous waste of resources and energy. All the 1990s 'mega-conferences', many would argue, 'produced watered-down, non-binding declarations and unfunded mandates to carry out action plans that are set within the policy framework of an expanded global economy based on enhanced corporate rights' – and diminished national capacity and resources (Menotti 2000). While the original documents themselves are worthy statements of principle, the UN system and UN diplomats are poorly equipped to engage in a meaningful process of monitoring and reviewing their implementation at the national level. As O'Neill writes, 'States sign these agreements in response to pressure from domestic women's groups as well as out of concern for their international reputation.' Their compliance through concrete legislation and policy mostly depends on the determination and positioning of women's NGOs and social movements to demand implementation and monitoring or, more likely, carry it out themselves (O'Neill 1995: 62). Silliman goes further, arguing that 'changes made at the international conference level are not structural' and, being non-binding, 'do not effect changes on a domestic level'. Moreover, she asserts, 'working to "monitor" the promises made at UN conferences ... often deflects NGO energies and sucks them into the orbit of governments and international lending agencies, where their impact is marginal and where too often their politics are compromised' (Silliman 1999: 152). But the reality, as we saw earlier, is more complex and differs widely depending on national and local contexts.

With regard to health, surveys conducted by both transnational women's NGOs and UN agencies provide ample evidence that free markets and current patterns of privatization are failing to deliver on the promises of Rio, Vienna, Cairo, Beijing and Copenhagen (see Chapter 5). Certainly they are not providing adequate reproductive and sexual health services for all who need them, nor assuring the realization of reproductive and sexual rights, much less the right to the highest available standard of health care for all. These surveys suggest the need for health reform programmes that strengthen, rather than weakening, *public* health systems, not only through increased investments but also through reorganization, retraining (in gender awareness, for example) and more effective management. At the same time, corruption, insensitivity and inefficiency in public-sector health services have been the constant complaint not only of international donor agencies but also of community groups and their constituencies – those who depend on the services most.[6] Given this dubious record in many countries, as well as the prevalence of markets everywhere, it is probably inevitable that (for-profit) private companies as well as (non-profit) charitable, NGO and community-based groups will often function side by side with public agencies to provide services. But in such hybridized (government/non-governmental) systems, privatization of *function* must be distinguished from privatization of *accountability* and *cost*. It is essential that the regulation and enforcement of universal standards of access and quality, including ensuring full coverage for those without means, remain the state's responsibility and be backed up by an effective system at the global level for enforcing basic human rights.

Women's NGOs can play an important role both as service providers and as civil society advocates who independently monitor health providers, both public and private. In some circumstances they can function effectively as 'partners' of the state, providing crucial advice and training of health officials and clinicians. But they should not take over the responsibilities of the state to provide overall regulation and assurance of basic health care for all, nor should they cede their independent critical role. The most successful models of national-level implementation of sexual and reproductive health programmes (such as Brazil and South Africa) exist in countries with strong state institutions that subscribe to principles of social solidarity and justice (across gender, race-ethnic and class divisions), along with strong civil society organizations and social movements that push the state forward and call it to account. In those societies, a high level of democracy and popular mobilization makes it possible for women's NGOs both to cooperate with and to critique, from a stance of independence, government policies and decision-making bodies. Yet these very conditions suggest that such 'best practice' models may not be easily transferable to societies where the political conditions are different, where authoritarian (as in Egypt and Malaysia) or US-lackey (as in the Philippines and Colombia) regimes prevail. Even in those societies with strong democratic institutions and social solidarity principles and where women's and other civil society organizations are robust, global economic constraints impede the implementation of avowed social justice and health care goals. This means that transformed institutions of global governance, including enforcement mechanisms for an economic enabling environment and promotion of human rights, are needed everywhere.

In fact, many civil society participants at all the UN conferences of the 1990s and early 2000s, including women's health and development NGOs, understood all too well that actualizing the promises of the conference action plans ultimately would depend on two kinds of fundamental structural trans-formation: in the *authority and decision-making processes within the UN system*, and in the *distribution of global resources*. They struggled bravely to incorporate such structural changes into the conference documents – and failed (see Chapter 2). Now, however – shaken by the Asian economic crises of the 1990s and those that followed in Latin America, and the evident failures of IMF-imposed 'shock therapy' – liberal neo-Keynesians have joined radical global justice activists in calling for structural reforms. Concerning the 'architecture' of global finance, critics of global capitalism have focused their proposals on the role and power of the IFIs, their self-prescribed autonomy from the rest of the UN system, and how to make them more transparent and accountable (Stiglitz 2002; Elson 2001; Menotti 2000; UNDP 2000a). Interpretations of the original mission of the Bretton Woods institutions and approaches to the problem of their non-accountability differ. Still, most critics would agree that (1) during the 1980s and 1990s the IMF and World Bank came increasingly to identify their mission with 'the interests of international financial corporations' (Elson 2001: 1); (2) their procedures, based on a process of weighted voting and closed-door decision making favouring wealthy countries, are inherently undemocratic; and (3) this has created 'a tragic institutional disconnect' between the goals of those institutions – to liberalize markets and contract national spending – and those of the UN's specialized agencies, treaty bodies and conference action plans, which typically urge member states to expand social programmes and human rights enforcement (Menotti 2000).[7]

In the case of the World Bank, as we saw earlier, except for a brief 'neo-Keynesian moment' embodied in the 2000 WDR, its policies favour narrowly defined, targeted social insurance schemes and 'safety nets' rather than broad redistributional measures. Moreover, as charged in a letter written in 2001 by a group of environmental and global justice NGOs to the executive directors of the Bank and the IMF, the conflicts between 'the macroeconomic and structural adjustment policies associated with their lending policies' and the 'poverty reduction objectives' create a 'two-track process'. The Bank urges governments to consult with their citizens and involve NGOs and CBOs in poverty-reduction strategies while negotiating SAPs and lending policies privately with finance ministers, in total secrecy from civil society organizations or elected representatives.[8] Even in regard to Poverty Reduction Strategy Papers (PRSPs), the Bank and the IMF conceive of civil society participation narrowly, in terms of 'monitoring and implementation' rather than policy planning and programme design (ActionAid *et al.* 2001). Finally, for all its recent emphasis on poverty reduction, gender equality and social sector investments, the Bank, like the IMF and the WTO, remains completely free from any formal accountability to the 'global citizens' whose taxes provide its revenues and whose lives are shaped by its decisions. Its 'constituency' is government finance ministers (themselves unelected), especially the US Treasury Secretary; and its deeply ingrained utilitarian values are those, not of a democracy, but of a bank.

To address this structural contradiction in the present UN system, one approach is to demand greater transparency in the proceedings of the IMF, World Bank and WTO. The 2001 Recommendations on Information Disclosure to the IMF and World Bank by ActionAid, Friends of the Earth, and other transnational NGOs, for example, urge those institutions to adopt a practice of public disclosure of all policies and documents related to macroeconomic and structural reforms, especially in poorer countries. These policy documents should be released, they argue, 'in draft form, *prior* to Board approval', to give 'sufficient time for the public to respond and provide input' (ActionAid *et al.* 2001). But the mechanisms and strategies through which such disclosure would occur and public response and input would be organized, especially in countries with heavy media censorship and unrepresentative or ineffectual legislatures, remain unclear. Stiglitz, in his indictment of globalization, seems to believe that democratization of the IFIs is as necessary as their transparency, but he is pessimistic about the chances of reforming their governance systems any time soon. His proposals for institutional reform thus also tend to emphasize the need for greater disclosure. Remarking the irony that the IMF, the US Treasury and the World Bank constantly call for 'greater transparency' on the part of recipient governments yet are themselves 'among the least transparent [institutions] that I had encountered in public life', Stiglitz proposes 'forcing the IMF to disclose the expected "poverty" and unemployment impact of its programs' (2002: xii, 240). Yet who will do the 'forcing' here, and how do we move from 'improving the information that citizens have about what these institutions do' to 'allowing those who are affected by the policies to have a greater say in their formulation' (2002: xii)? Clearly, 'transparency' is useless without enforcement and monitoring mechanisms, and public disclosure of policies after the fact is not the same as democratic participation in making those policies to begin with.

This raises very basic questions about what we even mean by 'democratization' at the level of global institutions. Echoing the sentiments of many African, Asian and Latin American governments, Stiglitz is disturbed by the patently undemocratic deliberations in the World Bank and the IMF, where 'votes are allocated on the basis of economic power' and the bankers and trade ministers of wealthy countries function like the dominant shareholders on a corporate board. But tinkering with the voting rules would not make these institutions more democratic, as Stiglitz himself is surely aware. The WTO has a 'one country, one vote' rule and requires consensus, but there too the US, Europe and Japan tend to exercise *de facto* domination (Stiglitz 2002: 225, 227). Stiglitz's answer, with regard to the IMF, is to narrow its mandate to short-term crisis management and to replace bail-out loans with bankruptcy proceedings over which the IMF (a major creditor) would have no control. But this 'solution' evades all the most critical issues: What kind of institutional framework should be in charge of global financial governance? Whose voices should be represented there? And how can superpower domination of these institutions be avoided without serious measures to redistribute resources and wealth?

Elson suggests 'the idea that the IMF should make a social impact assessment of its policies' is a step in the right direction (2001: 9), but, again, to whom or to what body should it be responsible for reporting such an assessment? Who will monitor its accuracy, what criteria will be used to determine an *unacceptable* social impact, and what authority can enforce changes in its practices if negative consequences (such as major increases in unemployment or clinic and hospital closures) occur? Relevant to this problem of self-assessment by institutions that remain unaccountable is a recent policy decision by the World Bank to evaluate all its projects – those having to do with foreign direct investment and infrastructure as well as health, education and poverty reduction – to assess their impact on women and girls. This extension of 'country gender analysis' to every country where the Bank maintains field offices grows out of its own research showing a strong positive correlation between a country's poverty level and the economic and social status of its women and between the level of women's participation in political life and 'good governance': 'societies that discriminate by gender pay a high price in terms of their ability to develop and to reduce poverty'.[9]

That the World Bank is now conveying the message to governments and other IGOs that 'gender equality is a core development issue' and that women are the key to reducing poverty and corruption is definitely good news for feminists. Both the new gender analysis policy and the Bank's published research are further indications that its openness to feminist thinking far exceeds that of the IMF and the WTO. At the same time, it is not at all certain that this policy will actually pre-empt the Bank's 'two-track process' by applying not just to its social development and poverty reduction projects but to all its lending practices as well. And this is because it is not at all sure that gender analysis has become a *holistic vision of social change* for the Bank, or that its officials actually understand what it is about women's lives that makes them a more reliable measure of community and national development than men's (Eisenstein 2004). Finally, on the matter of governance, this undeniably progressive internal policy change still hangs suspended in the ether of unaccountability and absence of formal outside monitoring.

Some critics have proposed a new body to oversee the IFIs and the WTO and 'manage systemic risk' – a World Financial Authority or a 'world tax organization'. Kapstein proposes a new Bretton Woods conference that would address the issues of labour mobility and migration, '[giving] workers a voice in international institutions', establishing 'an international social minimum' (in regard to living standards, education, health and wages), and regulating international capital flows (Elson 2001: 8; Kapstein 1999: 104–5). But piling on more layers of global governance institutions will change very little if 'public ownership' continues to mean accountability to investors and the wealthiest donor countries rather than to 'those who are affected by the policies'; just as 'one country, one vote' is meaningless if no reliable democratic processes exist at the national level to hold country representatives accountable to their citizens. If the IFIs and the WTO are 'public institutions' whose 'actions affect the lives and livelihoods of billions [of people]' (Stiglitz 2002: 228), then it becomes critical to identify what are the global publics that count and who is entitled to speak in their name.

Rao defines the problem as 'the absence of a global state organ with even a modicum of democratic representation'. He laments that, 'because the top security and financial agencies are grossly unrepresentative, weaker members of the world community are at a disadvantage in pressing their claims in other forums' (such as the General Assembly or UN conferences on women, the environment, racism, and financing) (Rao 1999: 80). Given the emergence over the past decade, however, of a dynamic though still evolving global civil society in both UN and alternative forums (described in Chapters 2–4), the narrow post-Second World War model of nation-states as the only legitimate 'members' simply will no longer do. Neither is it sufficient to tie 'global democracy' and the 'development of global citizenship' to the proposition that 'international agreements, such as those negotiated in the WTO, ought to be debated and approved by parliaments' (International Symposium 2000: 44), since truly democratic and representative parliaments are the exception rather than the rule in today's world.[10] The UNDP, in its 2000 *Human Development Report*, goes further, urging that more transparent, participatory decision making in the IFIs and the WTO requires inclusion not only of 'small and weak countries in the processes of negotiation' but also of 'civil society – including corporations, trade unions and global networks of NGOs – in a forum for open debate rather than in behind-the-scenes lobbying and on-the-street demonstrations' (UNDP 2000a: 85). But where is gender in all this, and what is to ensure the inclusion of women's voices, especially those of the most marginalized women? Moreover, should multinational corporations be considered equivalent to other civil society groups? Finally, can global justice activists ever afford to exchange 'on-the-street demonstrations' for participation in global governance forums – as if these were mutually exclusive rather than *interdependent* strategies for democratic expression?

Most of the proposals for reforming global governance raise more questions than they answer, leaving me eager to understand what a feminist analysis might add to the debate. Three key points are critical here: *structure*, *representation* and *resources*. Concerning the first – the appropriate structure for overseeing the economic, social and human rights consequences of global finance, trade and militarism – this structure, in fact, already exists, in a formal and 'constitutional' sense, in the present UN system. It consists of the General Assembly as the highest governing body within the UN; the Economic and Social Council (ECOSOC) and the Secretariat, which operate under the General Assembly; the human rights treaty bodies, which operate under ECOSOC and may receive individual and group complaints; and the International Court of Justice and the International Criminal Court (ICC), which have authority to interpret and apply the rules of international law.[11] Adding to this tripartite structure a world financial or tax authority responsible for regulating global capital flows and gathering global resources would not require a new Bretton Woods conference but only an act of the General Assembly and execution through ECOSOC; any such authority must, like the IFIs, be made clearly subordinate to the governing bodies that already constitute the UN system (Charter, Articles 57 and 63). In its paragraph on global governance reform put forward at WSSD+5 in 2000, the Women's Caucus directly addressed this need, but the US and other wealthy countries quashed it.[12] The main problem is not one of inventing new structures but rather of giving substantial resources and enforcement power to those that already exist – and this is largely a matter of political will.

In fact, a major reason why the existing UN governance structure has been weakened through consistent and systematic denigration and defunding by the US and some of its allies is precisely because its processes over the past decade have grown increasingly hospitable to the perspectives and partici- pation of women's, human rights and economic justice NGOs. If the ICC had not been 'engendered' through the criminalization of war rape and other sexual/reproductive abuses, the US might still have opposed it, but not as strenuously.[13] If the General Assembly and specialized agencies had not opened up the conferences on environment, human rights, population, social development, women and racism to a vast array of civil society – and especially feminist – groups, it is doubtful that the US right wing would have been so determined to discredit those conferences. If the UN Human Rights Commission and Mary Robinson, its High Commissioner, had not been sympathetic to feminist, anti-racist and global justice viewpoints, it is unlikely that the Bush administration would have worked so hard to push her out.

From a feminist standpoint, both ECOSOC and the human rights treaty bodies have shown themselves to have a lively and growing commitment to enforcing gender equality and economic and social rights, including sexual and reproductive rights and the human right to health (Center for

Reproductive Rights 2002). This commitment is far greater than that of the IFIs, whose primary concern is cost-effectiveness and securing markets and who have little understanding or love for human rights concepts. As we saw, CEDAW and CESCR have been responsive to reports and appeals by women's NGOs citing government violations of women's reproductive and sexual rights. In April of 2002, the UN Commission on Human Rights adopted resolutions to integrate the human rights of women throughout the UN system and all its activities, and inviting the human rights treaty bodies 'regularly and systematically to take a gender perspective into account in the implementation of their mandates'.[14] In some instances the treaty bodies have acted boldly to confront the existing power relations of global capitalism, as in the CESCR's statement to the WTO that 'international economic policy formulation' and 'trade liberalization' must serve the ends of economic, social and cultural rights as codified in existing international human rights instruments (see Chapter 3). But their lack of enforcement power and the widely held perception of their recommendations as essentially moral prescriptions, lacking any legal authority, prevent the treaty bodies from effecting systemic change. Like the other branches of the UN governance system, they are stymied by persistent claims of national sovereignty, strong resistance from the most powerful governments, and grossly inadequate human and financial resources.

All of this raises once again the question of whose voices count within the UN system and which interests they represent. A strong case can be made for representation of transnational civil society groups – especially women's, trade union, indigenous, refugee, economic justice, human rights, health, anti-racist and youth groups – as voting participants in major UN forums and deliberations, including: the General Assembly, ECOSOC, the Security Council, specialized agencies, the IFIs, and the WTO. Such a change in existing UN processes would of course amount to not just a reform, but a fundamental transformation of the post-war UN system, premised as it is on state members and the principle of national sovereignty. National governments will not accede to it soon or easily. Moreover, how such representation would be organized and authenticated among the infinite number of groups claiming some kind of global presence and interest would admittedly pose enormous challenges. But, leaving aside for a moment the criteria for representation, the ethical and political arguments for it seem clear:

• Nation-states are no longer the only major actors on the global scene. Organized civil society groups as well as TNCs and religious entities also play important roles in shaping global norms and policies in nearly every arena, from refugees and peacekeeping to labour and health, and this widely recognized reality is probably irreversible.

- Because such groups operate transnationally rather than within individual countries, particular governments cannot represent them; their global perspectives and concerns (except for those of TNCs – see below) are *de facto* excluded from a system based on nation-states as sole and sovereign actors.

- Civil society groups have already achieved a proven track record of institutional knowledge and substantive expertise in their decade or more of lobbying UN conferences and advising UN agencies, treaty bodies and even the Security Council. But such informal and 'behind-the-scenes' participation is no longer adequate. In fact, in many instances 'NGO lobbying' has become a kind of unpaid labour providing information and insights to governments and UN agencies without corresponding power or recognition. It needs to be replaced by effective forms of institutionalized representation with full speaking and voting rights.

- Above all, basic principles of democracy require that those whose lives and well-being are most affected by global policies have an authoritative voice in formulating those policies. This is especially true under conditions of the ascendance of global capitalism, militarism and fundamentalism and their tendency to undermine democratic participation at the national level.

Precise criteria and procedures for determining which groups have an authentic claim to representation within global governance forums and how that representation should be constituted are matters requiring complex debate, not only in the General Assembly, but even more importantly in the incipient venues where the germs of a global civil society have already begun to grow: the Internet, NGO forums attached to major international conferences, the World Social Forum and its regional offshoots, etcetera.[15] What I imagine is not an infinite plurality of small sectoral and identity-based groups but a process that would encourage the formation of larger coalitions across a variety of grids – economic justice, health, gender equality, anti-racism, peace, environment – and base voting rights on functional connections to community-based and popular movements. But my imagination is too parochial and limited to think this through alone. Here, I want to make just two central arguments: *for* the full representation and participation of women, especially those from poor and racially marginalized communities; and *against* any conception of global civil society that privileges or even gives equal weight to TNCs.[16]

In considering proposals to reform the 'international financial architecture', Diane Elson makes a strong argument that women, 'as provisioners of last resort' within households, are those who bear the greatest costs of the risky fiscal and monetary policies 'inherent in liberalized financial markets', with their resultant unemployment and loss of food, health and social security. Therefore reform efforts ought to '[ensure] that women representing poor and middle-income households play an equal role with men in holding providers and users of private and public finance to account' (Elson 2001: 4, 14). We can extend this kind of gender analysis to global governance generally, connecting issues of representation and voice to the World Bank findings regarding the contingency of economic growth, poverty eradication and good governance on gender equality and women's empowerment. Making sure women's groups – especially those representing poor and middle-income communities and the most vulnerable populations – are fully part of global (and also national and local) decision making about macroeconomics and health is not only a matter of justice and fairness. It is also grounded in the empirical reality that women across the globe are those most responsible for securing the health and survival of families and communities – and ultimately societies – when both markets and public provisioning fail, or when military violence results in social chaos. Everything feminists have written for twenty years about gender divisions and the hidden productivity of women's reproductive labour – now confirmed in studies by the World Bank – tells us why women's participation in global governance is indispensable for human development and survival.

Altogether different is the case of the TNCs. In trying to imagine the potential composition of an enfranchised global civil society, I listed four reasons above that can be applied to ground the 'credentialling' of a wide range of NGOs and other groups representing transnational social movements. As global actors whose agency has a direct impact on international policies and whose interests are surely affected by those policies, multinational corporations might also seem to qualify. But some obvious differences separate the TNCs and their kind of agency from groups representing women and the poor. First, corporations, unlike individual human persons, are not the *subjects* of fundamental human rights – to life, health, security of the person, an adequate standard of living, political participation, freedom from discrimination and coercion, and the like – but more often their *transgressors*. Years of attempts to draft corporate 'codes of conduct' and to devise mechanisms – still weak and unsuccessful – for enforcing corporate responsibility in international documents (Richter 2001) and two decades of human suffering from privatization and marketization of health care (see Chapters 3 and 4) are testament enough to the ways in which TNCs function as the problem rather than the solution within global power relations. The circus of Enronesque scandals in 2001–2 only made the corruption in giant corporate culture more nakedly visible (Block 2002; Bello 2002).

Second, in their lobbying of UN meetings, corporate interests have consistently taken a position opposed to serious mechanisms for enforcing human rights standards and international law in favour of 'voluntary, toothless agreements'; in other words, they stand in opposition to the very purposes of a transformed global governance system (TRAC 2000: 9). Finally, at the global as well as the national level, multinational corporations are already fully represented. Not only do they have the direct ear of governments (as in the drafting of TRIPS) or actually own the governments (through campaign contributions, bribes, the lure of investments and other levers), but in some cases, as in the contemporary United States where so many are headquartered, they *are* the government, moving back and forth between federal executive and corporate offices like migrating geese (Phillips 2002). In this respect, to lump an undifferentiated 'private sector' into 'civil society' without distinguishing the very special positioning of the multinational corporate giants is to re-enact the Rawlsian (and Hobbesian) fiction that simply pretends, for purposes of constituting that society, that we are all already equal and the same.

Despite these seemingly obvious realities, women's and other global justice NGOs have had to witness one of the most disheartening developments within UN politics to have emerged under global capitalism: the corporatization of the UN itself. This trend actually began in 1992 – the same year as the Rio conference on the environment – with the dismantling of the UN Centre on Transnational Corporations by then Secretary-General Boutros Boutros-Ghali (TRAC 2000). But its high point came in 2000 when Secretary-General Kofi Annan established the Global Compact, an arrangement coinciding with the organization's millennium activities and intended to formalize the relationship between the UN and 'the business community'. In theory the Global Compact is a set of nine principles, based on various

environmental, labour and human rights agreements, in whose promotion
and implementation a long list of corporations have been invited to join (see
http://www.unglobalcompact.org/; TRAC 2000). It thus gives a kind of moral
imprimatur to the directive toward 'public–private partnerships' between UN
agencies and corporations, like those we saw earlier between WHO,
UNAIDS and UNICEF and the giant pharmaceutical companies in the
matter of 'equity pricing'. In practice, however – as the Alliance for a
Corporate-Free UN and a 'Citizens' Compact' signed by dozens of transnational
NGOs attest – the Global Compact's invited participants include some of the
most egregious corporate violators of human rights and environmental and
labour standards, such as Nike ('symbol of sweatshops') and Royal Dutch/
Shell (oppressor of the Ogoni people in Nigeria), giving them an undeserved
mantle of legitimacy. More serious still, rather than a step towards corporate
accountability, the effect of the Global Compact is to substitute for an
effective monitoring and enforcement process that would regulate corporate
behaviour; it thus endorses voluntarism and self-regulation instead of international law (TRAC 2000; CorpWatch 2001).

The moves toward corporatizing the UN also embody the conceptual flaw
I alluded to above of defining 'civil society' as an undifferentiated mass, while
in practice privileging its most powerful members. In part because they look to
corporations for funds, UN leaders seem to feel a closer affinity to 'the
business sector' than to the part of civil society that actually represents the
people, especially the poor and women. At the UNGASS on HIV/AIDS in
2001, the General Assembly's invitation to 'civil society' participants included
not only health and AIDS groups but also 'the business sector, including
pharmaceutical companies' (IGLHRC 2001).[17] In a speech to the World
Economic Forum in New York in 2002, as thousands of protesters marched
outside, Kofi Annan warned the corporate élites gathered there that 'Business
cannot afford to be seen as the problem'; they should beware of 'the image
that the world had of them' (Schemann 2002). Whose voices count and who
gains recognition in global governance forums is heavily skewed by the
problem of inequitable resources.

In her *Justice Interruptus* (1997), Nancy Fraser admonishes us to give as
much attention to the 'injustices of recognition' as we give to the 'injustices of
distribution'. But ultimately the two are inextricably bound together. As
Rousseau understood two and a half centuries ago, if a small élite (in this case,
a handful of countries and corporate interests) monopolizes vast proportions
of the world's wealth and arms, that élite will also exercise disproportionate

control over votes, policies and political discourse (Rousseau 1987). If empowerment and public participation of women are necessary for economic growth, development, and thus a greater store of resources, it is also true that redistributive policies directing more resources toward women's health, education and reproductive and sexual rights are necessary to enable such participation. Borne down upon by HIV/AIDS, childcare burdens, malnutrition and illiteracy, how many women can participate effectively in public policy debates – even in their own home towns? And where will the resources come from to eliminate these barriers?

We have seen how inadequate and unreliable are voluntarist approaches and 'international cooperation' to generate resources for health care. While loans from multilateral development banks can prod governments to maintain social sector investments, and injections of private and public donor grants targeted at preventable, life-threatening diseases can help alleviate major health crises, these levels of aid can neither finance heavily under-resourced health delivery systems nor guarantee equal access. Moreover, most international assistance and humanitarianism – whether of Northern governments, drug companies, or the Bill and Melinda Gates Foundation – remain voluntary, discretionary in regard to funding levels and targets, and unaccountable to anyone. As in any other form of charity, the donors retain all the power – in the case of health, setting priorities for all the world's poor. Without human rights-based remedies spelled out in binding international documents, as we saw in relation to the case of access to essential medicines and the Global AIDS Fund (Chapter 3), there can be no legal mechanisms to uphold health rights over corporate profits and imperial military aims.

Even when governments sign on to commitments with time-bound targets – for example, the ICPD POA's promise of $21.7 billion for reproductive health by 2015, or the MDGs – there is still no effective machinery of global governance to enforce timely (or any) payments. That is why the first UN conference ever devoted solely to the problem of where and how to generate the resources to make good on the commitments of all the conferences of the previous decade – the Financing for Development (FfD) Conference, held in Monterey, Mexico in March 2002 – was, in the words of Jubilee South, a 'festival of words' but 'a disaster for development' (*DAWN Informs* 2002). The so-called 'Monterey Consensus' reaffirmed all the maxims of neoliberal global capitalism – trade liberalization and foreign direct investment as the main engines of economic growth, privatization of financing, macroeconomic policies that ignore gender realities, and a complete absence of references to human rights. It failed to make any real changes in the global economic governance system, merely 'encouraging' stronger 'coordination' between the UN and the IMF, World Bank and WTO while leaving the latter institutions virtually unaccountable. While providing a pre-conference NGO Global Forum and 'quadripartite' roundtables for exchanges between 'governments, civil society, the business community, and the institutional stakeholders', it left most NGO participants, particularly women, feeling silenced and betrayed.[18]

As for new resources, the FfD outcome document calls for a doubling of development aid to the poorest countries in order to meet the 2015 MDGs, yet puts the greatest responsibility for mobilizing resources on domestic governments. In fact, the international publicity surrounding the Monterey conference incited a promise by George W. Bush to create a 'millennium fund' that would double the US foreign aid budget from $10 billion to $20 billion over the next three years – an announcement hailed as the single most important achievement of the conference. Yet closer scrutiny reveals that, even with this (still to be realized) increase, the US still will be contributing well below 1 per cent of its GDP to foreign aid[19] – one-tenth the amount some members of the Bush administration projected for the cost of a war in Iraq. And the aid pledge comes with harsh strings attached: in order to get it, countries must prove they comply with whatever formula for free trade and economic and political reform the US chooses to dictate, including co-operation in the 'war on terrorism' (Bumiller 2002a, 2002b). Hence the shape of 'multilateralism' in the era of imperial war; hence the pitfalls of charity.

In relation to transforming global governance, the issue of resources poses a complicated train of chicken-and-egg dilemmas. As I argued in Chapter 4, a social and gender justice agenda requires that we return to the values of universal entitlement and universal access to health care, education and minimum incomes. But this is inconceivable without significant redistributive measures, both among and within countries, to rechannel excessive wealth and divert military spending into global and national social accounts. In turn, for such redistribution to happen at the global level would require the kinds of transformations in existing global governance institutions I have outlined, in order to democratize as well as strengthen and give enforcement power to the UN system and to subordinate the IFIs and the WTO to its jurisdiction. But such strengthening and democratizing will itself require substantial new resources, which comes back to the proposal of some kind of world finance or taxation authority to coordinate and enforce global revenue collection and redistributive measures through a variety of means – tithing not only wealthy governments but TNCs (through Tobin taxes, taxes on pollution, fines for trafficking in human labour or global public goods, etcetera) (Wachtel 2000). To complicate things further, the enforceability of such mechanisms will depend on replacing the outmoded and unreliable framework of charity or 'aid' with one of corporate and national duty – of distributive justice. And even then – assuming the establishment of an authority to generate revenues and a normative framework to support it – we cannot assume that merely identifying sources of new revenues will in itself guarantee gender and racial equity in how the benefits of those revenues are allocated. As Sonia Corrêa has written about Brazilian health groups' success in getting a new national tax on financial transactions dedicated to primary health care and HIV drugs,

> This suggests that the tax is not good in itself simply because it raises money from financial transactions. Its 'good' or 'bad' development meaning clearly depends on political conditions surrounding its adoption and on the ability of social stakeholders … to determine how it will be spent. (Corrêa 2002)[20]

So we come back to politics and the need for mobilized and persistent social movements – transnational, national and local – to continue pressuring institutions, occupying the streets, and organizing communities in the never-ending quest to democratize power and concretize social, racial and gender justice.

The strategic place of transnational NGOs and coalitions

In the previous section I tried to demonstrate the need for a radical restructuring of existing global governance institutions that will include both (a) effective means to assure accountability of the World Bank, IMF, WTO, TNCs and major donor countries to uphold international human rights; and (b) effective mechanisms of democratic participation for transnational civil society organizations, giving them a genuine place and voice within the UN system. But this kind of transformation cannot happen without the dynamic mobilization of transnational movements for social/economic/racial/gender justice world-wide *and* the organic connection of those movement, participatory community action in local settings. In this way, transnational movements and their organizational expressions become the critically situated nerve centres *in between* global governance and local (national as well as community-based) popular self-determination. I believe such a bridging function is vital for two reasons. First, contrary to the perspective of some anti-globalization voices, globalizing tendencies are here to stay and need to be democratized and socialized, since they can't simply be abolished and dismantled in favour of a return to some kind of pre-capitalist local autonomy.[21] This does not preclude many sorts of decentralization – of decision making, planning, monitoring and budgeting as well as service delivery (see discussion of people's and gender budgets, below). Such decentralization is in fact an essential condition for the democratic vision of global governance institutions I have endorsed, but its effectiveness in the twenty-first century depends on the integrity and authority of those institutions (compare Bello 2002).

This relates to my second reason, which is that, while states are still necessary to implement social welfare and human rights norms, the nineteenth-century concept of 'national sovereignty' is an anachronism. To revert to the national sovereignty principle in defence against the inequities of global capitalism is to deny women's experience almost everywhere of the nation-state and its historic roots in masculinism, racism and homophobia – even when it was the response to racist and masculinist colonialism.[22] In sum, we need transnational NGOs as the site of an operative global civil society, at the crossroads of the global and the local. Or, as Diane Otto puts it, we need a 'postliberal perspective' that 'decenters states and stresses the importance of local participation in the international community' (1996: 134).

Towards this end, it is critical that the site of the transnational be as multidimensional, varied and broadly coalition-based as possible – across all the vital movements for social change. This poses a serious dilemma for existing transnational NGOs, since often those with the greatest impact in the short run are those mobilized around the most focused, single-issue campaigns. One thinks of the campaigns for a landmine-free world, against sweatshops, and for codifying rape and other sexual and gender abuses as war crimes and crimes against humanity – all noble achievements and in many ways strategic models. In this book, I have tried to show the relative successes of transnational women's health groups in securing the conceptual legitimacy and, in some congenial national settings and pathbreaking experiments, the living reality of reproductive health and rights (Chapters 2 and 5). I have also explored the global campaign for access to essential HIV/AIDS medicines as a vital wedge opening up recognition not only of health as a human right but also of that right as superior to trade and property rights (Chapter 3). In each of these cases, as well as the other three mentioned, transnational NGOs have confronted the most powerful centres of global capitalism, militarism and fundamentalism – and held their ground.

The problem is that such campaigns, focused on particular rights and abuses, are limited in the constituencies they mobilize and too often do not encompass *long-term structural transformation* of global governance institutions. (The Women's Caucus for Gender Justice is an exception here, in so far as its momentous work to define gender-based war crimes was critical in constituting the ICC and determining its jurisdiction.) To encompass such a vision, issue-oriented organizations need to become part of large transversal/polyversal coalitions.[23] This means that groups advocating health as a human right, including women's groups committed to a reproductive and sexual rights agenda, must ally more closely with other transnational NGOs and CBOs that are utilizing human rights strategies – to eliminate poverty, secure a safe environment, challenge gender violence, racism and militarism, promote alternative models of social and economic development, and bring peaceful resolution to conflicts. Since this kind of broad and deep alliance in global activism is the only hope we have for a more just, equitable and healthy world, it is worth thinking about strategies to make its impact stronger and more lasting.

Building broader coalitions. Even within the health domain, numerous divisions exist that weaken the effectiveness of transnational activism. First, there are the divisions between 'inside' and 'outside' I discussed in Chapter 2. Political differences still divide transnational women's health NGOs – between, on one hand, those who tend to focus more on implementing reproductive and sexual health and rights and working to change the policies of IGOs and governments, and, on the other hand, those who tend to focus more on opposing population control policies and are suspicious of working within or with policy-making bodies. But, as I argued earlier, it is not particularly useful to dichotomize NGOs and social movements, or activists who work 'inside' and those who work 'outside' institutions ('lobbying' vs 'struggle politics'), since the long-term viability of any social movement clearly requires *both*. The distinction is better seen as a practical division of labour that also requires continual and organic links between these different levels or modes of seeking change, since each has its own built-in forms of insularity. For activists who work solely within global institutions (such as organizations that lobby UN meetings or file affidavits in courts or with UN treaty bodies), the space they inhabit and its inner dynamics become their entire world, and too often they become mesmerized by the power relations within that space. For those who engage in oppositional movements and protest, a moment of heightened media attention or a concession by those in power often becomes the end in view, without a transformative vision. And for community organizers and direct service providers – especially perhaps in the health field – their constituencies' immediate survival needs and the need to increase precious resources tend to overshadow everything else.

To cut through these different but related forms of myopia requires a more holistic and critical imagination. Coalition building requires explicit conversation across diverse levels of activism about common long-range goals as well as mapping of the ways that different approaches contribute to reaching those goals, so that strategies and tactics don't get mistaken for whole worldviews. The alliance between TAC, MSF, ACT-UP and CPT around treatment access in 2000–2001 is an admirable example of groups managing to bridge some of these kinds of 'inside'–'outside' divisions, bringing together lobbyists, advocates and community activists and working at local, national and global levels simultaneously. However, that alliance, whose members tend to be pragmatic and crisis-oriented, also failed to articulate a global vision of permanent mechanisms and processes for setting health care standards and *enforcing* health rights in the long term. In addition, the movement for treatment access has never fully incorporated a gender analysis into its campaigns and slogans – for example, the central importance not only for AIDS prevention but for social development and justice of addressing, not just access issues in the narrower sense, but also women's and girls' inequality and patterns of male violence and domination. Nor has it given the same attention to allying with and listening to women's health and reproductive and sexual rights groups as it has shown when dealing with trade unions, People with Aids (PWA) and medical groups, in order to mobilize a much broader coalition for health as a human right (see Chapter 3 above).

Transnational women's movements have also contributed their share to the pattern of movement fragmentation, or separate but parallel paths. Many women's health groups have expended little or no energy on organizing around women and AIDS, or on linking with HIV/AIDS and treatment access groups in what would seem to be an obviously common struggle for health and bodily integrity rights. This reticence, I believe, is in part related to persistent nervousness about sexuality even among some women's groups. In the familiar mantra of 'sexual and reproductive rights,' many women's health groups still feel more comfortable on the safer terrain of reproductive health; sexuality (except in relation to adolescents and sex education) remains something of an orphan, its 'rights' still awaiting thorough exposition on the global political stage (Corrêa and Parker 2001; Petchesky 2000). On the other hand, those women's health organizations that have asserted a more affirmative position on behalf of sexual rights for women and girls have avoided open confrontations around issues of sexual orientation rights and homophobia. And they have not actively sought alliances with transnational development and economic justice NGOs that are attempting to change global macroeconomic policies and structures. Conversely, organizations that focus primarily on macroeconomics – including gender-identified (WID, GAD and others) as well as mixed (like Third World Network, Jubilee South or ATTAC) organizations – show little interest in rights of sexuality, the body, or even health, unless convinced of their direct connection to trade or labour issues (as in the case of TRIPs and GATS).

All these multiple fragmentations contradict in practice the integral connectedness of the body, its health and sexuality, with the enabling – or disabling – macroeconomic, cultural and political environments it inhabits. They evade the lived reality I have tried to put at the centre of this book's analysis: the HIV+ pregnant woman who is poor and also sexually desiring, a worker or small farmer and also a mother; who may be living in southern Africa or southern Louisiana but in either setting has no health insurance or access to quality treatment and care and has to face shaming and abuse from family members and religious and state authority figures every day of her life; and whose chances of living longer and better will probably not improve without significant shifts in the global distribution of wealth and political power.

What if transnational women's health and reproductive/sexual rights movements, women's movements against violence, sexual abuse, FGM and other harmful practices, the movement for treatment access and access to essential medicines, and transnational movements for gay and lesbian rights – in short, all the NGOs and movements around bodily integrity and personal and health rights – were to forge stronger working alliances? Such a coalition would exert formidable power in the common effort to resist various fundamentalisms and to advance the human rights of health, sexuality and bodily self-determination. And what if this coalition joined forces with groups organized around peace, environment, anti-racist and economic justice issues for common goals related to global governance, human rights enforcement, generating resources and redistributing wealth? Then together they might secure a global governance system capable of enforcing those rights. This enlarged coalition – an authentic global civil society – would by definition be one that bridged (without erasing) differences of North and South, women and men, race/ethnicity/community, protester and lobbyist, and the many kinds of sexual orientation. It would constitute 'polyversal feminism' for the twenty-first century.

Strengthening organization and leadership, linking the global and the local. In fact, polyversal feminists are active today in organizations like DAWN, Articulación Feminista Marcosur and WEDO, who bring feminist leadership to the formation of a broad, multidimensional global civil society. These organizations work both inside the venues of UN conferences (such as the WCAR, FfD and the Johannesburg WSSD) and within alternative gatherings for 'another world', in the World Social Forums and their International Councils (see *Dawn Informs* May 2002). They help to remind development and economic justice NGOs about gender and the linkages between personal, social and economic rights (especially for women) and to build a strong countervailing pressure against both global fundamentalist and global corporate forces. The need for such leadership seems indisputable. As we saw in the experience of transnational women's NGOs working to implement reproductive and sexual rights as well as in the campaign for access to essential medicines, 'social movements do not sustain themselves without organizations' (Abdulhadi 1998). The effectiveness of women's health NGOs both nationally and internationally has depended on strong leadership, including effective secretariats or coordination centres. In the context of the UN conferences, usually this has meant one or two NGOs with extensive knowledge and a clear vision taking the lead in planning and strategizing on behalf of the Women's Caucus; in national contexts, it has more often meant a coordinating body that directs a coalition or network of women's NGOs who have worked together over time.

To maintain their legitimacy and their claim to be representative, on the other hand, NGOs and their leadership require organic ties to community-based social movements and organizations. Such ties cannot be taken for granted; they must be consciously nurtured. As the case studies in Chapter 5 illustrate, country-based efforts to implement women's reproductive and sexual rights have been most successful where NGOs have a strong history of connection to popular movements and CBOs (as in Brazil, the Philippines, South Africa or Peru). These examples show that NGOs can act as a bridge between social movements and governing institutions and can work effectively for popular participation in local and national health policy making. The challenge now is to make this kind of organic connection to the local and to popular self-determination the basis of transformative processes toward democratizing global governance. 'Localizing global politics' and informing the global with local knowledges are interrelated projects (Naples and Desai 2002: 37).[24] One potential source that might inform such local–global linkages is the proliferation of gender and participatory budgeting projects.

The gender and people's budget movements that have emerged in Brazil, South Africa and many other countries in recent years embody the possibility of creating democratic, participatory processes of financial decision making at the national and municipal levels (Elson 2001).[25] Although gender-responsive budgeting projects have existed since 1984, they began to flourish as a means of democratic participation in macroeconomic governance after 1995, when the concept was endorsed in the Beijing Platform for Action. Subsequently, gender budget initiatives have developed in over 40 countries stretching across all the world's regions. While not all these initiatives are conducted through participatory methods, they share the objectives of producing gender-disaggregated analyses of budgetary allocations and expenditures and more gender-egalitarian macroeconomic policies – for example, increases in social spending and reductions in military spending (UNIFEM/ Commonwealth Secretariat/IDRC 2001). The Alternative Federal Budget (AFB) exercise in Canada has a national steering committee open to representatives of any citizens' groups that accept its core principles, which include gender equality.[26] Its 'participatory approach [aims] to put financial policy at the service of social goals through a process of social dialogue' – in sharp contrast to World Bank and IMF forms of 'participation' that bracket financial policy and prescribe minimal public expenditure based on 'debt relief or social safety net funds' (Elson 2001: 13). Elsewhere, as in the municipality of Porto Alegre and nationally in South Africa, participatory and pro-poor budgeting that may not have a specifically gendered focus becomes a *de facto* vehicle for women's participation in macroeconomic policy making. This is because these projects assess budgetary priorities through a democratic process using such mechanisms as popular assemblies, in which women are over half the participants, and write-in campaigns among grassroots communities and organizations, where women's activity is much more prominent than in national elective bodies (Çağatay 2000; Fair Share 2000 and 2001/02; Budlender 1998).

Budgets are the most concrete public manifestation of distributive justice (or injustice), and democratic mechanisms to involve people directly in budgetary decision making are based on an assumption that people understand best their own and their communities' needs and are able, with some popular education, to make informed decisions about accessing and allocating resources. That conflicts about priorities will exist and necessitate extensive debate and compromise is a given; the point is the process itself and making it as participatory as one can imagine. As Gigi Francisco (2002) has written of national-level taxes on financial transactions, they have advantages over a global tax because they 'bring the debate on revenue utilization closer to the women and men that are directly affected by poverty'. We might see gender and people's budget projects as both a model and a vehicle for connecting grassroots women to global governance through participatory methods at the local level, where the poorest women often have a public voice. Indeed, it seems quite significant that gender and participatory budgeting arose in the context of democratic globalization, particularly after the Beijing Women's Conference. Without that context, it is unlikely that the idea for these projects would have spread so rapidly and shared a common framework of moral legitimacy. At the same time, popular decision making about local and national budgetary allocations can be an important resource to democratize and 'engender' global decision making about security, redistributive justice and health. The key here is the vibrancy of women's movements across the globe.

Epilogue: is another world possible?

At the end of this project, the state of the world leaves me teetering between pessimism of the intellect and optimism of the will. Earlier in my thinking I had reservations about the fitness of the language of empire, yet today I find myself unavoidably reverting to it all the time. The Bush government's designs on the Middle East, Central Asia and Africa, on the replacement of regimes and the redrawing of maps; its pronouncements of not only manifest destiny but also absolute, uncontestable dominion over all other countries and international organizations, have all the markings of classic imperialist behaviour (Armstrong 2002; Hardt and Negri 2000). As a citizen of this country, I will now have to work with many others to mobilize a huge mass movement at home to oppose this juggernaut that our government has become, and this will consume much of our energies and many (how many?)

years, as it did in the days of Vietnam. We'll put on hold the battles for health, gender equality, racial equality and human rights.

Earlier I thought it accurate to designate only certain governments in the rest of the world as imperial lackeys and copycats, assuming that some would still exercise their veto in the Security Council and their power in other UN forums to counter US domination and hubris. Today I wonder if there will be any objectors left (besides Cuba, and perhaps Brazil under the new government of Lula) after all fall in line behind the scramble for markets and investments and the relentless march towards armaments and war in Iraq and beyond. Will this become a failed test of the UN's 'relevance' as the Bush administration clearly wants? A whole world of lackeys and copycats.

Another scenario: on the last day of writing this book, there was a bomb scare in the famous Jewish delicatessen on the ground floor of the building where I live – where I have lived for the past eighteen years. As I left the building, suspended between fear and disbelief (probably it's all just a hoax), I remembered one thing I knew on 11 September a year ago: 'As an American, a woman, a feminist and a Jew, I have to recognize that the bin Ladens of the world hate me and would like me dead' (Petchesky 2001/2002). But I also remembered what every moment since that day has confirmed: Bush's America not only will not but cannot 'rescue' me, since its wealth and power and the hubris they generate do so much to foment the angers and hatreds that terrorists thrive upon. Why should I or any Americans have a privileged haven from the dangers and risks that menace the daily lives of so many others elsewhere?

Yet scattered among the grim and militaristic features of the post-9/11 world are also some hopeful signs, nourishing my optimism. In the wake of the corporate corruption scandals and the church paedophilia and sexual abuse scandals that crowded the headlines in 2001–2, these centres of power have lost some of their veneer of invincibility and holiness. Perhaps many more people will join the popular uprisings in Latin America, the women protesters who shut down the oil companies in Nigeria, and gay and lesbian, feminist and social justice groups everywhere in voicing their doubts about global capitalism and global fundamentalism.

In China a catastrophic HIV/AIDS epidemic has prompted a new social movement, including a petition from rural patients demanding 'that the government provide free medicine, or medicine we can afford, and [that it] … produce copies of Western medicines as quickly as possible'. Although the Chinese government jailed the principal organizer of the Chinese AIDS Action Project for nearly a month, it released him to continue his work after an international outcry and in order to pursue a desperately needed grant from the Global Fund to Fight AIDS. And, notwithstanding its eagerness to join the WTO, it promised to 'manufacture a full complement of AIDS drugs if Western patent holders did not lower prices within the next few months'. A not insignificant aspect of this story is that the activist in question, Dr Wan Yanhai, has been organizing around AIDS and gay and lesbian rights since the mid-1990s and is linked through the Internet and direct connections to gay and lesbian and treatment access groups in the US and around the world (Rosenthal 2002a, 2000b, 2000c).

This recent development in China represents yet another eruption of global movements and coalitions for health as a human right, in a society that has had little affinity with human rights strategies and concepts. It is one more among many, many indicators that transnational movements for social justice, health rights and gender and sexual equality are growing stronger and more effective all the time and will be the force that democratizes global governance and transforms global capitalism through local democratic partici-pation. Inevitably, women's movements are playing a leading role in this transformative process. As Eisenstein (2004) writes, 'although global capital, as such, is no friend to women and girls, it unsettles existing gender relations in ways it cannot simply control'.[27] Likewise, fundamentalisms have spawned resistance, however quiet, among women and girls in Iran, Afghanistan, India and Israel and within the Catholic Church. And global militarism too will create its own backlash, as resentment builds against US bullying and women's and peace and human rights groups throughout the world demand that the UN uphold the principles written in its own Charter.

I see this vision of global governance through civil society representation, women's empowerment and local participatory democracy. I see it in my mind's eye, though I hear, more loudly than ever, the drums of war.

Notes

1 See United Nations, World Summit on Sustainable Development (WSSD), Plan of Implementation (September 2002), Chapter VI ('Health and Sustainable Development'), paragraph 47; and United Nations, WSSD, 'The Johannesburg Declaration on Sustainable Development,' A/conf.199/L.6/Rev.2 (4 September 2002). Many thanks to Joan Ross Frankson and June Zeitlin for information on the outcomes at WSSD.

2 At this writing, rival groups still contended for power in most of the country; only the capital city of Kabul was considered stable; a car bomb had killed 28 bystanders in Kandahar; an assassination attempt on the US-backed president, Hamid Karzai,

had come within inches of succeeding; and the Bush administration was still hesitating to join the International Security Force set up to help stabilize the country.

3 President Bush signalled this new doctrine in the same State of the Union address of January 2002 in which he called Iraq, Iran and North Korea an 'axis of evil', when he announced: 'America will do what is necessary to ensure our nation's security…. I will not wait on events while dangers gather. I will not stand by as peril draws closer and closer. The United States of America will not permit the world's most dangerous regimes to threaten us with the world's most destructive weapons' (*New York Times*, 30 January 2002, p. A22). For further background to the doctrine, see the excellent article by Armstrong (2002).

4 The World Summit on Sustainable Development in 2001 added to this list the goal of cutting in half by 2015 the number of people in the world without access to sanitation.

5 Klare (2002), in an excellent overview of 'The New Bush Doctrine', makes a similar point.

6 Regarding abusive treatment of low-income women by public health services, see IRRRAG studies on Brazil (especially the North-east), Egypt, Mexico, and the United States, in Petchesky and Judd (1998); CRLP/CLADEM 1999; Mackintosh and Tibandebage 2000.

7 This 'disconnect' on the social development side of the UN is replicated on its security side, with the growing enfeeblement of Security Council resolutions and the systematic US effort to undermine the principles of collective security embodied in the Charter as well as the International Criminal Court and the Geneva Conventions. The quasi-unilateral US war on Iraq in early 2003 was aimed as much at usurping this collective system as it was at unseating Saddam Hussein.

8 This is the same contradiction I pointed out earlier with respect to the Bank's health policies and HSRs.

9 For original research, see King and Mason/World Bank 2001; *www.worldbank.org/gender/prr*; see also Moline 2002; UNDP 2000b.

10 Even in a formal democracy like the US, the two major political parties and all but a handful of Congressional representatives remain beholden to huge corporate interests for their campaign financing and supinely obeisant to these interests and an increasingly secretive and imperial Executive. See Phillips 2002.

11 See United Nations Charter, chapters IX–X and XIV–XV and the Rome Statute establishing the ICC in 1998. The Final Outcome Document of the Financing for Development (FfD) Conference (Mexico, March 2002) affirms this authority structure when it says: 'We reaffirm our commitment to enable the General Assembly to play effectively its central role as the chief deliberative, policy-making, and representative organ of the United Nations, and to strengthen further the Economic and Social Council to help it fulfil the role ascribed to it in the UN Charter' (paragraph 59). I omit from this analysis the special functions of the Security Council, spelled out in Chapter V of the Charter. Although the Council must report annually to the General Assembly, its deliberations are essentially separate and independent. Proposals for enlarging its permanent membership to include more of the world's developing countries and regions have floated around for years and would have to be implemented through an amendment of the Charter by a two-thirds vote in the GA and of 7 members of the Security Council (Chapter XVIII).

12 The Caucus paragraph stated: 'Reform the international financial structure, including a re-examination of current voting rights of the IMF and creation of mechanisms to assure accountability of the international financial institutions, including the World Trade Organization, to the United Nations system, through the human rights treaty bodies as well as ECOSOC, and the compliance of their policies and programmes with social development concerns and internationally agreed human rights principles.'

13 While a major motive behind US opposition is fear that US officials and former officials (like Henry Kissinger) may be prosecuted as war criminals, especially since the apprehension of Pinochet, there is also considerable worry in the Pentagon that US soldiers stationed around the globe will be subject to continual accusations of rape and other offences against women and girls living near US bases. Given the actual frequency of such incidents and of prostitution and sexual 'R & R' sponsored by US military authorities, this is a realistic concern. See Enloe 2000.

14 This resolution (E/CN.4/2002/L.59), adopted without a vote, may be found at the Commission's website: *http://www.unhchr.ch/Huridocda/Huridoca.nsf/*.

15 Such representation would also, of course, require substantial amendment of the UN Charter.

16 I am assuming that civil society representation in a reconstituted General Assembly would include religious as well as secular groups and that the inclusion of *all* religions that are organized transnationally would serve effectively to neutralize the vastly disproportionate status and influence the Vatican currently has in that body.

17 Corporate lobbyists hardly need a formal invitation to make their presence felt at UN meetings. At the WSSD+5 conference in Geneva, during contentious deliberations on TRIPS and human rights, American representatives of major pharmaceutical companies (many of them with Swiss offices) were very much in evidence in the halls.

18 It is an interesting development that, by the time of the Monterey conference, UN discourse was recognizing the separateness of these four constituencies; that 'the business community' is not just another part of 'civil society'. This piece of realism no doubt grows out of accelerating anti-corporate protests by civil society groups across the globe but also a more dubious intent to privilege business. To access the document, go to *http://www.un.org/esa/ffd/*. See also *DAWN Informs* May 2002 and FfD Women's Caucus Statements, 19 March 2002, available at *www.wedo.org*.

19 Apart from military spending, which consumes the lion's share of the total US foreign aid budget, US foreign assistance as a percentage of GDP is the lowest it has been since the Second World War and absolutely the lowest among all industrialized countries (Sokolsky and McMillan 2002).

20 Elson makes the same point when she warns that 'controls on international movements of capital are quite compatible with patriarchal control of women' and a failure to invest in gender-equitable policies (2001: 10). In a recent article stressing the ambiguous effects of globalization, Tina Rosenberg (2002) makes a compelling case that growth matters – and is most successful in countries (like Chile and Malaysia) that have regulated and taxed short-term capital inflows. But she completely ignores any questions of gender equity or who benefits from such taxes.

21 Even if 'abolishing' the IFIs and the WTO were a realistic possibility, I doubt that it is a more useful demand than calling for their radical reform and subordination to

both UN-based and local monitoring mechanisms (cf. Hardt and Negri 2000; Hardt 2002).

22 A very rich literature on gender, sexuality and nationalisms has emerged in recent years. Among others, see Alexander 1997; Eisenstein 1996; Grewal and Kaplan 1994; Heng 1997; Imam 1997; Kaplan *et al.* 1999; Moghadam 1994; Parker *et al.* 1992; Yuval-Davis 1997.

23 For interesting uses of the concepts of 'transversal' and 'polyversal' in the context of building transnational feminist movements, see Yuval-Davis (1997); Eisenstein (2004).

24 Keck and Sikkink offer an analysis of the synergestic relation between trans-national and local activism that is both eloquent and precise. They call it a kind of 'boomerang' effect, which curves around local state indifference and repression to put foreign pressure on local policy elites.... Thus international conacts amplify voices to which domestic governments are deaf, while the local work of target country activists legitimizes efforts of activists abroad' (1998: 200). This exactly describes the process that links the case studies in Chapter 5 to the women's coalition campaigns in Chapter 2, above.

25 The first women's budget was piloted by the Australian government in 1984, but 'the initiative really took off as a social movement in the context of social reconstruction in post-apartheid South Africa' (Standing 2002: 24). The 'people-centred budgeting' movement (which may or may not have a gender focus) began in 1989 in Porto Alegre, Brazil. Like the women's health and HIV/AIDS move-ments and the municipal health councils in that country (see chapters 3 and 5), participatory budgeting in Porto Alegre 'grew out of a long democratic tradition of civil society active [sic] in neighborhood organizing and negotiating with the city' (Çağatay 2000: 24).

26 The principles are 'full employment, a more equitable distribution of income, eradication of poverty, gender equality in economic life, the protection of civil, political, economic, social and cultural rights, improvement in the environment, strengthening of social programs and public services and the creation of a more just, sustainable and peaceful world order' (quoted in Elson 2001: 13).

27 Quoting Lisa Lowe, Naples (2002) makes a very similar point: 'Ironically "the very processes that produce a racialized feminized proletariat ... displace traditional and national patriarchies", thus generating "new possibilities precisely because they have led to a breakdown and a reformulation of the categories of nation, race, class, and gender"' (p. 9).

Bibliography

Abbot, F. (2002) 'Setting the Scene: A Historical Perspective on the Relation Between R & D and IPR, the TRIPS Agreement and the Concept of Public Goods', paper presented at Conference on 'The Crisis of Neglected Diseases: Developing Treatments and Ensuring Access', MSF/DND Working Group, New York, 14 March.

Abd el Salam, S. (1999) 'Language Is Both Subjective and Symbolic', *Reproductive Health Matters*, Vol. 7, No. 13, May.

Abdulhadi, R. (1998) 'The Palestinian Women's Autonomous Movement: Emergence, Dynamics, and Challenge', *Gender and Society*, Vol. 12, No. 6.

Abdullah, H. (1995) 'Wifeism and Activism: The Nigerian Women's Movement', in A. Basu (ed.), *The Challenges of Local Feminism: Women's Movements in Global Perspectives*, Westview Press, Boulder, CO.

AbouZahr, C. (1999) 'Disability Adjusted Life Years (DALYs) and Reproductive Health: A Critical Analysis', *Reproductive Health Matters*, Vol. 7, No. 14, November.

ActionAid *et al.* (2001) 'End Secrecy of Structural Adjustment Programs' (open letter to the World Bank and the IMF on information disclosure), *www.actionaid.org*.

AHI (Action Health Incorporated) (1999) *Growing Up, A Newsletter for Young People*, Vol. 7, No. 1.

Ahlberg, B. M. *et al.* (2001) 'Gendered Construction of Sexual Risks: Implications for Safer Sex among Young People in Kenya and Sweden', *Reproductive Health Matters*, Vol. 9, No. 17, May.

Aka-Dago-Akribi, H. *et al.* (1999) 'Issues Surrounding Reproductive Choice for Women Living with HIV in Abidjan, Côte d'Ivoire', *Reproductive Health Matters*, Vol. 7, No. 13, May.

Akhter, F. (1994) 'Resist Reduction of "Population" Issues into Women's Issues', *People's Perspectives*, No. 8.

Alexander, M. J. (1997) 'Erotic Autonomy as a Politics of Decolonization: An Anatomy of Feminist and State Practice in the Bahamas Tourist Economy', in M. J. Alexander and C. T. Mohanty (eds.), *Feminist Genealogies, Colonial Legacies, Democratic Futures*, Routledge, New York.

Alexander, M. J. and C. T. Mohanty (eds.) (1997) *Feminist Genealogies, Colonial Legacies, Democratic Futures*, Routledge, New York.

Allotey, P. A. and D. D. Reidpath (2002) 'Objectivity in Priority Setting Tools: Context and the DALY', *Reproductive Health Matters*, Vol. 10, No. 20, November.

Altman, D. (1995) 'Political Sexualities: Meanings and Identities in the Time of AIDS', in R. Parker and J. Gagnon (eds.), *Conceiving Sexuality: Approaches to Sex Research in a Postmodern World*, Routledge, New York.

—— (2001) *Global Sex*, University of Chicago Press, Chicago.

Altman, L. (2000) 'Africa's AIDS Crisis: Finding Common Ground', *New York Times*, 16 July.

—— (2002) 'Women with HIV Reach Half of Global Cases', *New York Times*, 27 November.

Alvarez, S. (1990) *Engendering Democracy in Brazil: Women's Movements in Transition Politics*, Princeton University, Princeton, New Jersey.

Amalric, F. (1994) 'Finiteness, Infinity and Responsibility: The Population–Environment Debate', in W. Harcourt (ed.), *Feminist Perspectives on Sustainable Development*, Zed Books, London.

Anand, S. and K. Hanson (1997) 'Disability-Adjusted Life Years: A Critical Review', *Journal of Health Economics*, Vol. 16.

Andrews, E. (2002) 'IMF Loan to Brazil Also Shields US Interest', *New York Times*, 8 August.

Annas, George J. (1997) 'Patients' Rights in Managed Care – Exit, Voice and Choice', *New England Journal of Medicine*, No. 337.

Anzaldúa, G. (ed.) (1990) *Making Face, Making Soul/Haciendo Caras: Creative and Critical Perspectives by Women of Color*, Aunt Lute Foundation, San Francisco.

Appadurai, A. (1996) 'Disjuncture and Difference in the Global Cultural Economy', in A. Appadurai (ed.), *Modernity at Large: Cultural Dimensions of Globalization*, University of Minnesota Press, Minneapolis.

Arkin, W. (2002) 'Secret Plan Outlines the Unthinkable', *Los Angeles Times*, 10 March.

Armstrong, D. (2002) 'Dick Cheney's Song of America', *Harper's Magazine*, October.

Assaad, M. B. (1999) 'Challenging the Terminology and Overcoming the Culture of Silence', *Reproductive Health Matters*, Vol. 7, No. 13, May.

Bandarage, A. (1997) *Women, Population and Global Crisis*, Zed Books, London.

Bang, R. *et al.* (1989) 'High Prevalence of Gynecological Diseases in Rural Indian Women', *Lancet*, No. 8629.

Barker, D. and J. Mander (1999) *Invisible Government – The World Trade Organization: Global Government for the New Millennium*, The International Forum on Globalization, Sausalito, CA.

Basu, A. (ed.) (1995) *The Challenges of Local Feminism: Women's Movements in Global Perspective*, Westview Press, Boulder, CO.

Batliwala, S. (1994) 'The Meaning of Women's Empowerment: New Concepts from Action', in G. Sen, A. Germain, and L.C. Chen (eds.), *Population Policies Reconsidered: Health, Empowerment and Rights*, Harvard

University, Cambridge, MA.

Bauman, Z. (1998) *Globalization: The Human Consequences*, Colombia University Press, New York.

Baxandall, R. (2001) 'Re-visioning the Women's Liberation Movement's Narrative: Early Second Wave African American Feminists', *Feminist Studies*, Vol. 27, No. 1, Spring.

Bayer, R. (2002) 'From the Bowels of an Epidemic: AIDS, Human Rights, and International Equity', *Macalester International*, Vol. 11, Summer.

Baylies, C. and J. Bujra (2000) *AIDS, Sexuality and Gender in Africa: Collective Strategies and Struggles in Tanzania and Zambia*, Routledge, London.

Bello, W. (2002) *De-Globalization: Ideas for a New World Economy*, Zed Books, London.

Bello, W. and A. Mittal (2001) 'The Meaning of Doha', *http://www.foodfirst.org/progs/global/trade/wto2001/index.html*.

Benmayor, R., R. Torruellas and A. Juarbe (1992) *Responses to Poverty Among Puerto Rican Women: Identity, Community and Cultural Citizenship*, Centro de Estudios Puertorriqueños, Hunter College, New York.

Berer, M. (1990) 'What Would a Feminist Population Policy Be Like?', *Women's Health Journal*, No. 8.

—— (1993) 'Population and Family Planning Policies: Women-Centred Perspectives', *Reproductive Health Matters*, No. 1, May.

—— (1999) 'HIV/AIDS, Pregnancy and Maternal Mortality and Morbidity: Implications for Care', in M. Berer and T. K. S. Ravindran (eds.), *Safe Motherhood Initiatives: Critical Issues*, Basil Blackwell, London.

—— (2000a) 'Safe Sex, Women's Reproductive Rights and the Need for a Feminist Movement in the 21st Century', *Reproductive Health Matters*, Vol. 8, No. 15, May.

—— (2000b) 'HIV/AIDS, Sexual and Reproductive Health at AIDS 2000, Durban', *Reproductive Health Matters*, Vol. 8, No. 16, November.

—— (2001) 'Images, Reproductive Health and the Collateral Damage to Women of and War', *Reproductive Health Matters*, Vol. 9, No. 18, November.

—— (2002) 'Health Sector Reforms: Implications for Sexual and Reproductive Health Services', *Reproductive Health Matters*, Vol. 10, No. 20, November.

Berer, M. and T. K. S. Ravindran (eds.) (1999) *Safe Motherhood Initiatives: Critical Issues*, Basil Blackwell, London.

Bermudez, J. *et al.* (2002) 'Access to Drugs, the WTO TRIPS Agreement, and Patent Protection in Developing Countries: Trends, Perspectives and Recommendations to Help Find Our Way', paper at conference on 'The Crisis of Neglected Diseases: Developing Treatments and Ensuring Access', MSF/DND Working Group, New York, March (*www.accessmed/ msf.org*).

Bhasin, K. and N. Khan (1986) *Some Questions on Feminism for Women in South Asia*, Kali, New Delhi.

Blasius, M. (ed.) (2001) *Sexual Identities, Queer Politics*, Princeton University Press, Princeton, NJ.

Block, F. (1987) *Revising State Theory: Essays in Politics and Postindustrialism*, Temple University Press, Philadelphia.

—— (2002) 'The Right's Moral Trouble', *The Nation*, Vol. 275, No. 10, 30 September.

Booker, S. and W. Minter (2001) 'Global Apartheid', *The Nation*, 9 July.

—— (2002) 'AIDS – Let's Get Real', *The Nation*, 8 July.

Brandling-Bennet, D. (2002) 'Defining the Crisis and Current Approaches', panel discussion at Conference on 'The Crisis of Neglected Diseases: Developing Treatments and Ensuring Access', MSF/DND Working Group, New York, March.

Brazil Ministry of Health (1999) *AIDS in Brazil*, Brazil Ministry of Health, World AIDS Conference, Geneva, June–July.

—— (2002) *National STD/AIDS Program*, Brazil Ministry of Health, Brasilia.

Brecher, J., T. Costello and B. Smith (2000) *Globalization from Below: The Power of Solidarity*, South End Press, Cambridge, Massachusetts.

Breen, N. (2000) 'Social Class and Health: Understanding Gender and Its Interaction with Other Social Determinants', Harvard Center for Population and Development Studies, *Working Paper Series*, Vol. 10, No. 3, March.

Bruce, J. (1990) 'Fundamental Elements of the Quality of Care: A Simple Framework', *Studies in Family Planning*, Vol. 21, No. 2, March.

Budlender, D. (1998) 'The South African Women's Budget Initiative', Background Paper No. 2, Community Agency for Social Enquiry, Cape Town, South Africa.

Bumiller, E. (2002a) 'Amid Talk of War Spending, Bush Urges Fiscal Restraint', *New York Times*, 17 September.

—— (2002b) 'Bush Urges $300 Billion For Health Care Changes', *New York Times*, 12 February.

Bunch, C. and N. Reilly (1994) *Demanding Accountability: The Global Campaign and Vienna Tribunal for Women's Human Rights*, Center for Women's Global Leadership, New Brunswick, NJ.

Business Week (2000) 'Global Capitalism – Can It Be Made to Work Better?', 6 November.

Butchart, A. (1998) *The Anatomy of Power: European Constructions of the African Body*, Zed Books, London.

Butegwa, F. (1995) 'International Human Rights Law and Practice: Implications For Women', in M. Schuler (ed.), *From Basic Needs to Basic Rights: Women's Claim to Human Rights*, Women, Law and Development International, Washington, DC.

Cade, T. (1970) 'The Pill: Genocide or Liberation?', in T. Cade (ed.), *The Black Woman*, New American Library, New York.

Çağatay, N. (2000) *Budgets as If It Mattered: Democratizing Macroeconomic Policies*, United Nations Development Programme, New York.

Cauvin, H. (2001) 'South Africa Court Orders Medicine for HIV-Infected Mothers', *New York Times*, 15

December.
—— (2002) 'AIDS Imperiling African Armies, Key to Stability of Many Nations', *New York Times*, 24 November.
Center for Reproductive Rights (2002) *Bringing Rights to Bear: An Analysis of UN Treaty Monitoring Bodies on Reproductive and Sexual Rights*, Center for Reproductive Rights, New York, and University of Toronto International Programme on Reproductive and Sexual Health Law, Toronto.
Center for Women's Global Leadership (1995) *From Vienna to Beijing: The Cairo Hearing on Reproductive Health and Human Rights*, Center for Women's Global Leadership, New Brunswick, NJ.
CFFC (Catholics for a Free Choice) (1998a) *When Catholic and Non-Catholic Hospitals Merge: Reproductive Health Compromised* (researched and written by Liz Bucar), Catholics for a Free Choice, Washington, DC.
—— (1998b) *Merger Trends: An Update to Reproductive Health Compromised* (researched and written by Liz Bucar), Catholics for a Free Choice, Washington, DC.
—— (1999) *Caution: Catholic Health Restrictions May be Hazardous to Your Health*, Catholics for a Free Choice, Washington, DC.
—— (2000) *The Holy See and Women's Rights: A Shadow Report on the Beijing Platform for Action*, Catholics for a Free Choice, Washington, DC.
CHANGE (Center for Health and Gender Equity) (1998) *The Implications of Health Sector Reform on Reproductive Health and Rights*, Center for Health and Gender Equality, Takoma Park, MD.
Cheah, P. (1997) 'Positioning Human Rights in the Current Global Conjuncture', *Public Culture*, Vol. 9.
Chen, M. A. (1996) 'Engendering World Conferences: The International Women's Movement and the UN', in T. Weiss and L. Gordenker (eds.), *NGOs, the UN, and Global Governance*, Lynne Rienner, Boulder, CO.
Ciarrocca, M. and W. Hartung (2002) 'Increases in Military Spending and Security Assistance since 9/11/01', Fact Sheet prepared by Arms Trade Resource Center, 4 October, World Policy Institute/New School University, New York.
CMH (Commission on Macroeconomics and Health)/WHO (2001) *Macroeconomics and Health: Investing in Health for Economic Development*, (ed.), Jeffrey Sachs, World Health Organization, Geneva.
CNPD (National Population and Development Commission, Brazil) (1999) *Cairo+5: Report on Brazil*, National Population and Development Commission, Brasilia.
Coe, A. B. (2001) *Health Rights and Realities: An Analysis of the ReproSalud Project in Peru*, Working Paper, CHANGE (Center for Health and Gender Equity), Takoma Park, Maryland, April.
Cohen, S. A. (2000) 'Abortion Politics and US Population Aid: Coping with a Complex New Law', *International Family Planning Perspectives*, Vol. 26, No. 3, September.
Conly, S. R. and J. E. Epp (1997) *Falling Short: The World Bank's Role in Population and Reproductive Health*, Population Action International, Washington, DC.
Cook, R. (ed.) (1994) *Human Rights of Women: National and International Perspectives*, University of Pennsylvania Press, Philadelphia, PA.
Copelon, R. (2000) 'Writing Gender into International Criminal Law: The International Criminal Court Statute', unpublished ms.
Copelon, R. and R. Petchesky (1995) 'Toward an Interdependent Approach to Reproductive and Sexual Rights as Human Rights: Reflections on the ICPD and Beyond', in M. Schuler (ed.), *From Basic Rights to Basic Needs*, Women, Law and Development International, Washington, DC.
CorpWatch (2001) Letter from Alliance for a Corporate-Free UN to Kofi Annan (draft), *http://www.corpwatch.org*, July.
Correa, C. M. (2000) *Intellectual Property Rights, the WTO and Developing Countries: The TRIPS Agreement and Policy Options*, Zed Books, London.
Corrêa, S. (1994) *Population and Reproductive Rights: Feminist Perspectives from the South*, Zed Books, London.
—— (1997) 'Empowerment in the Feminist Perspective: Theoretical Itineraries, Challenges Ahead', paper presented at the International Union for the Scientific Study of Population Seminar on Female Empowerment and Demographic Processes: Moving Beyond Cairo, Lund, Sweden, 21–24 April.
—— (1998) 'Reshaping the Brazilian Sexual and Reproductive Health Policy: The Role of Civil Society', paper presented at the Advanced Leadership Program, Princeton University, April.
—— (1999) 'ICPD+5: Back to the Future?', *DAWN Informs*, No. 1.
—— (2002) 'Financial Transaction Taxes: Evaluating National Experiences', Presentation at Second World Social Forum, Porto Alegre, Brazil, *DAWN Informs*, March.
Corrêa, S. and R. Petchesky (1994) 'Reproductive and Sexual Rights: A Feminist Perspective,' in G. Sen, A. Germain and L. C. Chen (eds.), *Population Policies Reconsidered*, Harvard University Press, Cambridge, MA.
Corrêa, S. and R. Parker (2001) 'Sexuality, Human Rights and Demographic Thinking: Connections and Disjunctions in a Changing World', paper presented at 24th IUSSP (International Union for the Scientific Study of Population) Conference, Salvador de Bahia, Brazil, August.
COSATU (Congress of South African Trade Unions) (2001a) 'Statement by the Central Executive Committee of COSATU on the AIDS Crisis', 26 April (*http://www.cosatu.org.za/press/latest.html*).
—— (2001b) 'COSATU Demands Treatment for HIV', press statement issued by COSATU, 27 June (*http://gate.cosatu.org.za/mailman/listinfo/press*).
Crenshaw, K. W. (1997) 'Beyond Racism and Misogyny: Black Feminism and 2 Live Crew', in D. Meyers (ed.), *Feminist Social Thought: A Reader*, Routledge, New York.
CRLP (Center for Reproductive Law and Policy) (1999) 'The Year of 6 Billion: The Rights behind the Numbers', CRLP, New York, 15 September.

—— (2001) *The Global Gag Rule – Take Action!*, CRLP, New York.
CRLP/CLADEM (Latin American and Caribbean Committee for the Defense of Women's Rights) (1999) *Silence and Complicity: Violence Against Women in Peruvian Public Health Facilities*, CRLP/CLADEM, New York.
Crossette, B. (1999) 'For the Poor, Water is Dirty Yet Costly, Experts Find', *New York Times*, 8 August.
—— (2001a) 'Brazil's AIDS Chief Denounces Bush Position on Drug Patents', *New York Times*, 2 May.
—— (2001b) 'New Determination Is Seen Emerging in AIDS Battle', *New York Times*, 28 June.
CWPE (Committee on Women, Population and the Environment) (1993) 'Women, Population and the Environment: Call for a New Approach', printed statement, CWPE, Newton Center, MA.
Dao, J. (2002a) 'Bush Sees Big Rise in Military Budget for Next 5 Years', *New York Times*, 2 February.
—— (2002b) 'In Quietly Courting Africa, White House Likes Dowry', *New York Times*, 19 September.
DAWN (Development Alternatives with Women for a New Era) (1999) *Implementing ICPD: Moving Forward in the Eye of the Storm – DAWN's Platform for ICPD+5*, DAWN, Suva, Fiji.
—— (2001a) 'Trade, AIDS, Public Health and Human Rights', *DAWN INFORMS Supplement*, August.
—— (2001b) 'DAWN Discussion Paper II on the WTO', *DAWN Informs Supplement*, November.
—— (2002), *Dawn Informs*, March.
De Barbieri, T. (1994) 'Gender and Population Policy', in L. A. Mazur (ed.), *Beyond the Numbers: A Reader on Population, Consumption and the Environment*, Island Press, Washington, DC.
De Jong, J. (1999) 'The Relationship between Research and Advocacy Work', *Reproductive Health Matters*, Vol. 7, No. 13, May.
Diniz, S. *et al.* (1998) 'Not Like Our Mothers: Reproductive Choice and the Emergence of Citizenship among Brazilian Rural Workers, Domestic Workers and Housewives', in R. Petchesky and K. Judd (eds.), *Negotiating Reproductive Rights*, Zed Books and St Martin's Press, London and New York.
Dixon-Mueller, R. (1993) *Population Policy and Women's Rights*, Praeger Publishers, Westport, CT.
Dugger, C. (2001) 'A Catch-22 on Drugs for the World's Poor', *New York Times*, 16 November.
Durano, M. (2001) 'Understanding Global Public Goods', *DAWN Informs*, August.
Dutt, M. (1998) 'Reclaiming a Human Rights Culture: Feminism of Difference and Alliance' in E. Shohat (ed.), *Talking Visions: Multicultural Feminism in a Transnational Age*, MIT Press, Cambridge, MA.
Dworkin, R. (1978) *Taking Rights Seriously*, Harvard University Press, Cambridge, MA.
Egypt National Population Council (1995) *Demographic and Health Survey*, EDHS, Cairo, Egypt.
Eisenstein, Z. (1996) *Hatreds: Racialized and Sexualized Conflicts in the 21st Century*, Routledge, New York.
—— (1998) *Global Obscenities: Patriarchy, Capitalism, and the Lure of Cyberfantasy*, New York University Press, New York.
—— (2004) *Feminisms Against Empire* (forthcoming), Zed Books, London.
El-Gibaly, O. *et al.* (2001) 'International Financial Architecture: A View from the Kitchen', paper presented at the International Studies Conference, Chicago, February.
Elson, D. and B. Evers (1998) *Sector Programme Support: The Health Sector – A Gender-Aware Analysis*, unpublished ms., University of Manchester, Graduate School of Social Sciences, January.
Elson, D. and N. Çağatay (2000) 'The Social Content of Macroeconomic Policies', *World Development*, Vol. 28, No. 7.
Emberson-Bain, A. (1994), 'Mining Development in the Pacific: Are We Sustaining the Unsustainable?' in W. Harcourt (ed.), *Feminist Perspectives on Sustainable Development*, Zed Books, London.
Enloe, C. (2000) *Maneuvers: The International Politics of Militarizing Women's Lives*, University of California Press, Berkeley, CA.
Epp, J. (2001) 'World Bank Strategic Approaches to Reproductive Health Commodity Security', The World Bank, Population and Reproductive Health Thematic Group, 10 January (unpublished).
Epstein, H. (2001) 'Time of Indifference', *The New York Review of Books*, 12 April.
Esiet, A. and B. Madunagu (1999) Interview, New York, March.
Evers, B. and M. Juárez (2002) 'Understanding the Links: Globalization, Health Sector Reform, Gender and Reproductive Health', in Ford Foundation, *Globalization, Health Sector Reform, Gender and Reproductive Rights*, Ford Foundation, New York.
Fabros, M. *et al.* (1998) 'From *Sanas* to *Dapat*: Negotiating Entitlement in Reproductive Decision-Making in the Philippines', in R. Petchesky and K. Judd (eds.)/IRRRAG, *Negotiating Reproductive Rights*, Zed Books and St. Martin's Press, London and New York.
Fabros, M. (1999) Interview, Belmont, Massachusetts.
Fair Share (2000) *Economic Justice Update*, Vol. 4, No. 4, December.
—— (2001/2002) *National Budget Handbook*, Fair Share, University of the Western Cape, South Africa.
Farmer, P. (1999) *Infections and Inequalities: The Modern Plagues*, University of California Press, Berkeley, CA.
Fathalla, M. F. (1999) 'Issues in Reproductive Health Care for Women', paper presented at the 43rd session of the United Nations Commission on the Status of Women, New York, 1–19 March.
Field, M., D. Kotz and G. Bukhman (2000) 'Neoliberal Economic Policy, "State Desertion", and the Russian Health Crisis', in J. Yong Kim *et al.* (eds.), *Dying for Growth: Global Inequality and the Health of the Poor*, Common Courage Press, Monroe, Maine.
Filmmakers Collaborative, Inc. (1999) 'Six Billion and Beyond' (brochure), PO Box 18654, Boulder CO.
Flanders, S. (2001) 'In the Shadow of AIDS, a World of Other Problems', *New York Times*, 24 June.
Fonn, S. *et al.* (1998) 'Reproductive Health Services in South Africa: From Rhetoric to Implementation', *Reproductive Health Matters*, Vol. 6, No. 11, May.
Ford Foundation (2000) *The Gender and Reproductive Health Impacts of Health Sector Reform in Asia*, Kunming

Medical College and Ford Foundation, Lijiang, Yunnan Province, China.

—— (2002) *Globalization, Health Sector Reform, Gender and Reproductive Health*, Ford Foundation, New York.

Forero, J. (2002) 'Still Poor, Latin Americans Protest Push for Open Markets', *New York Times*, 19 July.

Forman, S. and R. Ghosh (2000) *Promoting Reproductive Health: Investing in Health for Development*, Lynne Rienner Publishers, Boulder, CO.

Francisco, G. (1998) 'Reproductive Health Approach: The Philippine Experience since Cairo', unpublished paper.

—— (2002) 'Expanding the Debate on Global Tobin Tax', presentation at Second World Social Forum, Porto Alegre, Brazil, *DAWN Informs*, March.

Fraser, N. (1997) *Justice Interruptus: Critical Reflections on the 'Post-Socialist Condition'*, Routledge, New York and London.

Freedman, L. P. (1996) 'The Challenge of Fundamentalisms', *Reproductive Health Matters*, No. 8, November.

Freitas, A. (2001) 'Linking Through Closed Doors', *DAWN Informs Supplement on Trade, AIDS, Health and Human Rights*, August.

Fried, M. G. (ed.) (1990) *From Abortion to Reproductive Freedom: Transforming a Movement*, South End Press, Boston, MA.

Fried, S. T. (ed.) *The Indivisibility of Women's Human Rights: A Continuing Dialogue*, Center for Women's Global Leadership, New Brunswick, NJ.

Gaer, F. D. (1996) 'Reality Check: Human Rights NGOs Confront Governments at the UN', in T. Weiss and L. Gordenker (eds.), *NGOs, the UN, and Global Governance*, Lynne Rienner, Boulder, CO.

Gaidzanwa, R. (1999) *Voting With Their Feet: Migrant Zimbabwean Nurses and Doctors in the Era of Structural Adjustment*, Nordiska Afrikainstitutet, Uppsala, Sweden.

Galdos, S. and B. Feringa (1998) 'Creating Partnerships at the Grassroots Level: The ReproSalud Project, Peru', in HERA (Health, Empowerment, Rights and Accountability), *Confounding the Critics: Cairo, Five Years On*, Conference Report, Cocoyoc, Morelos, Mexico, November, International Women's Health Coalition, New York.

Galvão, J. (2001) 'Brazil – People First, Profits Later', *Dawn Informs*, Supplement on 'Trade, AIDS, Public Health and Human Rights', August.

Garcia-Moreno, C. and A. Claro (1994) 'Challenges from the Women's Health Movement: Women's Rights versus Population Control', in G. Sen, A. Germain, and L. C. Chen, (eds.) *Population Policies Reconsidered*, Harvard University, Cambridge, MA.

George, S. (2002) 'Another World is Possible', *The Nation*, 18 February.

Germain, A. and R. Kyte (1995) *The Cairo Consensus: The Right Agenda for the Right Time*, International Women's Health Coalition, New York.

Gevisser, M. (2001) 'AIDS: The New Apartheid', *The Nation*, 14 May.

Gill, K./World Bank (1999) *If We Walk Together: Communities, NGOs, and Government in Partnership for Health – the Hyderabad Experience*, The World Bank, Washington, DC.

Girard, F. (1999) 'Cairo +Five: Reviewing Progress for Women Five Years after the International Conference on Population and Development', *Journal of Women's Health and Law*, Vol. 1, No. 1, November.

—— (2001) 'Reproductive Health under Attack at the United Nations', *Reproductive Health Matters*, Vol. 9, No. 18, November.

—— (2002) 'UN Special Session on Children: Bush Administration Continues its Attacks on Sexual and Reproductive Health', *Reproductive Health Matters*, Vol. 10, No. 20, November.

Greenhalgh, S. (1996) 'The Social Construction of Population Science: An Intellectual, Institutional, and Political History of Twentieth-Century Demography', *Comparative Studies in Society and History*, Vol. 38.

Grewal, I. (1998) 'On the New Global Feminism and the Family of Nations: Dilemmas of Transnational Feminist Practice', in E. Shohat (ed.), *Talking Visions: Multicultural Feminism in a Transnational Age*, MIT Press, Cambridge, MA.

Grewal, I. and C. Kaplan (eds.) (1994) *Scattered Hegemonies: Postmodernity and Transnational Feminist Practices*, University of Minnesota Press, Minneapolis, MN.

Gupta, G. R. and E. Weiss (1995) 'Women's Lives and Sex: Implications for AIDS Prevention', in R. Parker and J. Gagnon (eds.), *Conceiving Sexuality: Approaches to Sex Research in a Postmodern World*, Routledge, New York.

Guttmacher, S. *et al.* (1998) 'Abortion Reform in South Africa: A Case Study of the 1996 Choice on Termination of Pregnancy Act', *International Family Planning Perspectives*, Vol. 24, No. 4, December.

Haberland, N. and D. Measham (eds.) (2002) *Responding to Cairo: Case Studies of Changing Practice in Reproductive Health and Family Planning*, Population Council, New York.

Hague Appeal *et al.* (2000) *Women Count, At Last!* Hague Appeal for Peace, The Hague, Netherlands.

Hankins, C. (2000) 'Preventing Perinatal HIV Transmission in Developing Countries: Recent Developments and Ethical Implications', *Reproductive Health Matters*, Vol. 8, No. 15, May.

Harcourt, W. (ed.) (1994a) *Feminist Perspectives on Sustainable Development*, Zed Books, London.

Harcourt, W. (1994b) 'Negotiating Positions in the Sustainable Development Debate: Situating the Feminist Perspective', in W. Harcourt (ed.), *Feminist Perspectives on Sustainable Development*, Zed Books, London.

Hardee, K. and J. Smith (2000) *Implementing Reproductive Health Services in an Era of Health Sector Reform*, The POLICY Project, March.

Hardt, M. (2002) 'Porto Alegre: Today's Bandung?', *New Left Review*, 14 March.

Hardt, M. and A. Negri (2000) *Empire*, Harvard University Press, Cambridge, MA.

Harris, C. (1998) 'Coping with Daily Life in Post-Soviet Tajikistan: The Gharmi Villages of Khatlon Province',

Central Asian Survey, Vol. 17, No. 4.

—— (1999) 'Health Education for Women as a Liberatory Process? An Example from Tajikistan', in H. Afshar and S. Barrientos (eds.), *Women, Globalization and Fragmentation in the Developing World*, Women's Studies at York Series, Hampshire, England.

Hartmann, B. (1994) '"The Cairo Consensus": Women's Empowerment or Business as Usual?', *Reproductive Rights Network Newsletter*, Fall.

—— (1995) *Reproductive Rights and Wrongs*, South End Press, Boston, MA.

—— (1999) 'Population, Environment, and Security: A New Trinity', in J. Silliman and Y. King (eds.), *Dangerous Intersections: Feminist Perspectives on Population, Environment, and Development*, South End Press, Boston, MA.

Häusler, S. (1994) 'Women and the Politics of Sustainable Development' in *Feminist Perspectives on Sustainable development*, W. Harcourt (ed.), Zed Books, London.

Health Watch (1998) 'From Contraceptive Targets to Reproductive Health: India's Family Planning Programme after Cairo', in HERA, *Confounding the Critics: Cairo, Five Years On*, Conference Report, Cocoyoc, Morelos, Mexico, November, International Women's Health Coalition, New York.

—— (1999) *The Community Needs-Based Reproductive and Child Health in India: Progress and Constraints*, Health Watch, Jaipur, India.

Heise, L. (1995) 'Violence, Sexuality, and Women's Lives', in R. G. Parker and J. H. Gagnon (eds.), *Conceiving Sexuality*, Routledge, New York.

Heise, L., K. Moore and N. Toubia (1995) *Sexual Coercion and Reproductive Health: A Focus on Research*, Population Council, New York.

Helmy, M. (1999), 'The Egyptian FGM Task Force: Creating a Social Movement', paper presented at the NGO Forum for ICPD+5, The Hague, Netherlands, 7 February.

Heng, G. (1997) 'A Great Way to Fly: Nationalism, the State, and the Varieties of Third-World Feminism', in M. J. Alexander and C. T. Mohanty (eds.), *Feminist Genealogies, Colonial Legacies, Democratic Futures*, Routledge, New York.

HERA (Health, Empowerment, Rights and Accountability) (1998) *Confounding the Critics: Cairo, Five Years On*, Conference Report, Cocoyoc, Morelos, Mexico, 15-18 November, International Women's Health Coalition, New York.

—— (n.d.) *Women's Sexual and Reproductive Rights and Health Action Sheets*, International Women's Health Coalition, New York (*www. iwhc.org*).

Hess, M. (2001) *When Religion Compromises Women's Health Care: A Case Study of a Catholic Managed Care Organization*, NARAL/NY Foundation, New York.

Heywood, M. (2001) 'Debunking "Conglomo-talk": A Case Study of the Amicus Curiae as an Instrument for Advocacy, Investigation and Mobilization', unpublished paper, AIDS Law Project, Centre for Applied Legal Studies, University of the Witwatersrand, Johannesburg, South Africa.

Heywood, M. and M. Cornell (1998) 'Human Rights and AIDS in South Africa: From Right Margin to Left Margin', *Health and Human Rights*, Vol. 2, No. 4.

Higer, A. J. (1999) 'International Women's Activism and the 1994 Cairo Population Conference', in M. K. Meyer and E. Prügl (eds.), *Gender Politics in Global Governance*, Rowman and Littlefield, Lanham, Maryland.

't Hoen, E. and S. Moon (2002) 'Pills and Pocketbooks: Equity Pricing of Essential Medicines in Developing Countries', paper at conference on 'The Crisis of Neglected Diseases: Developing Treatments and Ensuring Access', MSF/DND Working Group, New York, March (*www.accessmed/msf.org*).

't Hoen, E. and P. Chirac (2002) 'Don't Renege on Doha', *Le Monde*, 25 June.

hooks, b. (1989) *Talking Back: Thinking Feminist, Thinking Black*, South End Press, Boston, MA.

—— (1997) 'Sisterhood: Political Solidarity between Women', in A. McClintock, A. Mufti and E. Shohat (eds.), *Dangerous Liaisons: Gender, Nation and Postcolonial Perspectives*, University of Minnesota Press, Minneapolis.

Houston S. (2001) 'HIV Care in Africa: Anti-retrovirals in Perspective', *SAfAIDS News*, Vol. 9, No. 2.

Houtart, F. and F. Polet (eds.) (2001) *The Other Davos: The Globalization of Resistance to the World Economic System*, Zed Books, London.

IGLHRC (International Gay and Lesbian Human Rights Commission) (2001) 'Civil Society Is Not Corporate Society: Act Now to Participate in the UN General Assembly Special Session on HIV/AIDS', Action Alert, *www.iglhrc.org*, January.

Ikeji, N. (1996) 'The Emergence of the Silent Majority: Women NGOs Bridging the Health and Development Gap in Nigeria', paper presented at the Nigerian National Conference on International Health, June.

Imam, A. (1997) 'The Dynamics of WINing: An Analysis of Women in Nigeria (WIN)', in M. J. Alexander and C. T. Mohanty (eds.), *Feminist Genealogies, Colonial Legacies, Democratic Futures*, Routledge, New York.

International Symposium (2000) *Final Report and Summary of Proceedings*, International Symposium on Partnerships for Social Development in a Globalizing World, Geneva, Switzerland, 26–28 June.

IWHC (International Women's Health Coalition) (2002) 'Beijing Plus Five – Analysis of Negotiations and Final "Further Actions" Document', July.

—— (2002) 'Bush's Other War – The Assault on Women's Reproductive and Sexual Health and Rights', *www.iwhc.org*.

IWHIPPF (International Planned Parenthood Federation) (1995) *IPPF Charter on Sexual and Reproductive Rights*, International Planned Parenthood Federation, London.

—— (1999) *Real Lives: Promoting Dialogue and Highlighting Need in the South Asia Region*, Issue 3, January.

Ireland, D. (1999) 'AIDS Drugs for Africa', *The Nation*, 4 October.

IRRRAG (1999) *Catalysts and Messengers: The Story of the International Reproductive Rights Research Action Group*, IRRRAG, Hunter College, City University of New York.

Isis International (1993) *Women's Perspectives on Population Issues*, Isis International, Quezon City, Philippines.

Jackson, H. (2001) 'Comment', *SAfAIDS News*, Vol. 9, No. 2, June.

Jain, D. (1996) *Panchayat Raj – Women Changing Governance*, Gender in Development Monograph Series No. 5, UNDP, New York.

Jecker, N. S. (1994) 'Can an Employer-Based Health Insurance System be Just?', in *The Politics of Health Care Reform*, J. A. Marone and G. S. Belkin (eds.), Duke University, Durham, NC and London.

Joffe, C. (1995) *Doctors of Conscience: The Struggle to Provide Abortion before and after Roe v. Wade*, Beacon Press, Boston, MA.

Joffe, C., P. Anderson and J. Steinauer (1998) 'The Crisis in Abortion Provision and Pro-Choice Medical Activism in the 1990s', in R. Solinger (ed.), *Abortion Wars: A Half Century of Struggle, 1950–2000*, University of California Press, Berkeley, CA.

Jordan, W. D. (1968) *White Over Black: American Attitudes towards the Negro, 1550–1812*, W. W. Norton, New York and London.

Joseph, R. (1999) 'Flawed Human Rights-Based Approach to Health', *Vivant! Pro-Family News from the United Nations*, 23 March.

Kabeer, N. (1994) *Reversed Realities: Gender Hierarchies in Development Thought*, Verso, London.

Kahn, J. (2001) 'World Bank Presses Inquiry on Economist Who Dissents', *New York Times*, 7 September.

Kalavathy, M. C. *et al.* (2000) 'Roundtable: Disclosure of HIV Status and Human Rights', *Reproductive Health Matters*, Vol. 8, No. 15, May.

Kaplan, C. *et al.* (eds.) (1999) *Between Woman and Nation: Nationalisms, Transnational Feminisms, and the State*, Duke University Press, Durham, NC.

Kapstein, E. (1999) 'Distributive Justice as an International Public Good: A Historical Perspective', in I. Kaul, I. Grunberg and M. A. Stern (eds.), *Global Public Goods: International Cooperation in the 21st Century*, UNDP/Oxford University Press, New York.

Kaul, I., I. Grunberg and M. A. Stern (eds.). (1999) *Global Public Goods: International Cooperation in the 21st Century*, UNDP/Oxford University Press, New York.

Keck, M. and K. Sikkink (1998) *Activists Beyond Borders: Advocacy Networks in International Politics*, Cornell University Press, Ithaca, New York.

Kemp, A. *et al.* (1995) 'The Dawn of a New Day: Redefining South African Feminism', in A. Basu (ed.), *The Challenges of Local Feminism: Women's Movements in Global Perspective*, Westview Press, Boulder, CO.

Kerstenetzky, C. L. (2001) 'Brazil: The Violence of Inequality', *Social Watch Report 2001*, No. 5, Social Watch, Montevideo, Uruguay.

Keysers, L. (1994) 'Reflections on Reproductive and Sexual Rights during the ICPD', *Women's Global Network for Reproductive Rights Newsletter 47*, July–Sept.

—— (1999) 'Cairo + 5: Business as Usual', *Newsletter 65*, Women's Global Network for Reproductive Rights, No. 1.

Khan, M. E. and J. W. Townsend (1999) 'Target-Free Approach: Emerging Evidence', in S. Pachauri (ed.), *Implementing a Reproductive Health Agenda in India: The Beginning*, Population Council, New Delhi.

Kim, J. Y. *et al.* (eds.) (2000) *Dying for Growth: Global Inequality and the Health of the Poor*, Common Courage Press, Monroe, Maine.

King, E. and A. Manson/World Bank (2001) *Engendering Development Through Gender Equality in Rights, Resources and Voice*, World Bank, Washington, DC.

King Jr, M. L. (2000/1967) 'To Atone for Our Sins and Errors in Vietnam', in M. Marable and L. Mullings (eds.), *Let Nobody Turn Us Around: Voices of Resistance, Reform, and Renewal*, Rowman and Littlefield Publishers, Lanham, MD.

Kissling, F. and J. O'Brien (2001) 'Bad Faith at the UN: The Catholic Family and Human Rights Institute', *Conscience*, Vol. 22, No. 1, Spring.

Klare, M. (2002) 'Endless Military Superiority', *The Nation*, 15 July.

Klugman, B. (2000) 'Sexual Rights in Southern Africa: A Beijing Discourse or a Strategic Necessity?', *Health and Human Rights*, Vol. 4, No. 2.

Klugman, B. *et al.* (1998) *From Words to Action: Sexual and Reproductive Rights, Health Policies and Programming in South Africa 1994–1998*, Women's Health Project, Johannesburg, South Africa.

Koivusalo, M. and E. Ollila. (1997) *Making a Healthy World: Agencies, Actors and Policies in International Health*, Zed Books, London.

Kothari, S. and H. Sethi, (eds.) (1991) *Rethinking Human Rights: Challenges for Theory and Action*, New Horizons Press, New York/Lokayan, Delhi.

Kumar, R.S. (2000) 'Contradictory Discourses, State Ideology and Policy Interpretation: A Feminist Evaluation of the Reproductive and Child Health Programme (RCH) in Kerala, India', doctoral dissertation, The University of Waikato, New Zealand.

LACWHN (Latin American and Caribbean Women's Health Network) (1998) *The Cairo Consensus: Women Exercising Citizenship Through Monitoring*, LACWHN, Santiago, Chile.

Lamont, J. and D. Innocenti (2002) 'Mandela Joins South African AIDS Dispute', *Financial Times*, 18 February.

Lancaster, R. N. and M. di Leonardo (eds.) (1997) *The Gender/Sexuality Reader: Culture, History, Political Economy*, Routledge, New York.

Lang, S. (1997) 'The NGOization of Feminism', in J.W. Scott, C. Kaplan and D. Keates (eds)., *Transitions, Environments, Translations: Feminisms in International Politics,* Routledge, New York.

Le Carré, J. (2001) *The Constant Gardener,* Coronet/Hodder & Stoughton, London.

Leon, D. and G. Walt (eds.) (2001) *Poverty, Inequality and Health,* Oxford University Press, New York.

Lorde, A. (1984) *Sister Outsider: Essays and Speeches,* Crossing Press, Freedom, California.

Love, J. (2002) 'Paying for Health Care R & D: Carrots and Sticks', paper at conference on 'The Crisis of Neglected Diseases: Developing Treatments and Ensuring Access', MSF/DND Working Group, New York, March (*www.accessmed/msf.org).*

Macedo, M.F. (2002) 'What Is and/or Can Be the Role and Value of IPR for Developing Countries?', panel presentation, Conference on the Crisis of Neglected Diseases, MSF/DND (Drugs for Neglected Diseases Working Group), New York, March.

Mackintosh, M. and P. Tibandebage (2000) 'Sustainable Redistribution with Health Care Markets? Rethinking Regulatory Intervention in the Tanzanian Context', paper presented at conference on New Institutional Theory, Institutional Reform and Poverty Reduction, Development Studies Institute, London School of Economics, September.

Magdy, H. (1999) 'The Egyptian FGM Task Force: Creating a Social Movement', paper presented at the NGO Forum for ICPD+5, The Hague, Netherlands, 6–7 February.

Mallik, R. (2002) *The Two-Child Norm and Incentives and Disincentives in Population Policies in India: Analysis from a Gender Rights Perspective,* policy paper, Center for Health and Gender Equity, Takoma Park, MD.

Mann, J. (2000) 'Bush's Gag Rule Decision Will Speak Loudly', *Washington Post,* 20 December.

Marty, M. E. and R. S. Appleby (eds.) (1993) *North American Protestant Fundamentalism: Fundamentalism Observed,* Yale University Press, New Haven, CT.

Marx, K. (1994) *Selected Writings,* L. H. Simon (ed.), Hackett Publishing Co., Indianapolis, IN.

Matsabisa, M. G. (2002) Panel presentation at conference on 'The Crisis of Neglected Diseases: Developing Treatments and Ensuring Access', MSF/DND Working Group, New York, March (*www.accessmed-msf.org).*

Mazur, L. A. (1994) 'Beyond the Numbers: An Introduction and Overview', in L. A. Mazur (ed.), *Beyond the Numbers: A Reader on Population, Consumption and the Environment,* Island Press, Washington, DC.

Mbeki, T. (2002) 'Africa's New Realism', *New York Times,* Op-Ed, 24 June.

McGreal, C. (2001) 'Shamed and Humiliated, the Drugs Firms Back Down – Special Report: AIDS', *Guardian,* 19 April.

McNeil, D. (2000a) 'As Devastating Epidemics Increase, Nations Take on Drug Companies', *New York Times,* 9 July.

——— (2000b) 'Prices for Medicine Are Exorbitant in Africa, Study Says', *New York Times,* 16 June.

——— (2000c) 'Companies to Cut Costs of AIDS Drugs for Poor Nations', *New York Times,* 11 May.

——— (2001) 'Bush Keeps Clinton Policy on Poor Lands' Need for AIDS Drugs', *New York Times,* 22 February.

——— (2002) 'WHO Moves to Make AIDS Drugs More Accessible to Poor Worldwide', *New York Times,* 22 April.

Menotti, V. (2000) 'Globalization and the United Nations', unpublished paper, International Forum on Globalization (www.ifg.org).

Merrick, T. (2002) 'Short-Changing Reproductive Health', *Reproductive Health Matters,* Vol. 10, No. 20, November.

Meyer, M. (1999) 'The Women's International League for Peace and Freedom: Organizing Women for Peace in the War System', in M. Meyer and E. Prügl (eds.), *Gender Politics in Global Governance,* Rowman and Littlefield, Lanham, MD.

Meyer, M. and Prügl, E. (eds.) (1999) *Gender Politics in Global Governance,* Rowman and Littlefield, Lanham, MD.

Mies, M. and V. Shiva (1993) *Ecofeminism,* Zed Books, London.

Miliband, R. (1969) *The State in Capitalist Society,* Basic Books, New York.

Miller, A. (1999) 'Realizing Women's Rights: Nongovernmental Organizations and the Untied Nations Treaty Bodies', in M. Meyer and E. Prügl (eds.), *Gender Politics in Global Governance,* Rowman and Littlefield, Lanham, MD.

Moghadam, V. (ed.) (1994) *Gender and National Identity,* Zed Books, London.

Mohanty, C. T. (1997) 'Under Western Eyes: Feminist Scholarship and Colonial Discourse', in A. McClintock, A. Mufti and E. Shohat (eds.), *Dangerous Liaisons,* University of Minnesota Press, Minneapolis, MN.

Moline, A. (2002) 'World Bank to Rate All Projects for Gender Impact', *WOMENS NEWS,* Washington, DC (*www.aflcio.org).*

Mowlam, M. (2002) 'Comment', *Guardian,* 5 September.

MSF/DND (2002) *The Crisis of Neglected Diseases: Developing Treatments and Ensuring Access,* Working Group Expert Papers, MSF/DND (Drugs for Neglected Diseases Working Group), New York, March (at *www.accessmed-msf.org).*

Mukherjee, V. N. (2002) 'National and State Population Policies in India: Gender Matters', *Seminar,* No. 511, March.

Mukhopadhyay, S. and J. Sivaramayya (1999) 'Forging New Partnerships: Towards Empowerment', in S. Pachauri (ed.), *Implementing a Reproductive Health Agenda in India,* Population Council, New Delhi, India.

Murray, C. J. L. (1994) 'Quantifying the Burden of Disease: The Technical Basis for Disability-Adjusted Life Years', *Bulletin of the World Health Organization,* Vol. 72.

Murray, C. J. L. and A. K. Acharya (1997) 'Understanding DALYs', *Journal of Health Economics,* Vol. 16.

Murthy, N. (1999) 'Decentralised Participative Planning and Monitoring', in S. Pachauri (ed.), *Implementing a*

Reproductive Health Agenda in India, Population Council, New Delhi.

Musgrove, P. *et al.* (2002) 'Basic Patterns in National Health Expenditure', *Bulletin of the World Health Organization,* Vol. 80, No. 2.

Nahar, S. And A. Costello (1998) 'The Hidden Cost of "Free" Maternity Care in Dhaka, Bangladesh', *Health Policy and Planning,* Vol. 13, No. 4.

Nanda, P. (2000) 'Health Sector Reforms in Zambia: Implications for Reproductive Health and Rights', Working Paper, Center for Health and Gender Equity, Takoma Park, MD.

—— (2002) 'Gender Dimensions of User Fees: Implications for Women's Utilization of Health Care', *Reproductive Health Matters,* Vol. 10, No. 20, November.

Naples, N. (2002) 'Changing the Terms' and 'The Challenges and Possibilities of Transnational Feminist Praxis', in N. Naples and M. Desai (eds.), *Women's Activism and Globalization,* Routledge, New York and London.

Naples, N. And M. Desai (2002) *Women's Activism and Globalization: Linking Local Struggles and Transnational Politics,* Routledge, New York and London.

NARAL/NY Foundation (2001) *When Religion Compromises Women's Health Care: A Case Study of a Catholic Managed Care Organization* (Miriam Hess, principal author and researcher), NARAL/NY Foundation, New York, March.

Narayan, D. and P. Petesch (eds.) (2002) *Voices of the Poor: From Many Lands,* World Bank/Oxford University Press, New York.

Narayan, U. (1997) *Dislocating Cultures: Identities, Traditions and Third World Feminism,* Routledge, New York and London.

Navaratnam, V. (2002) 'Capacity Building and Technology Transfer: A Sustainable Solution?', panel presentation at conference on 'The Crisis of Neglected Diseases: Developing Treatments and Ensuring Access', MSF/DND Working Group, New York, March (*www.accessmed/msf.org).*

Nayyar, A. (1999) 'From Population Control to Reproductive Health: The Role of Advocacy', in S. Pachauri (ed.), *Implementing a Reproductive Health Agenda in India,* Population Council, New Delhi.

New York Times (2000) 'The Global Plague of AIDS', Editorial, *New York Times,* 24 April.

—— (2001) 'Africans Unite In Seeking More Funds to Halt Spread of AIDS', Editorial, *New York Times,* 28 April.

New York Times (AP) (2002) 'Nigerian Women, in Peaceful Protest, Shut Down Oil Plant', *New York Times,* 14 July.

Noel-De Bique, D. (1998) 'The Caribbean: NGO Partnerships for Advancing Male Responsibility in Implementing the Goals of the ICPD', in HERA, *Confounding the Critics: Cairo, Five Years On,* Conference Report, Cocoyoc, Morelos, Mexico, November, International Women's Health Coalition, New York.

NPU (National Population Unit) (1999) *South Africa's Progress Report for ICPD+5,* Republic of South Africa, National Population Unit, Department of Welfare, Pretoria, South Africa.

Nygaard, E. (2000) 'Is It Feasible or Desirable to Measure the Burdens of Disease as a Single Number?', *Reproductive Health Matters,* Vol. 8, No. 15, May.

Obermeyer, C. M. and R. Reynolds (1999) 'Female Genital Surgeries, Reproductive Health and Sexuality: A Review of the Evidence', *Reproductive Health Matters,* Vol. 7, No. 13, May.

Oduol, W. and W. M. Kabira (1995) 'The Mother of Warriors and Her Daughter: The Women's Movement in Kenya', in A. Basu (ed.), *The Challenge of Local Feminisms: Women's Movements in Global Perspective,* Westview Press, Boulder, CO.

Olliaro, P. and V. Navaratnam (2002) 'Technical Cooperative Networks in Developing Countries for Sustainable Access to Affordable, Adapted Medicines', paper presented at conference on 'The Crisis of Neglected Diseases: Developing Treatments and Ensuring Access', MSF/DND Working Group, New York, March (*www.accessmed/msf.org).*

Olsen, F. (1984) 'Statutory Rape: A Feminist Critique of Rights Analysis', *Texas Law Review,* Vol. 63, No. 7, November.

Olson, E. (1999) 'Free Markets Leave Women Worse Off, UNICEF Says', *New York Times,* 23 September.

—— (2002) 'US Backs New Trade Rules on Drugs', *New York Times,* 24 June.

O'Neill, M. (1995) 'Economic and Policy Trends: Global Challenges to Women's Rights', in M. A. Schuler (ed.), *From Basic Rights to Basic Needs,* Women, Law and Development International, Washington, DC.

Onishi, N. (2002) 'African Numbers, Problems and Number Problems', *New York Times,* 18 August.

Orbinski, J. (2002) 'Closing Remarks', Conference on the Crisis of Neglected Diseases, MSF/DND (Drugs for Neglected Diseases Working Group), New York, March.

Ortiz-Ortega, A. and J. Helzner (2003) 'Opening Windows to Gender: A Case Study of a Major International Population Agency', *Social Politics,* Vol. 10, No. 1, Winter.

Osakue, G. and A. Martin-Hilber (1998) 'Women's Sexuality and Fertility in Nigeria', in R. Petchesky and K. Judd (eds.)/IRRRAG, *Negotiating Reproductive Rights,* Zed Books and St Martin's Press, London and New York.

Otto, D. (1996) 'Nongovernmental Organizations in the United Nations System: The Emerging Role of International Civil Society', *Human Rights Quarterly,* Vol. 18, No. 1.

Oxfam (2001) 'Drug Companies vs. Brazil: The Threat to Public Health', Briefing Paper, Oxfam International, Oxford (*www.oxfam.org.uk),* May.

—— (2002) 'US Bullying on Drug Patents: One Year after Doha', Oxfam Briefing Paper 33, Oxfam International, Washington, DC, November.

Paalman, M. *et al.* (1998) 'A Critical Review of Priority Setting in the Health Sector: The Methodology of the 1993 World Development Report', *Health Policy and Planning*, Vol. 13, No. 1.

Pachauri, S. (1999) 'Moving Towards Reproductive Health: Issues and Evidence', in S. Pachauri (ed.), *Implementing a Reproductive Health Agenda in India,* Population Council, New Delhi.

Paiva, V. (2000) 'Gendered Scripts and the Sexual Scene: Promoting Sexual Subjects among Brazilian Teenagers', in R. Parker, R. Barbosa and P. Aggleton (eds.), *Framing the Sexual Subject: The Politics of Gender, Sexuality, and Power,* University of California Press, Berkeley, CA.

—— (2002) 'Beyond Magic Solutions: Prevention of HIV and AIDS as a Process of "Psychological Emancipation"', paper presented at meeting on Brazil's Programme on HIV/AIDS, Center for Gender, Sexuality and Health, Mailman School of Public Health, Columbia University, New York, April.

Parker, A. *et al.* (eds.) (1992) *Nationalisms and Sexualities,* Routledge, New York.

Parker, R. (1991) *Bodies, Pleasures and Passions: Sexual Culture in Contemporary Brazil,* Beacon Press, Boston.

—— (1999) *Beneath the Equator: Cultures of Desire, Male Homosexuality, and Emerging Gay Communities in Brazil,* Routledge, New York.

—— (2000) 'Administering the Epidemic: HIV/AIDS Policy, Models of Development and International Health in the Late-Twentieth Century', in L. Whiteford and L. Manderson (eds.), *Globalization, Health and Identity: The Fallacy of the Level Playing Field,* Lynne Reinner, Boulder, CO.

Parker, R. and R. M. Barbosa (eds.) (1996) *Sexualidades Brasileiras,* Relume-Dumara Esitores, Rio de Janeiro, Brazil.

Parker, R., R. M. Barbosa and P. Aggleton (eds.) (2000) *Framing the Sexual Subject: The Politics of Gender, Sexuality, and Power,* University of California Press, Berkeley, CA.

Parker, R. and J. Gagnon (1995) *Conceiving Sexuality: Approaches to Sex Research in a Post-Modern World,* Routledge, New York and London.

Partners in Population and Development (2001) 'Facilitating Access to Essential Health Commodities through South-to-South Collaboration: Kochi Declaration', *Reproductive Health Matters,* Vol. 9, No. 18, May.

Pear, R. (1999) 'More Americans Were Uninsured in 1998, US Says', *New York Times,* 4 October.

—— (2001a) 'Bush Plan Allows States to Give "Unborn Child" Medical Coverage', *New York Times,* 5 July.

—— (2001b) 'Health Care Is New Darling of Pork Barrel Spending', *New York Times,* 24 December.

—— (2002a) 'Budget Would Cut Medicaid Payments', *New York Times,* 1 February.

—— (2002b) 'After Decline, the Number of Uninsured Rose in 2001', *New York Times,* 30 September.

Pear, R. and R. Toner (2002) 'Amid Fiscal Crisis, Medicaid Is Facing Cuts from States', *New York Times,* 13 January.

Petchesky, R. (1990) *Abortion and Woman's Choice: The State, Sexuality and Reproductive Freedom,* Northeastern University Press, Boston, MA.

—— (1995a) 'From Population Control to Reproductive Rights: Feminist Fault Lines', *Reproductive Health Matters,* No. 6, November.

—— (1995b) 'The Body as Property: A Feminist Re-Vision', in F. Ginsburg and R. Rapp (eds.), *Conceiving the New World Order,* University of California, Berkeley, CA.

—— (2000) 'Sexual Rights: Inventing a Concept, Mapping an International Practice', in R. Parker, R. M. Barbosa and P. Aggleton (eds.), *Framing the Sexual Subject,* University of California Press, Berkeley, CA.

—— (2001/2002) 'Phantom Towers: Feminist Reflections on the Battle between Global Capitalism and Fundamentalist Terrorism', *The Women's Review of Books,* November 2001; *Economic and Political Weekly,* Vol. 36, No. 43, 27 October–2 November 2001; *Ms. Magazine,* December 2001. Reprinted in: S. Hawthorne and B. Winter (eds.), *September 11, 2001: Feminist Perspectives,* Spinifex Press, Australia (2002); K. Pollitt and B. Reed (eds.), *Nothing Sacred: Women Respond to Religious Fundamentalism and Terror,* Nation Books, New York (2002); R. Menon (ed.), *Feminist Perspectives on Peace and Terror,* Kali for Women, New Delhi (2002).

Petchesky, R. and K. Judd (eds.)/IRRRAG (1998) *Negotiating Reproductive Rights: Women's Perspectives Across Countries and Cultures,* Zed Books and St Martin's Press, London and New York.

Peters, J. and A. Wolper (eds.) (1995) *Women's Rights, Human Rights,* Routledge, New York and London.

Petersen, M. (2001) 'Lifting the Curtain on the Real Costs of Making AIDS Drugs', *New York Times,* 24 April.

Petersen, M. and L. Rohter (2001) 'Maker Agrees to Cut Price of Two AIDS Drugs in Brazil', *New York Times,* 31 March.

Petras, J. and H. Veltmeyer (2001) *Globalization Unmasked: The New Face of Imperialism,* Zed Books, London.

Phillips, K. (2002) *Wealth and Democracy: A Political History of the American Rich,* Broadway Books, New York.

Plesch, D. (2002) 'Why Bush's Deal with Putin Doesn't Make the World a Safer Place', *Observer* (London), 26 May.

Polatnick, R. (1996) 'Diversity in Women's Liberation Ideology: How a Black and White Group of the 1960s Viewed Motherhood', *Signs,* Vol. 21, No. 3, Spring.

Polish Federation for Women and Family Planning (1999) 'Gender Discrimination in Poland', independent report submitted to the United Nations Human Rights Committee, (prepared by Wanda Nowicka).

Pollack, A. (2001) 'Defensive Drug Industry: Fueling Clash Over Patents', *New York Times,* 20 April.

Press, E. (2002) 'Rebel with a Cause: The Re-Education of Joseph Stiglitz', *The Nation,* 10 June.

Preston-Whyte, E. *et al.* (2000) 'Survival Sex and HIV/AIDS in an African City', in R. Parker, R. Barbosa and P. Aggleton (eds.), *Framing the Sexual Subject,* University of California Press, Berkeley, CA.

Rahman, A. (1999) 'Church or State? The Holy See at the United Nations', *Conscience,* Vol. 20.

Raj, R., C. H. Leng and R. Shuib (1998) 'Between Modernization and Patriarchal Revivalism: Reproductive Negotiations among Women in Peninsular Malaysia', in R. Petchesky and K. Judd (eds.)/IRRRAG,

Negotiating Reproductive Rights, Zed Books and St Martin's Press, London and New York.

Ram, K. (1999) '*Ná Shariram Nádhi*, My Body Is Mine: The Urban Women's Health Movement in India and Its Negotiation of Modernity', *Women's Studies International Forum*, Vol. 21, No. 6.

Ramasubban, R. (1999) 'HIV/AIDS in India: Gulf between Rhetoric and Reality', in S. Pachauri (ed.), *Implementing a Reproductive Health Agenda in India*, Population Council, New Delhi.

Rao, J. A. (1999) 'Equity in a Global Public Goods Framework', in I. Kaul, I. Grunberg and M. A. Stern (eds.), *Global Public Goods: International Cooperation in the 21st Century*, UNDP/Oxford University Press, New York.

Ravindran, T. K. S. (2002) 'Understanding Health Sector Reforms and Sexual and Reproductive Health Services: A Preliminary Framework', *Reproductive Health Matters*, Vol. 10, No. 20, November.

Rawls, J. (1971) *The Theory of Justice*, Harvard University Press, Cambridge, MA.

Reidpath, D. *et al.* (2001) *Social, Cultural and Environmental Contexts and the Measurement of the Burden of Disease: An Exploratory Study in the Developed and Developing World*, Key Centre for Women's Health in Society, University of Melbourne, Melbourne.

RHM (1999) 'Round-Up', *Reproductive Health Matters*, Vol. 7, No. 14, November.

—— (2001) 'Round-Up', *Reproductive Health Matters*, Vol. 9, No. 18, November.

Richter, J. (2001) *Holding Corporations Accountable: Corporate Conduct, International Codes and Citizen Action*, Zed Books, London.

Rishyasringa, B. (2000) 'Social Policy and Reproductive Health', in R. Ramasubban and S. J. Jejeebhoy (eds.), *Women's Reproductive Health in India*, Rawat Publications, Jaipur, India.

Rivera, L. A. *et al.* (1997) 'What Is Managed Care?', *The Network News*, National Women's Health Network, Vol. 22, No. 3.

Roberts, J. (2002) Panel Presentation at Conference on the Crisis of Neglected Diseases, MSF/DND (Drugs for Neglected Diseases Working Group), New York, March.

Robinson, M. (2002) 'Globalization Has to Take Human Rights into Account', *The Irish Times*, 22 January.

Rodrique, J. M. (1990) 'The Black Community and the Birth Control Movement', in E. C. Dubois and V. L. Ruiz (eds.), *Unequal Sisters: A Multicultural Reader in U.S. Women's History*, Routledge, New York and London.

Rogow, D. (2000) *Alone You Are Nobody, Together We Float: The Manuela Ramos Movement, Quality/ Calidad/ Qualité*, Population Council, New York.

Rohter, L. (2001) 'Brazil Moves to Protect Jungle Plants from Foreign Biopiracy', *New York Times*, 23 December.

—— (2002) 'Brazil's Roller Coaster Market', *New York Times*, 24 June.

Rome Statute/United Nations (1998) *Rome Statute of the International Criminal Court*, adopted by the United Nations Diplomatic Conference of Plenipotentiaries on the Establishment of an International Criminal Court, A/CONF.183/9, 17 July (*http://www.un.org/icc/part1.htm*).

Rosenberg, T. (2001) 'The Brazilian Solution', *New York Times Magazine*, 28 June.

—— (2002) 'The Free-Trade Fix', *New York Times Magazine*, 18 August.

Rosenthal, E. (2002a) 'China Now Set To Make Copies of AIDS Drugs', *New York Times*, 7 September.

—— (2002b) 'China Frees AIDS Activist after Month of Outcry', *New York Times*, 20 September.

—— (2002c) 'AIDS Scourge in Rural China Leaves Villages of Orphans', *New York Times*, 25 August.

Ross, L. J. (1996) 'African American Women and Abortion: 1800–1970', in S. M. James and A. T. Busia (eds.), *Theorizing Black Feminism: The Visionary Pragmatism of Black Women*, Routledge, New York and London.

Rousseau, J.-J. (1987) *The Basic Political Writings*, Hackett Publishing, Indianapolis, IN.

Runyan, A. (1999) 'Women in the Neoliberal "Frame"', in M. Meyer and E. Prügl (eds.), *Gender Politics in Global Governance*, Rowman and Littlefield Publishers, Lanham, MD.

Rupp, L. J. (1997) *Worlds of Women: The Making of an International Women's Movement*, Princeton University, Princeton, NJ.

Russell, A. (2002) 'Victory and Betrayal: The Third World Takes on the Rich Countries in the Struggle for Access to Medicines', at *www.globaltreatmentaccess.org/content/press_releases/02*.

Sachs, J. (2001) 'The Best Possible Investment in Africa', *New York Times*, Op-Ed, 10 February.

Sachs, S. E. and J. Sachs (2002) 'AIDS and Africa – Where Is the US?', *Boston Globe*, 7 January.

Sadasivam, B. (1999) *Risks, Rights and Reform: A 50-Country Survey Assessing Government Actions Five Years After the International Conference on Population and Development*, Women's Environment and Development Organization, New York.

Sajor, I. (1995) 'Rape as a War Crime: A Continuing Injustice', in M. Schuler (ed.), *From Basic Needs to Basic Rights*, Women, Law and Development International, Washington, DC.

Salm, A. P. (2000) 'Promoting Reproductive and Sexual Health in the Era of SWAPs', *Reproductive Health Matters,* Vol. 8, No. 15, May.

Sanger, D. (1998) 'US and IMF Made Asia Crisis Worse, World Bank Finds', *New York Times*, 3 December.

—— (1999) 'World Bank Beats Breast for Failures in Indonesia', *New York Times*, 11 February.

—— (2002) 'Bush to Outline Doctrine of Striking Foes First', *New York Times*, 20 September.

Sassen, S. (1998) *Globalization and Its Discontents*, The New York Press, New York.

Schemo, D. (2002) 'Education Suffers in Africa as AIDS Ravages Teachers', *New York Times*, 8 May.

Schemann, S. (2002) 'Annan Cautions Business as Forum Ends', *New York Times*, 5 February.

Schiebinger, L. (1993) *Nature's Body: Gender in the Making of Modern Science*, Beacon Press, Boston.

Schneider, H. and L. Gilson (1999) 'The Impact of Free Maternal Health Care in South Africa: Safe Motherhood Initiatives, Critical Issues', in M. Berer and T. K. S. Ravindran (eds.), *Safe Motherhood*

Initiatives: Critical Issues, Basil Blackwell, London.

Schoofs, M. (2000) 'Proof Positive: How African Science Has Demonstrated that HIV Causes AIDS', *Village Voice*, 11 July.

Schrecker, T. (1998) 'Private Health Care for Canada: North of the Border, an Idea Whose Time Shouldn't Come?', *Journal of Law, Medicine and Ethics*, Vol. 26.

Scott, J. (1990) *Domination and the Arts of Resistance*, Yale University, New Haven, Connecticut.

Seif El Dawla, A. (1999) 'The Political and Legal Struggle over Female Genital Mutilation in Egypt: Five Years Since the ICPD', *Reproductive Health Matters*, Vol. 7, No. 13, May.

Seif, El Dawla, A., A. Abdel Hadi and N. Abdel Wahab (1998) 'Women's Wit Over Men's: Trade-offs and Strategic Accommodations in Egyptian Women's Reproductive Lives', in *Negotiating Reproductive Rights*, R. Petchesky and K. Judd (eds.), Zed Books, London.

Sen, A. (1993) 'Capability and Well-Being', in M. Nussbaum and A. Sen (eds.), *The Quality of Life*, Oxford University Press, New York.

—— (1994) 'Population: Delusion and Reality', *The New York Review of Books*, Vol. 41.

—— (1999) *Development as Freedom*, Alfred A. Knopf, New York.

—— (2001) 'Economic Progress and Health', in D. Leon and G. Walt (eds.), *Poverty, Inequality and Health*, Oxford University Press, New York.

Sen, G. (1994a) 'Women, Poverty and Population: Issues for the Concerned Environmentalist', in W. Harcourt (ed.), *Feminist Perspectives on Sustainable Development*, Zed Books, London.

—— (1994b) 'Development, Population and the Environment: A Search for Balance', in G. Sen, A. Germain and L. C. Chen (eds.), *Population Policies Reconsidered*, Harvard University, Cambridge, MA.

—— (1998) 'Cracks in the Neo-Liberal Consensus', *DAWN Informs*, No. 2.

—— (2000) 'Surviving Beijing+5', *Dawn Informs*, No. 2.

Sen, G. and S. Corrêa (2000) 'Gender Justice and Economic Justice: Reflections on the Five Year Reviews of the UN Conferences of the 1990s', paper prepared for UNIFEM for Beijing +5, *Dawn Informs*, No. 1, April.

Sen, G., A. Iyer and A. George (2002) 'Class, Gender and Health Equity: Lessons from Liberalization in India', in G. Sen, A. George and P. Ostlin (eds), *Engendering International Health: The Challenge of Equity*, MIT Press, Cambridge, MA.

Shah, S. (2002) 'Globalizing Clinical Research', *The Nation*, Vol. 274, No. 22, 10 June.

SHAAN Online (2002) 'UNGASS Declaration Champions Women's Empowerment', *SHAAN Online: IPS E-Zine on Gender and Human Rights, http://www.ipsnews.net/hivaids/uni_2612-1.shtml*, January.

Shapiro, T. (1985) *Population Control Politics: Women, Sterilization, and Reproductive Choice*, Temple University Press, Philadelphia, PA.

Shepard, B. (2000) 'The "Double Discourse" on Sexual and Reproductive Rights in Latin America', *Health and Human Rights*, Vol. 4, No. 2.

Shiva, V. (2001) *Protect or Plunder? Understanding Intellectual Property Rights*, Zed Books, London.

Shohat, E. (ed.) (1994) *Talking Visions: Multicultural Feminism in a Transnational Age*, MIT Press, Cambridge, MA.

Shohat, E. and R. Stam (1997) *Unthinking Eurocentrism: Multiculturalism and the Media*, Routledge, London and New York.

Shongwe, T. (1998) 'The Swaziland Schools HIV/AIDS and Population Education (SHAPE) Programme', in HERA, *Confounding the Critics: Cairo, Five Years On*, Conference Report, Cocoyoc, Morelos, Mexico, 15–18 November, International Women's Health Coalition, New York.

Silliman, J. (1997) 'Making the Connections: Women's Health and Environmental Justice', *Race, Gender and Class*, Vol. 5.

—— (1999) 'Expanding Civil Society, Shrinking Political Spaces: The Case of Women's Nongovernmental Organizations', in J. Silliman and Y. King (eds.), *Dangerous Intersections: Feminist Perspectives on Population, Environment, and Development*, South End Press, Cambridge, MA.

Silliman, J. and Y. King (1999) *Dangerous Intersections: Feminist Perspectives on Population, Environment, and Development*, South End Press, Cambridge, MA.

Silverstein, K. (1999) 'Millions for Viagra, Pennies for Diseases of the Poor', *The Nation*, 19 July.

Sims, C. (1998) 'Using Gifts as Bait, Peru Sterilizes Poor Women', *New York Times*, 15 February.

Sjfrup, L. (1997) 'Globalization: The Arch-Enemy?', *Reproductive Health Matters*, No. 10, November.

Smith, N. (1997) 'The Satanic Geographies of Globalization: Uneven Development in the 1990s', *Public Culture*, Vol. 10, No. 1.

Social Watch (2001) *Social Watch Report 2001*, No. 5, Social Watch, Montevideo, Uruguay.

Sokolsky, R. and J. McMillan. (2002) 'Foreign Aid in Our Own Defense', *New York Times*, Op-Ed, 12 February.

Soros, G. (2000) *Open Society: Reforming Global Capitalism*, Public Affairs/Perseus, New York.

Sparr, P. (ed.) (1994) *Mortgaging Women's Lives: Feminist Critiques of Structural Adjustment*, Zed Books, London.

Spivak, G. C. (1999) *A Critique of Postcolonial Reason: Toward a History of the Vanishing Present*, Harvard University Press, Cambridge, MA.

Stanchieri, J., I. Merali and R. J. Cook (eds.) (1999) *The Application of Human Rights to Reproductive and Sexual Health: A Compilation of the Work of UN Treaty Bodies*, Programme on Reproductive and Sexual Health Law, Faculty of Law, University of Toronto, Ontario.

Standing, H. (1999) *Framework for Understanding Gender Inequalities and Health Sector Reform: An Analysis and Review of Policy Issues*, Working Papers Series, No. 99.06, Harvard Center for Population and Development Studies, Cambridge, MA.

—— (2002a) *Towards Equitable Financing Strategies for Reproductive Health*, IDS Working Paper 153, Institute of Development Studies, Brighton, UK.

Steinhauer, J. (2001) 'UN Redefines AIDS as Political Issue and Peril to Poor', *New York Times*, 28 June.

Stevenson, R. (2002) 'New Study on Antiwar Spending is Fodder for Rival Camps', *New York Times*, 6 September.

Stienstra, D. (1999) 'Of Roots, Leaves, and Trees: Gender, Social Movements, and Global Governance', in M. Meyer and E. Prügl (eds.), *Gender Politics in Global Governance*, Rowman and Littlefield Publishers, Lanham, MD.

Stiglitz, J. (1986) *Economics of the Public Sector*, W. W. Norton, New York.

—— (1996) 'Keynote Address: The Role of Government in Economic Development', in M. Bruno and B. Plekovic (eds.), *Annual World Bank Conference on Development Economics*, World Bank, Washington DC.

—— (1998) 'Towards a New Paradigm for Development: Strategies, Policies and Processes', Prebisch Lecture at UNCTAD, Geneva, 19 October.

—— (2002) *Globalization and Its Discontents*, W. W. Norton, New York.

Stillwaggon, E. (2001) 'AIDS and Poverty in Africa', *The Nation*, 21 May.

Stolberg, S. (1999a) 'Racial Divide Found in Maternal Mortality', *New York Times*, 18 June.

—— (1999b) 'Black Mothers' Mortality Rate under Scrutiny', *New York Times*, 8 August.

—— (2001) 'Some Experts Say US is Vulnerable to a Germ Attack', *New York Times*, 29 September.

—— (2002) 'Buckets for Bioterrorism, but Less for Catalog of Ills', *New York Times*, 4 February.

—— (2003) 'Politics of Abortion Delays $15 billion to Fight AIDS', *New York Times*, 6 March.

Swarns, R. (1999) 'Health Care for South Africa's Poor Imperiled by Lack of Funds', *New York Times*, 16 November.

—— (2000a) 'Mbeki Details Quest to Grasp South Africa's AIDS Disaster', *New York Times*, 7 May.

—— (2000b) 'Dissent on AIDS by South Africa's President: Thoughtlessness or Folly?', *New York Times*, 8 July.

—— (2001a) 'South Africa's AIDS Vortex Engulfs a Rural Community', *New York Times*, 25 November.

—— (2001b) 'A South African Hospital Fights AIDS and Despair', *New York Times*, 26 November.

—— (2001c) 'Drug Makers Drop Suit over Aids Medicine', *New York Times*, 20 April.

—— (2001d) 'A Move to Force South Africa to Give AIDS Drug for Newborns', *New York Times*, 27 November.

—— (2002) 'In a Policy Shift, South Africa Will Make AIDS Drugs Available to More Pregnant Women', *New York Times*, 20 April.

Swarns, R. and L. K. Altman (2000) 'AIDS Forum in South Africa Opens Knotted in Disputes' *New York Times*, 10 July.

Tabb, W.K. (2001) *The Amoral Elephant: Globalization and the Struggle for Social Justice in the Twenty-First Century*, Monthly Review, New York.

TAC (Treatment Action Campaign) (2001a) *TAC E-Newsletter*, 12 February.

—— (2001b) *Equal Treatment*, Newsletter of the Treatment Action Campaign, Vol. 2, March.

Tangcharoensathien, V. (2002) 'ICPD Goals and Targets Worth Revisiting in the Context of Health Sector Reforms', *Reproductive Health Matters*, Vol. 10, No. 20, November.

Tax, M. (1999) 'World Culture War', *The Nation*, 17 May.

Taylor, V. (2000), *Marketisation of Governance: Critical Feminist Perspectives from the South*, DAWN and University of Cape Town, South Africa.

Teixeira, P. R. (2002) 'The Brazilian Response to the HIV/AIDS Epidemic', paper presented at meeting on Brazil's program on HIV/AIDS, Center for Gender, Sexuality and Health, Mainman School of Public Health, Columbia University, New York, April.

Terto Jr., V. (2000) 'Male Homosexuality and Seropositivity: The Construction of Social Identities in Brazil', in R. Parker, R. Barbosa and P. Aggleton (eds.), *Framing the Sexual Subject*, University of California Press, Berkeley, CA.

—— (2002) 'Access to ARV for HIV/AIDS: The Brazilian Experience', paper presented at Meeting on Brazil's Program on HIV/AIDS, Center for Gender, Sexuality and Health, Mailman School of Public Health, Columbia University, New York, April.

Thom, A. (2001), 'Millions Pin Hope on Drugs Hearing', *Independent Online*, 4 March.

Toner, R. (2001) 'Sagging Economy Threatens Health Coverage', *New York Times*, 12 November.

—— (2002) 'Administration Plans Care of Fetuses in Health Plan', *New York Times*, 31 January.

Torreele, E. (2002) 'From Louis Pasteur to J. Craig Venter: When Biomedical Scientists Become Bioentrepreneurs', paper presented at conference on 'The Crisis of Neglected Diseases: Developing Treatments and Ensuring Access', MSF/DND Working Group, New York, March (*www.accessmed/msf.org*).

Toubia, N. (1995) *Female Genital Mutilation: A Call for Global Action*, RAINBO (Research, Action and Information Network for the Bodily Integrity of Women), New York (*www.rainbo.org*).

TRAC (Transnational Resource and Action Center) (2000) *Tangled Up in Blue: Corporate Partnership at the United Nations*, CorpWatch, San Francisco, CA (*www.corpwatch.org*).

Tushnet, M. (1984) 'An Essay on Rights', *Texas Law Review*, Vol. 62, May.

UN (United Nations) (1998) *Rome Statute of the International Criminal Court*, A/CONF.183/9, 17 July (*http://www.un.org/icc/part1.htm*).

—— (2000) *The World's Women 2000: Trends and Statistics*, Social Statistics and Indicators Series K, No. 16 (ST/ESA/STAT/SER.K/16), United Nations, New York.

UNAIDS (Joint United Nations Programme on HIV/AIDS) (1999) *AIDS 5 Years Since ICPD: Emerging Issues and Challenges for Women, Young People and Infants*, UNAIDS, Geneva.

UNAIDS/WHO (2001) *AIDS Epidemic Update: December 2001*, UNAIDS and WHO, Geneva.

UN/CESCR (Committee on Economic, Social and Cultural Rights) (1999) 'Substantive Issues Arising in the Implementation of the International Covenant on Economic, Social and Cultural Rights: Statement of the United Nations Committee on Economic, Social and Cultural Rights to the Third Ministerial Conference of the World Trade Organization (Seattle, 30 November–3 December 1999)', CESCR, 21st Session, Geneva, 15 November–3 December, United Nations, Economic and Social Council, E/C.12/1999/9.

—— (2000) *Substantive Issues Arising in the Implementation of the International Covenant on Economic, Social and Cultural Rights*, General Comment No. 14, CESCR, 22nd Session, Geneva, 25 April–12 May, United Nations, Economic and Social Council, E/C.12/2000/4.

UN/CHR (Commission on Human Rights) (1998) *Guidelines on HIV/AIDS and Human Rights*, Second International Consultation on HIV/AIDS and Human Rights, Office of the UN High Commissioner for Human Rights and UNAIDS (HR/PUB/98/1), Geneva.

—— (2001) 'Access to Medication in the Context of Pandemics such as HIV/AIDS', Economic and Social Council, CHR Resolution 2001/33 (E/CN.4/RES/2001/33), Office of the United Nations High Commissioner for Human Rights, Geneva, April.

UNDP (United Nations Development Programme) (1998) *Human Development Report 1998*, Oxford University Press, New York.

—— (2000a) *Human Development Report 2000: Human Rights and Human Development*, Oxford University Press, New York.

—— (2000b) *Poverty Report 2000: Overcoming Human Poverty*, UNDP, New York.

UNFPA (United Nations Population Fund) (1997a) *Population and Sustainable Development: Five Years After Rio*, UNFPA, New York.

—— (1997b) *The State of World Population 1997 – The Right to Choose: Reproductive Rights and Reproductive Health*, UNFPA, New York.

—— (1999) *A Five-Year Review of Progress towards the Implementation of the Programme of Action of the International Conference on Population and Development*, background paper prepared for The Hague Forum (The Hague, 8–12 February), UNFPA, New York.

UN/General Assembly (1999) *1999 World Survey on the Role of Women in Development: Globalization, Gender and Work*, Report of the Secretary-General, General Assembly, 54th Session, A/54/227, United Nations, New York.

—— (2001a) 'HIV/AIDS and Human Rights', Special Session of the General Assembly on HIV/AIDS, Roundtable 2 (A/S-26/RT.2), 15 June.

—— (2001b) 'Global Crisis, Global Action', Declaration of Commitment on HIV/AIDS, Special Session of the General Assembly on HIV/AIDS, Final Declaration, 7 July.

—— (2001c) 'United Nations Millennium Declaration', General Assembly Resolution 55/2, 55th Session (A55/2), 8 September.

—— (2001d) 'Road Map towards the Implementation of the United Nations Millennium Declaration', Report of the Secretary-General, 56th Session (A/56/150, A/56/326), www.un.org/millenniumgoals..

UNICEF (1999) *Countries in Transition*, MONEE Project Regional Monitoring Report No. 6, Innocenti Research Centre, Florence, Italy.

UNICEF/UNAIDS/WHO/MSF (2000) *Selected Drugs Used in the Care of People Living with HIV: Sources and Prices*, Joint UNICEF/UNAIDS/WHO/EDM (Essential Drugs and Medicines Policy)/MSF Project, UNICEF Technical Services Centre, Geneva, October.

UNIFEM (United Nations Development Fund for Women) (1995) *Putting Gender on the Agenda: A Guide to Participating in UN World Conferences*, UNIFEM and UN/NGLS (United Nations Non-Governmental Liaison Service), New York.

—— (2000) *Progress of the World's Women 2000*, UNIFEM Biennial Report, (ed.) Diane Elson, UNIFEM, New York.

UNIFEM/Commonwealth Secretariat/IDRC (2001) *Gender Budget Initiatives,* UNIFEM, New York.

US Women of Color Delegation to the ICPD (1994) 'Statement on Poverty, Development and Population Activities', National Black Women's Health Project, Washington, DC.

Varmus, H. (2002) 'Keynote Address', Conference on the Crisis of Neglected Diseases, MSF/Drugs for Neglected Diseases Working Group, Graduate Center of the City University of New York, March.

Villanueva, V. and S. Galdos Silva (2000) Letter to President Clinton, Movimiento Manuela Ramos, Lima, Peru.

Visaria, L. and P. Visaria (1999) 'Field-Level Reflections of Policy Change', in S. Pachauri (ed.), *Implementing a Reproductive Health Agenda in India,* Population Council, New Delhi.

Wachtel, H. (2000) 'The Mosaic of Global Taxes', in J. Pieterse (ed.), *Global Futures: Shaping Globalization*, Zed Books, London.

Weisbrot, M. *et al.* (2001) *The Scorecard on Globalization 1980–2000: Twenty Years of Diminished Progress*, Center for Economic and Policy Research, Washington, DC.

Weiss, E. and G. R. Gupta (1998) *Bridging the Gap: Addressing Gender and Sexuality in HIV Prevention*, International Center for Research on Women, Washington, DC.

Weiss, T. and L. Gordenker (eds.) (1996) *NGOs, the UN, and Global Governance*, Lynn Rienner Publishers, Boulder, CO.

West, L. (1999) 'The United Nations Women's Conferences and Feminist Politics', in M. Meyer and E. Prügl (eds.), *Gender Politics in Global Governance*, Rowman and Littlefield Publishers, Lanham, MD.

WGNRR (Women's Global Network for Reproductive Rights) (1997) *Newsletter 47*, July– September, WGNRR, Amsterdam.

—— (1999/2000) *Newsletter 68-69*, Nos. 4, 1, WGNRR, Amsterdam.

—— (2002) *A Call for Action: International Trade Agreements and Women's Access to Health Care*, WGNRR, Amsterdam.

WHO (World Health Organization) (1978) *Alma Ata 1978: Primary Health Care*, World Health Organization, Geneva.

—— (1997) 'The DALY in Relation to the Global Burden of Disease Study and Global Health Situation and Trend Assessment', unpublished synthesis paper, March.

—— (2000) *The World Health Report 2000 – Health Systems: Improving Performance*, World Health Organization, Geneva.

—— (2002) 'WHO's Contribution to Achievement of the Development Goals of the United Nations Millennium Declaration', Fifty-Fifth World Health Assembly (WHA55.19), Geneva, 18 May.

WHO (with Commission on Macroeconomics and Health) (2001) *Macroeconomics and Health: Investing in Health for Economic Development*, World Health Organization, Geneva.

Wichterich, C. (2000) *The Globalized Woman*, Zed Books, London.

Wilks, A. (2000) 'Statement on Ravi Kanbur's Resignation as World Development Report Lead Author', www.brettonwoodsproject.org.

Williams, M. (2001a) 'The Doha Ministerial: Not Good for Development, Not Good for Gender Equality', *IGTN* (International Gender and Trade Network) *Bulletin* (*www.genderandtrade.net*; listserve: *secretariat@coc.org*).

—— (2001b) 'Imbalances, Inequities and the WTO Mantra', DAWN Discussion Paper II on the WTO, *DAWN Informs*, Supplement, November.

Williams, M. and G. Francisco (2002) 'Strategizing to Continue the WTO Battle', *DAWN Informs*, March.

Williams, P. (1991) *The Alchemy of Race and Rights: Diary of a Law Professor*, Harvard University Press, Cambridge, MA.

Wolfensohn, J. (1998) *The Other Crisis*, Address to the Board of Governors, The World Bank Group, Washington, DC, 6 October.

WOMENLEAD (Women's Legal Education, Advocacy and Defense Foundation) (2002), 'Petition to Reopen Proceedings and Review BFAD [Bureau of Food and Drugs] Bureau Circular No. 18, Quezon City, Philippines, May.

Women's Caucus for Gender Justice (1999) *Report on the November–December 1999 ICC PrepCom*, Women's Caucus for Gender Justice, New York, http://www.iccwomen.org.

—— (2000) *The International Criminal Court: The Beijing Platform in Action*, Women's Caucus for Gender Justice, New York.

Women's Groups/Philippines (2001) 'Statement of Women's Group at Protest Rally', 26 March.

World Bank.(1996) *World Development Report 1996: From Plan to Market*, World Bank, Washington, DC/Oxford University Press, New York.

—— (1997) *World Development Report 1997: The State in a Changing World*, World Bank, Washington, DC/Oxford University Press, New York.

—— (1998a) *Beyond the Washington Consensus: Institutions Matter*, by S. J. Burki. and G. E. Perry, World Bank, Washington, DC.

—— (1998b) *Nongovernmental Organizations in Bank-Supported Projects: A Review*, by C. Gibbs, C. Fumo and T. Kuby, World Bank, Washington, DC.

—— (1998c) *The Bank's Relations with NGOs: Issues and Directions*, Social Development Paper No. 28, World Bank, Washington, DC.

—— (1999a) *The World Bank Annual Report 1999*, World Bank, Washington, DC (*www.worldbank.org/ htm/extpb/annrep/bd.htm*).

—— (2000) 'Background Information: Poverty Reduction Strategies and the Poverty Reduction Strategy Paper', World Bank, United Nations, 12 April (*www.worldbank. org/poverty/strategies*).

—— (2000/2001) *World Development Report 2000–2001: Attacking Poverty*, World Bank, Washington DC.

——/HNP (1999b) *Population and the World Bank: Adapting to Change*, Health, Nutrition and Population Series, World Bank, Washington DC.

WTO (World Trade Organization) (2001) *Declaration on the TRIPS Agreement and Public Health*, Doha WTO Ministerial 2001 (WT/MN[01]/DEC/2), World Trade Organization, Geneva, 20 November.

Xaba, M. *et al.* (1998) 'Transformation of Reproductive Health Services Project, South Africa: A Collaboration between the Women's Health Project and Three Provincial Departments of Health and Welfare', in HERA, *Confounding the Critics: Cairo, Five Years On*, Conference Report (Cocoyoc, Morelos, Mexico, November), International Women's Health Coalition, New York.

Yuval-Davis, N. (1997) *Gender and Nation*, Sage Publications, London.

Index

abortion 1, 3-6, 9, 28n, 36-7, 39-40, 42, 44, 48, 60, 71n, 98, 170, 181n, 191-2, 198, 207-8, 216-17, 221, 226, 230-1, 239-42, 245n, 248, 252
Abzug, Bella 70n
Accelerated Access Initiative 110
accountability 27, 32, 44, 57, 59, 62, 68-70, 74n, 90, 111-13, 122, 151, 157, 174-80, 194, 201, 210, 213, 223, 227-8, 230-1, 236-7, 243-4, 248, 251, 254-6, 258-9, 263, 265-6, 268, 279n
Achmat, Zackie 85
Action Health Incorporated (AHI) 217
ActionAid 256
Afghanistan 123, 143, 249-50, 277, 277-8n
Africa 4-5, 8, 12, 14, 24, 32, 38, 54, 63, 67, 76, 79, 82-3, 86, 91, 97, 101-2, 104, 109-11, 114-15, 121, 123, 132n, 133, 137, 139, 149, 157, 165, 173, 178, 181n, 188, 192, 221, 238, 257, 275; African Union (AU) 133-4; New Economic Partnership for Africa's Development (NEPAD) 133; sub-Saharan 5, 12, 38, 63, 79, 83, 86, 97, 110-11, 132n, 137, 139, 149, 157, 165, 181n, 192, 221, 238
African National Congress (ANC) 89, 93-4, 127n, 230-1, 233
African Women's Leadership Institute 222
age 8, 21, 25, 116, 121, 167, 189, 217, 231-2, 251
agency 18, 24-7, 31, 141, 175
agriculture 107, 126n, 137, 143, 160, 163; agribusiness 78
aid 24, 57, 73n, 74n, 82, 114, 134, 154, 170-1, 178, 193, 267-8, 279n; see also donor agencies/countries
AIDS Coalition to Unleash Power (ACT UP) 82, 84-5, 126n, 271
AIDS Law Project (ALP) 87
Al Qaeda network 249, 278n
Alliance for a Corporate-Free UN 265
Alma Ata Declaration (1978) 71n, 118-19, 160, 170, 172, 175
Andhra Pradesh 21, 29n, 189, 199-200
Annan, Kofi 58, 68, 84-5, 88, 113, 264
apartheid 86-9, 94, 97, 109, 122-3, 165, 230, 232
Argentina 73n, 77, 79, 114, 180, 229
Asia 4, 7, 13-14, 23-4, 48, 67, 77, 101, 104, 114, 123, 137, 139, 181n, 188, 252, 255, 257; Central 123, 149, 275; East 137, 141, 181n; Pacific 67, 137; South 7, 48, 137, 181n, 252
Asmita Resource Centre for Women 29n, 189-90
Association for the Taxation of Financial Transactions for the Benefit of Citizens (ATTAC) 178-9, 187n
Australia 54, 59, 62, 166-7, 179, 280n
authoritarianism 145, 155, 201, 253, 255

Bangkok Declaration 23
Bangladesh 129n, 162, 184n, 192; Health and Population Sector Programme 184n
Barbados 102
Barzelatto, José 70n
basic needs 6-7, 12, 14-20, 26, 29n, 52, 111, 138, 173, 231
Behringer–Ingelheim 83, 91-2, 127n, 129n
Beijing *see* UN Conference on Women (Beijing)
biopiracy 78, 95, 103
Blair, Tony 249
body, age and 116; class and 116; control/integrity of 2-3, 8-11, 15, 28-9n, 34, 38-9, 189, 202-3, 230, 245n, 271-2; and development 15; feminism and 3, 8-9; HIV/AIDS as bodily mapping of global injustice 87; gender and 116; human rights violations of 34; and macroeconomic perspectives 272; men and 211, 214-15; race and 116; social markers on 116
Bolivia 39, 141, 191, 245n
Botswana 87
Boutros Ghali, Boutros 264
Brazil 4, 12, 19, 28n, 39, 53, 62, 81, 83-4, 86, 93-104, 107-9, 114, 122, 126n, 127n, 128n, 129n, 146, 177, 180, 183n, 188, 190-1, 224-31, 233, 238, 241-3, 245n, 254, 268, 273-4; Afro-Brazilian movement; 98; Citizens' Health Councils 177; Comprehensive Women's Health Programme (PAISM) 225-6; Homosexual Movement 98; law on access to AIDS drugs 95, 100, 129n, 229; Ministry of Health 94-6, 99-100, 102, 129n, 225; National Commission on Population and Development (CNDP) 226, 228; National Council of Women's Rights (CNDM) 225-6; National Feminist Health and Reproductive Rights Network (Rede Saúde) 225-6, 241; Oswaldo Cruz Foundation 129n; STD/AIDS programme 101, 103; Universal Health System (SUS) 97, 226-7, 229, 245n
Brazilian Interdisciplinary AIDS Association (ABIA) 99
Bristol-Myers Squibb 83, 125n
Bruce, Judith 70n
Brundtland, Gro Harlem 29n, 170
'burden of disease' approach 152-3, 157, 160, 164-72, 197
bureaucracy 99, 175, 196, 201, 211, 238
Bush, George W. 1, 40, 83-4, 107, 123, 143, 171, 179, 181n, 248-51, 260, 267, 275-6, 278n
Butegwa, Florence 17

Cairo *see* International Conference on Population and Development (ICPD)
Cambodia 191
Cameroon 166-7
Canada 14, 54, 59, 62, 90, 110, 129n, 133, 164, 183n, 251, 274; Alternative Federal Budget (AFB) 274

296

212, 226, 232; forced 34, 207, 212
Stiglitz, Joseph 144, 146-7, 151, 173, 181n, 257
structural adjustment 1, 5-6, 13, 28n, 29n, 43, 56-7,
    66, 74n, 135, 138-9, 144-5, 148, 150-1, 156,
    158, 160, 179, 180n, 191, 193-4, 205, 216, 229,
    242, 245n, 255-6
Summers, Lawrence 151, 182n
'survival sex' 87, 124, 126n
Swaziland 222-3, 237
Swedish International Development Agency (SIDA)
    238

Tajikstan 213-15, 237
Tamil Nadu 198
Tanzania 140, 180n
Target-Free Approach (TFA) 196-200, 244n
taxation 56, 74n, 138, 178-80, 229, 233, 256, 258,
    260, 267-8, 275, 279n
technology transfer 78-80, 101-2, 104, 111, 114-15,
    125n
Teixeira, Paulo Roberto 101
Thailand 81, 83, 85, 108, 114, 129n, 191
The Hague Forum 72n
Third World 6, 46, 78, 80, 82, 102, 109, 136, 149
Third World Network 62, 72n, 106
Tobin taxes 14, 55-6, 59, 150, 179-80, 268
Toubia, Nahid 202
trade 6, 9, 14, 19, 24, 54-8, 61-3, 66, 120, 122, 135,
    269, 272; liberalization 120, 122, 135-7, 140-1,
    145, 188, 219, 253, 256, 260-1, 266, 269
trade unions 64, 83, 88-9, 138, 148, 161, 219-20,
    259, 261, 271
traditional authority 5, 8-9, 13, 18-19, 24, 34, 36-7,
    50-1, 60-1, 120, 142, 193, 202-4, 214-15
traditional healers 129n, 161
Transformation of Reproductive Health Services
    Project (South Africa) 234-5
transformative politics 32, 59, 67-70, 72n, 97, 99,
    195, 215, 241, 252, 255, 267-71, 274, 277
transnational corporations (TNCs) 24-5, 27, 31, 55-
    6, 68-70, 76-95, 100-4, 106-14, 122, 124, 127n,
    128n, 130n, 137, 140, 150, 176-80, 216, 255,
    259, 261-4, 268
transparency 69, 144, 161, 182n, 194, 255-7, 259
transport 15, 18-19, 147, 159, 161, 215, 233
Treatment Action Campaign (TAC) 82-5, 88-92, 94,
    126n, 127n, 129n, 185n, 233, 235, 271
Trinidad and Tobago 219-20, 223
TRIPs (Trade-Related Intellectual Property Rights)
    61-2, 74n, 77-91, 100, 102-7, 111, 114-15, 122,
    125n, 126n, 128n, 141, 177, 264, 272
tubal ligation 240
tuberculosis 79, 84, 92, 105, 112, 128n, 139, 159,
    165, 168, 185n
Tunisia 129n
typhoid 214

Uganda 4, 93, 102, 129n, 161
Ukraine 12, 192
United Kingdom (UK) 115, 234
United Nations (UN) 4, 15, 20, 24-5, 31-70, 239,
    248, 273, 276-7, 278n; Cairo conference *see*
    ICPD; Commission on Human Rights 84, 117,

119, 121, 143, 260-1; Committee on Economic,
    Social and Cultural Rights (CESCR) 71n, 82,
    118-19, 121-2, 207, 261; Committee/
    Convention on the Elimination of All Forms of
    Discrimination Against Women (CEDAW) 71n,
    140, 181n, 189, 206-8, 261; corporatization of
    264; Decade for Women 32; Declaration of
    Commitment on HIV/AIDS (2001) 35;
    Declaration on the Elimination of Violence
    against Women (1993) 34, 171; General
    Assembly 34-5, 56, 58, 60, 62, 70n, 73n, 83-4,
    94-5, 101, 117, 120-3, 259-62, 265, 278n;
    globalization and 58-9, 248, 253; High
    Commissioner for Human Rights 117, 131n,
    260; human rights treaty bodies 17, 20, 24-5, 35,
    39, 56, 62, 71n, 74n, 148, 207, 256, 260-2;
    Millennium Declaration 69; Secretary-General
    58, 68-9, 84, 113, 264; Security Council 58-9,
    82, 120, 250, 261-2, 276, 278n; Special Session
    on AIDS (2001) 94-5, 101, 117, 120-3, 131n, 265
United Nations Centre on Transnational
    Corporations 264
United Nations Children's Fund (UNICEF) 82, 110,
    140, 165, 218, 222, 265
United Nations Conference on Environment and
    Development (UNCED) (Rio de Janeiro, 1992)
    29n, 33-5, 65, 70, 70n, 254, 264; Women's
    Caucus 34-5, 65, 70
**United Nations Conference on Women (Beijing,
    1995)** 5, 7, 17, 19, 27, 28n, 31, 34-42, 47, 50-1,
    53, 57-60, 66-8, 70, 70n, 73n, 74n, 75n, 120,
    142, 148, 153, 155, 159-60, 171, 187n, 188-90,
    192, 216, 228, 235, 248, 254, 274-5; five-year
    review (plus five) 36-8, 40, 50-1, 53, 57-60, 67-9,
    74n, 120; 'Further Actions' document 53;
    Platform for Action 35-9, 41-2, 51, 53, 59, 66,
    73n, 160, 171, 189, 216, 274; preparatory
    committee (Prep Com) meetings 36, 51;
    Women's Caucus 34-5, 50-1, 65, 70, 70n
United Nations Conference on Women (Nairobi,
    1985) 32, 70n
United Nations Development Programme (UNDP)
    17-18, 58, 76, 137, 146, 149, 159, 165, 172,
    182n, 259
United Nations Development Programme for
    Women (UNIFEM) 58, 70n
United Nations Economic and Social Council
    (ECOSOC) 56, 74n, 260-1, 278n, 279n
United Nations Financing for Development (FfD)
    Conference (2002) 73n, 179, 248, 266-7, 273,
    278n, 279n
United Nations Joint AIDS Programme (UNAIDS)
    82, 108-10, 112, 117, 131n, 165, 265
United Nations Population Fund (UNFPA) 32, 46,
    71-2n, 72n, 82, 110, 181n, 221-2, 234, 238
United Nations World Conference on Human Rights
    (Vienna, 1993) 17, 23, 33-5, 254;
**United Nations World Summit for Social
    Development (WSSD) (Copenhagen, 1995)**
    12-13, 35, 47, 50-2, 55-63, 70, 72n, 73n, 74n,
    77, 82-3, 160, 171, 179, 187n, 254, 260, 279n;
    Copenhagen Declaration and Programme of
    Action 51-2, 55-6, 59, 72n, 73n, 74n, 160, 171;